Islam and the Americas

New World Diasporas

UNIVERSITY PRESS OF FLORIDA

Florida A&M University, Tallahassee
Florida Atlantic University, Boca Raton
Florida Gulf Coast University, Ft. Myers
Florida International University, Miami
Florida State University, Tallahassee
New College of Florida, Sarasota
University of Central Florida, Orlando
University of Florida, Gainesville
University of North Florida, Jacksonville
University of South Florida, Tampa
University of West Florida, Pensacola

Islam and the Americas

EDITED BY AISHA KHAN

Kevin A. Yelvington, Series Editor

University Press of Florida
Gainesville · Tallahassee · Tampa · Boca Raton
Pensacola · Orlando · Miami · Jacksonville · Ft. Myers · Sarasota

Copyright 2015 by Aisha Khan
All rights reserved
Printed in the United States of America on acid-free paper

This book may be available in an electronic edition.

22 21 20 19 18 17   6 5 4 3 2 1

First cloth printing, 2015
First paperback printing, 2017

LIBRARY OF CONGRESS CATALOGING-IN-PUBLICATION DATA
Islam and the Americas / edited by Aisha Khan.
pages cm — (New world diasporas)
Includes bibliographical references and index.
Summary: This volume edited by Aisha Khan explores Muslims' lived experiences in the Western Hemisphere and the ways in which Islam has been codified in the New World by "Muslim minority" societies, using disparate case studies from the Caribbean, Suriname, Brazil, Mexico, and others in the Atlantic World.
ISBN 978-0-8130-6013-2 (cloth)
ISBN 978-0-8130-5405-6 (pbk.)
1. Islam—North America. 2. Islam—South America. 3. Muslims—North America.
4. Muslims—South America. I. Khan, Aisha, 1955- editor. II. Series: New World diasporas series.
BP67.A1I765 2015
305.6'97097—dc23
2014033318

The University Press of Florida is the scholarly publishing agency for the State University System of Florida, comprising Florida A&M University, Florida Atlantic University, Florida Gulf Coast University, Florida International University, Florida State University, New College of Florida, University of Central Florida, University of Florida, University of North Florida, University of South Florida, and University of West Florida.

University Press of Florida
15 Northwest 15th Street
Gainesville, FL 32611-2079
http://www.upf.com

Contents

List of Figures vii
Acknowledgments ix

1. Introduction: A Storied Hemisphere 1
   Aisha Khan

2. Contours: Approaching Islam, Comparatively Speaking 23
   Aisha Khan

PART I. HISTORIES: PRESENCE, ABSENCE, REMAKING

3. "Oriental Hieroglyphics Understood Only by the Priesthood and a Chosen Few": The Islamic Orientalism of White and Black Masons and Shriners 49
   Jacob S. Dorman

4. Locating Mecca: Religious and Political Discord in the Javanese Community in Pre-Independence Suriname 69
   Rosemarijn Hoefte

5. Fear of a Brown Planet: Pan-Islamism, Black Nationalism, and the Tribal Twenties 92
   Nathaniel Deutsch

6. Insha'Allah/Ojalá, Yes Yes Y'all: Puerto Ricans (Re)examining and (Re)imagining Their Identities through Islam and Hip Hop 115
   Omar Ramadan-Santiago

PART II. CIRCULATION OF IDENTITIES, POLITICS OF BELONGING

7. Between Terror and Transcendence: Global Narratives of Islam and the Political Scripts of Guadeloupe's Indianité 141
   Yarimar Bonilla

8. The Politics of Conversion to Islam in Southern Mexico   163
   Sandra Cañas Cuevas

9. Bahamian and Brazilian Muslimahs: Struggle for Identity
   and Belonging   186
   Jerusa Ali

PART III. SPATIAL PRACTICES AND THE TRINIDADIAN LANDSCAPE

10. "Up Against a Wall": Muslim Women's Struggle to Reclaim Masjid Space
    in Trinidad and Tobago   217
    Rhoda Reddock

11. Democracy, Gender, and Indian Muslim Modernity in Trinidad   249
    Gabrielle Jamela Hosein

12. More Than Dawud and Jalut: Decriminalizing the Jamaat al Muslimeen
    and Madressa in Trinidad   269
    Jeanne P. Baptiste

13. Island Currents, Global Aesthetics: Islamic Iconography
    in Trinidad   295
    Patricia Mohammed

List of Contributors   327
Index   331

Figures

1.1. "Islam Pou Lape, Viv ansanm pou lape," Haiti, 2013   3

3.1. Islam shrine invitation, San Francisco, 1890   59

7.1. Cartoon depicting Madassamy's arrest   143

13.1. "Newly Arrived Coolies," Trinidad, ca. 1987   299

13.2. Arabic reading of texts, wedding anniversary   303

13.3. Mosque at Valencia   303

13.4. Interior of Hindu temple, Chaguanas   304

13.5. Drawing of first surah by Ayoob Mohammed   305

13.6. Detail of Valencia Mosque surface decoration   305

13.7. Haji Gookool Meah Mosque, St. James   307

13.8. TML Islamic Mosque, St. Joseph   309

13.9. Crescent moon and star, Nur-e-Islam Mosque, San Juan   309

13.10. Charlieville Mosque.   311

13.11. Hosay festival, Trinidad, ca. 1910   312

13.12. Postcard of Hosay festival, 1930s   312

13.13. Tadjah from Hosay festival, St. James   313

13.14. Participatory event, Hosay festival, St. James   314

13.15. Obeisance before moon wreath, Hosay festival   315

13.16. Zuleikha Mohammed in shalwar chemise and ohrni   317

13.17. Two Afro-Trinidadian Islamic women in full burkha   318

13.18. A black Muslim family   319

13.19. Ornate headscarves and embroidered fabrics   319

13.20. Elder of the black Muslim group   321

13.21. Devotional stance of Ayoob Mohammed   322

Acknowledgments

This volume emerged from a series of conversations, impressions, and insights that I have had over a number of years with friends, colleagues, and students as we considered the practice and the study of Islam in the Caribbean. This journey of ideas began a couple of decades ago during my dissertation fieldwork and was enriched by early discussions with scholars at the University of the West Indies, St. Augustine, Trinidad—notably, at that time, with Brinsley Samaroo, Rhoda Reddock, and Patricia Mohammed. Since then, with further study and many more conversations, the journey has become increasingly multilayered and complex, broadening the aim and the scope of the subject matter both geographically and analytically and, in the process, revealing the exciting prospect of how much still remains to be learned and understood about Muslims and the lifeworlds that both shape and are shaped by their diverse populations and communities.

I am grateful to the contributors, who, with their carefully crafted and thoughtful work, have made this volume what it is. I am also grateful to the University Press of Florida for their early and unflagging support of the project and to Sally Antrobus for her conscientious editing. Our anonymous reviewers offered indispensable comments and suggestions. In addition, I would like to thank Allyson Purpura for her expert curatorial assistance with images for the volume's cover, and I extend special gratitude to Kate Crehan and Barbara Weinstein for generously providing invaluable feedback on my own two chapters. Finally, I thank the Humanities Initiative of New York University for awarding me a Research Fellowship and a Grants-in-Aid award, which allowed me to devote time to develop and complete this project.

1

Introduction

A Storied Hemisphere

AISHA KHAN

More than a quarter of a century ago Talal Asad called for scholars to dispense with the convention of approaching Islam in terms of "a fixed cast of Islamic dramatis personae, enacting a predetermined story," and instead to understand that the coherence of "the world of Islam is essentially ideological, a discursive representation" (Asad 1986: 10–11). Although scholars have come a long way in challenging essentialist representations of peoples and groups, our interventions have not come close to eliminating public sphere stereotypes of fixed casts of characters and predetermined stories, including those about Muslims and Islam.

This is a book about Muslims as they craft Islam in the "New World" of the Americas. It is a collection in which the authors encourage cross-cultural comparison through probing and challenging key presumptions about this religious tradition and its practitioners. We are not interested in Islam merely as an end in itself, a given traced from one place to another in the form of migration, diaspora, genealogical or kindred spirit, or conspiratorial alien. Our hope is to foster a better appreciation of the ways in which Islam *becomes* as well as *is*, as Muslims (however they may be defined) and those who are not Muslims (however they may be defined) bring Islam to bear on assertions of personhood, contestations of personhood, and the construction of this religious tradition as it serves community-building projects—whether neighborhood, national, or transnational.

As the chapters in this volume attest, Islam makes its presence felt in both direct and oblique ways; its definition and significance are matters of interpretation that vary with the historical moment, particular relations of power, social formation, and Zeitgeist. Islam's relationship with "the West" consists not of mutually exclusive categories hypothetically repelling each other but, rather, a relationship of interlacing encounters that are both face to face and fantasized. These and other considerations challenge standard images of Islam in the popular Western imagination, yet the reiteration of certain themes of mutual exclusivity persists. Still resonant are the stereotypical and allegedly adversarial dichotomies of Islam's patriarchy versus the West's gender equality; Islam's terrorism versus the West's rational democracy; Islam's destructive discord versus the West's reasoned forms of protest; Islam's parochialism versus the West's cosmopolitanism; Islam's inertia versus the West's advancement; Islam's traditionalism versus the West's modernity.

The project of this volume is to explore Islam *in* the West and the degrees to which that suggests Islam *of* the West: its multiple creations as an object of study, its modes of expression in local vernacular terms, and its development over time and territory. The idea is to explore simultaneously lived experience and the ways it is codified into its own subject matter, by both participants and observers, in "Muslim minority societies" (Kettani 1986) that emerged out of Western projects (notably Euro-colonialism) yet that have circuitous and uneven as well as distinctive connections to Western worldviews, pasts, and political economies. The challenge this presents is to consider relatively small populations located throughout the Americas, who have enjoyed comparatively little formal documentation and in some cases long but interrupted histories, significant cultural transformations, and consistent and animated debate about those transformations. At the same time, Islam's "whole"—its substance and its symbolism—is greater than the sum of its parts: its history, heterogeneity, geographical range, and the apprehensive imagery long associated with it from the Western gaze transcend Muslim individuals and communities of practitioners. Arif Dirlik puts it nicely when he reminds us that religion "comes in packages, one might suggest, that contain other social, political, and cultural anxieties and aspirations" (Dirlik 2003: 163). Our charge must include exploring how to understand what creates this whole and the cultural, social, and political implications it may have for individuals and communities.

In a good deal of contemporary discourse on Islam, "Islam is portrayed as inherently violent and Muslims are portrayed as desperately incapable of separating religion and politics" (Cesari 2010: 2). These sorts of separations, however, are indicative of the socially constructed categorization of human experience ("religion," "politics"), rather than a demonstration of inherent distinctions between them. It is simply a triumphalist discourse to claim the ability to know the difference between what is "religious" and what is "po-

Fig. 1.1. "Islam Pou Lape, Viv ansanm pou lape" (Islam for peace, live together for peace). Painted by the group Islam Pou Lape, Port-au-Prince, Haiti, June 2013. Photo courtesy Katherine Smith.

litical" when the alleged inability to make such distinctions is equated with backwardness and destruction. Yet as shorthand encapsulations of complex processes, such binary models are tenacious. A provocative suggestion for this tenacity lies in the comment by Haideh Moghissi, Saeed Rahnema, and Mark J. Goodman about the "enormous psychological power" that is exerted by such ideological oppositions, which present "a shimmering seduction: a permanent enemy" (2009: 13). The basic appeal of enmity can be debated, but the seductiveness of symbols is precisely their interpretive malleability; a fill-in-the-blank kind of power may be the greatest power of all.

In exploring the categorical boundaries of "Muslim" and "Islam," the case studies in this book address Kambiz Ghaneabassiri's critique that existing scholarship on Islam in the Americas has focused more on how Muslims are getting on than how they have shaped history (Ghaneabassiri 2010: 4). Each chapter in this volume presents Muslims as creative actors participating in the making of the societies of which they are a part. None approaches Islam at face value, as anything less than always and necessarily subject to debate and flux, nor Muslims as predictable or uniform subjects. The coverage is not comprehensive, nor is it meant to be. Research on Islam in this hemisphere reveals clear emphases and gaps in the subject matter, with the gaps far outnumbering the emphases. The collection reflects each contributor's particular research interests and sites of study, the availability of archival material, the accessibility of ethnographic material, and the empirical concentrations of Muslim populations (e.g., the Caribbean) or the symbolic "hot spots" of Islam irrespective of Muslim demographics (e.g., the United States). But comprehensive coverage would not be possible even if we aspired to it. For one thing, despite the relative paucity that continues to characterize scholarly research on Islam in this hemisphere, there is nevertheless far too much material for one volume. For another, "total coverage" necessarily implies finite and fixed criteria for defining a given subject. Among the intended lessons of this book is that we must unfailingly query our accepted epistemological criteria and, through what I call *creative skepticism*, push beyond our certainties. The point of scholarly endeavor should be to embrace the discomposure that can propel intellectual curiosity, not warm to the contentedness that reassures us we are right. Although the contributors do not individually echo my sentiments precisely or in unison, together their analyses should push readers not only to want to learn *more* about any given subject matter but also to think about *why* certain questions and issues arise and how they are constituted.

We do not provide a single theoretical approach or necessarily similar analytical conclusions. These studies and the scholars who conducted them are featured for their diversity: they are interdisciplinary, geographically dispersed, temporally wide-ranging, and written from religious commitment as well as from secular orientations. We do, however, mean to illustrate the wide, and perhaps unexpected, array of conditions of possibility that can lead to the emergence and unfolding of the ways Muslims embrace Islam and the ways that Islam can be both project and projection of—at times contentious—aspirations. Thus a baseline premise of the volume is that Islam is a discursive tradition (Asad 1993) that engages culture, religious discourse, class, gender, race, and realpolitik, through which Muslims and non-Muslims create identities of self and other, belonging and estrangement.

The scholarly literature on Muslims and Islam in North America has been growing exponentially, especially in the years since the attacks on September 11, 2001. However, in other parts of the hemisphere these communities—their assorted histories, cultures, ethnicities, and forms of religious identification—remain, in comparison, little studied. The important question of what topics enjoy formal study is not limited to Muslims and Islam; other significant New World populations also remain under-researched, such as Arab immigrant communities, the majority of which have historically been Christian. The exploration of how these diverse diasporic populations may be connected regionally and globally by shared worldviews, historical memory, values, and practices, or disengaged from them, and what the implications of such linkages and ruptures might be, reveals a focus of study still in its early stages. By emphasizing wide-ranging historical and ethnographic comparison, our broadest goal is to foster fresh dialogue, an imperative in the quest for equality and social justice. In calling attention to the contingent meanings and expressions of Islam among heterogeneous Muslim communities, and among those who observe and engage them, we encourage readers to examine in an informed and dispassionate way some ideas and assumptions about "the other" that are often taken for granted. This kind of approach rests on a commitment to begin by querying the very forms of knowledge we rely on and the conceptual categories that serve as our frames of reference.

The volume begins with my discussion of some key issues in the storied hemisphere of Islam that the New World presents. Contributors' chapters are organized into three thematic sections. Part I, Histories: Presence, Absence, Remaking, looks at the ways in which Muslim identities and the traditions, practices, and tensions that lend them substance are forged in the constant and inextricable relationship between history (social fact, sociohistorical process) and historiography (the recounting of facts and processes according to vantage point and perception of stakes involved). Historical narratives about and by Muslims in the New World are imperative correctives to the silences that distort our understanding of the past and distract from the basic problematic of "truth"; as Michel-Rolph Trouillot has observed, "the production of historical narratives involves the uneven contribution of competing groups and individuals who have unequal access to the means for such production" (Trouillot 1995: xix). Knowledge of the histories and historiographies of Muslims in the New World is also imperative in order to appreciate both the range and the reach of influences, forces, and creative forms of agency that produce Islam and its practitioners.

The four chapters in part I are stories of a hemisphere's becoming: the confluence of diverse and often unexpected forces and events that create place, person, and group, identified or self-identified as "Muslim," in the process shaping the histories of this part of the world. The proposal of this section is not only that Islam comes in numerous expressions but that these expressions are not limited to what is anticipated and obvious: delimited, identifiable national or ethnic groups engaging in recognizable religious practices. Of course these communities contribute to the cultural, political, and social landscapes of their places of settlement. But as these case studies show, critically important are the unexpected uses and interpretations of Islam, whose practitioners are necessarily, unavoidably in dialogue with a host of immediate and distant, empirical and imagined interlocutors. These far-ranging, indeed, global, dialogues produce profound—if at times unintended, unanticipated, or unappreciated—consequences for Muslims' belief and practice that are not merely carry-over transplants in diaspora but are embedded into the generative currents that make Muslims in the New World, that make New World Islam, and that in turn make the histories of the Americas. The latter are much more than the sum of accumulating (incoming) parts; rather, they are the discursive consequences of these parts in dialogical relation to one another.

Jacob Dorman discusses nineteenth-century U.S. public culture as it was shaped by the appropriation of Islamic history and the performance of Islamic ritual by white and black Shriners. In their initial incarnation as a white male fraternal organization, the Shriners developed a gendered persona of ribald parody of both the post–Civil War American (allegedly feminizing) fascination with the "Oriental" East and the increasing public presence of women in the social movements of the day—religious, reform, suffrage. Using parody as a masculinist agenda, the Shriners drew from compiled "facts and fancies" about Muslims and their countries, cultures, and histories, emphasizing the exotic and erotic; suitable game for ridiculing what these Shriners saw as the hypocritical Victorian valorization in the United States of the mystical Orient.

In this midcentury moment, Americans of African descent were subject to new systems of segregation and disfranchisement. Thus, by contrast, when founding their own Shriners organizations, black Shriners treated their role and activities with solemn respect. Like black churches, black lodges provided one of the few means of self-determination and social mobility available. Evoking both Islamic and Judeo-Christian imagery, and performing secret and public rituals based on a global imagined community of Muslims (and Shriners and Masons), black Shriners established historical and mythical genealogies to the Holy Land. Their white Shriner counterparts may have treated their narrative and employment of Islam as "an elaborate joke," but both engaged Islam. Dorman shows that white and black Shriners' distinctly American version of fraternalism was informed to great extent by their reliance on the documented and putative characteristics and traditions of Islam, whether in jest or with respect. They did so by analogy and metaphor rather than literally through text-based doctrine, but the effects have been palpable:

for example, the Shriners' well-known children's hospitals, and black Shriners' rites as important inspiration for the rise of Black Muslim sects in the United States. No matter how perhaps attenuated, or distinct from each other, neither group could be what it is without their various engagements, for better or worse, with (what they thought to be) Islam. And as Dorman concludes, not only have there been occasions when Americans identified with the Muslim Orient—they have not always imagined Muslims as enemies.

Moving forward a few decades and turning to the Dutch Caribbean, Rosemarijn Hoefte considers the case of mid-twentieth-century Muslim Javanese—"Asian"—immigrant labor in Suriname. Arriving in the 1920s and 1930s, these immigrants brought with them a divided interpretation of Islam: reformist and traditionalist. Reformists emphasized the clearing away of cultural traditions and non-Islamic ceremonies from their practice of Islam, emphasizing a strict adherence to the Five Pillars of Islam and critiquing what they saw as corruptions in the form of belief in spirits and deities (influences from Hinduism, Buddhism, and animism) and partaking in alcohol, gambling, and other forms of perceived immorality. A key symbol of the reformists' religious orthodoxy was facing east for prayer. The traditionalists rejected what they interpreted as the reformists' "Arabization" and emphasized prayer facing west. As Hoefte shows, by the 1940s and 1950s this opposing East versus West stance about prayer could not be understood as simply a matter of religious conflict; rather, it also represented larger and more complex issues about the ways that these Muslim Javanese and their progeny imagined, and struggled over, their economic and political futures, both as settlers in Suriname and, via an ultimately unsuccessful repatriation effort, in Java.

The growing ethnic consciousness among Javanese in Suriname was based both on Islam and on Indonesian nationalism, of which migrants in Suriname kept abreast through the print media as well as by word of mouth from new arrivals from Java. The cohesion of community solidarities based on these ethnic and religious sentiments abraded against local postwar assimilationist ideals, made concrete with the advent in 1948 of universal suffrage and the formation of political parties. Stakeholders in these dialogues were Muslim "East" reformists, Muslim "West" traditionalists, those who wished to repatriate to Java (fueled in part by an idealized vision of their past), those who wished to secure their future in Suriname, with Afro-Surinamese calling for only a gradual introduction of universal voting rights (thereby avoiding the swelling of other power bases), and politicians grappling with demands (and objections to those demands) for the recognition of non-Christian religions, notably via the Asian Marriage Law. Although all-encompassing, Surinamese assimilation ideology still sought to maintain the dominance of Christianity, a wholesale application of the law, and the depression of Asian (Javanese) influence, especially considering the activities of political entities like the influential Indonesian Islamic Organization.

It was not until changes in the political economy at the turn of the twenty-first century that new immigration of Javanese Surinamese was spurred, this time to the Netherlands. And although east- and west-facing Muslims in Suriname continued to differ about their interpretations of Islam, the rancorous tone of these debates diminished as the political economy improved the life chances of all Surinamese. As Hoefte makes clear in her detailed analysis, what is understood at first blush to be a "religious question," involving ideological disagreements about the place of cultural practices in worship and belief among Javanese Muslims in Suriname, is also deeply implicated within colonial and postcolonial politics, economics, and sovereignty struggles among Indonesian, Dutch, and Surinamese stakeholders. It is all of these forces in simultaneous play that have created the Suriname that knows Islam today.

The relationship between Islam and an Asian or "Asiatic" identity takes on a different cast in the context of the first half of the twentieth century in the United States, as part of the racialization processes of the period. Nathaniel Deutsch examines the complex connections between race and Islam through tackling the fascinating and difficult question of how Lothrop Stoddard, one of the best-known early twentieth-century white racists in the United States, became a key source of knowledge for Malcolm X, one of the nation's most influential African American social justice activists of the 1960s. The answer lies in an intricate historical narrative that binds the century's global thought, notably science and scientific racism, and Pan-African, Pan-Asian, and Pan-Islamic movements. All are deeply implicated in global discourse about the past, present, and future of Islam, including Islam's relationship to race. This conversation, Deutsch argues, contradicts the idea of North American isolation from the broad intellectual currents of the day. Rather, it reveals a century of transnational interchange between modern Islamic and non-Islamic thinkers that drew together the Islamic world, Europe, and North America.

This global conversation about Islam—its history, its present, and its future—is an important window onto the influences that the intellectual cross-pollination between modern Islamic and non-Islamic thinkers had on the formation of the American landscape in terms of contemporary notions of national and cultural identity among Americans and others. Middle Eastern

Muslims in the first decades of the twentieth century were engaged in a process of redefining Islam through the combined lenses of Islamic and Western categories; Western (European and American) Orientalists were sympathetic to Islam as they envisioned it, not as "primitive" or "savage" but as a producer of civilization with identifiable historical achievements and capable, as Deutsch reports Stoddard's term, of a "Renaissance."

The fertile American dialogues of the early twentieth century revealed ideas about the compatibility between Muslim and non-Muslim worlds. As Deutsch argues, while Lothrop Stoddard concurred with the view of Islam's alleged historical decline, he espoused the belief that drawing from its intellectual traditions and historical achievements, Islam was worthy of Western attention and engagement. One important characteristic of Islam identified by Muslim, non-Muslim, Pan-Islamic, and Pan-Asian thinkers alike was Islam's affinity with and incorporation of the world's different races and cultures. Yet these were not merely sanguine acknowledgments. Subject to the racial and other logics of the day, Islam's bridging capacity took on important distinctions. On the one hand, African American intellectuals like Hubert Harrison and Malcolm X viewed Islam as the better alternative to Christianity, given what they saw as its lack of historical association with enslavement and racism in the Americas. In this American era, Pan-Islamism had explicitly linked itself to the struggle of peoples of color against white supremacy and European colonialism, significantly influencing the black nationalism that emerged. On the other hand, this linkage between Islam and subaltern populations, perhaps not surprisingly, was interpreted in white racist thought as a threat to white dominion. Yet as Deutsch's analysis persuasively reveals, the seemingly strange intellectual fellowship of Stoddard and Malcolm X is not idiosyncratic or strange at all when understood in the context of global conversations about Islam among interlocutors who saw themselves as sharing as well as lacking commonalities, and thus, for a time, imbricated identities.

Creative fellowship ties together Puerto Rico and the United States in Omar Ramadan-Santiago's chapter on Muslim Puerto Rican hip-hop artists. Working to form for themselves a cohesive triptych of Muslim, Puerto Rican, and hip-hop identities, these young men engage in self-taught cultural and religious history to ground their claims of belonging in multiple arenas and to challenge their experience of social marginalization. Hip-hop art is where their identities converge and are imaginatively asserted. The activities and philosophies of these artists resonate with the present post-9/11 moment of religious identity transformation and the rise of what some call the "new

Islams." Unexpected convergences and perceived affinities among these domains of identity construction illustrate multiple and simultaneous Muslim identities in continuous creation.

In their goal to expand what it means to be Muslim, Puerto Rican, and hip-hop artists, Ramadan-Santiago's informants (interlocutors, as he refers to them) seek ownership of identities from which they are otherwise excluded or marginalized. Hegemonic imagery portrays this particular religion, culture, and art form as mutually exclusive, or at least in uneasy juxtaposition. In asserting their legitimate claim to all three simultaneously, Muslim Puerto Rican hip-hop artists deconstruct the stereotyped representations that encase identities into distinct, isolable essences. Key to this reconstruction is pedagogy: the reeducation by Muslim Puerto Rican hip-hop artists, for themselves and for others (Muslims and non-Muslims alike), through religious and secular means. One mode of their auto-didacticism is treating hip-hop as a form of *da'wah*, an invitation to Islam (or Islamic proselytizing), writing and performing hip-hop lyrics in which the message educates listeners about Islam and in the process strives to correct misperceptions. As one artist put it, "Islam was evangelized by hip-hop." Another pedagogical mode is availing themselves of academic scholarship on the histories of Africans and Muslims in the Americas in general and in Puerto Rico in particular. Both modes are seen by these young men as compatible and equally effective in what might be viewed as identity reclamation projects.

The standard by which their identity claims are deemed legitimate and therefore irrefutable is "authenticity." These young men rely on the same tropes of authenticity that also differentiate them from what is purportedly "real." In a sense, they dismantle, to a point, the master's house with the master's tools.[1] It is only to a point because an idea of what Ramadan-Santiago calls "naturalness" is a desired outcome of the pedagogical projects of da'wah and secular academic scholarship. Here "natural" connotes appropriate or valid, but it can also carry an implication of essence. In arguing that history proves Islam is not a "foreign" religion in Puerto Rico, that Muslims in Muslim minority societies are as Muslim as those from Muslim majority societies, that there is a more "pure" Islamic past as well as an originary hip-hop to which to return, that the "religio-cultural synthesis" of which Ramadan-Santiago speaks does not change their culture, religion, or identities as Puerto Rican, and that the rightful occupation of these identities is the measure of "authenticity," Islam is simultaneously construed as responsive yet deep-seated, fluid yet definitive, without borders yet situated. This thinking does not indicate contradictory logic. Instead it reveals the creative agency evinced by these artists, who, to borrow from Karl Marx's famous comment, are remaking histories of their own making but of which they have been denied a part.

Part II, Circulation of Identities, Politics of Belonging, moves readers into the current moment of late twentieth- to early twenty-first-century globalization, particularly in the form of migration and settlement, encounters among immigrant and indigenous or local communities, and the social structures that are transformed or that emerge from these processes. Strategies of distancing and belonging characterize these interactions, as representations, ways of knowing, and competing claims to those ways of knowing are marshaled and collide. The salient question becomes what the *ummah*, or global Muslim community, means in a deterritorialized world. Will local ways of knowing be subsumed by universalizing canons, or will the vernacular take precedence, and what might that mean for both the evaluation and the practice of Islam? Also brought to the fore is the question of what it means to be "indigenous" or "immigrant," foreign as opposed to local, irrespective of historical trajectory or century of arrival. Mediated symbols circulate across the globe with or without their embodied travelers. Customs and traditions become scrutinized according to new and different perspectives (assumptions and expectations). And beliefs and practices are called upon to make other kinds of sense, both to practitioners and to observers.

The global ramifications of the post-9/11 "war on terror" take a fascinatingly figurative turn in Yarimar Bonilla's analysis of the "Madassamy Affair" in Guadeloupe and the symbolism of Osama Bin Laden applied to labor activism there. Exploring how and why this analogy—otherwise without any religious or political substance—was possible, and resonant, Bonilla shows that being necessarily embedded in broader contexts of practice and meaning, Islam is always global in its local manifestations, and as such, it can reveal a great deal about phenomena only ostensibly unrelated.

In this case the salient context of practice and meaning is the current "war on terror" and its associated iconographies. Although at first glance perhaps a seemingly unlikely arena, the Francophone world of Overseas Departments, including France's Caribbean possessions, is not exempt from the circumstances in other parts of the world where terror, Islam, policing, and judicial concerns have fused. In this widespread climate, an (ersatz) Islamic "other" is posed in opposition to the fundamental universalist values of the French Republic, and by extension the "free world," not the least basis for this being an emphasis on a shared encompassing nationality rather than disaggregated interest groups—religious, ethnic, racial. (See Hoefte's essay in this volume for a similar tension.) As Bonilla's analysis reveals, freedom and democracy can be as much floating signifiers as can terror. Her discussion highlights one example of terror's iconography, a cartoon that represented as Osama Bin Laden a major local Guadeloupean labor activist, Michel Madassamy.

As an Indian (that is, of South Asian descent), Madassamy is not an Arab. But as a Guadeloupean of Indian descent, like Indian-descended peoples in other parts of the Caribbean, he occupies what is locally a culturally ambiguous, and ambivalent, space. As a labor activist, he has no affiliation with Bin Laden, Al Qaeda, or so-called jihadist movements, yet his circulated image of long beard and frontal stare was a model of Muslim-terrorist-Arab (despite the majority of Indo-Caribbean people being Hindu). It was also a model of charismatic, Gandhi-like spirituality (irrespective of that Hindu majority), as the success of the labor union activism grew. Centered within the conflation of global discourse about Islam and about terror and local discourse about labor activism and Indian-Guadeloupeans, the "Madassamy Affair" exemplifies the ways in which an iconic figure such as Bin Laden can signify the West's war on terror, bringing the war home both metaphorically in terms of the connotations conveyed and literally in terms of the disciplining, prosecutorial arm of governance. Globally circulated images can make locally defined "enemies" of the state. But this case also illuminates how hegemonic narratives and counter-narratives engage each other. Labor activists exercised their own agency as they emphasized Madassamy's charismatic qualities in service of other key symbols, like solidarity and justice, rejecting his denigration (and by extension, that of labor activists and Indians), in promotion of their own values and goals.

In her chapter on Maya Muslim converts in Chiapas, Sandra Cañas Cuevas underscores the larger context of recent transformative processes that have been taking place in Latin America in general and Mexico in particular, to show how conversion to Islam among indigenous Maya is a multilayered, global phenomenon involving unexpectedly disparate interests and complicated agendas. Among these are several interlaced factors. One is the crisis in the Catholic Church having to do with an ongoing decline in its membership, not unrelated to competition from Protestant denominations. Another is the Zapatista uprising, among the responses to the structural adjustment policies of neoliberal economies, which in Mexico included the privatization of land (land reform). A third factor is the increasing diversification of non-Catholic religions in Mexico, including proselytizing by overseas Muslims, such as those from Andalusia, Spain, who saw in their Islamic critique of state and market oppression a resonance with the Zapatista mission. A fourth key factor is a fluid conversion environment, where prior to Islam local Maya had embraced forms of Protestantism, notably in Presbyterian and Seventh Day Adventist congregations. Finally, the 1992 recognition of Mexico's multicultural composition in its constitution reinforced the country's ethnic groups as possessing distinct cultural rights. These diverse but connected forces have created a social, political, and economic environment that has both encouraged Chiapas Maya conversion to Islam and reshaped its contours.

Contending with historical marginalization, increasing political-economic disfranchisement, and being undermined in pervasive land struggles, Chiapas Maya work to rebuild and improve their lives. They do this to a significant degree in their embrace of Islam. As Cañas Cuevas thoughtfully discusses, however, although Muslim Maya have found in Islam important means to reconstruct their communities, it is not without challenges and difficulties. These complications center largely on differences in interpretation, and valorization of certain Islamic precepts between Spanish Muslim converts and Chiapas Maya Muslim converts. At the heart of these tensions is the problematic of *culture*: the representational substance of Islam (also see Dorman, Hoefte, Deutsch, and Ramadan-Santiago, this volume). Spanish Muslim converts disapprove of the use of the indigenous Maya language Tsotsil, and their style of dress, their main cuisine items (including maize), and their inclination to cultivate social and political networks with other indigenous but non-Muslim Maya. Fission resulted between 2004 and 2007, and Maya Muslims who formed new communities practice Islam, as Cañas Cuevas puts it, according to their own cultural logic.

Had this been the end of the story it would in actuality be just the beginning. Particularly through a consideration of Maya Muslim women's experience, it is clear that selective appropriation of certain aspects of Islam render it into what these practitioners see as a more inclusive religion. Their choices, Cañas Cuevas argues, fly in the face of stereotypical assumptions about Islam—for example, that ethnic identification is subsumed by Islam—or such assumptions as those posited in some feminist critique, which has Muslim women as at best, passive, and at worst, victims, and Muslim men as their oppressors. Like the speciousness of a universal explanation of Islam vis-à-vis ethnic identity, Maya Muslim women's expressions of agency shape it as much as it shapes them (see Ali, Baptiste, this volume).

These specificities are due in no small part to the contact between the Chiapas Maya worldview of their culture and their view of Islam. For example, these Maya put a (cultural) premium on gender segregation that does not derive from Islam. Contrary to initial expectations, perhaps, gender segregation therefore need not be a point of contention or a key indicator of women's status. Maya ideas about marriage, however, are not in concert with Islamic allowances for polygamy, which was encouraged by the Spanish Muslims and directed toward the Maya. In Maya communities, Cañas Cuevas explains, the interpretation of such arrangements is adultery and is punishable, with women and men being entitled to the same rights. That said, perhaps another unexpected effect is that Spanish Muslims promoted the idea of friendship and courtship among the Maya, which is not their traditional practice (although not unknown among them since Protestant conversions). As a result, Maya Muslim women's ability to choose a partner was reinforced as common rather than anomalous practice. Finally, Islamic teachings have influenced Maya Muslim approaches to the environment and preserving their natural resources, encouraging another, perhaps unexpected, global conversation. These and other examples show that "culture" and "religion," in debates about Islam or any other religious tradition, are at odds only in ideological terms—vernacular or dominant. Some aspects of culture are compatible with religious precepts, and others are not. Decisions about what is and is not acceptable do not emanate only from religious strictures but may be generated by cultural predilection as well.

Jerusa Ali focuses on the lives and perceptions of *Muslimahs*, or Muslim women, in the Bahamas and Brazil as she examines the relationship between religious faith and identity construction in these two localities. Through extensive interviews that give her Muslimah informants a central voice, Ali is able to show that coherence in Islamic canons is a fundamental value among practitioners, yet is not imagined in reductive or uniform ways. This nuanced view lends important support to Ali's argument that it is within changing global as well as local networks of power relations that these women's aspirations to present themselves as exemplary Muslimahs are shaped simultaneously by context-contingent Islamic religious ideals and the fluid exigencies of their locally ensconced daily lives.

The Muslimahs with whom Ali worked self-identify with their country of origin; thus they are "Bahamian" and "Brazilian," respectively. Their ethnicity is a mixture of African, European, South Asian, and/or Amerindian heritage, which differentiates them from first, second, and third generation Arab and South Asian diasporic communities in the Bahamas and in Brazil. Most of the women are either converts to Islam or are first generation Muslims. They represent a range of social and class backgrounds and have been influenced by a number of Islamic schools of thought. Ali is interested in Muslimahs' perspectives on what it means to be Muslim in contexts where social and religious belonging and legitimacy involve ideas about what is foreign and what is local vis-à-vis Islam, what is mixed and what is pure vis-à-vis Muslim genealogies, and hence what the ideal Muslimah is in aspiration and in lived practice.

As Ali argues, these considerations, configured from the local, mean that women in these "mixed" Muslim minority communities are not necessarily firmly, incontestably embedded within the ummah, given what one might call their "creole" identities, the distinctions made between "immigrant" and "foreign" (which are not always synonymous), and the discourses of authenticity that circulate among and about them. Various experiences of alienation work to dislodge the feelings of rootedness upon which belonging and other forms of what can be called cultural citizenship depend. Among these immigrant and local communities the dedication of some to da'wah, in this case meaning orthodox religious observance, is posed against charges against others of over-commitment to such worldly concerns as commercial enterprise. An ostensibly *a*-cultural Islam is posed against an Islam that is (inappropriately) saturated with cultural practices. Critique of the "Arabization" of Islam is contrasted with the possibility for other constructions of the ideal Muslimah. And conversion to Islam among a number of these Muslimahs can result in feelings of estrangement from their families and also from immigrant Muslim communities, not only in religious terms but in terms of differences in language and customs as well.

These women negotiate their feelings about belonging and alienation, their ideas about the relationship between culture and religion, and their subscription to ideal as opposed to idealized Islamic identities by redefining the terms of these conversations. Many resist being identified as a particular kind of Muslim (e.g., Sunni, Shi'a), reject the premise that an Arab pedigree translates as more authentic Islam, and, in their fashion, argue for a conceptually deterritorialized ummah where "Muslim" is an overarching indicative rather than a label associated with a particular ethnic homeland. The unifying theme in the narratives of her informants, Ali explains, is that the Muslim ummah should be increasingly deterritorialized and thereby be progressively more open-minded and transformative.

Part III, Spatial Practices and the Trinidadian Landscape, focuses on a single site, Trinidad, to consider Islam in its relation to the practice and meaning of visibility in Muslim minority societies. The case of Trinidad is particularly apt because it is such a society and is also organized according to and permeated by its colonial social formation. In Trinidad's colonial origins, a system of stratification based on a class-race-color hierarchy—beginning with slavery and continuing through emancipation and indenture—laid the foundations for an independent republic, the hallmark of which has been ethnic group competition fostered by class inequalities and state control of certain resources. Having implemented a parliamentary system of communal politics, notably voting blocs organized along ethnic/racial group lines, post-independence nationalism operates within clear ethno-racial political divisions (primarily Afro-/Indo-Trinidadian) while promoting a discourse of "callaloo" (mixed) harmony that is said to characterize this multiculturally diverse population. The organization of state patronage and distribution of resources follows communally defined groups who define themselves according to what Raymond Williams (1977), in another context, has termed "selected traditions," and who make their social presence felt by public performance of those traditions—typically construed as religious or cultural. These politics of visibility engendered by the state-nation relationship influence the meaning of space and spatial practices: the everyday actions through which spaces are made and challenged, the interactions and power dynamics among people, objects, acts, and their forms of representation that carve out symbolic and literal domains that, in turn, assert various strategies of identification. The four chapters in part III ask readers to question the binary dividing "public" and "private," to reflect on what can equate the "personal" and the "political," and to apprehend some key ways in which spatial practices are necessarily linked to identity construction.

Looking at the changing position of Muslim women in Muslim worship practices in Trinidad, particularly access to and use of *masjid* (mosque) space, Rhoda Reddock frames her discussion with an exploration of the historical role of Muslim reformer Moulvi Ameer Ali and with a recent example of activism by a female member of a major local *jamaat* (congregation). Reddock then presents three contemporary examples of women's ongoing struggle over the use of masjid space. Their varied engagement with global Islamization projects shapes their demands as well as the multilayered meanings women give to "visibility" in religious practice. Reddock argues that the liminal space of identity construction and the congregational space of worship together provide the conditions of possibility to challenge patriarchal forms of religious power.

As is also the case among Muslim women in other parts of the world, Muslim women in Trinidad have a history of investment in diverse forms of struggle about their relationship to Islam in gendered terms. In Reddock's analysis, the crux of these concerns is in the problematic of space and its access—restricted, public, liminal, private. Muslim women challenge hegemonic meanings of gendered space by pressing for the right to congregational worship, rights that Reddock suggests have been notably curtailed since the rise of Islamist movements and their influence in Trinidad. The issue of masjid access is, among other things, a generational one, whereby Muslim women who grew up in a more gender-equitable time in Trinidadian Islam (prior to the 1980s) had a different religious experience and orientation to Islam than do new converts. "Islamist-influenced women," as Reddock identifies them, tend not to be discontented with gender-segregated masjid worship space and remain within a patriarchal understanding of Islam (although we must also remember that these women may not necessarily concur with other aspects of patriarchal Islamic codes).

In posing the question of why there was in Trinidadian Islam's early history a greater autonomy for Muslim women than there is today, or at least the expectation of it, Reddock looks to the material conditions particular to the sugar plantation system, a system that in general did not valorize women's equal rights. Her point is instructive: spatial practices are not only a form of agency, in this case Muslim women's, but they can grow in the unexpected liminal spaces and pockets of systems-within-systems—that is, Islam on the British colonial plantation. Rather than thinking only in terms of a double oppression (but certainly not rejecting its effects), Reddock asks readers to consider acts of piety as both conforming and noncompliant at the same time.

Muslim women's bodies become their own spatial practices when thrust into gender-segregated, or gender-prohibited, arenas like the masjid, or when thrust into the public sphere presenting a sartorial message of religiously defined modesty, as Reddock also discusses with respect to wearers of the *hijab* (head covering) and *niqaab* (face veil). In the context of a relatively new Islamic orthodoxy (Islamization), women negotiate between conformity to a relatively new, globally linked, and more visible Islam, of which they want to be a part, and their long-familiar traditions of collective worship, whose message of gender equity also happens to be a part of a relatively new, globally linked, and more visible human rights discourse. As Reddock concludes, the contact zones where these different agents, objectives, representations, and strategies meet provide the possibilities for challenges to patriarchal power, of which women's masjid struggles are an important part.

Taking a 2004 election of executive officers in the Jama Masjid, the city of San Fernando's major jamaat, affiliated with Trinidad's leading Indo-Muslim organization, the Anjuman Sunnat ul-Jamaat (ASJA), Gabrielle Hosein analyzes the relationship between democratic practices derived from the parliamentary politics of the republic and the "spiritual correctness" for which ASJA members strive. At stake is the perpetuation or disruption of local ideas about Muslim forms of modernity, as male and female members of the jamaat seek to reconcile religious and secular ideas about what participatory democracy means. Hosein's analysis shows that although universalist in theory, democracy, as a model of rights and belonging, is in practice an experience made particular according to differential gender norms, definitions of religious piety, and investments in modernity.

Hosein highlights a conflict embedded in this election, which hinged on the exclusion of women from involvement in the election process. Expressed as debate and as mutual accusation, the conflict reveals anxieties about exercising the prerogatives of a secular-rational, democratic society based on the British parliamentary system—campaigning, holding elections—while keeping the realm of the sacred free of the corruptions of politics. These corrupting influences were perceived to be channeled through processes of creolization, which, as Hosein shows, have different implications for (proper) femininity and masculinity, if also being the inevitable consequence of modernity and thus threats to the alleged purity of unworldly concerns (even those concerns dealing with the issue of organizational leadership). Jama Masjid women and men are oriented in distinct, gendered ways to the worldly, modern concerns of equal enfranchisement and representation and to the "spiritual," traditional concerns about correctly expressed piety and appropriate gender roles in Islam. As Hosein argues, Indo-Trinidadian Muslim modernity must be understood as a "lived meaning" created in the intersections of religious and secular forms of authority, normative gender role expectations, and competing claims to belonging. These are configured, in part, by the recuperation of creolization as more indicative of modernity than as a tarnishing agent.

Jeanne Baptiste offers a case study of the members of the Jamaat al Muslimeen, a Trinidadian Muslim community about which much less is known relative to their prominence in the entwined political and racial discourse of the country. Exploring the relationship among nation-building, governmentality, the Zeitgeist of post-9/11 fear of Islam, and the gendered criminalization of blackness and the Muslim body, Baptiste argues that the Muslimeen is more socially incorporated within Trinidadian society than has typically been perceived. This social incorporation is particularly significant because it exists in conjunction with and in spite of a prevailing local discourse separating the Muslimeen from mainstream Trinidadian society. This separateness is construed in spatial terms: there is the physical compound that delineates (or warns of, depending upon one's point of view) the Muslimeen's presence. But its dimensions also symbolize another kind of presence, one personifying a contemporary global imaginary that draws together Islam and blackness with the common thread of dangerous other.

Baptiste tackles the ideological tensions between the Muslimeen as a place of possibility for the disempowered and disfranchised (a positive crucible of resistance) and as a negative signifier of criminality (where racialization conveys the same message of blackness vis-à-vis members both Afro- and Indo-Trinidadian). In focusing on the ordinary lives of Muslimeen members, Baptiste presents these women and men as agentive actors rather than as passive spectacle. In the process, she posits, we will be better able to understand Muslims in Muslim minority societies as real persons living by Islamic doctrine, as they understand it, rather than as reduced to a stereotyped ideal, or model, of Islam that is far from "ideal." As Baptiste recounts it, Muslimeen members lace efforts to meet the expectations of their religious convictions with their own perspectives and idiosyncrasies. These creative acts produce new—or perhaps to observers unfamiliar—formations of the person. Notable are the care with which many Muslimeen men seek to follow Islamic precepts about harmonious relations with wives, dispelling the image of the aggressively over-sexualized, racialized (black) Muslimeen man, and the *pious sexuality*, as Baptiste terms it, through which many Muslimeen women understand what is thought of as an unproblematic intertwining of spirituality and carnality. Baptiste suggests that the worlds of everyday life are enigmatic and therefore that the Muslimeen is an evocative example of Muslims' lives being much more than simply a Dawud versus Jalut (David vs. Goliath) metaphor. More productive is to look at the spaces of creative, ordinary living between the binaries.

Patricia Mohammed considers the emergence of an Islamic iconography in Trinidad, starting with the Indians brought there during the nineteenth and twentieth centuries under the British colonial indentured labor project and continuing into the current moment. Although the Islamic iconography that Mohammed discusses is largely of Indian immigrant origin, she also recognizes both the pre-emancipation role of Africans in the Americas in casting Caribbean Islamic aesthetics and the present-day contribution to those aesthetics of Afro-Caribbean Muslims returning to what some of them see as their earlier African Islamic heritage (see Ramadan-Santiago, this volume). Focus on key arenas of public presentation in Trinidad illustrates how the different aesthetic spaces within which Islam works are created by spatial practices that have emerged from the multiculturalism-generated politics of representation, which have become the trademark of many New World creolization sites, island and mainland.

Diverse spatial practices shape and reflect different forms of consciousness, as Mohammed's historical trajectory suggests. On the one hand, indentured

Indian Muslims dressed in what were the common, and commoners,' clothes of their day, largely indistinguishable from those of their Hindu counterparts. Although not perhaps deliberately, against the backdrop of Trinidad's "Western" peoples of African and European descent, this clothing tradition made its own sartorial statement. On the other hand, the meditative donning of the hijab and niqaab adopted later creates a different kind of public visual space around the wearers, including a more explicitly religiously gendered one, and a more obliquely racialized one (see also Baptiste, this volume). Dotting the landscape with humble and grand masjids is another practice of visual space making. Still another is the insistent remembrance of mourning and fortitude represented by the street procession of the Hosay commemoration.

As Mohammed points out, Trinidad has no self-identified "Islamic" artists or locally produced public Islamic art other than the architecture of masjids and the event of Hosay. In Trinidadian Muslims' private settings, particularly their domestic arenas, the aesthetic is more austere, following the Islamic injunctions against representations of the human form; Mohammed suggests that this may have contributed to a lack of development of experimental artistic forms that, according to her thinking, could lead to more robust reckonings of iconic markers. Pointing to the stark contrast between this private tendency toward austerity and the public exuberance of the colors and emotions of Hosay, Mohammed raises the interesting idea that color and affect are mutually evocative, reminding us that spatial practices involve all of the senses.

* * *

Islam is never simply a self-referential story about itself. Steering us away from hoary debate about the demise of religion, the emptying of spirituality, reversion back to a darker age, and globalization as a particular imaginary of progress, this volume circles us back to the real issue: interpretive categories organize experience by collating and congealing all that we see, hear, and feel into the production of knowledge, but in their work of creating meaning, interpretive categories flex to an innumerable *possibility* of factors. This makes them able to do all kinds of ideological work that employs many and unpredictable interlocutors. Focused on local values, practices, traditions, and tensions, this collection places these within larger questions about what kinds of histories, social dynamics, and meaning production make Islam significant, or deny its significance, in a part of the world that largely has not recognized Islam as belonging to its historical foundation, that cannot claim majority Muslim populations, and yet in which configurations of Islam loom large. A number of the issues and conundrums presented in these pages share similarities with other Western contexts and the West's historical and contemporary engagement with Muslims and Islam. The volume does not make a case for an Ameri*cas* exceptionalism any more than it does for an Ameri*can* (U.S.) exceptionalism. At the same time, the New World is not simply reducible to "the West"; it represents one variation. This hemisphere constitutes both a Global North and a Global South, built in part by Muslims whose journeys span at least half a millennium (enslaved, indentured, educated, unlettered, activist, entrepreneurial, refugee), hailing from tremendously varied cultural and social terrains spanning much of the globe. As we seek to underscore in this collection, the relationship and relevance of Muslims to the New World is a dialogue of mutually constitutive presences—both figurative and literal. The New World is made and remade by the company of its "Muslim minority" populations. And Muslims, their identities embodied as immigrants and in their lifeways, are themselves being remade in the process. It has always been a dance of partners.

Notes

1. I am borrowing from Caribbean-American writer and activist Audre Lorde: "The master's tools will never dismantle the master's house."

References Cited

Asad, Talal
1986 "The Idea of an Anthropology of Islam." Occasional Paper Series. Center for Contemporary Arab Studies, Georgetown University.
1993 *Genealogies of Religion: Description and Reasons of Power in Christianity and Islam.* Baltimore: Johns Hopkins University Press.
Cesari, Jocelyne
2010 "Introduction." In *Muslims in the West after 9/11: Religion, Politics, and Law*, ed. Jocelyne Cesari, 1–6. London: Routledge.
Dirlik, Arif
2003 "Modernity in Question? Culture and Religion in an Age of Global Modernity." *Diaspora* 12(2): 147–68.
Ghaneabassiri, Kambiz
2010 *A History of Islam in America: From the New World to the New World Order.* Cambridge: Cambridge University Press.
Kettani, M. Ali
1986 *Muslim Minorities in the World Today.* London: Mansell Publishing.

Moghissi, Haideh, Saeed Rahnema, and Mark J. Goodman
2009 *Diaspora by Design: Muslims in Canada and Beyond.* Toronto: University of Toronto Press.
Trouillot, Michel-Rolph
1995 *Silencing the Past: Power and the Production of History.* Boston: Beacon Press.
Williams, Raymond
1977 *Marxism and Literature.* Oxford, UK: Oxford University Press.

2

Contours

Approaching Islam, Comparatively Speaking

AISHA KHAN

When he gave his tours of Park51, or the "Ground Zero mosque," to tourist groups in New York City, most of whom were not Muslim, American Muslim activist and former Park51 employee Rashid said he liked to emphasize a message of "*un*learning Islam and Muslims as strange or foreign people." It was July 2012 when we spoke, and tours had recently ceased to be offered by Park51, but Rashid kindly agreed to give me a recap of his presentation's central themes. Most important to him was a message of kinship, broadly conceived. He recounted one of his favorite examples, about the Prophet Mohammed, whom Rashid felt it imperative to convey "was not a random, crazed prophet, he's all the way back to Abraham. The *lineage* is what makes 'strange' or 'foreign' the wrong way to think." He went on to explain that as he sees it, "Islam is primordial, [it is] for everybody. 'Primordial' means it precedes or transcends ethnic groups or religions; Adam is the first prophet, and so [he] is part of the *human* story. Everything is Muslim, everything submits. Islam is universally applicable; things can be Muslim even if they're not affiliated with the *religion*."

In his understanding of the universal application of Islam, Rashid made a clear distinction between what he called "lower case islam" and "the big I Islam." The former might be viewed as generic: "if you are trying to get closer to the one God it's 'islamic' but not necessarily 'Islam.'" The "big I Islam" is particular, achieved "through the Prophet Mohammed; it's the institutionalized Islam." For this well-educated middle-class twenty-something American Muslim, Islam in a sense is dual: on the one hand, it is universal, it is about human striving for spirituality and toward God, recorded by the genealogical maps of human/God history; on the other hand, it is also particularized into code: the standardized expectations and canons of tailored belief.

On an August night in 1791, at an alleged, perhaps apocryphal, secret meeting of fellow slaves in Saint Domingue's Bois-Caiman forest, the religious and political leader Boukman purportedly held a Vodou ceremony, which, as the narrative goes, launched the Haitian Revolution. Boukman is celebrated in the Atlantic World by scholars, activists, artists, and ordinary people as a Haitian religious and political leader whose skill, charisma, commitment, and knowledge helped to change history and assert the dignity and authority of Vodou in the face of its detractors. This representation of Boukman—as a Haitian Vodou priest—is pervasive. However, Boukman also had a—less well known—relationship with Islam. What sparse historical records there are tell us that he was an English-speaking Jamaican, brought to Saint Domingue by a British slaver. Some historians (e.g., Buck-Morss 2009; Diouf 1998; Gomez 2005) suggest that the name Boukman was the French approximation of his sobriquet in English, "Book Man," called this because he was literate and purportedly owned a copy of a particular book, the Quran. Other respected Vodou leaders who, like Boukman, are indispensable emblems of slave revolts and the making of the Afro-Atlantic were François Mackandal and Boukman's contemporary Cecile Fatiman. Also like Boukman, both are associated with Islam and Muslim identity.

In 1999, when she was twelve years old, a young girl, let us call her Yasmin, emigrated with her family from Pakistan to Toronto, Canada. According to Canada's 2001 census, Muslims were 2 percent of the total population (Moghissi et al. 2009: 7). Although not presenting the specter of Muslim immigrant millions that prompts some in Europe to worry about an emerging "Eurabia," in the ten years between 1991 and 2001 the Muslim population in Canada grew by 128.9 percent (Moghissi et al. 2009: 7). Four years after her arrival, when she was sixteen, Yasmin voluntarily began to wear a *niqaab*, or veil, over her face, something her mother and her sisters do not do. Talking with her in August 2012, I asked her about her decision. She explained her reasons in this way: "My decision to wear the niqaab, similar to my sisters' and mother's decision to wear the hijab, is first and foremost in accordance with the verses of the Quran, which obligate women to cover themselves. Some scholars believe that along with hair, these verses also include the face. I decided to cover my face first and foremost because I felt that these scholars had strong arguments and evidence to prove this and thus it was mandatory according to the Quran." Another motivation that Yasmin explained in our conversation was her experience of trying to fit in at school and "desperately failing," which made her "realize that everyone is different and we shouldn't be afraid of expressing our thoughts, values, and beliefs regardless of what others think. Although some people like the niqaab [and] want to adopt it, they feel scared that they will be too different from the norm. In my case, because I had already gone through this experience of 'being too different,' I was not afraid of being shunned once again. By this time I had also developed strong friendships among my peers, who supported my decision and stuck by me even if I was met with criticism from time to time. Once I started wearing the niqaab, I realized that some people judged niqaabis to be uneducated or backwards or a nuisance. I decided to take it upon myself to prove people wrong." Yasmin continued that this "added goal" was meant to show that niqaabis, like other women, pursue "good careers," seek "nice futures," have "good manners," are "neat and tidy," and "can love and excel in computer programming"—as Yasmin herself does. "So, basically," she said, "my niqaab made me more conscious of my actions in high school and university because I felt like whatever I did, I was doing it on behalf of all the other niqaabis and Muslim girls out there." Yasmin concluded that "Toronto is actually a very nice multicultural city," due in part to the protections offered by Canada's *Charter of Rights and Freedoms*, which, she said, "back me up."

At the turn of the seventeenth century John Smith had brought with him to the colony of Virginia extensive experience fighting Turks in Ottoman Europe, long before he crossed the Atlantic: "he prided himself as a hearty crusader against the Muslims" (Marr 2006: 2). As Timothy Marr remarks, Smith's involvement in the Islamic orient foreshadowed his point of view toward peoples and places in America, including his relationship with Pocahontas (Marr 2006: 3). Moreover, Smith's story reveals one way "old world patterns of disdaining 'others' were imported into new world spaces as a strategy to situate the strangeness of cultural difference" (Marr 2006: 3; Schueller 1998). Although no monolithic framework satisfactorily accounts for the array of discourses about the East generated in the West (Toner 2013: 17), multiplicity typically was congealed into predominant binary oppositions.[1] During its colonial and nationalist periods, America invented its moral legitimacy partly through comparison with the Islamic world: Islam was antichristian, America embodied Christian purity; Islam meant barbaric despotism, America was an enlightened democracy; Islam exuded immoderate sensuality, indolence, and irrational fatalism, America valued public chastity, hard work, and progressive reform (Marr 2006: 10). As is all too familiar, negative contrasts often serve as handy substitutes for actual substance.

These four narratives span more than two centuries, cross thousands of miles, and present a number of different perspectives. Yet they are tied together by a central problematic: the practice and representation of Islam, an

Old World religious tradition in the New World of the Americas, on the part of those who live or strive to live within its canons and by those who have been their interlocutors (both known and unseen). In these dialogues, "Old" and "New" worlds are connected by common themes that point both to the contentious permeation of worldviews and to the emergence of alternative social and cultural spaces from those permeations. One theme involves enlisting Islam to engage a powerful other, whether through self-explanation and justification, as in Rashid's and Yasmin's expositions, or through organized resistance, as in the Boukman story, the Haitian Revolution, and other slave rebellions. When we include experiences that pattern behavior and expectations, as in John Smith's prefigured attitudes, we see Islam as a means of agency within structures of power that are specific to the conquest of the New World and development of the Americas, striking in their variation yet belonging to similar projects and logics. Thus the examples point to another theme in the bridges between Old and New worlds that Muslims and their non-Muslim interlocutors build: how to understand the flow of religious traditions across space and time; how to assess their transformations and the efforts to prevent or deny those transformations; how to generalize through comparison of commonalities without losing sight of the contrasts posed by particulars; how to create from religious traditions such delimited territories as "the New World," "the Americas," and "the West" as well as ascertain the meaning and significance of these bounded entities.

Approaching Islam as a medium that interlocks Old and New worlds while contributing to the creation of those new worlds underscores another theme: the twin ideas of modernity and the "West." Both ideas symbolize conditions of being, measures of progress, and modes of valuation, about which I will say more momentarily. Abiding and tenacious notions, they have retained their core definitive features yet have also been put to the test—of validity, of usefulness—in sites that are not self-evidently "non-Western." That is, one might say that *wests* are embedded within *the West*, which raises the question of how we approach Islam and Muslims who have over decades or centuries become *of* the West and not simply *in* the West. And, in turn, what might considering Muslims in the Americas suggest about what "the West" signifies?

Such a range of practitioners, observers, places, times, and circumstances illustrates what we might call the connected specificities of this hemisphere, the New World Americas. It also raises the question of how commonalities and distinctions might be established among such wide-ranging cases. They share histories of colonization by Europeans who were themselves linked in complex relationships involving colonial objectives; they share population diasporas of colonized others; and they share contemporary political-economic and social realities that carry legacies of those historical relations of power. Common denominators are the bases upon which interpretive categories like "hemisphere" and "world" and "region" are constructed. But the work of rubrics is to group and generalize, which still leaves the issue of how to deal with the particularities that lie within delineated borders.

In defining what ostensibly already exists, all interpretive categories create the realities they are meant to represent. Hence, as Edward Said (1978) and many others since have argued, conceptualized as a particular kind of place in the world, the "West" itself relies on an oppositional "East." Together they form an entrenched paired polarity that stands for and summarizes the opposing force between them—that draws them together even as they are distinguished as opposites. Although we cannot ascertain a definite genealogy of the innumerable global influences that eventually came to be absorbed under the umbrella concept "Western" (Graeber 2008: 291), the results of that coalescence are clear in the sway that Western epistemology still exercises. The forcefulness of that sway encourages us to think of each side of a paired polarity (each side of a "versus") in terms of particular cohesive and undeviating common denominators, which allows them to be more easily juxtaposed against each other. But these sorts of juxtapositions are self-fulfilling prophecies, in that the contrasts presume a condition of opposition, a stance of conflict. Other kinds of epistemologies, or modes of interpretation, would be created if assumptions about cohesiveness and common denominators were exchanged for a focus on particularities and indeterminacies. Yet such an approach is not a simple solution because we create meaning by constructing interpretive categories from the vastness of experienced particularities and indeterminacies, categories that, again, become meaningful only when posed in relation to each other.

The challenge is not to lose sight of the power of dominant ways of knowing while not reifying the premise of antagonistic opposition. The narratives opening this chapter portray Muslims in diverse expressions across time and place. How might we make sense of their practice of Islam, their identification as Muslims, and their identification by others, all of which are subject to changing milieus and variable methods (and possibilities) of access? The Americas are simultaneously a boundaried and porous entity, an imagined rubric and an empirical context: the New World, at times the Atlantic World, always the former colonial (and some current) territories of Europe. It comprises "the West" and also multiple "wests" and "easts" together. Given this, how might we undertake comparative analysis pushing against or even abandoning paired polarities? If opposition is inherent in comparative exercises, how might we construe that opposition in productive, generative terms rather than as self-affirming reifications of prefigured suppositions? And what then, if anything, is distinctive about Muslims and Islam in the Americas, in the Western hemisphere, from those in other arenas of the Old World's West, or from arenas in its designated East? These questions are important, too complex to be resolved in a single chapter. But we can trace them through a discussion and critique of some scholarly and popular approaches to Islam and the Muslims who practice it. In doing so, my objective is to point to some useful considerations for scholars, sundry publics, and policymakers as we each attempt to understand Muslims' historical and contemporary presence in and contributions to this hemisphere.

* * *

The paired polarity of "tradition" versus "modernity" is inseparable from contemporary discussion of Islam. Deceptively simple in its conventional definition, tradition is understood as abiding customs that carry the force of unspoken law, in the sense of unchallenged, consistently enacted, and virtually inescapable rules. Tradition can be treasured or denigrated, depending on perspective; for example, as moral justifications for certain worldviews or as ignominious forms of conduct. Although modernity has no standardized definition, there is some consensus about what it means. This logic has European origins and, some argue, greatest traction in European and North American worldviews. Basically referring to a kind of logic about human progress and civilization, modernity signals a period in world history, either the European Renaissance and the "discovery" of America, or the European Enlightenment (Mignolo 2005: 5). During this period, which saw the "emergence of a new continent, the navigation as well as physical and conceptual appropriation of the globe, and the subsuming of all other forms of knowledge," the Christian perspective became preeminent "over the other religions of the Book" (Mignolo 2005: 105). Debates about the degree of compatibility between different religions and various forms of modernity have formed a discursive tradition in their own right, generated from Enlightenment thinking about freedom of thought, individual agency, self and other and the relation of each to the universe and to the idea of progress—cultural, as in "civilization," and intellectual, as in "rational" thought. Commandeered by ruling elites, these discourses also are woven into the philosophical questions of subordinated peoples, who made them their own, changing them and changed by them in the process.

It is both remarkable yet not surprising that the power of this modernity/tradition lens on religion still serves as a framework in scholarship, and certainly in popular wisdom. Almost two decades ago Talal Asad argued that tradition and modernity are not mutually exclusive conditions but rather different aspects of historicity. Nor are they developmental stages but rather dimensions of social life (Asad 1996: 1–2). Despite his insight about Islam and its study, the discourse about Islam today seems as intent as ever upon defending or critiquing Islam vis-à-vis this binary opposition. A few abbreviated examples should make my point.

Widely discussed in popular as well as scholarly circles, Benjamin Barber offered the image of the "opposing forces" of jihad and McWorld (Barber 1996: 5). Jihad is driven by "parochial hatreds" and "pursues a bloody politics of identity" (Barber 1996: 6, 8); McWorld is driven by "universalizing markets" and "a bloodless economics of profit" (Barber 1996: 6, 8). Contrasts, and yet in a "paradoxical interdependence," neither is what the world needs, Barber argues, given their antinomy to democracy, citizenship, and civil liberty (Barber 1996: 6). In a word, jihad is antimodern and McWorld is modernity gone bad. And thus they sustain the split between tradition and modernity. More commonly, modernity in relation to Islam or to religion in general is not subjected to such a critique. Akbar Ahmed, for example, posits that Islam's global population (over a billion), distribution (across five continents), and relationship with the United States make it "the perfect subject for a case study of a traditional civilization undergoing change in the age of globalization" (Ahmed 2007: 26). Pankaj Mishra's analysis of writer Ayaan Hirsi Ali's work asserts that "the problems she blames on Islam ... are to be found wherever traditionalist peoples confront the transition to an individualistic urban culture of modernity" (Mishra 2010: 70). While Christianity also has its flaws, states Jon Meacham in an essay about the debates over the Ground Zero (Park51) mosque, "large parts of the Christian universe have managed to adapt to modernity in ways that have at least discouraged the worst excesses of religiously motivated believers." Islam, he surmises, "needs reform" (Meacham 2010: 4). In a panel discussion on Islam and immigration in the spring of 2010, Tariq Modood commented that despite the social conservatism with which some Muslims are likely to be in accord, Islam is certainly compatible with democracy.[2] And finally, in the fall of 2012 Salman Rushdie lamented in a National Public Radio interview that "something has gone wrong inside the Muslim world"; that in his own living memory cities like Beirut, Tehran, Damascus, and Baghdad were "cosmopolitan," "outward-looking," and "cultured," but "in the last half-century these cultures seem to have slid backwards into medievalism."[3] Contrary to Asad's point, tradition and modernity remain treated not so much as contingent ideas as barometers of value (about development, progress, aspiration) across the divide of oceans and continents—another linkage between Old and New worlds and an assessment tool in the Americas targeting Muslim populations where these sorts of disappointments might be perceived.

By contrast to Christianity, which is commonly considered to be the only Western religion (despite its emergence in the "Near East"), Islam is not conceptualized as being of the West in its origins. Yet both religions, and Judaism, share monotheistic theologies, binding the three under one rubric of kinship, commonly known as the "People of the Book." Islam's historical longevity and widely acknowledged early role in scientific discoveries in astronomy, mathematics, and medicine confirm for many, Muslim and non-Muslim alike, Islam's original contribution to "civilization." Despite present day detractors decrying *contemporary* Islam's "strong resistance to modernization" (Harrison 2006: 96), this obduracy at times is viewed as a regression from a more admirable, free-thinking, creative past. The idea is that somewhere along the way a devolution occurred, where "the vanguard role of Islam during its first several centuries" (Harrison 2006: 96) was transformed from being "progress prone" to "progress resistant" (Harrison 2006: 119).

Enlightenment-derived ideas about individual will, freedom of thought, and the power of rationality and logic certainly bequeath an agentive power to "modern" peoples to make, build, and create, in contrast with "premodern" peoples' stymied energies that simply conform to, replicate, mimic (Mamdani 2002). Islam's historical "vanguard role" has been negated or eclipsed in much of today's terror-focused discourse. However, among scholars and, arguably, in the popular rhetoric of political correctness, that negation has not been complete. Combined with the kinship of monotheism and fourteen hundred years of interaction with the "Western" religion of Christianity,[4] Islam also retains, even if at times grudgingly in some perspectives, a measure of comparability with Western-Christian subjectivity that polytheistic and animist religious traditions, for example, are by no means necessarily granted by Western-Christian worldviews, or by Islamic worldviews, for that matter. These narratives of historical loss—initial cultural creativity and subsequent cultural mummification (Mamdani 2002)—belong to a broader Liberal discourse, one that is "increasingly prevalent in Western discussions of relations with Muslim-majority countries" (Mamdani 2002: 767), and with which the West congratulates its own tolerance and universalism and at the same time protects itself from their imagined consequences.

Yet the Americas complicate any neat divisions between the two. As the first European colonies—the site of burgeoning industrial production for a world market based on budding capitalism, and the site of massive, continuous encounters among culturally diverse peoples—the Americas have been identified as the crucible of modernity, not as its recipient but as its generator (e.g., James 1989 [1963]; Mignolo 2005; Mintz 1996; Trouillot 1998). The racial hierarchies that helped buttress Euro-colonial agendas in the Americas, however, kept the connotations of "premodern" tenacious as it was applied to indigenous, enslaved, and indentured subjects. Thus the premodern overlapped with rather than entirely succumbed to the modern, and these categories became entangled and refashioned accordingly. The ostensible inertia of the premodern flies in the face of the particular energy that New World societies are imagined to exude—an energy anything but conforming and lifeless—even while they are peopled by those understood from Euro-colonial perspectives to have originated from premodern or regressive places. When thinking about Islam and the Americas, then, not only are we presented with Muslim minority societies and the issues that distinguish them from Muslim majority societies; we also must contend with the region's troubling of such binaries as traditional (or premodern) versus modern, and cultural creation versus cultural replication.

Defining a "Muslim minority" as a part of a population who are Muslim (bound by affirmation of certain Islamic precepts) and who are often subjected to differential treatment by those who do not share these precepts, M. Ali Kettani (1986: 2) emphasizes that the meaning of "minority" goes beyond numerical factors. Key is social position and the ability to avoid being subject to differential treatment or to demand its redress. Demographically, in no society of the Americas are Muslims the majority population. Equally significant to population numbers is the differential treatment that comes in the form of recognition (or its absence). Although Muslims have a centuries-long historical presence in the Americas, Islam is not officially recognized to be a foundational religion of any nation in the hemisphere (regardless of its history). Rather, in the narratives of nation formation, Islam enters from outside and after the fact, brought by the enslaved, the indentured, the migrant. Although these figures represent empirical historical moments when Muslims arrive in the hemisphere, their contribution of Islam to the region is largely depicted in terms of once vibrant but eventually subsiding heritage (Africans), minor or secondary presence (South Asians), or newly developing, "foreign" communities (South Asians, Africans, Arabs).

Despite European, African, Asian, and Middle Eastern histories in the

Americas all being, as it were, outsider-in histories, they are not equally foundational in narratives of the region's establishment in the world. That role is generally reserved for indigenous populations, Europeans, and Africans, where religion foundational to nation-building is assigned primarily to Christianity. In virtually every instance the religious hegemony of Christianity has had to contend with non-European religious traditions (in many cases amalgamating with them in some fashion), yet Christianity, or more broadly the Judeo-Christian tradition, remains predominant across the region. We might say that a *culture* of Christianity persists, since the countries of the Americas are all, in one way or another, committed to secular governing. Although tensions are not expressed as those of "religious versus secular," or "secular modernism versus faith-based traditionalism," there remain relevant political questions about what the state ought to be promoting (or prohibiting) among non-Christian populations—from labor protections to education, legal marriage, land use, and immigration policies.

Over time, the ratio between Muslims' actual numbers and their significance in the hemispheric imagination has maintained a lopsidedness that clouds understanding of Muslims' presence in this region. Scholarship has not devoted attention to these populations and their religious traditions equal to that expended on other topics of research (notwithstanding important exceptions, cited in this chapter and throughout this volume). For example, in his review of the recent 268-page introductory text *Caribbean Religious History: An Introduction* (Edmonds and Gonzalez 2010), N. Samuel Murrell writes that "Islam and Hinduism are trivialized in five paltry pages" (Murrell 2012: 161). By my own count it is six pages, the difference still not explaining the comment by Edmonds and Gonzalez that Islam and Hinduism "forever changed Caribbean religion. Though Christianity and African diaspora religion often receive all the attention, the presence of [Islam and Hinduism] alters the religious and cultural landscape of the region" (Edmonds and Gonzalez 2010: 201). Murrell's point underscores an unfortunate missed opportunity; besides the recognition of the impact of Islam (and Hinduism), by 2010 there was ample scholarship on the region's Muslim (and Hindu) traditions and communities. And Daniel Varisco's (2009) generally very useful bibliography of works on Muslims and Islam includes a detailed parsing of the world into Muslim countries and regions, for example, "America" (i.e., the United States), "Africa," and "Afghanistan and Central Asia," as well as key themes like "History of Islam," "Ritual Celebrations," and "Terrorism." Absent without comment, however, are such appropriate thematic subheadings as Diaspora, and such Islam/Muslim-relevant regional divisions as the Americas, the Atlantic World, the Caribbean, or Latin America. These areas of the world may not be places where one would conventionally look for Muslims, particularly if historical longevity (earlier than 1492) and demographics (majority populations) are the primary criteria. But looked at in another way, it is for precisely these reasons that these sites lend themselves to questions about how it is decided who Muslims are and, reciprocally, what Islam is. Everywhere we look should be treated as an open question, and this is perhaps even more imperative for places or circumstances where we are not likely to find what we already know.

Omissions also necessarily lend importance to what is not neglected in research and scholarly discussion, irrespective of demographics; for example, the role of Muslims in resistance struggles against slavery (e.g., Diouf 1998; Gomez 2005; Reis 1993). As significant as this role was, its emphasis can exaggerate our certainties about what Islam meant in the first place and how it was constituted, in turn obscuring possible alternative understandings and forms of practice on the part of Muslim enslaved Africans and others (e.g., Khan 2012). Recent currents responsive to the post-9/11 moment now emphasize in popular wisdom a different kind of Muslim presence irrespective of demographics, notably what might be called the post-9/11 terror talk (borrowing from Mamdani's [2002] notion of "culture talk"). This emphasis also exaggerates certain kinds of importance vis-à-vis Muslims—much of which, needless to say, is not admiring. In both instances, however, Muslims remain in a sense larger than life. This unevenness is yet another factor to unravel as we seek to understand better the still largely untold ways in which Muslims in the Americas have reconstituted Islam, defined themselves, and been defined by others.

* * *

Vast geographical expanses, extensive passage of time, great cultural heterogeneity, and religious variability characterize the flow of Muslims and Islam to the Americas. As diasporic populations, Muslims in the Americas, whether arriving in the New World centuries or decades or just days ago, form communities (residential, occupational, or educational enclaves) that can suggest to observers self-defined, enclosed entities within which the beliefs and practices of Islam are expressed and contained. These sorts of aggregations exist. They are based on sharing customs and cultural values about dress, cuisine, kinship rules, etc.; sharing language, from myriad possibilities; a common religious philosophy within Islam, such as Sunni, Shi'a, Ahmadiyya, or Sufi; or memorialized pasts (e.g., the partition of India in 1947, the Battle of Kerbala in Iraq ca. 680 AD, or the Middle Passage from West Africa to the Western hemisphere from the sixteenth century—all meaningful to Muslims in some part of the Americas).

The farther back in time one reaches, the less certain is our information. Some scholars take the position that there was pre-Columbian exploration of North and South America by Africans, including Muslims from West Africa (Abdur-Rashid 2010; Van Sertima 1976). Other scholars contend that Muslims from Andalusia, Spain, visited North America well before Columbus, as reported for example by twelfth-century North African geographer Al-Idrisi (Kettani 1986: 191). Inferences and speculations are even more common when it comes to places like Mexico, where the history of Islam is largely undocumented and clues must be sought in such sources as the sixteenth-century novel *Un Hereje y un Musulman* (A Heretic and a Muslim), attributed to Pascual Almazan (McCloud 2005: 4684). An early literary work that exercised great influence on the ways Islam was imagined in the Americas (and in the West in general) was *The One Thousand and One Nights* story of Scheherazade. First published in the United States in the 1790s, it was as important as the Quran in shaping Western attitudes toward Islam, its impact no less significant for its emphasis on romantic exoticism (Marr 2006: 13).

Islam made its early presence felt in other less speculative ways besides exploration and literary fiction: through individuals' life stories and the points of view generated from their experiences. Fifteenth- and sixteenth-century Portuguese and Spanish ships were probably manned by Andalusian Muslim mariners, some of whom were also Moriscos (Kettani 1986: 191).[5] Increasingly reliable information about Muslims and Islam in the Americas becomes available as the sixteenth century moves into the seventeenth, and focus shifts to European colonization of the New World and the development of forced labor projects—slavery and indenture. Yet there still remains the question of how the interpretive categories "Muslim" and "Islam" are defined. Who, for example, comprises the early Muslim community that Michael Gomez (1998) argues made important contributions to the creation of African American identity? What kind of contribution is Mooretown, with Jamaica's Maroon Council members continuing to use the phrases "*As-Salamu-'alaikum*" and "*Allahu Akbar*" into the mid-nineteenth century (Afroz 2000)? By that time, most scholars agree, a vibrant Muslim presence in the Caribbean had critically diminished (e.g., Campbell 1974; McCloud 2005; Samaroo 1988). Joao Jose Reis remarks that after Brazil's abolition of slavery in 1888, formerly enslaved Muslims could still be seen but "as isolated practitioners of their faith" (Reis 2001: 308). These communities and their relationships create palimpsests of culture, politics, religion, and the like—creolization, if you will—that not only make *Muslim* and *Islam* relative terms but also involve much broader processes not easily managed by simply tracking a religious tradition and its adherents. Recognition and interpretation depend entirely on the criteria that identify both "religion" and "community."

These issues become even more nuanced when we reflect on the fact that we cannot separate the historiography about Islam and Muslims from the prolonged and curious (in both senses of the term) gaze of Europe onto the Middle East and Asia. As Dale Eickelman observes, the numerous features of shared heritage between West and Middle East/Islam and their intricately entangled histories mean that the Middle East/Islam "has never appeared to Westerners as safely different and exotic" (Eickelman 1997: 27). Particularly interesting here is the idea of "safely different." What this suggests is that difference presents itself in degrees of discomfort, and that more similar, more recognizable, or more familiar is not necessarily preferable to greatly dissimilar, unrecognizable, or unfamiliar. Perhaps analogous with the "uncanny valley" effect described in reference to animation and other forms of replication of the human subject, being too similar yet not identical is disquieting; difference requires enough perceived distance to be viewed as innocuous. Counterintuitively, *like* us but not of us can feel more threatening than *not* like us and not of us.

Narratives about Muslim diversity, meant to signal that Muslims cannot be reduced to predictable beliefs, dispositions, or actions, perhaps attain their greatest implication of urgency in diasporic contexts, particularly in Muslim minority societies, where contrasts between local and immigrant populations are starkest and often most troubling to both local and immigrant in terms of resource distribution, opportunity, and justice. In his address at the Iftar (breaking fast) dinner hosted by the White House on August 13, 2010, during the month of Ramadan, President Barack Obama differentiated Muslims in an effort to homogenize them more broadly into the U.S. mainstream. He noted that Muslims in the United States were "like so many other immigrants": farmers, merchants, mill and factory and railroad workers, who "helped to build America."[6] Highlighting Muslim heterogeneity is empirically more faithful to the on-the-ground realities of Muslims' lives; such emphasis also counters culturalist models that reinforce stereotypes of Islam's incongruity (Abu-Lughod 2002; Mamdani 2002). Scholars have pressed this point about diversity among Muslims by raising such considerations as who has the authority to identify a Muslim; by whom that authority is bequeathed; how important religion in general and orthodoxy in particular are in determining who is a Muslim; and how being a Muslin is defined (see, e.g., Gilsenan 1982; Ouzgane 2006; Shivley 2006; Smith 2010).

Reaffirming Muslims' heterogeneity can also counteract a common image of the Orient as a place "where all aspects of life—culture, politics, economics and personal relationships—could be explained by reference to the religion of Islam ... [which] offered an explanatory touchstone for the behaviour of people from otherwise diverse cultures, ethnic groups and social classes" (Graham-Brown 1988: 6). The term *Islam* is itself a sizable generalization, encompassing among other referents Arab, Ottoman, North African, Spanish, Indian, and Far Eastern (Toner 2013: 21). And that is just in the Old World. The image of a metonymic Islam has not been much dispelled. Yet the corrective that assertions of heterogeneity intend relies on addition, on identifying forms of difference among Muslims without necessarily inquiring into what *Muslim* is. In other words, it is rarer to question the basis of social categories than simply to expand their inclusiveness. Reflecting on why difference matters suggests an irony embedded within the notion of multiculturalism: that the idea of difference actually promotes (a reassuring) similarity. "They" are different, just like "us."[7] Diversity is an ostensibly empirical truth (it is obvious, we can see it), yet it establishes a greater, encompassing sameness that unites diversity into a cohesive whole. The idea of difference in service of similarity—that is, difference that reaffirms the social or cultural (categorical) norm—is politically desirable in these times because it seems to hinder or repel stereotyping, essentializing, or profiling—practices that although persistent also are decried, at least in theory. But if in embracing difference the message is that "they" are just like "us," then we ultimately simply confirm our own worldviews and perspectives, homogenizing even as we distinguish.[8] What if Muslims were viewed as heterogeneous but not, therefore, just like us? What if "heterogeneity" and "progress" were not synonymous? What other kinds of narratives and ways of knowing might appear?

In the context of the Americas a hyper-awareness of difference is ideologically built into the region as one of its central motifs. As the conventional wisdom has it, the Americas are nothing if not all about diversity—mixed, mestizo, rainbows, mosaics, multicultural, creole, callaloo. This complicates challenges to reductionist, essentialized representations of the "Muslim world" because merely being sensitive to difference and cultivating our appreciation of difference (and labeling others as backward who repudiate difference, such as, for example, religious heterodoxy) are not enough. Difference in itself is not necessarily either an admirable or unworthy quality; rather, it is imbued with certain meaning and significance well beyond its immediate message of distinctiveness or uniqueness. A useful example is Islam's relationship to "racecraft," what Karen and Barbara Fields (2012: 18, 261) call the "mental terrain," "pervasive belief," and "social alchemy" that create race from racism.

In North America, particularly the United States, the attacks on September 11, 2001, brought Muslims living in the United States, the West, and the East into popular discourse in an unprecedented way (Ewing 2008: 1). The ensuing policy measures and legal nuancing that came on the heels of 9/11 in the name of national security threw into relief the racial formation of the United States as Muslims became subject to profiling and the Bush Administration's "special registration" project, which according to some observers "turned a religion, namely Islam, into a race" (Bayoumi 2006: 270).[9] The racialization of Islam in the United States, however, long preceded the intensified scrutiny of Muslims after 9/11. The connection between citizenship status and race has a centuries-long history in the United States. Fluctuations in the definition of "white" as applied to Arabs, South Asians (e.g., Indians), and East Asians (e.g., Japanese) meant that applicants had varied classifications (and results), depending on the moment and court in question. A different sort of racialization of Islam is associated with the Nation of Islam, founded in 1930, historically one of the largest Islamic movements among African Americans and important in the development of the civil rights movement of the 1960s (Ewing 2008: 3). This particular Muslim contribution to American history, however, pales in comparison to Muslims' connotation of terrorism in the United States, an association that began globally about the 1980s.

In her survey of research on Muslims in the United States, Karen Leonard (2003) discusses the racialization of Muslims in terms of their construction as a category that "if not racial as traditionally understood, is at least racial in that Muslims experience discrimination and are not given full access to opportunities" (Leonard 2003: 58; Kettani 1986). Leonard is drawing an interesting distinction at the same time as pointing to commonalities in the ways that category construction—in this case, racial categories—works. Let us consider African American Muslims and immigrant Arab, Asian, and European Muslims in terms of different expressions of racialization. Muslim religious traditions can be thought of as a suffix to African Americans' racial identity; Islam is enraced by virtue of association with African Americans/blackness. The arrival of Muslims into the North American racial formation from parts of the world other than Africa—for example, Turks, Arabs, Iranians, Eastern and Central Europeans—enraced Islam differently. By this same accounting, these groups can be perhaps racially ambiguous, typically not "black" and often not "white."

Thus Islam in the Americas undergoes racialization not only through racial genealogies but also through the ideological process of analogy: being made "like" or "equivalent to" those already enraced by virtue of certain structures and practices of discrimination, begun in the colonial era and particularly the case in the post-9/11 climate. The Boston bombings of April 2013 underscored ambiguity rather than definitiveness as debates unfolded about whether the alleged perpetrators, the Tsarnaev brothers, are white. On the one hand, as journalist Peter Beinart remarked, "the Tsarnaevs hail from the Caucasus, and are therefore, literally, 'Caucasian.' You can't get whiter than that" (Beinart 2013). Other commentators echoed this view. On the other hand, Beinart observed that in "public conversation in America today, 'Islam' is a racial term. Being Muslim doesn't just mean not being Christian or Jewish. It means not being white" (Beinart 2013). The connections between race and religion are deep and complex everywhere; in this part of the world they should motivate us to consider the dynamics by which difference is imagined to become racial difference for some, paired with the allegedly fixed quality of race that is assumed to inhere in others.

* * *

The challenge of locating and interpreting Muslims and Islam is in part empirical, but as we have seen, drawing precise lines around our categories is a vexed issue to start with. And culturally and religiously heterogeneous populations of Muslims in the Americas make for themselves diverse ways of being Muslim. The larger point is that this diversity, although interesting in itself, calls for serious reflection about forms of recognition. And querying forms of recognition requires nuancing as well. Some scholars have argued that research on Muslims in the Americas gets short shrift because focus on other populations, religions, or diasporas overshadows them (e.g., Bal and Sinha-Kerkhoff 2005; Diouf 1998; McCloud 2005). These critiques are important reminders against scholarly complacency, but they also illustrate the tension that can arise between empirical data and the way data are interpreted, the way "significance" is construed. Ellen Bal and Kathinka Sinha-Kerkhoff (2005), for example, posit that South Asian diaspora studies in the Dutch Antilles have favored Hindu populations, to the detriment of learning about Muslims' history there. Yet the population numbers of Hindus as compared to Muslims in this part of the world's diasporas are much higher, which some might argue justifies the uneven attention. The caution that can be gleaned from their position is not to assume the merits of quantity; that is, importance should not be a matter reducible to numbers.

More provocative is Aminah Beverly McCloud's contention that Indo-Caribbean Muslims "made no efforts to blend into and strengthen the existing Muslim community" (McCloud 2005: 4683). If Afro-Caribbean Islam was vastly diminished by the time Indian indenture began in the Caribbean in 1838, as most scholars agree (including McCloud), then we must ask who would have comprised this "existing Muslim community." Were they aggregated into community groups—neighborhoods, organizations, etc.? And given the planters' penchant for segregating Afro-Caribbeans and Indo-Caribbeans on sugar estates and curtailing Indos' mobility as much as was useful for production, how might Muslim blending and strengthening have occurred? Drawing attention to the distinctions between Muslim populations in the Caribbean and in the Americas in general has great historiographical value. However, it is imperative to approach religion as necessarily articulated with all other social domains—the plantation mode of production, labor control, diminution of Afro-Caribbean Muslim populations (or at least of the practice among them of what today is defined as Islam), and so on—not as somehow transcending or existing independently of them.

* * *

Muslims in the Americas, as elsewhere, appeal to certain common denominators, typically taken from the Quran and the Hadith, and at the least including some observation of the Five Pillars, by which they define and interpret Islam (Asad 1996; Leonard 2003). Muslims also come in many forms, some recognizable to other Muslims or to non-Muslims, and others contested or unrecognized. These kinds of assessments are as constitutive of religious traditions as are common denominators that establish definitive parameters. Thus there is, on the one hand, the standardization of common denominators that together serve as a shorthand rubric identifying a religion, for example, Islam; and on the other hand, there is the lived religion that gives these rubrics their animation, plasticity, and meaning. In other words, the study of Muslims and Islam (or any religious tradition) requires investigation of a number of related considerations at the same time.

The first is the category of religion itself and how it is being defined. As Asad, among others, has pointed out, definitions determine "the kinds of questions one thinks are askable and worth asking" (Asad 1986: 12). Second is the "historicality" (Guha 2002) of religious traditions, taking account of which helps to dislodge the fused and standardized common denominators of authorizing discourses. Finally, what must be investigated are the ways in which "particular people, in particular places and times, live in, with, through, and against the religious idioms available to them in culture—*all* the idioms, including (often enough) those not explicitly their 'own'" (Orsi 1997: 7). I would add that determining which religious and cultural idioms are "their 'own,'" and what the consequences of that ownership are, is a project in itself.

We must therefore take seriously Asad's rejection of the idea that Islam is simply what Muslims say it is, because there will always be Muslims who challenge other Muslims' opinions and claims (Asad 1986: 2). No isolated subject, or representative of that subject, can be bracketed: a "Muslim's beliefs about the beliefs and practices of others *are* his own beliefs," which "animate and are sustained by his social relations with others" (Asad 1986: 2). Thus, as Asad proposes, Islam should be approached as a discursive tradition that "relates itself to the founding texts of the Qur'an and the Hadith" and "addresses itself to conceptions of the Islamic past and future, with reference to a particular Islamic practice in the present" (Asad 1986: 14). Discursive traditions authorize various instituted practices as being Islamic by way of teaching and socialization, and it is these instituted practices that offer "the proper theoretical beginning" for studying Islam (Asad 1986: 15).

Yet it is precisely because Muslims come in many forms—recognizable, contested, and unrecognized—that we must approach as multilayered the instituted practices that make up this discursive tradition. Such an approach, in turn, calls for flexible criteria in conceptualizing such traditions. Incorporation must include all of those who engage meaningfully with the discourse and the practice (in whatever way), not simply Muslim-to-Muslim. Particularly in the context of diaspora and residence in Muslim minority societies, the means of addressing canonical Islam may be indirect, may be by non-Muslims, may be concerned with divergent aspects of a text or a practice, or may be occasional rather than regular. And over time, some canons may take on different emphases and others may be momentarily silent. Discursive traditions, including Islamic ones, do aspire to coherence (Asad 1986: 16-17), but given the heterogeneity of traditional practices and the relations of power involved in debating the inculcation and performance of those practices, coherence is never complete. It is the unpredictability of coherence, one might say, that makes the exploration of Muslim epistemologies a rich and imperative project of cross-cultural exploration. In the New World of the Americas this exploration of the Islam that Muslims craft asks us to approach Islam as something truly new in the sense of generative capacities, yet also in some significant ways remaining consistent through shared histories and points of reference. Islam in Muslim minority societies is neither diminutive nor merely reiterative. Approaching Islam as a medium that interlocks Old and New worlds while contributing to the creation of those new worlds moves comparative analysis beyond the binaries. This kind of comparative study can tell us about the ways in which a focus on Islam reveals the logics and methods whereby the Americas and their constituent parts are constructed. Such efforts can also tell us about how the Americas produce Muslims. The rich yield is suggested in the work of this volume.

Notes

1. As Jerry Toner points out, the "East" and the "Orient" were "plastic concepts," broadly including "the Maghreb, the Levant, the Middle East, India, China, Japan, and other countries of the Far East" (Toner 2013: 20–21).

2. "Islam and Immigration," panel discussion with Tariq Modood, Aristede Zohlberg, and Jose Casanova, moderated by Chase Robinson, City University of New York Graduate Center, New York, March 8, 2010.

3. National Public Radio, *Morning Edition*, September 18, 2012.

4. One can argue that historically Judaism has for the most part been ambivalently considered a "Western" religion.

5. Moriscos were Muslims who had been converted to Christianity in Spain and Portugal and were generally suspected (by Christians) of continuing to practice Islam.

6. *Washington Wire*, August 14, 2010, http://blogs.wsj.com/washwire/2010/08/14/text-of-obamas-address.

7. Taking up "the issue of how to speak of collectivities while at the same time noting the diversity of perspectives" when discussing Islam in a post-9/11 world, Cheryl Mattingly, Mary Lawlor, and Lanita Jacobs-Huey (2002: 744) employ Stanley Fish's notion of "interpretive community" to emphasize that knowledge is "situational" and therefore cannot be reduced to stable or unvarying certainties. In a different context, Segal and Handler (1995) offer an early and insightful discussion about the implicit limitations of multicultural politics of "difference."

8. Albeit in a different vein, apposite here is David Scott's argument that it is our questions that must be queried (notably, historicized) and not simply the answers that are produced (Scott 1999: 9).

9. "Special Registration" was a program implemented on September 11, 2002, by the U.S. Department of Justice through the Immigration and Naturalization Service (INS). It required "certain non-immigrant aliens"—men over the age of sixteen from twenty-three Muslim-majority countries (or twenty-five; reports vary)—to "register with the U.S. immigration authorities, be fingerprinted and photographed, respond to questioning, and submit to routine reporting" (Cainkar 2002: 73; Asian American Legal Defense and Education Fund 2003: 1).

References Cited

Abdur-Rashid, Imam Al-Hajj Talib
2010 "A Brief History of the Afro-Islamic Presence in New York." *Souls* 12(1): 3–12.
Abu-Lughod, Lila
2002 "Do Muslim Women Really Need Saving? Anthropological Reflections on Cultural Relativism and Its Others." *American Anthropologist* 104(3): 783–90.
Afroz, Sultana
2000 "The Moghul Islamic Diaspora: The Institutionalization of Islam in Jamaica." *Journal of Muslim Minority Affairs* 20(2): 271–89.
Ahmed, Akbar
2007 *Journey into Islam: The Crisis of Globalization*. Washington, D.C.: Brookings Institution Press.
Asad, Talal
1986 *The Idea for an Anthropology of Islam*. Occasional Paper Series. Center for Contemporary Arab Studies, Georgetown University.
1996 "Modern Power and the Reconfiguration of Religious Traditions" (Interview with Saba Mahmood). *Stanford Electronic Humanities Review* 5(1): 1–13.
Asian American Legal Defense and Education Fund
2003 *Special Report, Special Registration: Discrimination and Xenophobia as Government Policy*. Asian American Legal Defense and Education Fund. http://www.aaldef.org.
Bal, Ellen, and Kathinka Sinha-Kerkhoff
2005 "Muslims in Surinam and the Netherlands, and the Divided Homeland." *Journal of Muslim Minority Affairs* 25(2):193–94.
Barber, Benjamin R.
1996 *Jihad vs. McWorld*. New York: Ballantine Books.
Bayoumi, Moustafa
2006 "Racing Religion." *CR: The New Centennial Review* 6(2): 267–93.
Beinart, Peter
2013 "Are the Tsarnaevs White?" April 24. http://www.thedailybeast.com/articles/2013/04/24/are-the-tsarnaevs-white.html#url=/articles/2013/04/24/are-the-tsarnaevs-white.html.
Buck-Morss, Susan
2009 *Hegel, Haiti, and Universal History*. Pittsburgh, Pa.: University of Pittsburgh Press.
Cainkar, Louise
2002 "Special Registration: A Fervor for Muslims." *Journal of Islamic Law and Culture* 7(2):73–101.
Campbell, Carl
1974 "Jonas Mohammed Bath and the Free Mandingos in Trinidad: The Question of their Repatriation to Africa 1831–1838." *Pan-African Journal* 7(2): 129–52.
Diouf, Sylviane A.
1998 *Servants of Allah: African Muslims Enslaved in the Americas*. New York: New York University Press.
Edmonds, Ennis B., and Michelle A. Gonzalez
2010 *Caribbean Religious History: An Introduction*. New York: New York University Press.

Eickelman, Dale
1997 *The Middle East and Central Asia: An Anthropological Approach*. 3rd ed. Upper Saddle River, N.J.: Prentice Hall.
Ewing, Katherine
2008 "Introduction." In *Being and Belonging: Muslims in the United States Since 9/11*, ed. Katherine Ewing, 1–11. New York: Russell Sage Foundation.
Fields, Karen E., and Barbara J. Fields
2012 *Racecraft: The Soul of Inequality in American Life*. London: Verso.
Gilsenan, Michael
1982 *Recognizing Islam: An Anthropologist's Introduction*. London: Croom Helm.
Gomez, Michael
1998 *Exchanging Our Country Marks: The Transformation of African Identities in the Colonial and Antebellum South*. Chapel Hill: University of North Carolina Press.
2005 *Black Crescent: The Experience and Legacy of African Muslims in the Americas*. New York: Cambridge University Press.
Graeber, David
2008 "On Cosmopolitanism and (Vernacular) Democratic Creativity: Or, There Never Was a West." In *Anthropology and the New Cosmopolitanism*, ed. Pnina Werbner, 281–305. Oxford: Berg.
Graham-Brown, Sarah
1988 *Images of Women: The Portrayal of Women in Photography of the Middle East 1860–1950*. London: Quartet Books.
Guha, Ranajit
2002 *History at the Limit of World-History*. New York: Columbia University Press.
Harrison, Lawrence E.
2006 *The Central Liberal Truth: How Politics Can Change a Culture and Save It from Itself*. New York: Oxford University Press.
James, C.L.R.
1989 [1963] *The Black Jacobins: Toussaint L'Ouverture and the San Domingo Revolution*. New York: Vintage.
Kettani, M. Ali
1986 *Muslim Minorities in the World Today*. London: Mansell Publishing.
Khan, Aisha
2012 "Islam, Vodou, and the Making of the Afro-Atlantic." *New West Indian Guide* 86(1–2): 29–54.
Leonard, Karen
2003 *Muslims in the United States: The State of Research*. New York: Russell Sage Foundation.
Mamdani, Mahmood
2002 "Good Muslim, Bad Muslim: A Political Perspective on Culture and Terrorism." *American Anthropologist* 104(3): 766–75.
Marr, Timothy
2006 *The Cultural Roots of American Islamicism*. Cambridge, UK: Cambridge University Press.

Mattingly, Cheryl, Mary Lawlor, and Lanite Jacobs-Huey
2002 "Narrating September 11: Race, Gender, and the Play of Cultural Identities." *American Anthropologist* 104(3): 743–53.
McCloud, Aminah Beverly
2005 "Islam in the Americas." *Encyclopedia of Religion*, 2nd ed. Vol. 7, ed. Lindsay Jones, 4682–91. Detroit: Macmillan Reference.
Meacham, Jon
2010 "Let Reformation Begin at Ground Zero." *Newsweek*, September 6, 4.
Mignolo, Walter
2005 *The Idea of Latin America*. Malden, Mass.: Blackwell.
Mintz, Sidney W.
1996 "Enduring Substances, Trying Theories: The Caribbean Region as Oikumene." *Journal of the Royal Anthropological Institute* 2: 289–311.
Mishra, Pankaj
2010 "Islamismism." *New Yorker*, June 7, 68–73.
Moghissi, Haideh, Saeed Rahnema, and Mark J. Goodman
2009 *Diaspora by Design: Muslims in Canada and Beyond*. Toronto: University of Toronto Press.
Murrell, N. Samuel
2012 Review of *Caribbean Religious History: An Introduction*, by Ennis B. Edmonds and Michelle A. Gonzalez. *New West Indian Guide* 86(1–2): 159–62.
Orsi, Robert
1997 "Everyday Miracles: The Study of Lived Religion." In *Lived Religion in America: Toward a History of Practice*, ed. David D. Hall, 3–21. Princeton, N.J.: Princeton University Press.
Ouzgane, Lahoucine
2006 *Islamic Masculinities*. London: Zed.
Reis, Joao Jose
1993 *Slave Rebellion in Brazil: The Muslim Uprising of 1835 in Bahia*. Baltimore: Johns Hopkins University Press.
2001 "Quilombos and Rebellions in Brazil." In *African Roots/American Cultures: Africa in the Creation of the Americas*, ed. Sheila S. Walker, 301–13. Lanham, Mass.: Rowman and Littlefield.
Said, Edward
1978 *Orientalism*. New York: Vintage.
Samaroo, Brinsley
1988 "Early African and East Indian Muslims in Trinidad and Tobago." Paper presented at Conference on Indo-Caribbean History and Culture, May 9–11, Centre for Caribbean Studies, University of Warwick, Coventry, England.
Schueller, Malini Johar
1998 *U.S. Orientalism: Race, Nation, and Gender in Literature, 1790–1890*. Ann Arbor: University of Michigan Press.
Scott, David
1999 *Refashioning Futures: Criticism after Postcoloniality*. Princeton, N.J.: Princeton University Press.

Segal, Daniel, and Richard Handler
1995 "U.S. Multiculturalism and the Concept of Culture." *Identities* 1: 391–407.
Shivley, Kim
2006 "Looking for Identity in the Muslim World." *American Anthropologist* 108(3): 537–42.
Smith, Jane I.
2010 "Islam in America." In *Muslims in the West After 9/11: Religion, Politics, and Law*, ed. Jocelyne Cesari, 28–42. London: Routledge.
Toner, Jerry
2013 *Homer's Turk: How Classics Shaped Ideas of the East*. Cambridge, Mass.: Harvard University Press.
Trouillot, Michel-Rolph
1998 "Culture on the Edges: Creolization in the Plantation Context." *Plantation Society in the Americas* 5(1): 8–28.
Van Sertima, Ivan
1976 *They Came Before Columbus*. New York: Random House.
Varisco, Daniel
2009 "Islam: Sociology and Anthropology." Oxford Bibliographies Online. http://www.oxfordbibliographies.com.

I

HISTORIES

Presence, Absence, Remaking

3

"Oriental Hieroglyphics Understood Only by the Priesthood and a Chosen Few"

The Islamic Orientalism of White and Black Masons and Shriners

JACOB S. DORMAN

Black nationalist and freemason Martin R. Delany reported to a meeting of African American freemasons in 1853 that before the construction of King Solomon's Temple, Masonry was originally taught through "Egyptian, Ethiopian, Assyrian, and other oriental hieroglyphics understood only by the priesthood and a choosen [sic] few" (Delany 1853: 19). Delany's comments are one example of the many ways in which nineteenth-century Black Americans sought to recover hidden knowledge of their past by delving into Freemasonry as well as Hebrew, Ethiopian, Egyptian, and Islamic histories, conceptualized under the broad banner of "the Orient."

The Orientalist Mythology of Shriners

No secret society was more deeply immersed in Orientalist mythology and legends than a uniquely American order known as the Shriners, or the Ancient Arabic Order of the Nobles of the Mystic Shrine for North America. Open only to those who had achieved the highest levels in one of the branches of Masonry, the Shriners called themselves the "playground of Freemasonry" and sought to embody a spirit of Oriental decadence and frivolity, balanced by charitable works. Well-known New York thespian William J. "Billy" Florence and a prominent Masonic and "devoted Arabic" scholar, Dr. Walter M. Fleming, founded the Shriners in 1872 (Ross 1906: 1–2; Walkes 1993). The order took off in 1878 when the founders hired Albert Rawson, an Orientalist "expert" who determined to "decorate it with all the mysticism of the Orient," and "a certain degree of mystery" (Melish 1921: 12; Nance 2009:

158). Perhaps searching for ways to make fun of the increasing feminization of American public culture after the Civil War, Shriners mocked the solemnity of the Western Orientalist quest for authenticity in the East and the absurdities of fraternal regalia and hullabaloo. At a time when women were making their voices heard in religious movements, reform movements, suffrage campaigns, and the appreciation of all things "Oriental," from consumer goods to loose-fitting "harem" pants to religious ideals, the Shriners' rude masculine games embraced the East satirically (Carnes 1989; Clawson 1989; Douglas 1998 [1977]; Nance 2003, 2009). The Shriners created a blatantly fraudulent legend linking their secret order back to the nephew and son-in-law of the Prophet Mohammed and the city of Mecca in 644. In the twentieth century the silly miniature bicycles that fez-wearing Shriners rode in their parades invited their audiences to release their Westernized workaday woes and enjoy a carefree, absurd Orientalist spectacle (International Shrine Clown Association 1989: 59).

Intent on having a good time, supporting charitable projects, and enjoying the fleshpots of Egypt as literally as possible, the Shriners seldom took their own legends very seriously. Even their own historians speak of the "fancies" and other liberties taken with their origin stories: "The placing of the origin of this Order at Mecca is a fancy of the imagination which historians in general have a license to claim use of," one Shriner historian wrote in 1906, referring to the rites of the order as a "compilation of facts and fancies which subsequently were handed out to a waiting and anxious constituency" (Ross 1906: 1).

The Shriners' fancies had a distinctly Orientalist flavor, describing Muslim lands with exotica and erotica, as in the following passage:

> Looking backward toward the home of the Order, we find the Brotherhood in Egypt flourishing and fruitful in good works, as beautiful as are the queenly palms which wave their feathery arms in the soft airs that crinkle the surface of the lordly Nile into rippling lines of loveliest corrugations, or cast their cooling shadows upon the star-eyed daughters of Egypt. (Ross 1906, 47)

This kind of Orientalist fantasy was so overwrought that it did not disguise its air of winking and slightly salacious irreverence, which matched the air of droll irony that became part of American masculine culture in the wake of the horror of the Civil War (Carnes 1989; Nance 2003, 2009). As American cities grew with new migrants and immigrants, men responded to the increased anonymity of the city by forming new fraternal organizations. These all-male organizations often mixed secret passcodes and costumes with all-male dinners and titillating after-dinner entertainment. At a time when progressive reformist women were advocating for the right to vote and expressing feminism through religious movements that elevated the "mystical" East against the "materialistic" West, the Shriners' frivolity attracted the most prominent men in America and made sport of reformers, progressivism, and even other all-male fraternal organizations.

The order's costumes also embodied Western Orientalist ideas of the East. The Nobles wore rich costumes "of Eastern character," made of silk and brocaded velvet "of oriental intensity of color," topped with a fez. According to the Shriners, the wearing of the fez originated from the time when the Crusades interrupted the *hajj* pilgrimage to Mecca around 960 CE, and "Mohammedans west of the Nile" journeyed to the city of Fez in Morocco instead (Ross 1906: 47). Shriner myths were loosely based in Islamic history but included many inaccuracies. As a center of Islamic learning, Fez has long been a destination for travelers searching for knowledge (*talabal'ilm*). Jerusalem was sometimes used as a hajj destination when Muslims were unable to visit Mecca, but Fez never served a similar purpose (Abun-Nasr 1987; Eickelman and Piscatori 1990: 69; Riley-Smith 1995: 223).

As Susan Nance (2003) writes, the Shriners' rites were not a simple mockery of Islam but were part of a late nineteenth-century masculine burlesque of reverence and the feminizing influence of Western admirers of Eastern spirituality. In fact, Albert Rawson, who wrote the Shriner initiation rites, was a friend and supporter of Madame Blavatsky, who founded the Theosophical Society in 1875. Blavatsky's movement practiced spiritualism and looked to India and the writings of ancient Eastern philosophers for religious inspiration. Rawson may have respected Blavatsky and Islam, but later white Shriners were prone to viewing their order's Orientalist history of Islam irreverently. "Like many popular arts and amusements in the nineteenth century the Shrine ritual could be all things to all men," Nance writes. "Whether an initiate sought relief from the seriousness of Masonry, a humorous interpretation of exotic travel narratives, or just a lighthearted elite fraternal experience, whether they despised the Muslim Arabia, romanticized it, or were indifferent to it, they could all find their own meaning in the tricks and skits of the Muslim Shrine" (Nance 2003: 104–79; see also Marr 2006: 178).

Orientalism in America

Orientalism was a protean and plastic phenomenon, not simply a derogatory one. At this time Orientalism resonated with an American public increasingly becoming habituated to "Oriental" consumer goods, whether Chinoiserie from China or Persian rugs from Iran (Tchen 1999). Orientalism provided a dis-orienting and luxurious feeling among patrons of department stores and, later, movie theaters (Bernstein and Studlar 1997; Jackson Lears 1981; Leach 1993). Scholars have speculated that popular Orientalism in consumption and leisure activities was therapeutic for workers habituating themselves to the deadening sameness of work during the Industrial Revolution (Jackson Lears 1981; Nance 2009).

While these materialist motives might explain some of the U.S. fascination with the Orient in the Gilded Age, they do not explain the phenomenon in its entirety. Fascination with the "East" extended before the Industrial Revolution and had contexts in religious and cultural discourses that combined ideational and materialist elements. In particular, American Orientalism in its many various venues—consumerism, cinema, religion, and leisure—not only presented the Orient as "other" but may also have propagated alternative gender roles, racial hierarchies, political systems, and, of course, religious systems.

In the Muslim Orient all roads lead not to Rome but to Mecca, and the Shriners appropriately began with Mecca Temple in New York City on September 26, 1872. It would be four years before they expanded, but when they did they swept across the land, adorning America with a strange poetry of Arabic-named shrines. In 1876, the year that a disputed presidential election led to the withdrawal of federal troops from the South and the end of Reconstruction, Shriners founded Damascus Temple in Rochester, New York, Mt. Sinai in Montpelier, and Al Koran in Cleveland. The year of the Compromise of 1877 brought Cyprus Temple in Albany, Oriental in Troy, New York, Syrian in Cincinnati, Pyramid in Bridgeport, Syria in Pittsburgh, and Ziyara in Utica. Then came Kaaba in Davenport, Moslem in Detroit, Aleppo in Boston, and Medinah in Chicago (Melish 1906: 280–82).

The Shriners spread to the West Coast in 1883 with the opening of Islam Temple in San Francisco on March 6, but the center of the movement remained the East Coast and Midwest, where there were four or five new temples almost every year of the 1880s, starting with Philadelphia's Lu Lu Temple, Murat in Indianapolis (1884), Bourmi in Baltimore, Kosair in Louisville and Tripoli in Milwaukee (1885). New Orleans, that "Big Easy" city famous for good times, incongruously named its shrine after the holy city of Jerusalem. St. Paul chose Osman, Minneapolis took Zuhrah, and in 1886 the nation's capital picked Almas. Palestine landed, strangely, in Providence, Rhode Island, while El Kahir took up residence in Cedar Rapids. The party lodge of

"Furniture City," Grand Rapids, Michigan, was called Saladin. St. Louis's shrine was Moolah, Richmond's was Acca, and in 1887 Leavenworth, Kansas, chose Abdallah. There also was a spate of ancient Egyptian names: Wheeling, West Virginia, picked Osiris; Salina, Kansas, chose Isis; and Toronto dubbed its temple Rameses. The odd Orientalist naming process continued: Dallas, Hella; Albuquerque, Ballut Abyad; Lincoln, Nebraska, Sesostris; Brooklyn, Kismet; Buffalo, Ismailia; Denver, El Jebel; St. Joseph, Missouri, Moila; Kansas City, Missouri, Ararat. Finally in 1888 three more lodges joined San Francisco's Islam Temple on the West Coast: Al Kader in Portland, Al Malaikah in Los Angeles, and Afifi in Tacoma, Washington. That year also saw the birth of Algeria in Helena, Montana; Morocco in Jacksonville, Florida; and El Riad in Sioux Falls. In 1889 the Sahara came to Pine Bluff, Arkansas; Tangier to Omaha; the Alhambra to Chattanooga, Tennessee; Yaarab to Atlanta; and El Zagal to Fargo, North Dakota. The year 1890 witnessed the Battle of Wounded Knee, the last major battle with and massacre of American Indian people by U.S. soldiers, while in other parts of the West, men playing Muslims founded El Kalah in Salt Lake City and El Katif in Spokane. By the end of the year there were 16,980 Shriners nationwide and new chapters in Erie, Pennsylvania, and Birmingham, Alabama, with many more to follow (Melish 1906: 105).

By the time the World's Columbian Exposition opened in Chicago in 1893 there were sixty-three shrines nationwide, with almost 23,000 members, and by the time it closed there were sixty-seven (Melish 1906: 108). The year of the World's Fair, India landed in Oklahoma City and the Mohammed shrine played in Peoria. The Shriners continued at this pace in the following decades, planting shrines in almost every large and medium-sized city in the country. By the time the Shriners published their official *History of the Imperial Council* in 1921, there were 154 chapters at a time when the country as a whole had only fifty-eight metropolitan districts (Thompson 1976: 17). They sported such exotic names as Bedouin, Arabia, Kazim, Sudan, Egypt, Tigris, Oasis, Salaam, Luxor, Cairo, Crescent, Gizeh, El Mina, Khartum, Vektash, Omar, Nile, Midian, Al Shah, Alcazar, and perhaps strangest of all given recent political developments, Wahabi in Jackson, Mississippi, founded on July 12, 1911. Notably, they all remained in the continental United States, except for Hawaii's Aloha temple (1900), Khartum in Winnipeg (1904), Anezeh in Mexico City (1906), Mocha in London, Ontario (1908), and the Canal Zone's Abou Saad (1917).

Unlike other streams of Freemasonry, which started in Scotland and embellished upon legends drawn from Central Europe, the Shriners were a distinctively American version of fraternalism that drew on romantic Orientalist legends at a time when America itself was bursting onto the world's stage as a major industrial, cultural, military, and colonial power while simultaneously suppressing Americans of African descent through new systems of segregation and disenfranchisement. There is no simple correlation between Shrinerdom and the new imperialism, however. Through subversive laughter and ribald parodies of Islam, some of the country's most prominent men ridiculed the Victorian hypocrisies of their own society, using the gay, potent, and appealing mythology of the Muslim East.

The carnivalesque display of exotic peoples on the Midway in Chicago during the 1893 World's Columbian Exposition also provided opportunities for intercultural and interracial interaction and even friendship. As writer Julian Hawthorne reported, "the ends of the earth were meeting, and finding one another good fellows" (Hawthorne 1893: 35, 38, 77, 150; Reed 2000: xxvi).

Over time, visitors to the fair were able to strike up friendships with the visitors from foreign lands: "We shake hands with the Soudanese [sic], and ask them how mother is; we walk arm-in-arm with the Moslem, poke the Dahomeyans in the ribs," wrote the son of Nathaniel Hawthorne (Hawthorne 1893: 150). The Midway's Muslim diaspora in general and its "Street in Cairo" in particular contained all the elements of Egyptology and romantic Orientalism that were the stock-in-trade of the Shriners, whose legends and rituals fetishized and romanticized both the contemporary Muslim world and the mysteries of ancient Egypt. If the Shriners were the "playground of Masonry," then the ersatz Arabia of the World's Fair was a veritable playground for Shriners. Hence it is particularly appropriate that the World's Fair was the place where Shriners passed on the twenty-one-year-old traditions of the Ancient Arabic Order, launched in New York City's Mecca Temple, to Black Freemasons.

The Advent of Black Prince Hall Shriners

The key figure in the transmission of Shrinerdom to African Americans was a Black attorney from Chicago named John George Jones, who was born on September 18, 1849, in Ithaca, New York. When he was aged seven his family moved to Chicago, and when Jones came of age he studied law under the tutelage of W. W. O'Brien, a noted criminal attorney. Jones passed the bar in the State of Illinois in 1881 and was later elected to the state legislature from Chicago.

Jones was a man of considerable eloquence and organizational acumen who became a prominent member of the local Prince Hall Masonic lodge, rising to the rank of deputy grand master in 1875. In 1887, however, he began to stray from Prince Hall orthodoxy, finding himself suspended on the charge of ignoring the orders of a Masonic court and then reinstated in the same year (Bey n.d.; Commission of Masonic Information 1954: 11, 14; Walkes 1993: 23–40). Around 1890 he began representing himself as the "Sovereign Grand Commander of the United Supreme Council of the Southern and Western Masonic Jurisdiction, United States of America," and began petitioning the Shriners' "Grand Council of Arabia," seeking to be initiated into the Shrine and to be vested with the power to organize temples in the United States.

On June 1, 1893, Jones got his wish when a Shriner delegation in town for a Shriner convention timed to coincide with the World's Fair conferred on Jones the degree of Ancient Arabic Order of the Nobles of the Mystic Shrine, in impressive ceremonies at Chicago's eighteen-story Masonic Hall. Along with the initiation, the Shriners gave Jones the power and authority to confer the degree of the Mystic Shriner, to found temples, to create Grand Imperial Councils, and to call himself Imperial Potentate of the Imperial Grand Council in the United States of America. The head of the Shriner delegation called himself "Noble Rofelt Pasha, Deputy of the Shriner's Grand Council of Arabia." He was assisted by three others, who likewise claimed to be from the Orient (Secret Ritual n.d.:7; Ferguson 1937: 189; Nuruddin 2000: 240). According to one of Jones's successors, the others were "S. Hussein of Syria, Turkey, Amel Kadar of Palestine, Turkey, and A. B. Belot of the north of Africa, while representing their various countries at the Chicago World's Fair" (Walkes 1993: 58). The following day Jones convened thirteen members of the local Prince Hall Masons in Chicago, just as thirteen white Masons had met in New York to form the Mystic Shrine twenty-one years previously, and together Jones and his associates founded the Black version of the Shriners, beginning appropriately enough with Palestine Temple (Walkes 1993: 24–25; Ferguson 1937: 189; Nuruddin 2000: 239). They followed that up before the end of the year with Mecca Temple in Washington, D.C., Jerusalem Temple in Baltimore, Medina Temple in New York, Pyramid Temple in Philadelphia, and Persian Temple in Indianapolis, thus mapping ancient Egypt, the Orient, and the holy cities of the Islamic world onto some of the major Black cities of the late nineteenth century.

Black Masons were already well enshrined in African American social life. Along with Black churches, Black Masonic lodges provided one of the few venues controlled by African Americans. At a time when most African Americans were effectively disenfranchised, lodges provided the opportunity to vote for officers, run organizations, and network with prominent members of "the race." Perhaps equally important, practicing Freemasonry allowed African Americans to imagine themselves into its narrative, which begins with the great builders of the Holy Land and Egypt and continues through the Scottish Enlightenment and the fall of tyranny in the United States, Europe, and Haiti. Accepting the Mystic Shrine allowed prominent Black men to join a network that included many others like themselves. It also tied African Americans into fictive networks that were not simply transnational but joined them, at least in the legends of their initiation ceremonies, with people of color in the Islamic Orient.

The white Shriners noted the advent of a "colored" group as early as 1894, when Imperial Potentate Thomas J. Hudson reported the existence of "organizations of our colored fellow citizens, who have pirated our title almost verbatim" (AEAONMS 1901: 12–13). Prince Hall Shrine historian Joseph Walkes concludes that a member of the white Shrine "was directly involved with Jones and his organizing the Prince Hall Shrine" (Walkes 1993: 45). Despite protests from some white Shriners in succeeding decades, others continued to supply their Black counterparts with regalia and meeting places. With the intensification of Jim Crow in the early twentieth century, such cooperation worked to the detriment of segregationists when the U.S. Supreme Court ruled against white Shriners in southern states who were attempting to bar African Americans from using the name and symbol of the order.

The Prince Hall Masons faced dissension from within and without from the beginning, when a rival named Milton F. Fields emerged and began conferring the mysteries of the Mystic Shrine on Black Masons. With the order split between a "Jones Faction" and a "Fields Faction," Jones lost a bid for reelection as Imperial Potentate in 1895 and organized a rival Supreme Council (AEAONMS 1909: 1). In 1897 Prince Hall Shrinerdom became further fragmented when Jones began expelling members en masse. In order to quell dissension between what had become three separate Black Shriner organizations, representatives of three of the first temples met in December 1900 and formed the Imperial Council of the Ancient *Egyptian* Arabic Order Nobles of the Mystic Shrine of North and South America and Its Jurisdictions (emphasis added). By placing "Egyptian" in their name, the Black Shriners were distinguishing themselves from the white organization with a reference to Africa that connoted both the contemporary Egypt and the ancient glories of the pharaohs that had long played a central role in Masonic legend (Walkes 1993: 54). The Prince Hall Shriners' founder, Jones, got himself expelled from "regular" Prince Hall Masonry in 1903 for setting up a fraudulent Grand Lodge of Illinois and spent the remainder of his life until his death in 1914 feuding with other Black Masons (Walkes 1993: 23–39).

Prince Hall Shrine temples spread rapidly, from twenty-five in 1895 to sixty-one in 1899. As with white Shriners, the Black Shriners' choice of temple names reflected their fascination with Islam and the Muslim Orient. There was Allah Temple in Kansas City, Missouri, Magnus in Alexandria, Virginia, and Sahara Temple in Pittsburgh. Black Shriners in Baltimore met in Jerusalem Temple and those in Los Angeles chose the name Egyptian. Koran Temple was founded in Kansas City, Kansas; Mohammed Temple in Forrest City, Arkansas; and Sinai Temple in Gulfport, Mississippi. Other temple names included Constantine, Medina, Golconda, Syria, Rabban, Arabia, El Hassa, Emuth, Damascus, Adel Kader, Kalif Aloe, Midianah, Moses, Mecca, Mount Ararat, Mount Olive, Marracca, Palestine, Red Sea, and two called Mosslem [*sic*]. Of the thirty-two temples on the roster for the annual convention in 1909, only Birmingham's St. Joseph Temple and Oklahoma City's Great Western Temple lacked identifiably Arabic or Oriental names (AEAONMS 1909: 41).

African American Shriner Orientalism

African Americans interpreted the Orientalist myth at the heart of Shrinerdom differently than did their white peers, just as Joanna Brooks has argued that African Americans developed their own interpretations of Freemasonry in general (Brooks 2000). Whereas the white Shrine tradition had been mainly a ribald mockery of the stuffy hypocrisy of the Gilded Age, Black Shriners invested the ritual with considerably more solemnity. While the white Shriners tended to treat their origin legend as an elaborate joke, Black Shriners took a more reverent approach.

As the decades progressed and Black Shriners started to come under attack from their white counterparts, they became even more deeply invested in their origin story, which they used to argue that white Shriners lacked authority to practice the ritual of the Mystic Shrine. Black Shriners used their origin story to distinguish themselves from white Shriners, arguing that they had received the ritual directly from the mysterious Noble Rofelt Pasha and the "Grand Council of Arabia" (Jones 1901, in Walkes 1993: 429). In a speech given at the establishment of Jerusalem Temple at Baltimore, Maryland, in September 1893, John G. Jones claimed: "The Ancient Arabic Order of Nobles of the Mystic Shrine of Masonry is possibly the most profound of all the mysteries of Masonry, for its origins bears internal evidence of its existence soon after the creation of the world." Likewise, Jones emphasized the uplifting and morally edifying nature of its ceremonies and principles, which promised to unite men, to teach "solemn and important lessons of truth and justice for all," and to promote "the evangelization of man and the promotion and practice of Christian faith" (Jones 1893, in Walkes 1993: 419). These sentiments of justice, uplift, and expansionist evangelization were common for "colored" men and women of Jones's era and social station, who frequently advocated spreading the gospel of Christianity to foreign lands in general and Africa in particular (Campbell 1998; Higginbotham 1994).

Blacks and whites also related to the Orient very differently in the era known as the "nadir" for Black Americans, when lynching and Jim Crow segregation attained a new ferocity. The most common attitude in white Shrine literature is one of overwrought reverence for Islam and the Orient. However, it was not uncommon for white Shriners to associate Arabs with Africans and to connect both with denigrating stereotypes of Black Americans. In one illustration for a function of the white Islam Temple in San Francisco, California, an elephant threatens an "Arab," drawn with the cartoonish bulging eyes and exaggerated lips, both tropes of American racist caricatures of Black people (Islam Shrine 1890).

On the other hand, Black Shriners used the mystique of the Orient to advance the cause of the uplift and progress of "the race." At the twelfth annual session of the Imperial Council of the Black Shriners, held at the "Oasis" of Detroit in the "Desert" of Michigan in 1910, Imperial Potentate Jacob F. Wright melded the vocabulary of Islam into the language of the Exodus narrative. "Many years ago," he said, "there lived in the minds of a people, who had for years been driven by hard task-masters, that somewhere on the northern boundary of our country situated between two lakes, was the gateway to a country of human liberty," he pronounced, referencing the poetic language of Black American spirituals that turned the South into Egypt and the North into a metaphorical Promised Land. Yet the Shriners superimposed the Holy Land of Islam on top of the Holy Land of Judaism, Christianity, and Negro spirituals: "Many struggled in vain for this Mecca," Potentate Wright continued, "but to many others the dream became a living reality." For Black Americans living in an age of lynching and Jim Crow in the South, the struggles for the "Mecca" of Detroit were very current. The warm reception "our caravan of the faithful" received there made "each pilgrim" feel that "life is worth living in Detroit" (AEAONMS 1910: 22). As Shriners, Black men were metaphorically pilgrims to the Mecca of the North, living Judeo-Christian and Islamic mythology simultaneously.

African American Shriners consciously used the language of uplift to describe the mission of their organization, which Imperial Potentate Eugene

Fig. 3.1. Oriental banquet invitation, San Francisco's (white) Islam Shrine, 1890. Courtesy of Asiya (formerly Islam) Shrine headquarters, San Mateo, California.

Phillips stated in Atlantic City in 1911 "means so much for the advancement and uplift of our race." Conversely, the factionalism among Prince Hall Shriners was a "retardation not only of the progress of our order but of the race as well" (AEAONMS 1911: 19, 22). Prince Hall Shriners endowed their organization with a seriousness of purpose that was commonly lacking among their white counterparts.

In 1913 Imperial Potentate Phillips defined the work of the order as allaying the suffering of humanity, "which is so wretched and so sadly in need of love." The duty of members was never to "lull their conscience to sleep while there is one soul suffering from the injustice of his brother, whether that brother be black or white." Rather, they should "give a cool drop of water of encouragement to every effendi, oh yes, to every man, be he Seyyid or be he Fellah whenever he needs our assistance as he journeys by the oases of our desert. Illustrious Sons of the Desert," Phillips continued, at full stride, "the day is now here upon us and about us when we must confer and consult for the good of the race to which we have the honour to belong." Rather than simply making merry in Indianapolis, the gathering was a time to "consecrate" to "the solution of the great questions of Justice and Righteousness of the Unity of Allah and the Brotherhood of Man." And all of this was to be done in the "Spirit of that lowly One, the Man of Sorrows" (AEAONMS 1913: 20). African American Shriners transposed the familiar Christian and Hebraic imagery of the spirituals and the Exodus into the Islamic poetic vocabulary of Orientalism, translating a desire for freedom, racial uplift, and human rights into the language of the pilgrimage to Mecca.

For Black Americans not only was the African-ness of Moorish and Islamic peoples a source of pride, but the foreignness of the Orientalist rituals of the Mystic Shrine provided a lifeline outside the racism of American shores. As Masonic historian Joseph C. Walkes explains, some of the motivation for the creation of the Shriners "came from the need of African-Americans to be recognized outside of their own communities, and such recognition coming from a 'Grand Council of Arabia,' from a mysterious foreign land, perhaps was the spark" (Walkes 1993: 41). For Black Americans, the Mystic Shrine was a way of staking a claim to the world's most ancient mythology while also building fictive ties to a global imagined community of Shriners, Masons, and Muslims.

In a 1901 address Jones referred to both halves of the Masonic mythic dyad when he spoke of "the ancient mysteries of Judea and Egypt" (Jones 1901, in Walkes 1993: 429). Yet the main referent for the initiation rituals of both branches of the Mystic Shrine was not Judaism or Christianity but Islam. The rites of the Nobles of the Mystic Shrine became an important inspiration for the rise of Black Muslim sects in the United States because the rites were suffused with Islamic legends, myths, and passwords. Initiates were hustled from station to station by Nobles dressed as Arabic soldiers carrying curving scimitars. The opening words of the Shriner ceremonial explaining their initiation rites were: "My friends or Nobles of the Mystic Shrine, the order with which you have become united was founded by Mohammed and has as its background the trackless desert of Arabia and the fearless, devoted, and barbaric Arab." All initiates were made to "cross the hot sands," which represents the perilous journey of the first Muslim pilgrims to Mecca. Initiates promised to "worship at the Shrine of Islam" and cleanse themselves in a pool meant to represent the Well of ZemZem (or ZamZam), where Islamic tradition teaches that Hagar and her son Ishmael quenched their thirst when they were expelled from Abraham's tent. The "Illustrious Potentate" who leads the ceremony asks, "Who is he who hath professed to have conversed in person with the Supreme and maketh himself mightiest of the mighty? Mohammed, the Prophet of the Arab's creed." The High Priest proclaims, "There are Moslems among us; there are others who swerve from propriety: but who so seeketh Islam earnestly seeks true direction; but those who swerve from truth and justice shall merit and reap abundance of chastisement." Candidates, referred to as "Sons of the Desert," were made to swear a solemn oath "as did the elect of the Temple at Mecca, the Moslem and the Mohammedan" on the Bible "and on the mysterious legend of the Koran, and its dedication to the Mohammedan faith." Initiates gave a "Grand Salaam" and bow in imitation of Muslim prayer, and they kissed a representation of the Kaaba, the black stone that is the focal point of the annual Muslim pilgrimage to Mecca (AEAONMS 1973).

The Shriners taught reverence for the Koran and the Prophet Mohammed, who they claimed was the founder of their secret society. "The Koran is the unique history of our founder Mohammed," both white and Black Shriners learned upon initiation:

> The work is absolutely unique in its origin and in its preservation, upon the authenticity of which no one has ever been able to cast a serious doubt. The Koran is the actual text as dictated by Mohammed himself, day by day and month by month, during his lifetime. It is the reflection of this master-mind, sometimes inartistic and self-contradictory, more often inspiring and lyrical, and always filled with great ideas which stand out as a whole. (AEAONMS 1973: 1)

In sum, the heart of the secret ritual of the Shriners was Islamic history and Islamic ritual. As they explained themselves, "our whole ritualistic system is based upon these kindly attributes [such as refinement, education, and moral integrity] together with an unflinching faith in Allah." One part of the initiation was intended "to teach you to always renounce the wiles and evils of the world and promise to ever worship at the Shrine of Islam, where the air is rich with the wisdom of Allah" (AEAONMS 1969: 6–7). Shriners swore a "Moslem's oath" to "Allah, the God of Arab, Moslem, and Mohammed," and they used "Moslem Greetings" such as "Aleikum Es Salaam"—Peace be with you—and "Es Salamu Aleikum"—with you in Peace (AEAONMS 1969: 62).

Through the alchemy of the performance of intense theatrical rituals, which were intended in part to disorient and frighten initiates, the Nobles became fictive Muslims in a theatrical Arabia. The lecture given upon initiation proclaims that "this city in which you now stand is the Holy City of Islam ... situated in the Desert of Arabia" (AEAONMS 1969: 1–2). This use of present tense make-believe was not uncommon in Shriner ceremonies, portions of which they explicitly identified as "sacred." Shriners both Black and white luxuriated in this Orientalist role playing. "You have made the road clear for the journey of your camels," the Black imperial potentate told his charges in 1909; "I find it an easy task to ride through the Desert of burning sand to an Oasis of success" (Walkes 1993: 64). In the lecture given to initiates upon their entry into the order, the speaker referred to those present as "we, as true Arabs" (AEAONMS 1969: 3). In their ceremonies, Shriners professed reverence for the Holy Prophet, the Holy Koran, and the holy city of Mecca, they reenacted Islamic history, they spoke Arabic phrases, and they imagined themselves into a global community of Muslims stretching back vertically in time to the sixth century and horizontally in the present across the chasm of oceans to foreign countries.

Religion in Black Shrinerdom

The religious aspect of Masonry was particularly noticeable during the late nineteenth and early twentieth centuries, in the fraternity's elaborate rituals and highly symbolic initiation processes. The world of irregular Prince Hall Freemasonry was especially attractive to men of the cloth and became fertile ground for the growth of religious sects (Fels 1985: 370). Propagated by expelled Masons or by hucksters, who sold the secret mysteries of the order for material gain, irregular Freemasonry lacked doctrinal standards and encouraged the embellishment and mutation of Masonic mysteries. This process of centrifugal variations affected Prince Hall Shriners as much as Prince Hall Masons.

Sometime between 1913 and 1925, the twentieth century's first large African American sect practicing Islam began with a man named Timothy Drew, who adopted the Shriner designation of "Noble" and the Shriner fez and rituals to become "Noble Drew Ali." He called his organization the Canaanite Temple and later dubbed it the Moorish Science Temple (Curtis 2002:45–62; Gomez 2005: 203–75). In 1914, the year after the Canaanite Temple began, Shriner Noble W. O. Murphy of Medina Temple No. 19, New York, remarked on the splinter groups, or "spurious lodges," being formed around the country, and suggested that the Prince Hall Shriners take some action to eradicate them (AEAONMS 1914: 7). Forty years later the situation was very much the same: "It is an amazing circumstance to realize that so many ministers of the gospel are either the heads of such 'unrecognized' organizations in the capacity of a Grand Master, or are actively associated with propagating the work of unscrupulous individuals," wrote leading Prince Hall historian Harry Williamson, who listed seventy-three "so-called clergymen" connected to the alternative African American Masonic organizations in 1954. "If we're not careful," he warned, "these spurious lodges threaten to overwhelm us" (Williamson 1930: 38). Disputes between African American Masons over their legitimacy or lack thereof continue to the present day, when one Prince Hall Web site, founded by Masonic Prince Hall historian Joseph A. Walkes, notes that there are more African American "Bogus" Grand Lodges in the United States than there are legitimate Grand Lodges worldwide (Walkes 1993).

Masonry and its rituals, myths, costumes, and esoteric and magical beliefs saturated the sphere of Black alternative religions. Prince Hall Masons may not have accepted or liked the fact that Freemasonry was permeating this alternative and somewhat shadowy religious sphere, but there was little that they could do about it. The so-called bogus, spurious, clandestine, irregular, and unrecognized African American Masonic movements outnumbered but did not overwhelm Prince Hall Masons. They did, however, provide an important mechanism by which greater numbers of less privileged African Americans could participate in fraternalism. Even more important, they provided organizational structures, esoteric myths, and a potent tradition of Orientalism that formed a critical part of the web of ideas and organizations that led to the creation of alternative African American religions—religions as major as Black Islam and Black Israelism. It was this alternative Black Masonic and Shriner Orientalism that provided one of the most important vehicles by which African Americans in the early twentieth century reimagined their past and reshaped their worlds.

Orientalism acquired an unsavory reputation with the postwar publications of critics of Western Orientalism, such as Anouar Abdel-Malek (1963), A. L. Tibawi (1964), and of course Edward Said (1978). But as Michel Foucault noted, the matrixes of power and knowledge within discourses admit alternative and even oppositional ideas as well as oppressive ones. Foucault wrote that "discourse transmits and produces power; it reinforces it, but also undermines and exposes it, renders it fragile and makes it possible to thwart it" (Foucault 1978: 101). Shriners' secret rituals included ideas about Islam that were inaccurate, and their vision of the Muslim Orient was often fanciful and always Orientalist. But the fact that tens of thousands of prominent Americans—white as well as Black—identified with Islam, learned about the life of the Prophet Muhammad, and created an imagined community as "true Arabs" suggests that Romantic Orientalism offered opportunities for Americans to identify with the Muslim Orient. Some Shriners no doubt viewed their rituals as being farcical, but others absorbed Shriner myths and rituals and gained respect for Islam and the East. African Americans endowed their Orientalist rituals with considerably more solemnity than the white originators of the order, and the spread of Islamic rituals within African American communities contributed to the 1925 founding of the first Black-directed Islamic religious movement in America, the Moorish Science Temple (Nuruddin 2000: 222).

Today Shriners of all races are aging, and their numbers are dwindling. San Francisco's old Islam Shrine is no longer in San Francisco and is no longer called Islam. The white lodge moved to suburban San Mateo, where they produce the East-West Shrine football game, a fundraiser for the twenty-two Shriner children's hospitals, which offer free medical care. After the attacks of September 11, 2001, when bigots harassed and even murdered people they thought might be Muslims, chauvinists sometimes mistook Shriners sporting fezzes for Muslims and harassed them as well. Emphasizing the need to protect their members, two Shrines changed their names: the Palestine Shrine became the Rhode Island Shrine, and Islam Temple became Asiya, which they understood to be an Arabic word meaning "those who heal" but which native speakers suggest might be translated as "coldheartedness" (Neidorf 2002).

Identification with the dress, the beliefs, the statements of faith and the Arabic names of Muslims and the Islamic world might seem incredible after the attacks of September 11, 2001, and the two wars that followed in Iraq and Afghanistan, killing more than 200,000 civilians and 6,650 U.S. and Allied soldiers and producing more than a million Iraqi and almost 3 million Afghan refugees (Costsofwar.org 2013). But the United States has had a long fascination with the Islamic world. After September 11, as in the past, romantic American Orientalist knowledge is not very accurate, but neither is it always malicious. The "coldhearted" might have been trying to call themselves "those who heal." Often oppressive and hegemonic discourses also contain resistant ones, lying just below the surface of a myth or a mistranslation. The story of the (white) Ancient Arabic Order and the (Black) Ancient Egyptian Order of Nobles of the Mystic Shrine tells us that Americans have not always imagined Muslims and Arabs as enemies. In fact, the United States has long produced romantic and multivalent forms of Orientalism, teaching Americans to identify as Muslims and Arabs through the transformative power of secret rituals even as they produced both reverent and irreverent identification with the Islamic world.

Acknowledgments

Thank you to the New Faculty General Research Fund Grant from the University of Kansas that supported the research in this chapter, and the National Endowment for the Humanities long-term fellowship at the Newberry Library in Chicago that supported its writing.

References Cited

Abdel-Malek, Anouar
1963 "Orientalism in Crisis." *Diogenes* 11 (44): 103–40.
Abun-Nasr, Jamil M.
1987 *A History of the Maghrib in the Islamic Period.* Cambridge, UK: Cambridge University Press.
AEAONMS (Ancient Egyptian Arabic Order of Nobles of the Mystic Shrine of North and South America), Archives of the Headquarters, Memphis, Tennessee.
1901 *Proceedings of the Ninth Annual Session of the Imperial Council of the Ancient Arabic Order of Nobles of the Mystic Shrine of North and South America, Canada and Dependencies,* Buffalo, New York, August 1, 1901. (Cited in Walkes 1993, 45.)
1909 AEAONMS Imperial Council, *Proceedings of Eleventh Annual Session Held at Newark, New Jersey.* Baltimore, Md.: Afro-American Company.
1910 "Imperial Potentate's Address," by Jacob F. Wright. In *Proceedings of the Twelfth Annual Session of the Imperial Council Ancient Egyptian Arabic Order of Nobles of the Mystic Shrine of North and South America, Detroit.* Baltimore, Md.: Afro-American Company.
1911 "Imperial Potentate's Address," by Eugene Phillips. In *Proceedings of the Thirteenth Annual Session of the Imperial Council Ancient Egyptian Arabic Order of Nobles of the Mystic Shrine of North and South America, Atlantic City, N.J.* Baltimore, Md.: Afro-American Company.
1913 "Imperial Potentate's Address," by Eugene Phillips. In *Proceedings of the Fifteenth Annual Session of the Imperial Council Ancient Egyptian Arabic Order of Nobles of the Mystic Shrine of North and South America, Indianapolis.* Baltimore, Md.: Afro-American Company.
1914 *Transactions of the Sixteenth Annual Session of the Ancient Egyptian Arabic Order of Nobles of the Mystic Shrine,* Pittsburgh, Pennsylvania, August.
1969 *Ritual of the Ancient Egyptian Arabic Order Nobles of the Mystic Shrine of North and South America and Jurisdictions, Inc.* Revised 1958; 10th ed., 1969. http://www.phoenixmasonry.org/masonicmuseum/History_of_the_Shrine.htm. (Identical to early twentieth-century versions in AEAONOMS archives.)
1973 Mystic Shrine Ceremonial Lectures. http://www.phoenixmasonry.org.
1993 *History of the Shrine* (see Walkes 1993).
Bernstein, Matthew, and Gaylyn Studlar (eds.)
1997 *Visions of the East: Orientalism in Film.* New Brunswick, N.J.: Rutgers University Press.
Bey, Ezekiel M.
N.d. John G. Jones: The Father of Bogus Masonry. http://www.thephylaxis.org/bogus/johnjones.php.
Brooks, Joanna
2000 "Prince Hall, Freemasonry, and Genealogy," *African American Review* 34 (2): 197–216.
Campbell, James T.
1998 *Songs of Zion: The African Methodist Episcopal Church in the United States and South Africa.* Chapel Hill: University of North Carolina Press.

Carnes, Mark C.
1989 *Secret Ritual and Manhood in Victorian America*. New Haven, Conn.: Yale University Press.
Clawson, Mary Ann
1989 *Constructing Brotherhood: Class, Gender, and Fraternalism*. Princeton, N.J.: Princeton University Press.
Commission of Masonic Information, Prince Hall Grand Lodge
1954 *Freemasonry among Men of Color in New York State*. New York: Prince Hall Grand Lodge Free and Accepted Masons, State of New York.
Costsofwar.org
2013 Costs of War. Eisenhower Study Group, Brown University. http://www.costsofwar.org.
Curtis, Edward E., IV
2002 *Islam in Black America: Identity, Liberation, and Difference in African-American Islamic Thought*. Albany: State University of New York Press.
Delany, Martin R.
1853 *A Treatise in The Origin and Objects of Freemasonry, Its Introduction Into the United States, and Legitimacy Amoung Colored Men: A Treatise Delivered Before St. Cyprian Lodge, no. 13, June 24th, A.D. 1853*. Pittsburgh: Privately published.
Douglas, Ann
1998 [1977] *The Feminization of American Culture*. New York: Noonday Press.
Eickelman, Dale F., and James P. Piscatori (eds.)
1990 *Muslim Travellers: Pilgrimage, Migration, and the Religious Imagination*. Berkeley: University of California Press.
Fels, Tony
1985 "Religious Assimilation in a Fraternal Organization: Jews and Freemasonry in Gilded-Age San Francisco." *American Jewish History* 74 (4): 369–403.
Ferguson, Charles W.
1937 *Fifty Million Brothers: A Panorama of American Lodges and Clubs*. New York: Farrar and Rinehart.
Foucault, Michel
1978 *The History of Sexuality*. Vol. 1: *An Introduction*. Translated by Robert Hurley. New York: Vintage Books.
Gomez, Michael A.
2005 *Black Crescent: The Experience and Legacy of African Muslims in the Americas*. Cambridge, UK: Cambridge University Press.
Hawthorne, Julian
1893 *Humors of the Fair*. Chicago: E. A. Weeks.
Higginbotham, Evelyn Brooks
1994 *Righteous Discontent: The Women's Movement in the Black Baptist Church, 1880–1920*. Cambridge, Mass.: Harvard University Press.
International Shrine Clown Association
1989 *Sahib Temple Clown Unit*. Nashville, Tenn.: Turner Publishing.

Islam Shrine, San Francisco
1890 Oriental Banquet Invitation, March 19. Archives of the Asiya Shrine Temple, San Mateo, Calif.

Jackson Lears, Kenneth
1981 *No Place of Grace: Antimodernism and the Transformation of American Culture, 1880–1920*. Chicago: University of Chicago Press.

Jacob, Margaret C.
1991 *Living the Enlightenment: Freemasonry and Politics in Eighteenth-Century Europe*. Oxford, UK: Oxford University Press.

Jones, John G.
1893 "Speech of John G. Jones, 33rd Delivered at the Establishment of Jerusalem Temple at Baltimore, Maryland, September 30, 1893." In Walkes 1993.
1901 "Address of John G. Jones Imperial Grand Potentate Ninth Annual Session, Imperial Grand Council, August 1, 1901, Buffalo, New York." In Walkes 1993.

Kantrowitz, Stephen
2010 "'Intended for the Better Government of Man': The Political History of African American Freemasonry in the Era of Emancipation." *Journal of American History* 96(4): 1001–26.

Leach, William
1993 *Land of Desire: Merchants, Power, and the Rise of a New American Culture*. New York: Vintage.

Marr, Timothy
2006 *The Cultural Roots of American Islamicism*. New York: Cambridge University Press.

Mclish, William B.
1921 *The History of the Imperial Council, 1872–1921*. 2nd ed. Cincinnati: Abingdon Press.

Nance, Susan
2003 "Crossing Over: A Cultural History of American Engagement with the Muslim World, 1830–1940." PhD diss., University of California, Berkeley.
2009 *How the Arabian Nights Inspired the American Dream, 1790–1935*. Chapel Hill: University of North Carolina Press.

Neidorf, Shawn
2002 "Harassed, Insulted, Shriners Pay Price for Islam Imagery." *San Jose Mercury News*, repr. *Chicago Tribune*, October 21, 2002. http://articles.chicagotribune.com/2002-10-21/news/0210210200_1_shriners-hospitals-orthopedic-problems-harassed.

Nuruddin, Yusuf
2000 "African American Muslims and the Question of Identity: Between Traditional Islam, African Heritage, and the American Way." In *Muslims on the Americanization Path?*, ed. Yvonne Yezbeck Haddad and John Esposito, 215–62. New York: Oxford University Press.

Reed, Christopher Robert
2000 *All the World is Here!: The Black Presence at White City*. Bloomington: Indiana University Press, 2000.

Riley-Smith, Jonathan
1995 *The Oxford Illustrated History of the Crusades*. New York: Oxford University Press.

Ross, Noble William, Recorder and Historian, "Lu Lu" Temple, Philadelphia
1906 *A History of the Ancient Arabic Order of the Nobles of the Mystic Shrine for North America*. Library of Freemasonry vol. 5, ed. Robert Gould. London: John C. Yorston Publishing Company.

Said, Edward
1978 *Orientalism*. New York: Pantheon.

Secret Ritual
N.d. *The Secret Ritual of the Secret Work of the Ancient Arabic Order of the Nobles of the Mystic Shrine*. New York: Masonic Supply Company.

Skocpol, Theda, Ariane Liazos, and Marshall Ganz
2006 *What a Mighty Power We Can Be: African American Fraternal Groups and the Struggle for Racial Equality*. Princeton, N.J.: Princeton University Press.

Stevenson, David
1988 *The Origins of Freemasonry: Scotland's Century, 1590–1710*. New York: Cambridge University Press.

Summers, Martin
2004 *Manliness and Its Discontents: The Black Middle Class and the Transformation of Masculinity, 1900–1930*. Chapel Hill: University of North Carolina Press.

Tchen, John Kuo Wei
1999 *New York before Chinatown: Orientalism and the Shaping of American Culture, 1776–1882*. Baltimore: Johns Hopkins University Press.

Thompson, Warren Simpson
1976 *Population: The Growth of Metropolitan Districts in the United States, 1900–1940*. Manchester, N.H.: Ayer Publishing.

Tibawi, A. L.
1964 "English-Speaking Orientalists," *Islamic Quarterly* 8(1–4): 25–45.

Walkes, Joseph A., Jr.
1993 *History of the Shrine (Ancient Egyptian Arabic Order Nobles of the Mystic Shriner, Inc., Prince Hall Affiliated): A Pillar of Black Society*. Detroit: Ancient Egyptian Arabic Order Nobles of the Mystic Shrine of North and South America.

Wilder, Craig
2001 *In the Company of Black Men: The African Influence on African American Culture in New York City*. New York: New York University Press.

Williamson, Harry A. C.
1930 "Unrecognized Negro Masonic Bodies." Masonic Collection, Schomburg Center for Research in Black Culture, New York Public Library, Astor, Lenox, and Tilden Foundations.

4

Locating Mecca

Religious and Political Discord in the Javanese Community in Pre-Independence Suriname

ROSEMARIJN HOEFTE

Rukun or harmony is one of the central values in Javanese life (De Waal-Malefijt 1963: 57–58).[1] This principle remained in force in the Javanese migrant communities in Suriname in the twentieth century.[2] Solidarity, cooperation, and peace were important notions when adjusting to a new life in a not very receptive environment. As the last migrants to arrive before World War II, the Javanese occupied the lowest rungs of the social-economic ladder, behind the Creole (descendants of former enslaved) and Hindustani populations. Javanese culture, with its emphasis on the ideals of harmony and cooperation, was, however, a source of pride.

Yet in the 1940s and 1950s *rukun* seemed to have lost its significance when the Javanese community was bitterly divided. The overwhelming majority of the Javanese were Muslims, yet intra-religious strife split the group. The argument between worshippers who prayed as in Java, thus facing westward, and those facing east toward Mecca was also a dispute involving Javanese culture, politics, and whether the future of the Surinamese Javanese was in Suriname or in newly independent Indonesia.

This study addresses the schisms in the Javanese community in Suriname in the 1940s and 1950s. Traditionally this division is presented as a cultural-religious conflict with strong ideological and socioeconomic overtones (see Breunissen 2001; Suparlan 1995). Thus the social-economic dimension has been recognized, but it has not featured in the analyses of the weakening of the controversy.

Central to this topic is the repatriation of one group of Javanese to escape the discord in Suriname. They built a new village in Indonesia named Tongar, but the lack of success there meant that for future potential migrants, the escape route to Indonesia was not a viable option anymore; the population in Suriname was now forced to focus on life there. Only in the last decades of the twentieth century did emigration to the Netherlands, traditionally a destination only for students and professionals, become an option for Surinamese with little education. Insufficiently recognized in studies on twentieth-century Suriname, I argue, is that gradual sociocultural and socioeconomic advancement followed in the wake of the political emancipation of the Javanese after World War II. The growing economy and the expanding civil service sector in particular offered employment opportunities besides agriculture, thus offering the Javanese social mobility as well. Eastward- and westward-facing worshippers continued to differ on the interpretation of Islam, but the acrimonious tone about the future and the position of the Javanese was gone.[3]

Another aspect to be considered here is that since avoidance of conflict is also part of the principle of *rukun*, the remigration to Indonesia can be seen as a typical Javanese solution to the problem. Escapism and avoidance protest have been part and parcel of Javanese peasant culture (Adas 1992) and played a significant role in a number of Javanese designs to leave Suriname for a more hospitable place.[4] The first time was in 1933, when the Creole political activist Anton de Kom was rumored to have promised the Javanese that ships were waiting offshore to take them back to Java. The arrest of De Kom ended in a bloodbath, and the disillusioned Javanese turned back to their plantations and smallholdings (Hoefte 1998: 180–82). The second was in 1954, when more than a thousand people left for Tongar in Indonesia, as discussed later in this chapter. The final episode took place in the 1970s, when tens of thousands of Javanese left for the Netherlands in the years preceding Suriname's independence in 1975.

This chapter is focused on the religious, cultural, and socioeconomic schisms in the Javanese community in the 1940s and 1950s and is partly based on interviews recorded in 2009–2010 with Surinamese Javanese in Indonesia, Suriname, and the Netherlands.

Javanese Migration and Settlement

On August 9, 1890, the first Javanese migrants arrived in Suriname to work as indentured laborers on the colony's largest plantation. The government and the planters recruited these temporary workers to replace emancipated slaves. Against expectations the majority of these workers turned out not to be temporary at all. Slightly less than 80 percent of the almost 33,000 Javanese who arrived between 1890 and 1939 (compared to approximately 65 percent of the more than 34,000 British Indians or Hindustani who came between 1873 and 1916) did not return to their homeland but stayed, for many reasons, in Suriname.[5] One reason was government policy: already in the late nineteenth century time-expired immigrants could receive a plot of land and a small amount of money in exchange for their free return passage. Thus the colonial government started to change its focus from large-scale agriculture to smallholdings farmed by Hindustani and Javanese settlers.

Around 1930 a new stage of immigration began with the recruitment of free Javanese smallholders, who quite literally lived in the shadow of the plantations: they worked on the estates only when the management demanded extra hands. Fewer laborers were needed now that scarcely any plantations were left. The worldwide economic crisis of the 1930s, including mass unemployment, only reinforced this downward trend.

The final stage in Javanese immigration was the Welter-Kielstra plan, named after the colonial minister and the governor of Suriname, respectively. Its architect was Suriname governor J. C. Kielstra, who had two goals in mind when he designed this grand project in 1937: the formation of a permanent smallholding population and the creation of a labor reserve for the remaining plantations. The other aim was to "Indianize" (*verindischen*, as in the Netherlands East Indies) or more precisely "Javanize" the colony by transferring 100,000 immigrants from Java to Suriname in a ten-year period and to have them cultivate rice for domestic consumption and export. The colonists would settle in *desa* (villages), complete with their religious and civil leadership, including a *lurah* (village leader) and a *kaum* (religious leader), on new lands provided by the government.[6] Under this program 990 Javanese moved to Suriname in 1939; World War II prevented further execution of the plan.

This policy was an extension of earlier programs, but Governor Kielstra added a new element: rather than the individual interests of the colonist, the communal interests of a tight, effectively supervised group were to prevail, as was the case in Java. The inhabitants of the five *desa* were dependent on the village leader for the distribution of rental plots and had fewer rights than individual smallholders. This emphasis on community and harmony reflected Kielstra's political philosophy, which was based on his earlier career as a civil servant in the Netherlands East Indies (Hoefte 2011: 198–99; Ramsoedh 1990). His experiences in this plural society and his theories about colonial political economy informed his policies in Suriname. Kielstra's ideas were based on an "organic" ideology that valued existing differences between the different populations on their own merits. Local customs and traditions, including the administration of justice, should play a prominent role in colonial society. In contrast, official policy in Suriname was aimed at assimilation, based on one language, one law, and one Christian culture.

Kielstra's emphasis on smallholdings and *desa* is not surprising given his conservative ideology. He firmly believed in the maintenance of local customs, the self-reliance of different population groups, and "organic" ties between them. Not only economic interests should tie an individual to a village. The *lurah* would be responsible for the financial, legal, and material order in the *desa*. As one interviewee outlines it, "Everything had to go through the *lurah*. For example, if you wanted to cultivate new land or build a dam. The *lurah* was powerful and had to report to the district commissioner."[7] Another informant, born in 1929, describes how in his Surinamese *desa* the *masyarakat* (the people) elected the leadership, trying to judge their honesty and fairness. He then explains the commanding position of the leader: "A *lurah* got 2,5 hectares of land as compensation (*bengkok*). He didn't have to cultivate the land himself; that had to be done by the *masyarakat*."[8]

Kielstra (1927: 190) was critical about the role of education: "Denying existing cultural differences makes those who are successful in school become unbalanced." He thus promoted the diversification of education to suit the needs of different population groups. This ideological argument had a strong economic component: Javanese and Hindustani pupils were trained to become peasants and should be taught not to look down on manual or agricultural labor. According to the government, education was not an avenue for social mobility but rather a mode to maintain and strengthen a society based on smallholder agriculture.

The governor broke with the attempts by earlier administrations at assimilation of the various population groups. Kielstra respected existing ethnic values, traditions, cultural expressions, and non-Christian religions. The governor's policies ran into strong opposition, among the Creole population in particular. His critics accused him of "divide-and-rule" strategies. The prewar Creole elite, and to a lesser degree the small middle class, fiercely objected to the liquidation of the assimilation idea. These groups feared that Christianity would be undermined, that the unity of law (meaning that the same law applied to all population groups) would be broken, and that the Asian groups would increase their cultural and political influence. To that end, Kielstra had appointed Hindustani to the colonial parliament to represent the interests of the Hindustani and Javanese. The introduction of the so-called Asian marriage law in 1940 was the straw that broke the camel's back. This new regulation legitimized Javanese and Hindustani marriages if they were solemnized in accordance with the Muslim or Hindu religion. It thus broke the unity of law, undermined Christian churches, and added to the self-confidence of the Javanese and Hindustani in general and their religious leaders in particular.

However, Kielstra was not alone in undermining the assimilationist ideal. The immigrants themselves subverted this concept by voicing their ethnic interests. Indeed, the marriage law was a case in point: as early as 1913 an immigrant organization had requested the recognition of weddings conducted according to Hindu or Muslim rites. This request gained some support in the Dutch parliament, but Governor Kielstra was the first to act upon it in his zeal to recognize ethnic and religious differences.

The growing ethnic consciousness of many Javanese was based on Islam and Indonesian nationalist sentiments that had been imported from the homeland. Migrants in Suriname could keep abreast of developments in their homeland through newly arrived immigrants and publications imported from Java.

Notions such as *sambatan* (mutual assistance) and *rukun* remained in force in Suriname.[9] Islam was a significant element of Javanese culture.[10] In both Java and Suriname, however, only a small minority of mostly elderly men— *santri* (learned or religious men)—upheld a Shafiitic, Sharia-centered interpretation of Islam and faithfully fulfilled the religious duties.[11] They lived according to the Muslim guidelines and were familiar with the Quran, which they recited in Arabic. *Santri* were the main source of religious information in Suriname.

Most Javanese—often known as *wong Islam* (Islamic men), *wong Agami Jawi* (people adhering to Javanese religion), or more pejoratively *abangan* (followers)—had incorporated many pre-Islamic Javanese traditions and mystical notions into their religion. Known as *kejawèn*, it combined elements of Buddhism, Hinduism, and animism. The spirits played a key role, and communication with them through offerings of food, flowers, or tobacco formed an essential part of life. Life's milestones such as birth, circumcision, marriage, and death or other important social occasions were commemorated with a *slametan*, a ritual meal to foster *rukun*. The *slametan* and the complex of spirit beliefs are the core of the religious system (Geertz 1960: 5–16). For this group, both in Java and in Suriname, Islam was part of the "Javanese sociocultural system" (Suparlan 1995: 140).

The wish to establish a place in an alien world and the resulting ethnic solidarity in a not very welcoming society enabled the Javanese to hold onto their own cultures, which in part were newly constructed.[12] The fact that immigrants originated from different areas with diverse traditions often led to the amalgamation of several cultures and languages into one "Javanese" culture and language, which served to strengthen the ethnic identity. The geographical and social isolation of most immigrants facilitated the process of constructing and maintaining this identity.

In the early twentieth century the Javanese followed the Hindustani example by founding immigrant organizations to defend their interests. These organizations were established on an ethnic basis and promoted the welfare of members within colonial structures.[13] The first immigrant organizations did not have a religious character, but as I show later, this would change when politics and religion in Java (and Suriname) became more entwined.

The Javanese increasingly expressed their growing Indonesian nationalist sentiments: the modernist Muslim organization Sarekat Islam (SI, the Islamic Union, founded in Java in 1911) and Indonesian nationalist leader Sukarno enjoyed support in Suriname as well. The arrival of SI members after World War I fired nationalist sentiments among some Javanese in Suriname. In Java the organization promoted the social and economic progress of the rural population, emphasizing Javanese identity. SI's most influential leader, Tjokroaminoto, tried to combine Islam and European political ideologies, such as socialism. In 1917 the annual congress discussed SI's attitude toward the capitalist system. It proposed to differentiate between "rightful" (i.e., native) and "sinful" (i.e., foreign) capitalism. For example, in 1919 SI took on the "sinful capitalism" of the sugar industry. After 1917 SI radicalized and became openly critical of the colonial government. The leadership, however, did not support militant action by the revolutionary wing of SI. Instead Tjokroaminoto called for passive resistance. However, in an effort to keep the movement together Tjokroaminoto embarked on a more radical course. The alliance between religious reform and political self-awareness did not last, and SI split: the majority of the revolutionaries joined the Partai Kommunis Indonesia (PKI, Indonesian Communist Party), founded in 1920, and others would later join the Partai Nasional Indonesia (PNI, Indonesian National Party).[14]

This pro-independence PNI party, advocating harmony among nationalism, religion, and socialism to establish a united Indonesia, was founded by Sukarno in 1927. Sukarno had been a lodger in a boarding house managed by Tjokroaminoto. Coming soon after the disintegration of SI in the early 1920s and the crushing of the PKI after their failed rebellion of 1926, PNI began to attract a large number of followers, to the growing anxiety of the colonial authorities. They arrested Sukarno and other PNI leaders in December 1929. At his trial in 1930, Sukarno made a series of political speeches attacking the injustices of colonialism and imperialism. These received wide press coverage, and due to pressure from more liberal individuals in the Netherlands and the Netherlands East Indies, Sukarno was released early from prison in December 1931. By then he had become a hero who was widely known throughout Indonesia and also Suriname.

Among the Javanese in Suriname religion and politics were similarly intertwined. The goal of Perkumpulan Islam Indonesia (PII, Indonesian Islamic Organization) was to "unite the Indonesian Muslims in Suriname and to look after their religious and social interests" formally and legally. This organization had the official blessing of the governor and counted five hundred mostly rural members in 1934. The office was decorated with a large painting of Sukarno. Despite the prosecution of Sukarno in Java, the Surinamese chief of police did not label the PII as dangerous.[15] In the period 1933–35 PII's most important project was the building of a mosque, named Nabawi, in the capital of Paramaribo. The worshippers in this mosque would face east, while most Javanese followed the custom from their homeland and faced west during prayer.[16] One informant noted: "My biological father's name was Somantri. He was a respected Muslim and an east worshipper. That caused problems with the Javanese Muslims, the west worshippers. He cooperated with the Hindustani Muslims in the Surinaamse Islamitische Vereniging [SIV, Surinamese Islamic Association]. He was one of the first to argue that Mecca was located east of Suriname and that it was the correct direction for praying."[17] As is shown in this chapter, the choice in the direction of prayers also stood for a choice between traditional Javanese culture (west) and religious orthodoxy (east). This choice affected not only religion but also politics and socioeconomic views.

The SIV, founded in 1929, was an umbrella organization of local *jamaats* (communities). Most of its members were not Javanese but of Indian origin. Less than one-fifth of the Indian migrants were Muslims, mostly adhering to the Sunni tradition. These Hindustani Muslims adhered to the Hanafitish Sharia, while their literature and ritual language was based on Urdu.[18] The Ahmadiyya reformist movement, which started in Lahore, India, in the late 1880s, progressively guided the SIV leadership.[19] Suparlan underlines the importance of the link with the Hindustani Muslims as they were instrumental in the formation of some Javanese political parties in the 1940s when the "Javanese Islamic leaders who had close relationships with Hindustani Muslims [. . .] laid the foundation for the formation of Javanese parties in Suriname, for activating Islamic sentiments in the political arena, and for building an affiliation with Hindustani Muslims" (Suparlan 1995: 224).

The building of the mosque facing east was a confrontation that was part of a number of disputes about proper behavior expected from Muslims. "Real"

Muslims "should strictly follow Islamic teachings as written in the Koran. They should pray toward the East, the actual direction of Mecca" (Suparlan 1995: 141).

In the 1920s and 1930s, newly arrived immigrants emphasized the importance of Islam's Five Pillars and rejected the rituals and offerings and other cultural expressions by the "traditionalists" (Suparlan 1995: 140–54). This difference between east (*wong ngadep ngetan*) and west worshippers (*wong ngadep ngulon*) divided the Javanese community as it also represented a conflict between reform-minded (mostly lower- and middle-class) and traditionalist (often smallholding) Javanese. The conflict within the Javanese community would only intensify with the advent of universal suffrage in 1948 and the formation of political parties.

Suriname on the Road to Autonomy

World War II produced profound social, economic, and political changes in Suriname. Employment opportunities in defense construction work and in bauxite mining lured thousands from the rural areas to the capital, Paramaribo. Often little education or experience was needed to obtain a relatively well-paid job. The economy was booming, and for the first time in decades a budget surplus was achieved.

Politically, Suriname behaved as a colony loyal to the Dutch government in exile in London. Yet the economic growth, coupled with decreased involvement of the Dutch administration, stimulated nationalist feelings among the light-skinned, educated Creole population. The goal was to move to more autonomy within the existing political structure. Further boosting nationalist sentiments were the unpopularity of Governor Kielstra, at least among the Creoles; the Atlantic Charter championing the right of self-determination for colonies; and a speech in December 1942 by the Dutch queen proposing the creation of a commonwealth of the Netherlands, the Netherlands East Indies, Suriname, and the Netherlands Antilles, with autonomy for each overseas territory.[20]

In 1943 a group of Creoles founded Unie Suriname (Union Suriname) in support of the quest for autonomy. Later the union became the Nationale Partij Suriname (NPS, National Party Suriname). Three years later the Hindostaans-Javaanse Centrale Raad (Hindustani-Javanese Central Council) was founded to represent the interests of thirteen Hindu and Muslim religious and trade organizations. The demands included respect, socioeconomic advancement, and state support for religious activities similar to the funding of Christian churches (Gobardhan-Rambocus 2001: 322–30). Soon specific ethnic and religious interests led to fragmentation, and a number of ethnic-religious parties were founded. A few years later the dust settled, and fusions of different groups led to the formation of the Kaum Tani Persatuan Indonesia (KTPI, Indonesian Peasants Union) in 1947 and the Verenigde Hindostaanse Partij (VHP, United Hindustani Party) in 1949.[21] For decades to come these two parties would represent the interests of the majority of Javanese and Hindustani. Their basis would remain ethnic and religious, not ideological. The main goal was to guard the interests of their own population group, leading to patron-client relationships between politicians and their voters. Since the 1950s elected politicians have been able to provide civil service jobs, housing, scholarships, licenses, or land for their constituents.[22]

Meanwhile, the Netherlands showed little inclination to meet the Surinamese politicians, as the metropolis was focusing on the separation of Indonesia.[23] Pressure from its Caribbean colonies forced discussions about a new order. In 1954 The Hague formally recognized the autonomy of Suriname and the Netherlands Antilles.

Earlier, in 1948, universal suffrage was introduced to elect a parliament. General elections in 1949 and 1951 gave the NPS an edge, as the voting law favored candidates in the urban areas, which at that time were still dominated by Creoles. Internal divisions within NPS between the light-skinned elite and the working class, however, gave coalitions of other parties a chance to govern after the elections of 1955. The Creole and Hindustani political leaders broadened their support by working together. The so-called *verbroederingspolitiek* (fraternatization politics) enabled the NPS and the VHP, a few years later in conjunction with the KTPI, to dominate politics from 1958 to 1967. This coalition combined the emancipation of the Creole working class with the political and economic ascent of the Javanese and Hindustani (Ramsoedh 2001: 96). This class and ethnic emancipation was based on patronage: an increasing number of Javanese and Hindustani joined the expanding ranks of the civil service.

Schisms in the Javanese Community

In an analysis of postwar Suriname politics Hans Ramsoedh (2001: 91–92) argues that in light of client-patron relationships, the epithet "political entrepreneurship" is more fitting than political leadership. A second characteristic is that this system based on person-oriented networks is unstable, as personal feuds may lead to secession and the founding of new parties, thus explaining the fragmentation of the political tableau, as will be shown in the case of Javanese politics.

In the postwar years the Javanese openly expressed their social dissatisfaction and feelings of inferiority regarding other population groups, the urban Creoles in particular. They blamed the government for limited Javanese participation in society (Derveld 1982; Ismael 1950; Suparlan 1995).[24] On account of the poor quality of education in the districts where between 80 and 90 percent of the Javanese lived, the majority of inhabitants were illiterate. The situation improved little in the following years because of lack of funding and the pupils' limited ability to understand Dutch, the official medium of instruction (Breunissen 2001: 166; Gobardhan-Rambocus 2001: 381; 486; Grasveld and Breunissen 1990: 30). In the years before the introduction of universal suffrage only sixty-two Javanese (out of a total of 34,272 Javanese, or one-fifth of the colony's population) had voting rights (Derveld 1982: 34); at that time there were one Javanese teacher and two assistant teachers, four police officers, and three nurses, plus a few lower-level civil servants and *lurahs*.[25] The frustration manifested itself in two ways: the desire to return to Indonesia or the demand for socioeconomic advancement in the colony.

In 1946 Persatuan Indonesia (Association of Indonesians) was founded to organize the return to Indonesia. The movement demanded that the government grant a free passage to all individuals who already had given up their right of free return. Developments in Indonesia and the slow negotiations with the Netherlands had an impact on Suriname as well. In reaction to the Linggadjati Agreement of 1946, with the Netherlands agreeing to recognize Republican rule over Java, Sumatra, and Madura, the Pergerakan Bangsa Indonesia Suriname (PBIS, Movement of the Indonesian People in Suriname) was founded in Paramaribo in 1947.[26] In contrast to Persatuan Indonesia, the PBIS did not advocate a return to Indonesia but cooperation with the government to improve the position of the Javanese in Suriname itself. That did not lessen its members' respect for Indonesia. One informant tells about his father: "He was the PBIS representative in Vreeland. On 17 August [Indonesian Independence Day] he always hoisted the *merah-putih* [red-white, Indonesian flag] and he always attached *melati* [jasmine] to the flag, that is how much *hormat* [respect] he had for the flag."[27] In that same year the *Tabian*, carrying 769 people, was the last ship repatriating former contract laborers free of charge.

Meanwhile in Suriname there were fierce debates regarding the introduction of universal voting rights. The light-skinned Creole establishment opted for a gradual introduction, while parties with an Asian constituency demanded immediate rights to increase their power base. The exception was the PBIS, as the movement feared the manipulation of the masses. This stance was a direct challenge to Persatuan Indonesia (since 1947 KTPI) and initiated a power struggle between the two parties that went beyond politics. The KTPI appealed to traditional Javanese values and a longing for Java, while the PBIS demanded more active policies to improve the situation of the Javanese in Suriname.

Most KTPI supporters were west worshippers, who included non-Muslim rituals such as *sajèn* (food offerings to the ancestors) and *slametan* ritual meals in their religious observations. The east worshippers strove to ban what they defined as non-Islamic ceremonies. According to Suparlan (1995: 140), they "saw the practice of Islam by the Surinamese Javanese as having been corrupted by belief in spirits and deities. They also observed that many Javanese did not strictly follow the Five Pillars of Islam, the most important of which is praying five times a day, and indulged in behavior strongly prohibited by Islamic law: drinking, gambling, concubinage, adultery."

PBIS adherents were a mix of east and west worshippers and Christians. The PBIS rejected large *slametans*—and also *tayub(an)* parties with hired female dancers, drinking, and gambling—with the argument that the money would be better spent on education or business ventures. Regularly, PBIS leaders pointed at the Hindustani example and argued that the Javanese could make progress only by working hard and saving, traits generally attributed to Hindustani. Many regarded the PBIS stance as an attack on the core of Javanese culture in general and *slametans* in particular. The rivalry was personified in the battle between Salikin Hardjo of PBIS and Iding Soemita of KTPI for the leadership of the Javanese community.

Iding Soemita was a Sudanese born in West Java in 1908 who arrived in Suriname as a contract worker in 1925. Later he became a hospital aide and a shopkeeper in Paramaribo. He was not well educated, but his emotional speeches in Javanese enthralled his audiences. His message of returning to Java (*mulih nDjawa*) was extremely popular. Salikin Hardjo was also born in Java, in 1910, and came to Suriname with his parents; his father was a contract laborer in the bauxite industry. Salikin Hardjo became a printer but never realized his dream of becoming a journalist.[28]

Soemita and the KTPI were the clear winners in the first general elections. Both men were candidates in the same district, and Soemita beat Hardjo with 2,325 to 884 votes, leaving the PBIS empty-handed. In the wake of this defeat the PBIS withdrew from active politics, yet this move did not ease the rivalry within the community. To the contrary, the KTPI-PBIS strife bitterly divided the Javanese. Sakri Ngadi, born in 1941 and member of a PBIS family, recalls:

> The KTPI were dressed in black ... they were showing off. The PBIS were less visible, but the PBIS people were more intellectual. [KTPI] was present at parties; if you weren't a supporter they wouldn't let you in. At that time, 1950, 1951, 1952, even families were divided. I have always experienced that. They told me 'don't look at him, he is the son of a KTPI man,' but we children had nothing to do with it and didn't see any difference.... Even though no physical confrontations took place, the tension was palpable because relationships were broken off; young people in love or already engaged were forced to split up.[29]

How the PBIS-KTPI fight divided families is also told by an informant who supported the PBIS and was repatriated: "I no longer was in contact with my parents and brothers in Suriname. Actually we broke communication already there, as they had joined the other party, KTPI. Party politics were very confrontational back then.... When I think about it, I feel very sad how things with my family have gone, but there is no way back."[30]

Militant youth organizations with warlike names such as Banteng Hitam (Black Wild Bull) introduced physical violence to the mix. F. Derveld (1982: 42) notes in his case study of the Surinamese Javanese town of Tamanredjo that a number of PBIS followers moved to ethnically mixed areas. Parsudi Suparlan (1995: 154) records that in the 1950s and 1960s east worshippers who participated in a *slametan* openly tossed their *berkat* (blessed food to take home) to chickens or dogs.

In addition to the return to Java, a second issue split the community: the question of nationality. After the Netherlands in 1949 finally recognized the Republic of Indonesia, the Surinamese Javanese had two years to choose between Indonesian and Dutch citizenship. The first option implied the loss of suffrage in Suriname. The KTPI strongly advised its supporters to become Indonesians, yet Soemita himself opted for Dutch citizenship in 1950, claiming that it would help him to defend the interests of his followers. In PBIS circles the opposite took place, with Hardjo choosing Indonesian nationality while most followers remained Dutch citizens.[31]

Soehirman Patmo in an interview aptly summarizes the situation: "Thus there were political and religious divisions—Muslims and non-Muslims, east worshippers–west worshippers, Protestants-Catholics—that had great influence on the community. It undermined the existing harmony. Suddenly people had to make choices and such a small community suffered."[32]

Returning Home

Surprisingly, it was not the KTPI but the PBIS that organized the return to Indonesia. The KTPI never realized its dream. KTPI members could buy *kartu idjo* (green cards) for a passage to Indonesia. Some Javanese sold all their possessions to get a card or stopped tilling their land on the assumption that they would soon leave. The expected KTPI ship never came. Suparlan (1995: 234) notes that the "victims of the scam" saw that "some KTPI leaders had become prosperous. Although they knew where their money had gone, they did not pursue the matter."

The reason the PBIS now pursued the return to Indonesia is partly explained by the fact that PBIS supporters felt intimidated by the KTPI. On May 1, 1951, Salikin Hardjo and Johannes Kariodimedjo, a highly regarded Javanese Christian politician, founded Yayasan Tanah Air (Back to the Fatherland). Their goal was to build a village including agricultural cooperatives in Indonesia. Soon more than two thousand families joined; members could save for the journey and paid for a multiparty delegation of eight men to negotiate with the government in Jakarta. Twice President Sukarno received this delegation, yet ultimately the Indonesian government was less than forthcoming.

In March 1953 the Indonesian government informed another three-man delegation that it would accommodate repatriation to the island of Sumatra, northwest of Java. Back in Suriname the PBIS leaders selected some 300 families or 1,000 individuals, including approximately 100 Christians, for the first voyage to the east.[33] The leadership preferred skilled workers rather than farmers, to set up the village as quickly as possible. Only a fraction of the return migrants had enough money to pay for the journey; it was decided that individuals repatriating later would co-pay the passage of the first group. These pioneers would then repay them to finance the second trip.

More than half of the 1,018 migrants (316 families) were born in Suriname. Homesickness drove the older generation, while the younger migrants looked for opportunities in building a new nation. The repatriation physically divided families. Also because of financial obstacles, some family members would join the first group; other relatives were expected to follow later.

Sent off by revelers celebrating this triumph of the PBIS, the migrants aboard the *Langkoeas* departed Paramaribo on January 5, 1954, to arrive in Sumatra a month later.[34] The reception in Sumatra was not very cordial, and conditions were more primitive than in Suriname. Almost immediately disappointment eclipsed the original enthusiasm. Soon a number of migrants accused the PBIS and Hardjo in particular of deception. Their new village of Tongar was not suited for mechanized agriculture and was geographically isolated. Within one year many, especially those without an agricultural background, left for cities like Medan, Pekanbaru, and Jakarta in search of work. Monetary problems trumped solidarity. Financial disputes further undermined Tongar. Kariodimedjo left for Medan as he felt threatened by Hardjo supporters.[35]

In short, Tongar was an economic failure and the atmosphere was poisoned. Word of this reached Suriname, and a second voyage would never take place. Debts incurred to travel on the *Langkoeas* often could not be repaid. Some had paid five hundred guilders and never went to Indonesia.[36] To the contrary, a number of the *Langkoeas* migrants returned to Suriname.

The final blow to Tongar was a civil war in the western part of Sumatra between 1957 and 1959. Only the elderly and some smallholders remained in Tongar. Conflicts about land ownership made that the only economic activity; agriculture also collapsed.[37] Tongar had been a failure; in his memoirs, published in Indonesian in 1989 and Dutch in 2001, Salikin Hardjo blames outsiders for all these problems (Breunissen 2001: 200–11).

The repatriation to Indonesia had repercussions in Suriname besides internal strife. Many competent individuals, often local leaders, had migrated, thus decapitating numerous organizations(Derveld 1982: 43; Ismail in Djasmadi et al. 2010: 41).

The Aftermath

With the virtual elimination of the PBIS, the KTPI and its leader, Iding Soemita, came to dominate Javanese politics until 1967.[38] However, "a lack of administrative talent and intellectual cadre" and persistent rumors about corruption undermined the party's effectiveness and the confidence of its following (Meel 2011: 101). Soemita gained no seats in the elections of 1967 and 1969. Most Javanese turned to a new party, the Sarekat Rakyat Indonesia (SRI, Union of Indonesians), founded in 1966 by KTPI dissenters. The new party resembled the PBIS as it promoted socioeconomic progress and a more urban outlook (Derveld 1982: 44–46; Suparlan 1995: 237–40). However, besides incompetence and corruption eroding KTPI's base, the base itself was changing as well. Soemita's core constituency was the poor smallholders living in the outlying districts. Yet urbanization and modernization did not bypass the upwardly mobile younger generations. In 1972 Iding Soemita passed the mantle to his son Willy, who quickly managed to rebuild the KTPI.

He actively supported the quest for Suriname's independence, thus dividing the Javanese community once more. Many Surinamese feared independence and Creole domination in particular.[39] Willy Soemita's main rival, Paul Somohardjo, threatened to send thousands of Javanese to the Netherlands if the Dutch handed over sovereignty. In the uncertain years immediately preceding independence in 1975 an estimated 20,000 to 25,000 Surinamese Javanese boarded planes for Amsterdam.[40] Willy Soemita and Paul Somohardjo almost seemed to reenact the scenario that had played out twenty years earlier when Iding Soemita and Salikin Hardjo divided the Javanese community.

Political strife may have made the headlines, but the cultural-religious emancipation of the various populations continued. Muslim and Hindu organizations played a vital role in the emancipation of the Javanese and Hindustani population. Modeling themselves after Christian churches, they set up schools, orphanages, hospitals, and social funds. These socio-religious activities were successful attempts to counteract efforts by Catholic and Protestant missionaries who had built boarding schools for non-Christian students, enabling them to get a secondary education in Paramaribo. Pointing at religious freedom, Muslims and Hindus claimed the same rights as the major Christian denominations and demanded state funding for Hindu and Muslim schools.[41] After strong Creole/Christian opposition, the first Hindu secondary school was opened in 1960. Later other Hindu and Muslim schools followed (Gobhardan-Rambocus 2001: 494–95).

A decade later in 1970, Bada (Bodo) or Id ul Fitre and Holi Phagwa were recognized as national holidays.[42] This was but one aspect of the increased recognition and self-assurance of Islam and Hinduism. A growing number of mosques along main roads attest to this heightened self-confidence of the Muslim population. Moreover, Javanese media outlets offer room for religious programming.

During his fieldwork in the early 1970s Parsudi Suparlan (1995: 141–62) observed that the conflict had abated and that a middle road between east and west worshippers, which he defines as "moderate reformism," had emerged. These worshippers pray to the east but do not reject Javanese cultural expressions, particularly the *slametan*, which they interpret as the giving of alms, a key aspect of Muslim practice. To the contrary, these moderates tie together Muslim and Javanese identity by changing the meaning of the ritual, but not the ritual itself, and they repudiate "Arabization."[43]

Thus a form of *rukun*, often by means of not mentioning differences, has reappeared in the Javanese community now that the divisions between west and east worshippers or traditionalists and progressives have become less pronounced. Yet in strongholds of east worshippers, often villages with a strong Javanese majority, Javanese cultural expressions such as dance and certain musical styles were still rejected in the 1970s. As one female informant, born in 1966 and growing up in Koewarasan, tells,

> I was raised strictly according to the Islamic rules. In the afternoon we recited from the Quran, *ngaji*. . . . It wasn't really mandatory, but it was part of your upbringing. I was ten or eleven years old. And we also went to the mosque. Everybody went there, it was a rule of life during that time. . . . As a Muslim you had little access to, for example, Javanese cultural expressions. *Lèdèk* [female dancer, as at a tayub party] and *gamelan* [Indonesian music style or musical ensemble] were not part of the Muslim life style. Islam was really strict. . . . Then I had no interest in learning Javanese dances, now as an adult I miss it, as it is part of Javanese culture.[44]

The census of 2004 counts approximately 72,000 Javanese, 15 percent of the total population in Suriname. Islam is the third largest religion, after Christianity and Hinduism, but is losing support: in 1980 close to 20 percent of the population was Muslim, and in 2004 this had dropped to slightly more than 13 percent. In 2004 more than 64 percent of the Javanese adhered to Islam—down from 93 percent in 1977, while close to 14.5 percent were Christian—up from 7 percent in 1977 (Hendrix and van Waning 2009: 22–23, 36). Most recent converts to Christianity joined Pentecostal churches. The division between east and west worshippers is unclear, but Suparlan (1995: 162) states that in the early 1970s, *wong Islam* were the majority of Javanese Muslims in Suriname.[45] Hendrix and van Waning (2009: 23–24) estimated that in 2009 the west worshippers were still the larger group by a slight margin. This division is also visible in the organizational structure of Muslims, with the Federatie van Islamitische Gemeenten in Suriname (Federation of Islamic Congregations in Suriname) uniting the west worshippers, while the Stichting Islamitische Gemeenten in Suriname (Foundation of Islamic Congregations in Suriname) unifies the east worshippers. The Stichting Islamitische Gemeenten plays a significant role in the Madjlies Muslimin Suriname (Council of Muslims in Suriname), the council that initiated the national Bada prayer meeting (Jap-A-Joe et al. 2001: 211; Meel 2011: 110).

Conclusion

The religious differences between east and west worshippers surfaced in the 1930s with the building of an east-facing mosque in Paramaribo, but it was the east worshippers' rejection of Javanese traditions such as *slametan* and *sajèn* that affronted the majority of Javanese. Suparlan (1995: 225) states that the government's recognition of Islam and the legitimation of the *kaum* in the marriage law of 1940 precipitated the conflict. I would argue that the marriage law, and by extension the recognition of non-Christian religions, was the product of a longer process of Hindustani and Javanese identity formation. Already in 1913 the SIV had requested the legal recognition of marriages solemnized by Hindu priests or Muslim officials (Hoefte 1998: 177). To be sure, the passing of the law boosted the position of Hindu and Muslim religious leaders.

This religious-cultural conflict was further deepened by an ideological clash between people looking back to an idealized past in Java and those looking forward to a brighter future in Suriname. This conflict was at its height in the 1940s and 1950s; here I disagree with Suparlan, who states that the open conflicts occurred in the 1950s and 1960s (Suparlan 1995: 154). I argue that the apex of the hostilities between the KTPI and PBIS parties and their respective leaders was in the 1940s and 1950s, ending with the departure of PBIS supporters. After their return to Indonesia in 1954 and the almost immediate failure of the Tongar experiment, the acrimony gradually subsided, without completely disappearing, however. For example, until today the community has been split between different Javanese political parties.

Avoidance by minimizing challenges to opponents (cf. Adas 1992: 217) was part of the strategy to calm the waters. At least three times the underlying party left the scene to escape discord: the political withdrawal of the PBIS after the election loss; the repatriation of PBIS members; and the departure of Kariodimedjo from Tongar.

The controversy between east and west worshippers went to the heart of the Javanese community, but after the disappointment of Tongar the options for Surinamese Javanese were restricted. If return to Indonesia was not feasible, Suriname was, at that point in time, the only place where the population could advance. Javanese social and economic emancipation took shape in the 1960s and 1970s, when more and more people moved to Paramaribo. As Ad de Bruijne and Aart Schalkwijk (2005: 259–60) show, it was not ethnicity but the time of arrival in the city and access to formal education that determined socioeconomic advancement of Hindustani and Javanese: "Their increased level of education has in turn allowed them to take advantage of better economic opportunities so that they can participate in a broader range of economic activities. Second, access to government jobs has been very important. Improved access to civil service jobs for all of the ethnic groups, resulting in part from rising educational levels, appears mainly to be a consequence of the way political parties have consistently used their administrative apparatus as a means to further the emancipation of their ethnic basis." The religious question was also a socioeconomic question, and I would argue that political *cum* socioeconomic emancipation took away some sharp edges.

The conflict between Iding Soemita and Salikin Hardjo seems to have been replayed in the 1970s with the rivalry between Willy Soemita and Paul Somohardjo. Both conflicts turned on the question of migration to better places. However, there were two fundamental differences: first, in the 1950s it was the discontent of a specific Javanese group that led to emigration, whereas in the later case the anxiety surrounding Suriname's independence touched all ethnic groups and led to mass migration to the Netherlands. Second, the migration to the Netherlands lacked the strong cultural-religious overtones that embittered the Javanese community in the 1940s and 1950s.

Notes

1. I want to thank Hariëtte Mingoen, Amorisa Wiratri, Ayumi Malamassam, and Jo Moestadja for conducting or translating the interviews used in this article. All interviews can be found at http://www.javanenindiaspora.nl.

2. Suriname, one of the three Guianas, was a Dutch plantation colony. After the abolition of slavery in 1863 contract laborers from Asia were imported to provide the estates with docile labor. With the arrival of the indentured workers the population consisted of Afro-Surinamese—Creoles and Maroons (descendants of refugees from slavery), British Indians or Hindustani (called Hindostani in Suriname), Javanese, Chinese, American Indians, and smaller groups of Europeans and Lebanese or Syrians. According to the first census in 1921, the colony counted 55,138 Creoles (49.7 percent); 30,530 British Indians (27.5 percent); 18,529 Javanese (16.7 percent); 1,313 Chinese (1.2 percent); and 1,396 Europeans (1.3 percent). In addition, there were an estimated 18,400 Maroons and 2,600 American Indians; they were not included in this census.

3. I use the terms east and west worshippers as this is how these groups refer to themselves in Suriname. Parsudi Suparlan (1995) uses "reformists" and "traditionalists," respectively, to identify these groups.

4. Michael Adas (1992: 217) defines avoidance protest as a way in which "dissatisfied groups seek to attenuate their hardships and express their discontent through flight, sectarian withdrawal, or other activities that minimize challenges to or clashes with those whom they view as their oppressors."

5. For an English-language history of contract labor in Suriname see Hoefte 1998; for a history of Javanese immigration see Ismael 1949; and for a cultural-political history up to independence see Suparlan 1995.

6. *Indisch* is the adjective in Dutch for "from or in the Netherlands East Indies." The goal was the demographic, socioeconomic, and cultural Javanization of Suriname. The words *desa* and *kaum* are Malay, and *lurah* is Javanese; the use of these words emphasizes the Javanese or *Indisch* character of the project.

7. Soeki Irodikromo, interview by Jo Moestadja—this informant describes the last *lurah* of Koewarasan; see also Djasmadi et al. 2010: 28–29.

8. Ngadimin Saridjo, interview by Amorisa Wiratri and Ayumi Malamassam, translated by Hariëtte Mingoen, March 17, 2010. He describes Leiding Vijf, southwest of Paramaribo.

9. De Waal-Malefijt 1963, Suparlan 1995, and Van Wengen 1975 are the main sources on Javanese culture and religion in English and inform my study.

10. See, for example, Geertz (1960: 124–27) for a history of Islam in Java. Merchants from India brought Islam to Indonesia and "completely dominated" Java by the end of the sixteenth century (Geertz 1960: 125). Indonesian Islam, however, was isolated from the centers of orthodoxy until the mid-nineteenth century. Arab traders introduced reform movements, but the "drift toward orthodoxy was slow" (Geertz 1960: 125). The majority of Indonesians are Sunni Muslims.

11. Sharia is Islamic law. Lane and Redissi (2009) distinguish four schools of law that are referred to by the names of their founders. The Shafiite is named after Shafii (died 820). Shafii "put into his *Risala* (Letter) the principle of hierarchy of the legal sources and the way of reasoning in order to find the appropriate judgment (first the Koran, the Sunna [of the prophet] being complementary)" (Lane and Redissi 2009: 95). The Shaffii schools are also commonly found in Arabia, Malaysia, Egypt, Somalia, Eritrea, Yemen, and southern parts of India (Lane and Redissi 2009: 96).

12. The Creole population was not enthusiastic about indentured immigration. Besides feeding xenophobia and racial prejudice, it increased labor competition, thus lowering wages (Hoefte 1998: 102–6).

13. The action programs concentrated on wage questions, maltreatment, and immediate social issues, such as the lack of drinking water (Hoefte 1998: 179–81).

14. On Sarekat Islam and subsequent political developments see Petrus Bloemberger (1987: 55–89) and Lowensteyn, "Indonesia between 1908 and 1928" (http://www.lowensteyn.com/indonesia/sarekat.html).

15. National Archives, The Hague, Kabinet Geheim 1887–1951, vol. 53, no. 4, May 29, 1934.

16. After the completion of the mosque, most of the members withdrew because of its eastern direction (Breunissen 2001: 15, 169). A second organization, Sahabutal Islam (Friendship of Islam) established in 1935, wanted to purge Islam of all foreign elements. It was influenced by the Muhammadiyah movement (Van Wengen 1975: 8). The orthodox Muhammadiyah was founded in Java by a returning pilgrim in 1912 (Geertz 1960: 126; Petrus Bloemberger 1987: 90–101). Sahabutal Islam maintained cordial relations with the PII, but according to Suparlan (1995: 225), "PII was more gentle and refined in dealing with traditionalists [west worshippers]."

17. Joesoef Ismail, interview by Hariëtte Mingoen, February 5, 2010; Djasmadi et al. 2010: 40.

18. The Hanafi school is found in South Asia and also in Central Asia, China, Turkey, Egypt, and the Balkans. It is named after Abu Hanifa, who died in 767. He gave prominence to *ijitihad* (the solution by personal "effort" to problems not covered by the Quran) rather than the Sunna of the prophet (Lane and Redissi 2009: 95–96).

19. Jap-A-Joe and colleagues (2001: 205–6) state that Ahmadiyya teachings appealed to relatively young, upwardly mobile Hindustani Muslims. These Muslims were more likely to move to Paramaribo than were Hindus. When the news reached Suriname that Ahmadiyya's founder, Mirza Gulam Ahmad, was revered as a prophet, a growing number of *jamaats* distanced itself from the SIV. On the political significance of Ahmadiyya in Indonesia see, for example, Petrus Bloemberger 1987: 102–5.

20. In 1941 the United States and Great Britain called for self-determination in all colonial societies.

21. The first genuine political party was the Surinaamse Moeslim Partij (Surinamese Muslim Party), founded in 1946. Other parties were the Hindostaans-Javaanse Politieke Partij (HJJP Hindustani-Javanese Political Party) and the Surinaamse Hindoe Partij (SHP, Surinamese Hindu Party). These three merged into the VHP. In 1973 this party changed its name to Vooruitstrevende Hervormings Partij (Progressive Reform Party), still abbreviated as VHP.

22. After World War II the government became the largest employer, financed by bauxite revenues and Dutch development funds.

23. The Republic of Indonesia unilaterally declared its independence on August 17, 1945. The Netherlands accepted Indonesia's independence four years later.

24. The main obstruction to social mobility was the lack of education, but it was also well known that to obtain a government clerical job, for example, it was an advantage to be Christian (Hoefte 1998: 173).

25. Voting was based on taxes and education. This means that sixty-two Javanese had an income of more than eight hundred Suriname guilders or an education beyond the elementary level.

26. On Javanese politics see Breunissen (2001), Derveld (1982), and Suparlan (1995).

27. Antonius Dasimin Senawi, interview by Amorisa Wiratri and Ayumi Malamassam, trans. Hariëtte Mingoen, April 9, 2010.

28. For information on Soemita (who died in 2001) see Choenni 2009. For Hardjo (who passed away in 1993) see Breunissen (2001), which also includes Hardjo's autobiography.

29. Sakri Ngadi, interview by Amorisa Wiratri and Ayumi Malamassam, trans. Hariëtte Mingoen, April 15, 2010; Djasmadi et al. 2010: 76.

30. Samingat, interview by Amorisa Wiratri and Ayumi Malamassam, trans. Hariëtte Mingoen, March 14, 2010.

31. In the course of time, an increasing number of Surinamese Javanese opted for Dutch citizenship, but in 1973, two years before Suriname's independence, 20 percent of the 58,863 Surinamese Javanese were still citizens of Indonesia (Derveld 1982: 22).

32. Soehirman Patmo, interview by Hariëtte Mingoen, July 17, 2009; Djasmadi et al. 2010: 91.

33. This percentage of Christians is considerably higher than the 3 percent of Javanese in Suriname who were Christians.

34. The *Langkoeas*, owned by the Dutch shipping company Rotterdamsche Lloyd (1883–1970), was primarily used for the transportation of pilgrims to Mecca (Breunissen 2001: 66).

35. According to Wongsodikromo-Flier (2009: 51), Kariodimedjo left because of tensions between Muslims and Christians. Only five Christian families remained, but later they also left Tongar. See Breunissen (2001: 86–89) on religious strains in Tongar.

36. Joesoef Ismail, interview by Hariëtte Mingoen, February 5, 2010; Djasmadi et al. 2010: 40.

37. The basic question was whether the land belonged to the migrants and their offspring or to Yayasan Tanah Air, read Salikin Hardjo. It was rumored that he had sold land to third parties and pocketed the money. It appears that Hardjo behaved like a *lurah*, responsible for the distribution of land. His daughter Haryanti gives her version of the conflict in an interview with Amorisa Wiratri and Ayumi Malamassam, trans. Hariëtte Mingoen, March 17, 2010; Djasmadi et al. 2010: 13–22.

38. In 1969 the PBIS as an organization collapsed after the death of its leader Sadikoen Djojoprajitno, a board member since 1947.

39. Javanese and Hindustani viewed independence as a Creole project. The administration in Suriname that had called for independence ignored the objections by Hindustani, Javanese, Maroons, and American Indians. In Suriname's parliament nineteen members were in favor of independence and exactly as many were against. A Hindustani parliamentarian broke the tie. Thus in Suriname independence did not gain great political or popular support.

On the physical threat by Creoles and the submissiveness to Creole culture see Suparlan 1995: 108–9. He observes that in the early 1970s Javanese argued that "Suriname is the country of Creoles, so in order to survive, they must behave like Creoles or be ill-treated by them."

40. One-seventh of the Surinamese population left for the Netherlands in the years 1974–1975.

41. See Gobardhan-Rambocus (2001: 359–76) for a description of *desa* schools, the involvement of Christian missionaries, and the efforts to improve education.

42. Bada or Id ul Fitre celebrates the end of Ramadan, while Holi Phagwa is the Hindu festival of spring, also known as the festival of color. On the morning of Bada/Id ul Fitre a prayer meeting is held on Paramaribo's central square.

43. Arabization stands for (orthodox) religious influence from Arabia, including the learning of Arabic. For a fieldwork report on relations between east and west worshippers in 2009 see Hendrix and Van Waning 2009.

44. Rita Tjien Fooh-Hardjomohamad, interview by Jo Moestadja, 2010; Djasmadi et al. 2010: 132–33.

45. More in-depth research is needed to study the strength of orthodoxy and the spiritual and material influence of Arab countries in twenty-first-century Suriname.

References Cited

Adas, Michael
1992 "From Avoidance to Confrontation: Peasant Protest in Precolonial and Colonial Southeast Asia." *Comparative Studies in Society and History* 23(2): 217–47.
Breunissen, Klaas
2001 *Ik heb Suriname altijd liefgehad: Het leven van de Javaan Salikin Hardjo.* Leiden: KITLV Press.
Choenni, Chan E. S.
2009 *Bapak Iding Soemita (1908–2001): De innemende leider van de Javanen in Suriname.* Haarlem: no publisher.
De Bruijne, Ad, and Aart Schalkwijk
2005 "The Position and Residential Patterns of Ethnic Groups in Paramaribo's Development in the Twentieth Century." *New West Indian Guide* 79: 239–71.
Derveld, F.E.R.
1982 *Politieke mobilisatie en integratie van de Javanen in Suriname: Tamanredjo en de Surinaamse nationale politiek.* Groningen: Bouma's Boekhuis.
De Waal-Malefijt, Annemarie
1963 *The Javanese of Surinam: Segment of a Plural Society.* Assen: Van Gorcum.
Djasmadi, Lisa, Rosemarijn Hoefte, and Hariëtte Mingoen
2010 *Migratie en cultureel erfgoed: Verhalen van Javanen in Suriname, Indonesië en Nederland.* Leiden: KITLV Press.
Geertz, Clifford
1960 *The Religion of Java.* Glencoe, Ill.: Free Press.
Gobardhan-Rambocus, S. L.
2001 *Onderwijs als sleutel tot maatschappelijke vooruitgang: Een taal- en onderwijsgeschiedenis van Suriname, 1651–1975.* Zutphen: Walburg Pers.
Grasveld, Fons, and Klaas Breunissen
1990 *Ik ben een Javaan uit Suriname.* Hilversum: Stichting Ideële Filmprodukties.
Hendrix, Noor, and Marjoleine van Waning
2009 "De Javaanse moslims in Suriname: Een kwalitatief onderzoek anno 2009." MA thesis, University of Utrecht.
Hoefte, Rosemarijn
1998 *In Place of Slavery: A Social History of British Indian and Javanese Laborers in Suriname.* Gainesville: University Press of Florida.
2011 "Learning, Loving and Living in Early Twentieth-Century Suriname: The Movement of People and Ideas from East to West." *Journal of Caribbean History* 45(2): 190–211.
Ismael, Joseph
1949 *De immigratie van Indonesiërs in Suriname.* Leiden: Luctor et Emergo.
1950 "De positie van de Indonesiër in het nieuwe Suriname." *Indonesië* 4: 177–93.
Jap-A-Joe, Harold, Peter Sjak Shie, and Joop Vernooij
2001 "The Quest for Respect: Religion and Emancipation in Twentieth-Century Suriname." In *Twentieth-Century Suriname: Continuities and Discontinuities in a New*

World Society, ed. Rosemarijn Hoefte and Peter Meel, 198–219. Kingston: Ian Randle, Leiden: KITLV Press.

Javanen in Diaspora

2010 Interviews (various interviewers and dates). http://www.javanenindiaspora.nl.

Kielstra, J. C.

1927 "Nieuwe mogelijkheden voor Suriname." *De Economist* 76: 181–96.

Lane, Erik-Jan, and Hamadi Redissi

2009 *Religion and Politics: Islam and Muslim Civilization*. 2nd ed. Burlington, Vt.: Ashgate.

Meel, Peter

2011 "Continuity through Diversity: The Surinamese Javanese Diaspora and the Homeland Anchorage." *Wadabagei* 13(2): 95–134.

Petrus Bloemberger, J. T.

1987 [1931] *De nationalistische beweging in Nederlandsch-Indië*. Dordrecht: Foris.

Ramsoedh, Hans

1990 *Suriname 1933–1944: Koloniale politiek en beleid onder gouverneur Kielstra*. Delft: Eburon.

2001 "Playing Politics: Ethnicity, Clientelism and the Struggle for Power." In *Twentieth-Century Suriname: Continuities and Discontinuities in a New World Society*, ed. Rosemarijn Hoefte and Peter Meel, 91–110. Kingston: Ian Randle, Leiden: KITLV Press.

Suparlan, Parsudi

1995 *The Javanese in Suriname: Ethnicity in an Ethnically Plural Society*. Tempe: Arizona State University.

Van Wengen, G.

1975 *The Cultural Inheritance of the Javanese in Surinam*. Leiden: Brill.

Wongsodikromo-Flier, J.

2009 *Javaanse zending der Evangelische Broedergemeente in Suriname*. No publisher.

5

Fear of a Brown Planet

Pan-Islamism, Black Nationalism, and the Tribal Twenties

NATHANIEL DEUTSCH

On March 1, 1961, Malcolm X, then the national spokesman for the Nation of Islam, delivered a broadcast from the organization's Mosque #7 in New York City in which he condemned Christianity for creating a slave mentality among African Americans. Rather than citing the teachings of Elijah Muhammad, the Nation's prophet and longtime leader, however, Malcolm X invoked a different source for his critique of Christianity: Lothrop Stoddard, whom he described as a "noted white scientist [who] explains how the black man, when Christianized, becomes docile towards his masters, and is more inclined to look toward the white man for his education, even food, clothing and shelter."[1]

By the early 1960s Lothrop Stoddard (1883–1950) had largely disappeared from public discourse, but during the 1920s—a nativist period that the American historian John Higham evocatively dubbed "the Tribal Twenties"—Stoddard was, in the words of Jonathan Spiro, "the second most influential racist in the country," only surpassed by his mentor Madison Grant, author of *The Passing of the Great Race* (Spiro 2009: 172). Indeed, at his height, Stoddard was so notorious that he even inspired a fictional character named Goddard—parodied as the author of a racist tome called *The Rise of Coloured Empires*—in F. Scott Fitzgerald's novel *The Great Gatsby*.

How did one of America's most prominent and prolific white racists during the 1920s become transformed into "a noted white scientist" and key source of knowledge for the country's best known and most influential African American Muslim during the 1960s? At first glance, the very question may provoke cognitive dissonance. And yet, as I argue in this essay, its answer is embedded within a complex historical narrative that not only links the emergence of the Nation of Islam's ideology in the 1930s to American intellectual developments of the 1920s but also links both phenomena in the United States to a wider—indeed, global—network of intellectual encounters between European and Euro-American racist thinkers and the founding theorists of the Pan-Islamic, Pan-Asian, and Pan-African movements.

The resulting portrait is one in which American intellectuals who engaged with Islam during the 1920s cease to appear as isolated figures with little connection to broader intellectual currents within the Islamic world or Europe and, instead, are revealed as profoundly imbricated in a series of transnational conversations concerning the history, present, and future of Islam, including its ongoing relationship to race. Against this backdrop, Malcolm X's invocation of Lothrop Stoddard—who, among his many works, published *The New World of Islam* in 1921—should not be seen as idiosyncratic but, rather, as emblematic of a history of intellectual cross-pollination between modern Islamic and non-Islamic thinkers extending back to the middle of the nineteenth century.

European Orientalism and the Rise of Pan-Islamism

In a brilliant study of the genesis of Pan-Islamic and Pan-Asian thought—and their eventual intersection—Cemil Aydin has argued that European Orientalism and Pan-Islamism developed dialectically in two distinctive phases over the course of the nineteenth century. During the first phase, which lasted through the middle of the century, conservative Orientalists asserted the cultural and racial superiority of Europe over the rest of the globe, including its proximate rival, the Ottoman Empire, but they did not yet frame their approach in the scientifically racist terms that would dominate in the post-Darwinian era. In response, Ottoman intellectuals were initially nonplussed for two reasons: "First, the Ottomans viewed themselves as belonging to the Caucasian race and thus were not offended by racist perceptions of the natives in Australia, Africa, and the Caribbean. Second, they could rely on the universalism of the Islamic tradition to embrace and modify Enlightenment universalism. The Muslim leaders of the Ottoman state thus believed they should encounter no religious, cultural, or racial obstacles to being as civilized as the Europeans, as long as they completed a set of reforms that would allow them to reach a higher level on the universal ladder of progress" (Aydin 2007: 22).

Thus Ottoman intellectuals initially saw themselves as natural collaborators in a civilizational project rooted in a shared heritage—rather than essential conflict—between Christian Europe and the Muslim Ottoman Empire. Significantly, the identification of Ottoman elites with this project was grounded, in part, in an assertion of racial solidarity with Europeans over and against supposedly less civilized peoples in sub-Saharan Africa, Oceania, and elsewhere. As Aydin has noted (drawing on essays published by Ottoman intellectuals during the 1860s): "Muslim intellectuals could accept that the Caucasian race was unique in terms of its high intellectual capacity and contribution to civilization, as long as they could count the Turks and Arabs as belonging to this superior Caucasian race. Hence some Muslim intellectuals even contended that the black race, 'by its very nature and creation, was not capable of grasping the issues of science and philosophy'" (Aydin 2007: 49, 215, n. 32).[2]

Although this feeling of racial and civilizational solidarity was not reciprocated by European intellectuals, we should nevertheless pause at this juncture to note that both European Christian and Ottoman Muslim elites could share a belief that they were superior to Africans and their diasporic descendants. The supposedly inferior racial status of Africans to both Europeans and, once the category was articulated, Asiatics, would become a leitmotif of racialist discourse over the next century, eventually contributing to a profound sense of racial ambivalence toward sub-Saharan Africa among members of both the Moorish Science Temple and the Nation of Islam.

A major turning point in the evolving relationship between nineteenth-century European and Muslim intellectuals came in 1883, when the noted French Orientalist Ernest Renan (1823–92) delivered a lecture at the Sorbonne entitled "L'Islamisme et la science" (Islam and science), which was published in the *Journal de Débats* on March 29, 1883. In a pioneering example of what Aydin has termed the "new Orientalism," Renan linked race and civilization, arguing for an essential contrast between the categories of white, Aryan, Christian, and European, on the one hand, and Semitic, Turco-Mongolian, and Muslim on the other. More specifically, Renan claimed that Islamic civilization was incompatible with science and philosophy and that the low status of these disciplines within the Ottoman Empire was due to the Turks' "total lack of the philosophic and scientific spirit" (Renan 1883: 16).[3]

In his lecture Renan made two overlapping assertions that would have a profound and long-lasting influence on the perception of Islam among both Europeans and Americans in the coming years. First, he argued that Islam was incompatible with, even hostile to, the very notion of progress as embodied by science and technology. Second, he racialized Islam, figuring it as both a racial and a religious identity.[4] As we will see, the racialization of Islam—and its link to an "Asiatic" racial identity in particular—would influence attitudes in the United States among both white racists and black nationalists during the first few decades of the twentieth century.

In 1883 Renan's remarks inspired Muslim intellectuals in the Ottoman and Russian empires, India, Egypt, and Europe itself to publish refutations. Most important, Jamal ad-Din al-Afghani (1838–97)—a founding figure of the Pan-Islamic movement who was then living in Paris, where, along with Muhammad Abduh, he had begun to print the influential Pan-Islamist journal *al-Urwa al-Wuthqa* (The firmest bond)—published a response to Renan in the *Journal de Débats* on May 18, 1883.[5] Significantly, al-Afghani did not denounce Renan personally, nor did he deny the currently low status of science within Islamic societies. Indeed, in a harbinger of the reaction of black nationalist figures like Hubert Harrison and Malcolm X to the writings of Lothrop Stoddard, al-Afghani had only kind words for Renan, referring to him as "an eminent philosopher" and praising him as "the great thinker of our time, the illustrious M. Renan, whose renown has filled the West and penetrated into the farthest countries of the East.... I find in his talk remarkable observations, new perceptions, and an indescribable charm.... He receives my humble salutation as an homage that is due him and as the sincere expression of my admiration" (Keddie 1983: 181–82).

Concerning the content of Renan's lecture, al-Afghani expressed ambivalence. On the one hand, he asserted, "M. Renan has not at all tried, we believe, to destroy the glory of the Arabs which is indestructible," while on the other, he acknowledged Renan sought to prove that "the Muslim religion was by its very essence opposed to the development of science, and that the Arab people, by their nature, do not like either metaphysical sciences or philosophy" (Keddie 1983: 182). In response, al-Afghani admitted that Islam currently held back scientific development, but he charged that this was not unique among religions—indeed, he asserted that Christianity had an even worse historical record—and argued that if reformed, Islam could once again become a fertile environment for science and philosophy.[6]

In what Aydin (2007: 51) has described as "a rare instance in which a late nineteenth-century European intellectual directly responded to a critique by a Muslim intellectual," Renan published a rejoinder to al-Afghani in the *Journal des Débats* on May 19, 1883, writing patronizingly that "there was nothing more instructive than studying the ideas of an enlightened Asiatic in their original and sincere form" (Keddie 1972: 196). Renan conceded al-Afghani's point that Christianity had also hindered the progress of science: "Christianity in this respect is not superior to Islam. This is beyond doubt. Galileo was no better treated by Catholicism than Averroes by Islam" (Keddie 1972: 197). But he reiterated his earlier position that Muslims possessed a civilizational and, in most cases, racial, antipathy toward science and technology—and therefore to progress—unless they belonged to the minority of Muslims who, like al-Afghani himself, supposedly possessed "Aryan" racial roots: "Sheikh Jemmal-Eddin is an Afghan entirely divorced from the prejudices of Islam; he belongs to those energetic races of Iran, near India, where the Aryan spirit lives still energetically under the superficial layer of official Islam" (Keddie 1972: 197).

This seminal exchange between Renan and al-Afghani would mark the beginning of a series of intellectual encounters over Islam's relationship to the hardening geographic-civilizational categories of East and West as well as over the place of Islam within an increasingly hegemonic racial taxonomy in which the peoples of the world were divided into "white," "brown," "yellow," and "black" races. Concomitantly, during the first few decades of the twentieth century, Pan-Islamic and Pan-Asian intellectuals began to articulate a common set of interests and even a common Asiatic identity that they formulated in opposition to European civilization and its imperialist project. Thus Aydin observes that whereas the earliest formulations of Pan-Asianism initially "classified Muslims as one of the outsider occupiers of Asia, whose boundaries were defined by Buddhist legacy and the yellow race ... the trend was toward a more global consciousness of belonging to an Eastern and Asian unity.... Similarly, Muslim intellectuals extended their vision of solidarity beyond the scope of the Islamic world, showing interest in the fates of Japan and China" (Aydin 2007: 86).

The New World of Islam and the Fear of a Brown Planet

With the 1914 publication of his first book, *The French Revolution in San Domingo*, Lothrop Stoddard, then a newly minted PhD in history from Harvard University, embarked on his decades long career as an indefatigable promoter of white racial supremacy and an important intellectual progenitor of what has more recently become famous as the "clash of civilizations" model.[7] Stoddard signaled the ideological orientation of all his future work when, in the first line of his study of the Haitian Revolution, he claimed: "The world-wide struggle between the primary races of mankind—the 'conflict of color,' as it has been happily termed—bids fair to be the fundamental problem of the twentieth century" (Stoddard 1914: vii).

A number of historians have already examined Stoddard's role as the foremost popularizer of race theory in the United States between the World Wars; unlike his patrician mentor Madison Grant, Stoddard wrote his works in a more accessible, journalistic style. Matthew Guterl, in particular, has also identified and explored the complex intellectual exchanges between Stoddard and several leading figures of what became known as the "New Negro Movement" (after Alain Locke's eponymous 1925 book), including W.E.B. Du Bois, with whom Stoddard engaged in a series of electrifying public debates (Guterl 2001: 142–43). Rather than simply focusing on the ideological opposition between Stoddard and these interlocutors, Guterl has perceptively noted their constitutive relationship: "Stoddard, Nordicism, and white world supremacy had become, by the 1920s, thoroughly intertwined with the New Negro movement. . . . Stoddard helped to remake Du Bois even as Du Bois made Stoddard the leading popular advocate of Nordicism" (Guterl 2001: 142–43).

By comparison, Stoddard's intense interest in Islam, his polemical writings on the topic, and the reception of this work by a range of Muslim and non-Muslim intellectuals—both within the United States and elsewhere—has received relatively little scholarly attention. Islam not only served as the subject for Stoddard's 1921 book *The New World of Islam* but also played a critical role in his 1920 best-seller *The Rising Tide of Color against White World-Supremacy*, for which he gained great fame during the 1920s.

In this section I examine Stoddard's complex attitudes toward Islam and its relationship to race theory, revealing in the process Stoddard's place within an ongoing set of conversations about the status of Islam in the modern world, including the previously examined literary debate between Renan and al-Afghani. I then turn to the writings of Hubert Harrison, one of the most important African American intellectuals of the day, who published several sympathetic reviews of Stoddard's work, including *The New World of Islam*, and whose stance helps us to understand the seemingly incongruous praise of Stoddard by Malcolm X with which I opened this essay. Rather than being isolated from contemporary global debates concerning Islam during the first few decades of the twentieth century, this discussion illuminates the degree to which some American intellectuals—possessing widely different backgrounds and perspectives—actively participated in the debates.

In *The Rising Tide of Color against White World-Supremacy*, Lothrop Stoddard lamented the suicidal impact of World War I—an event he described as a "Modern Peloponnesian War"—on white supremacy. Influenced by both

Madison Grant's racial taxonomy in *The Passing of the Great Race* (1916) and Oswald Spengler's theory of civilizational decay in *The Decline of the West* (1917), Stoddard warned that European hegemony was under threat by the "brown and yellow worlds of Asia" (Stoddard 1920: 229). Rather than simply dismiss "Asiatics" as inherently inferior to Europeans, however, Stoddard consistently praised them for their high level of civilizational achievement. While Asiatics had experienced a long period of decline, they were now undergoing "a real renaissance" that would eventually result in the expulsion of European imperialists from Asia, or as he put it: "White men must get out of their heads the idea that Asiatics are necessarily 'inferior.' . . . The Asiatics have by their own efforts built up admirable cultures rooted in remote antiquity and worthy of all respect. . . . That this profound Asiatic renaissance will eventually result in the substantial elimination of white political control from Anatolia to the Philippines is as natural as it is inevitable" (Stoddard 1920: 229).

According to Stoddard, Asiatics consisted of both "brown" and "yellow" peoples. Although Stoddard wrote that "there is no generalized brown culture like those possessed by yellows and whites," he nevertheless claimed that "there is a fundamental comity between the brown peoples. . . . Its salient feature is the instinctive recognition by all Near and Middle Eastern peoples that they are fellow Asiatics, however bitter may be their internecine feuds" (Stoddard 1920: 55). Significantly, the other factor uniting brown peoples, according to Stoddard, was Islam: "The great spiritual bond is Islam. . . . that spiritual factor, Islam, from which the brown renaissance originally proceeded, and on which most of its present manifestations are based" (Stoddard 1920: 55, 58–59). In analyzing the factors that had helped to bring about the current Islamic/brown renaissance, Stoddard praised the Wahabi movement for "purging Islam of its sloth," but he was wary—if respectful—of Pan-Islamism, which he characterized as hostile to European power: "Such is the vast and growing body of Islam, to-day seeking to weld its forces into a higher unity for the combined objectives of spiritual revival and political emancipation. This unitary movement is known as 'Pan-Islamism'" (Stoddard 1920: 59, 66).

In *The Rising Tide of Color*, therefore, Stoddard linked the categories of "brown," "Asiatic," and "Islamic" into a unified and politically potent racial and civilizational grouping, which he placed in opposition to white world supremacy. By dramatic contrast, Stoddard depicted sub-Saharan Africans and their descendants in crudely racist terms, describing them, for example, as "widely addicted to cannibalism," people whose "native religions were usually sanguinary, demanding a prodigality of human sacrifices" (Stoddard 1920:

90–91). And Stoddard persistently contrasted Africans not only with Europeans but also with Asiatics:

> From the first glance we see that, in the negro, we are in the presence of a being differing profoundly not merely from the white man but also from those human types which we discovered in our surveys of the brown and yellow worlds. The black man is, indeed, sharply differentiated from the other branches of mankind. His outstanding quality is superabundant animal vitality.... Never having evolved civilizations of their own, they are practically devoid of that accumulated mass of beliefs, thoughts, and experiences which render Asiatics so impenetrable and so hostile to white influences. (Stoddard 1920: 90–92)

Stoddard's claim that "Asiatics" were civilizationally superior to Africans—which, as we will see, was a motif throughout his published work—reflected a widely held contemporary view. Indeed, the newly founded League of Nations had formalized this hierarchical relationship in Article 22 of its Covenant when it placed former imperial holdings in three mandates, designated by the letters A, B, and C. Territories in Africa and the South Pacific Islands were placed in Mandates B and C and, due to their supposedly lower level of development, required various degrees of direct oversight by the Mandatory established by the league. Mandate A, by contrast, consisted of "certain communities" that had formerly belonged to the Ottoman Empire and had "reached a stage of development where their existence as independent nations can be provisionally recognised subject to the rendering of administrative advice and assistance by a Mandatory until such time as they are able to stand alone. The wishes of these communities must be a principal consideration in the selection of the Mandatory" (League of Nations 1924).

Because of their supposedly inferior racial makeup and low level of civilizational achievement, Stoddard did not view sub-Saharan Africans as a threat to white hegemony on their own. Nevertheless, they constituted a profoundly dangerous threat if their large numbers and "animal vitality" were harnessed by the "brown" enemies of European imperialism. The key element in such an alliance, according to Stoddard, was Islam. As he put it, "Islam is, in fact, the intimate link between the brown and black worlds.... Islam is militant by nature, and the Arab is a restless and warlike breed. Pan-Islamism once possessed of the Dark Continent and fired by militant zealots, might forge black Africa into a sword of wrath, the executor of sinister adventures" (Stoddard 1920: 86, 102).

So important was the theme of Islam to Lothrop Stoddard that only a year after *The Rising Tide of Color* appeared in print, he published an entire monograph devoted to the subject. Even the title, *The New World of Islam*, suggests that Stoddard intended to take a radically different approach from many other Orientalists—including, as we have already seen, Ernest Renan—who viewed Islam as hopelessly and irrevocably mired in a civilizational decline that precluded modernization. To these critics, Stoddard responded as follows:

> Before discussing the ideas and efforts of the modern Moslem reformers, it might be well to examine the assertions made by numerous Western critics that Islam is by its very nature incapable of reform and progressive adaptation to the expansion of human knowledge. Such is the contention not only of Christian polemicists, but also of rationalists like Renan and European administrators of Moslem populations like Lord Cromer.... Yet an historical survey of religions, and especially a survey of the thoughts and accomplishments of Moslem reformers during the past century, seem to refute these pessimistic charges.... As a matter of fact, Mohammed reverenced knowledge. His own words are eloquent testimony to that. (Stoddard 1921: 26–29)

Rather than dismiss Islam as intrinsically unable to change or adapt—and therefore fundamentally at odds with modernity—Stoddard instead constructed a genealogy of modern Islamic reformers. Even more strikingly than in *The Rising Tide of Color*, in *The New World of Islam* Stoddard singled out the Wahabi movement as the first stage in the modern reformation of Islam.[8] Stoddard depicted the Wahabis as a "strictly puritan reformation," and he clearly sympathized with its moral dimension, writing approvingly: "The Wahabi leaven has destroyed abuses and has rekindled a purer religious faith. Even its fanatical zeal has not been without moral compensations" (Stoddard 1921: 21, 36). Yet according to Stoddard, "despite their moral earnestness," the Wahabis were "excessively narrow-minded, and it was very fortunate for Islam that they soon lost their political power and were compelled thenceforth to confine their efforts to moral teaching" (Stoddard 1921: 25).

In Stoddard's view the current hope for Islam lay with a different group, one he termed the "liberal reformers," and in particular a "nucleus of Indian Moslem liberals" (e.g., Moulvie Cheragh Ali and Syed Amir Ali) who "form the part of evolutionary progress in Islam. They are in the best sense of the word conservatives, receptive to healthy change, yet maintaining their hereditary poise. Sincerely religious men, they have faith in Islam as a living, moral force, and from it they continue to draw their spiritual sustenance" (Stoddard 1921: 31–32). Stoddard emphasized the "hereditary poise" and "elite character" of these Muslim liberals and portrayed them as classic progressives, which is to say, much like Stoddard himself. They were therefore natural allies, despite their racial difference from Stoddard.

In contrast to the Muslim liberal reformers with whom he clearly identified, Stoddard warned his readers about other contemporary developments and forces that might hamper or even reverse progress within the Islamic world, such as the Iknathan in Arabia or the Salafis in India and elsewhere (Stoddard 1921: 72). But his real concern was with the threat posed to the West by Pan-Islamists like al-Afghani, whom he described as "endowed with a keen intelligence, great personal magnetism, and abounding vigour," and whose "teachings may be summarized as follows: 'The Christian world, despite its internal differences of race and nationality, is, as against the East and especially as against Islam, united for the destruction of all Mohammedan states'" (Stoddard 1921: 52–53).

Elsewhere in the text Stoddard argued that the future of Islam would be determined by an internecine struggle between Muslim liberals and Pan-Islamists. As he put it, "Islam is, in fact, to-day torn between the forces of liberal reform and chauvinistic reaction" (Stoddard 1921: 35). Nevertheless, Stoddard remained optimistic about the ultimate ability of Muslim reformers to defeat "the fanatical, reactionary aspects of the political Pan-Islamic movement" (Stoddard 1921: 64). He observed: "The liberals are not only the hope of an evolutionary reformation, they are also favoured by the trend of the times, since the Moslem world is being continually permeated by Western progress and must continue to be thus permeated unless Western civilization itself collapses in ruin. . . . The spread of liberal principles and Western progress goes on apace. If there is much to fear for the future, there is also much to hope" (Stoddard 1921: 36).

As in *The Rising Tide of Color*, Stoddard framed the relationship between Islam and the West in racial as well as civilizational terms in *The New World of Islam*. Although he devoted less space to denigrating Africans than in his earlier book, Stoddard once again stressed the fundamental division between Europeans and Asiatics, on the one hand, and Africans, on the other, cautioning his readers, "We must always remember that the Asiatic stocks which constitute the bulk of Islam's followers are not primitive savages like the African negroes or the Australoids, but are mainly peoples with genuine civilizations built up by their own efforts from the remote past. In view of their historic achievements, therefore, it seems safe to conclude that in the great ferment now stirring the Moslem world we behold a real *Renaissance*" (Stoddard 1921: 75).

Stoddard's use of the term *Renaissance* to describe contemporary cultural developments within the Islamic world is significant for a number of reasons. First, it reflects his general historiographical tendency to view Muslim history through the lens of European categories, including periodization—for example, in likening the Wahabi movement to an Islamic "Reformation." Second, by employing the term *Renaissance*, Stoddard was implying that contemporary Muslim societies were currently emerging out of a kind of Dark Ages and, just as important, that they were doing so by drawing on their own classical sources of inspiration. Thus while Stoddard essentially accepted the standard view of Islam's historical decline, he rejected the notion that Islam was inherently anti-intellectual, and he was even decidedly optimistic about the potential for cultural rebirth.

Also as in *The Rising Tide of Color*, Stoddard reiterated in *The New World of Islam* that "the great brown spiritual bond is Islam" (Stoddard 1921: 103). Unlike "yellow," "black," or "white" people, the "brown" people of the world did not possess a unified "racial type-norm" (Stoddard 1921: 103). Instead, they were Asiatic, a hybrid racial identity or racial "melting pot"—in Stoddard's formulation—that had historically incorporated "black," "yellow," and "white" racial elements. For these reasons, the world of Islam was able to accommodate a range of racial and national identities more easily than could Christian Europe or the United States: "In Moslem eyes, a man need not be born or formally naturalized to be a member of a certain Moslem 'Nationality.' Every Moslem is more or less at home in every part of Islam, so a man may just happen into a particular country and thereby become at once, if he wishes, a national in good standing" (Stoddard 1921: 171).

Islam, according to Stoddard, was a culturally and racially hybrid phenomenon, which meant that Muslims from different parts of the world could find common cause and even identify profoundly with one another, despite differences in origin, skin color, and language. In this way Islam, like the related categories of "brown" and "Asiatic," both bridged and incorporated elements of the more reified—for Stoddard, at least—racial categories of "white," "black," and "yellow." It should be noted, however, that Stoddard's statement "Every Moslem is more or less at home in every part of Islam" ignored significant historical differences between Arabs and non-Arabs, Middle Easterners and sub-Saharan Africans, and so on. Yet it also anticipated Malcolm X's later perception, as exemplified by the now-famous account of his pilgrimage to

Mecca, that Islam was more racially harmonious, if not more diverse, than Christianity (Malcolm X and Haley 1964: 350).

During the 1960s, the presumed cultural and racial hybridity of Islam (especially as compared to Christianity) would profoundly appeal to Malcolm X once he had abandoned the Manichean racial taxonomy of the Nation of Islam in favor of a more orthodox Muslim identity. By contrast, in the 1920s, this same perception signified something radically different for Lothrop Stoddard: a profound threat to Euro-American hegemony, particularly in places like sub-Saharan Africa where Islam and Christianity were competing for converts.

Despite the fact that brown people already constituted a racial melting pot, members of which Stoddard admitted had made great contributions to world civilization, and despite his oft-expressed hope that Western and Muslim reformers could engage in peaceful and constructive intellectual encounters, Stoddard nevertheless rejected the contemporary sexual integration of brown and white people. In so doing, Stoddard once again revealed the primacy of racial separatism in this thinking, for as he put it: "To unite physically would be the greatest of disasters.... Ethnic fusion would destroy both their [white and brown peoples'] race-souls and would result in a dreary mongrelization from which would issue nothing but degeneration and decay" (Stoddard 1921: 104).

Although he did not acknowledge it, a profound contradiction lay at the heart of Stoddard's depictions of brown people. An amalgam of white, black, and yellow races, according to Stoddard, brown people had produced many cultural achievements over the centuries. This despite what should have been the negative impact of their supposedly "dreary mongrelization," a view of racial hybridity that was shared by many anthropologists, eugenicists, and others from the nineteenth century on, as Robert Young has demonstrated (Young 1995: 1–26). Ironically, Stoddard's own history of brown people, including their crucial role in the emergence of Islam, served as powerful evidence for the potential cultural advantages rather than disadvantages of racial hybridity. Phrased differently, why would the "ethnic fusion" of white and brown people be problematic at the beginning of the twentieth century, if the fusion of black, white, and yellow peoples that had produced brown people in the first place had not resulted in their "degeneration and decay"? Ultimately Stoddard could not escape from the kind of racist thinking that dominated white supremacist circles during the 1920s, even when he himself produced evidence to the contrary.

Black Nationalism, Islam, and the Tribal Twenties

As John Higham demonstrated in his now classic work *Strangers in the Land*, in the United States the "Tribal Twenties" were a period of intense "racial nativism," the chief "prophet" of which was Madison Grant (Higham 1955: 300). Within this historical context it is not surprising that the work of Lothrop Stoddard, Grant's most important protégé, found a receptive audience among many native-born white Americans and was favorably reviewed by venerable national publications such as the *Saturday Evening Post*, which had begun to publish Norman Rockwell's idealized images of American life only a few years earlier in 1916. Less predictable, perhaps, is that Stoddard's writings, including his extensive work on Islam, were avidly read—and in a number of cases even positively reviewed, at least in part—by a variety of contemporary Pan-Asian, Pan-Islamic, and Pan-African thinkers.

Thus, for example, Cemil Aydin has noted that the Japanese intellectual Ôkawa Shûmei, who published *Fukkô Ajia no Shomondai* (Problems of a resurgent Asia) in 1922, "often referred to Stoddard's work in his writings" and approvingly described the first two decades of the twentieth century as "the era of 'the rising tide of color against the white world supremacy'" (Aydin 2007: 150–51). Ôkawa was part of a broader pan-Asian movement during the 1920s that sought to expand the civilizational concept of Asia beyond either the Chinese or Buddhist cultural spheres—as some earlier formulations had done—to include areas such as Persia and Turkey, thereby establishing linkages with contemporary Pan-Islamism.

Meanwhile, Stoddard's *The New World of Islam* was almost immediately made available to a wider Muslim readership when it was translated by Ajjaj Nuwayhid into Arabic (he later described how he stayed up all night reading the book after struggling to acquire it from a British library) and published in an expanded multivolume edition along with a lengthy commentary by the important Pan-Islamic intellectual Shakib Arslan, a close associate of Muhammad Abduh.[9] The first edition of *Hadir al-Alam al Islami* (The new world of Islam) appeared in Cairo in 1924, and thereafter several editions were published over the next half-century, testifying to the work's lasting impact.[10]

In his commentary Arslan expanded on Stoddard's work and provided corrections in a respectful rather than dismissive or combative tone. Nuwayhid, who would later publish an Arabic edition of the notorious anti-Semitic fabrication *The Protocols of the Elders of Zion*, praised Stoddard in the preface to a 1971 edition of the book: "[God willed that] in this book two geniuses [Arabic, *'abqariyyatan*] would be brought together: the genius of the author, the composer [i.e., Stoddard] and the genius of the encyclopedic, the singular, al-Amir Shakib Arslan. And when these two geniuses were brought together in one arena, the book achieved what no other book like it achieved in this age" (Studard 1971: 6–7).[11] Indeed, Nuwayhid was also deeply impressed by Stoddard when the two met in Jerusalem in 1924 during a trip that the American took to the Middle East, and the two continued to correspond until the outbreak of World War II made it impossible to continue (Studard 1971: 44).

The cordial relations between Stoddard and Arab interlocutors like Arslan and Nuwayhid should be seen within the broader context of the extensive intellectual and personal interactions between European and American Orientalists who were sympathetic to Islam—or at least, to a certain vision of Islam—and Middle Eastern counterparts during the first few decades of the twentieth century, who were themselves engaged in a process of reimagining and redefining Islam through the lens of traditionally Islamic and Western categories alike. Henri Lauzière, for example, has explored the complex network of figures—including Louis Massignon, Rashid Rida, Stoddard, and Arslan—who contributed to the modern construction of Salafism (*al-salafiyya*). Concerning Stoddard and Arslan in particular, Lauzière writes:

> In the Arabic version of Stoddard's *The New World of Islam*, for example, the passage about *salafiyya* did not elicit any reaction from the polemical Shakib Arslan (d. 1946), whose lengthy commentaries on other passages doubled the size of the book. The so-called Prince of Eloquence, who was not a religious expert per se, stood strangely mute in the face of Stoddard's confused description of the Salafi movement as a fanatical trend dominated by dervishes. For all their oddities, both Stoddard's glaring errors and Arslan's silence reflect the lack of clarity about *salafiyya* in the 1920s, when the notion was being worked out simultaneously in the West and the Muslim world." (Lauzière 2010: 381)

Rather than focus on the reception of Stoddard's work on Islam by intellectuals in the Middle East, however, for the reminder of this essay, I turn to a source closer to home, namely Hubert Harrison, one of the most important African American intellectuals during the first quarter of the twentieth century and a founding figure of the New Negro movement, who took a special interest in Islam. After emigrating to the United States from the island of St. Croix in the Danish West Indies at the age of seventeen, Harrison moved to Harlem, where he became involved in a number of causes. From 1912 to 1914 Harrison was a member of the Socialist Party of America and the most prominent black socialist in the country. Related to his involvement in radical politics, Harrison also became involved in the Freethought Movement—an intellectual current that emphasized free inquiry and critical thinking, sympathizers with which included Susan B. Anthony, Eugene V. Debs, Herbert Spencer, Margaret Sanger, A. Philip Randolph, and other prominent figures—and he began to identify himself publicly as an atheist (Perry 2009: 186, 232, 333; Perry 2001: 35).

Harrison (1914) was especially critical of Christianity, which he viewed as playing a crucial role in the historical enslavement and ongoing persecution of blacks in the United States, publishing an article entitled "The Negro a Conservative: Christianity Still Enslaves the Minds of Those Whose Bodies It Long Held Bound," and commenting in the margins of his copy of Stoddard's *The Rising Tide of Color*, that "Xtianity and race prejudice go together" (see Perry 2009: 40, n. 39). In this regard Harrison was not alone among early twentieth-century black intellectuals, many of whom found fault with the way that Christianity had been deployed in order to enforce racial oppression, and who explicitly rejected depictions of Jesus as a white man. Nevertheless, Harrison went further in the intensity of his critique of Christianity than most of his contemporaries—including Marcus Garvey, with whom he would work closely for a period and who maintained a Christian identity despite absorbing influences from Islam.

Significantly, Harrison's sentiment would later be echoed by Elijah Muhammad, leader of the Nation of Islam, in *The Message to the Black Man in America*: "Christianity is one of the most perfect black-slave-making religions on our planet. It has completely killed the so-called Negroes mentally" (Muhammad 1965: 70). Although I have not uncovered evidence that Elijah Muhammad was directly influenced by Harrison's writings on Christianity, a number of scholars have noted the profound impact of Garveyism—and more broadly, of Caribbean radicalism—on the Nation of Islam. Within this intellectual milieu, it is possible that Muhammad was exposed to Harrison's writings through his involvement in Garvey's movement during the early 1920s. As Winston James has noted: "Elijah Poole, better known as Elijah Muhammad, was substantially influenced if not formed ideologically by Garveyism in his native Georgia and later in Detroit" (James 1998: 260).

In dramatic contrast to his negative attitude toward Christianity, Hubert Harrison evinced a profound sympathy for Islam. Harrison praised the pioneering work of Edward Wilmot Blyden, one of the founding figures of Pan-Africanism, who had argued as early as 1887 in his book *Christianity, Islam and the Negro Race* that Islam was better suited to Africans than was Christianity, and as his biographer Jeffrey Perry has noted, Harrison eventually "decided to write the Sheik-ul-Islam of England in order to 'get in touch with organized Mohammedanism in the United States and to learn the Arabic language'" (Perry 2009: 372). And in his book *When Africa Awakes*, Harrison explicitly praised "the brown man's show of resistance in Egypt, India and elsewhere under Islam" (Harrison 1997 [1920]: 143). Thus Islam appealed to Harrison as an alternative to Christianity, not tainted by the latter's historical association with slavery and racism in the Americas, and which in the contemporary period, under the banner of Pan-Islamism, had explicitly linked itself to the struggle of people of color against European colonialism and white supremacy.

In 1920 Harrison became the editor of the *Negro World*, the newspaper of Marcus Garvey's United Negro Improvement Association (UNIA). As Richard Turner has demonstrated, "significant cross-fertilization between the UNIA and black American Islam occurred during the World War I era, as the former became an important source for Islamic ideas in America" (Turner 1997: 81). Of particular importance was the influence on Garvey of Duse Mohammed Ali, a Sudanese-Egyptian Muslim, while both men were living in London. According to Turner, "the young Garvey learned much about African history and politics and Islam from Duse Mohammed Ali, and he contributed an article to *The African Times and Orient Review* [an influential journal published by Ali]" (Turner 1997: 84).

This context helps to explain Hubert Harrison's decision to review Lothrop Stoddard's work on Islam in the pages of the *Negro World*, since it was a topic that appealed to many members of Garvey's organization, who were searching for religious alternatives to Christianity in Islam and elsewhere (for instance, the prominent Garveyite Arnold Josiah Ford's promotion of black Judaism within the movement). In addition, Harrison, like Ajjaj Nuwayhid, developed a personal relationship with Stoddard, and the two corresponded with each other extensively during the early 1920s (Perry 2009: 321).

Given the crude racism that Lothrop Stoddard exhibited toward black people in his writings, it may be surprising that Harrison interacted with him so cordially in private and, as we shall see, publicly praised both him and his work.[12] Nor, as Matthew Pratt Guterl has observed, was Harrison alone in his positive stance toward Stoddard: "The shriller Stoddard's cries for a renewed race-consciousness became, the more fervently New Negro admirers lauded his work" (Guterl 2001: 141). For example, Guterl (1999: n. 83) notes that "Garveyites in Los Angeles were encouraged to read Stoddard," and Cyril

Briggs, another West Indian immigrant to the United States who founded the African Blood Brotherhood and edited its publication the *Crusader,* "often cited Stoddard as an expert in support of its opinion" (Tolbert 1975: 240–41).

Unlike W.E.B. Du Bois, who dismissed Stoddard as a rank dilettante because of his popularizing approach and tendentious assertions, Harrison respected Stoddard's scholarship, claiming that "Mr. Stoddard as a historian is quite competent" (Harrison 1921, quoted in Perry 2001: 319). In a review of *The Rising Tide of Color,* Harrison drew a sharp contrast between the work of Stoddard, which he respected, and that of Madison Grant, which he dismissed: "The difference in value and accuracy between Mr. Stoddard's text and the pseudo-scientific introduction of Dr. Grant would furnish material for philosophic satire" (Perry 2001: 307). Indeed, Harrison gave *The Rising Tide of Color* a ringing endorsement: "The book should be widely read by intelligent men of color from Tokio [*sic*] to Tallahassee. It is published by Charles Scribner's Sons at $3 and is well worth the price" (Perry 2001: 309).

Harrison had even kinder words for *The New World of Islam,* to which he devoted a two-part review in the *Negro World* in 1921 before breaking with Garvey and leaving the newspaper: "Mr. Stoddard's book is a masterly epic of the facts of international Islam and as such is a welcome handbook onto which the readers of *The Negro World* can devise with pleasure and profit" (Perry 2001: 319). Elsewhere in his review Harrison made clear what he liked about Stoddard's approach in *The New World of Islam.* First, Harrison reiterated Stoddard's identification of Islam with peoples of color and his assertion that all Muslims were brothers whatever their racial background: "[The] earlier world-domination of Islam was in many respects superior in moral and spiritual values to that of the white man. In the first place it was not eaten by the corroding canker of race prejudice. In political and civic matters character counted for much; color and race for nothing at all. As Mr. Stoddard remarks, 'All true believers were brothers'" (Perry 2001: 313).

This supposed lack of race prejudice was only one way in which Harrison claimed the "spiritual superiority of rejuvenated Islam over obsolescent Christianity" (Perry 2001: 317). As he put it, "Black and brown and yellow were not, as in the Christian system, brothers in theology only but they were genuinely so in practice before the magistrates and in all the relations of daily life" (Perry 2001: 313). In a gesture that recalled the earlier literary exchange between Renan and al-Afghani, Harrison also quoted Stoddard to support his view that "it is in another and no less important respect that Islam's superiority is demonstrated. . . . While Christianity as an ecclesiastical system controlled Europe's educational systems and institutions, no thinker dared to think a new thought.... On the other hand, despite the huge cairn of lies that have risen on the graves of Islam's reputation in the Western world, the Mohammadan system from its very beginning strove to promote knowledge and free inquiry" (Perry 2001: 313).

Perhaps most important, Harrison reiterated Stoddard's view that Islam was the chief unifying force for people of color around the world in their unfolding struggle against white supremacy: "Such was the religion that linked together and still links the souls of hundreds of millions of black, brown, and yellow peoples from the Senegal to the shores of the Yellow Sea. And it is this multitudinous mass that is now on the move, struggling upward to their 'place in the sun,' under the impact of white arrogance, greed, and race prejudice which call to their aid the forces of religion, business, imperialism and war" (Perry 2001: 313).

In praising Stoddard's work, Harrison ignored the distinction that Stoddard consistently drew between brown and yellow peoples, whom he depicted as culturally advanced, and blacks, whom he denigrated en masse as "savages." It appears that Harrison was willing to overlook this significant detail because so many of Stoddard's other views resonated with his own. Both men saw the world through the prism of race and were convinced that in the wake of World War I, global white supremacy was under imminent threat. As Harrison observed in his review of *The Rising Tide of Color*, "Here is a book written by a white man that causes white men to shiver. For it calls their attention to the writing on the wall" (Perry 2001: 306). However, whereas Stoddard lamented this situation, Harrison celebrated it, writing in a letter to Stoddard on June 24, 1920, "Since I am a Negro, my sympathies are not at all with you: that which you fear, I naturally hope for" (Perry 2009: 473, n. 32). Finally, Harrison agreed with Stoddard's portrait of a contemporary Islamic renaissance, even though unlike Stoddard's, his sympathies extended to Pan-Islamism since it sought to undermine European hegemony.

Conclusion

As the Tribal Twenties gave way to the 1930s, many of the ideas that circulated among the thinkers examined here would become part of the ideology adopted by the Nation of Islam, including the racialization of Islam, the critique of Christianity as helping to enslave blacks both mentally and physically, the link between Islam and an Asiatic identity (i.e., the concept of the Asiatic Black Man), and a concomitant ambivalence toward sub-Saharan Africa (see Deutsch 2001, 2009). It may also be argued that just as the Pan-Islamic movement was largely displaced in the Middle East by Arab nationalism during the 1930s, so in the United States the Pan-Islamic currents of the 1920s were increasingly replaced by a narrower black nationalist perspective on Islam that would dominate the American Islamic scene and characterize the Nation of Islam until the late 1950s and early 1960s, when the movement began to undergo what Edward Curtis (2006: 13) has described as a process of "Islamization"—that is, an increasing identification with "the Islamic beliefs, rituals, ethics, and symbols of 'mainstream' Islam."

Along with this religious transformation, elements within the Nation of Islam itself, as well as many voices within the broader Islamic world, began to identify with anti-colonialism and with the post–World War II emergence of the "Third World," as exemplified by international gatherings such as the 1955 Afro-Asian Conference in Bandung, Indonesia (Curtis 2006: 38).[13] Thus in a 1965 interview with the *London Times,* Malcolm X declared: "At the Bandung Conference . . . one of the first and best steps toward real independence for nonwhite people took place. The people of Africa and Asia and Latin America were able to get together. . . . All of the fear had left the African continent and the Asian continent" (Clark 1992: 56–57). Concomitantly, during this period more mainstream Muslim figures outside the United States were often able to "put aside their theological disagreements with Elijah Muhammad in order to emphasize Muslim unity in the face of neocolonial threats to Muslim self-determination" (Curtis 2006: 38).

This is the wider historical context for the 1961 speech by Malcolm X with which we began this essay. Against the backdrop of contemporary anti-colonialist movements, a growing sense of international Islamic unity, and the emerging articulation of a common "Third World" identity, the vision articulated by Lothrop Stoddard in *The Rising Tide of Color against White World-Supremacy* and *The New World of Islam* must have seemed remarkably prescient or at least strikingly relevant to Malcolm X, just as this vision had earlier appealed to Hubert Harrison, even as both men rejected Stoddard's virulently racist view of sub-Saharan Africans.

Notes

1. Quoted in Malcolm X, Muhammad Speaks Broadcast from Mosque #7, March 1, 1961, Malcolm X Collection Papers, New York Public Library, Schomburg Center for Research in Black Culture, box 6, folder 3, Script XIV, as cited in Abdat, 92.

2. Citing Ayd Münif Efendi, "Mahiyet ve Aksam-I Ulum," *Mecmua-ı Fünun,* no. 13 (June 1863): 7. Aydin notes, "For similar racist comments on blacks and natives of the

West Indies, see Mehmed Sevki, "Avrupa Devletlerinin Ahval-I Hazirrasi," *Mecmua-ı Fünun*, no. 32 (October 1864): 305."

3. As cited in Hourani, *Arabic Thought in the Liberal Age*, 120. Hourani notes that "Renan admitted indeed the existence of a so-called Arabic philosophy and science, but they were Arabic in nothing but language, and Greco-Sassanian in content. They were entirely the work of non-Muslims in inner revolt against their own religion."

4. As Aydin (2007: 52) has written: "Similar to the identity of being Jewish, being Muslim was [now] a quasiracial category. It is due to this racial implication that Muslim modernists had to defend Islam against Orientalist critiques of inferiority and backwardness, while conceding a certain level of civilizational backwardness and working for the 'revival' of their fellow coreligionists."

5. For an English translation, see Keddie (1983).

6. Hourani (1983: 122–23) argues that in his response to Renan, al-Afghani understated his real views, and that in fact al-Afghani "not only believed that Islam was as true or false as other religions, but that it was the only true, complete, and perfect religion, which could satisfy all the desires of the human spirit. Like other Muslim thinkers of his day, he was willing to accept the judgement on Christianity given by European free thought: it was unreasonable, it was the enemy of science and progress. But he wished to show that these criticisms did not apply to Islam; on the contrary, Islam was in harmony with the principles discovered by scientific reason, was indeed the religion demanded by reason."

7. Frank Wu (2002: 120) has noted the link between the clash of civilizations model of Samuel Huntington and the earlier work of Madison Grant and Lothrop Stoddard. Unlike their predecessors, however, neither Huntington nor Bernard Lewis, who originally coined the phrase, explicitly frame the clash in racial as well as civilizational terms.

8. See, for example, Stoddard (1921: 21): "Yet, in this darkest hour, a voice came crying out of the vast Arabian desert, the cradle of Islam, calling the faithful back to the true path. This puritan reformer, the famous Abd-el-Wahab, kindled a fire which presently spread to the remotest corners of the Moslem world, purging Islam of its sloth and reviving the fervour of olden days. The great Mohammedan Revival had begun."

9. On Arslan, see Cleveland 1985; Haddad 2004; Adal 2008.

10. Luthrub Studard, *Hadir al-Alam al-Islami*. The second edition was published privately in Cairo in 1963 by a patron named 'Aysa al-Baabi al-Halabi. The third edition was published in 1971 in Beirut by the well-known Arabic press Dar al-Fikr.

11. My thanks to Joel Blecher for his translation from the Arabic and for the many illuminating conversations we had about Arslan's edition of Stoddard's work.

12. In contrast, as Guterl (1999: 348) has noted, W.E.B. Du Bois "had nothing but scorn . . . concluding that 'Lothrop Stoddard has no standing as a sociologist. . . . [He] is simply a popular writer who has some vogue now.'"

13. See Curtis's discussion of this phenomenon as well as the Bandung Conference, in particular.

References Cited

Abdat, Fathie Bin Ali
"Malcolm X and Christianity," MA thesis, Department of History, National University of Singapore.

Adal, Raja
2008 "Shakib Arslan's Imagining of Europe: The Coloniser, the Inquisitor, the Islamic, the Virtuous, and the Friend." In *Islam in Inter-War Europe*, ed. Nathalie Clayer and Eric Germain. New York: Columbia University Press.

Aydin, Cemil
2007 *The Politics of Anti-Westernism in Asia: Visions of World Order in Pan-Islamic and Pan-Asian Thought.* New York: Columbia University Press.

Clark, Steve, ed.
1992 *Malcolm X: February 1965, The Final Speeches.* New York: Pathfinder.

Cleveland, William L.
1985 *Islam against the West: Shakib Arslan and the Campaign for Islamic Nationalism.* Austin: University of Texas Press.

Curtis, Edward, IV
2006 *Black Muslim Religion in the Nation of Islam, 1960–1975.* Chapel Hill: University of North Carolina Press.

Deutsch, Nathaniel
2001 "The Asiatic Black Man: An African American Orientalism?" *Journal of Asian American Studies* 4 (3): 193–220.
2009 *Inventing America's Worst Family: Eugenics, Islam, and the Fall and Rise of the Tribe of Ishmael.* Berkeley: University of California Press.

Guterl, Matthew
1999 "The New Race Consciousness: Race, Nation, and Empire, in American Culture, 1910–1925." *Journal of World History* 10(2): 307–52.
2001 *The Color of Race in America, 1900–1940.* Cambridge, Mass.: Harvard University Press.

Haddad, Mahmoud
2004 "The Ideas of Amir Shakib Arslan Before and After the Collapse of the Ottoman Empire." In *Views from the Edge: Essays in Honor of Richard W. Bulliet*, ed. Neguin Yavari, Lawrence Potter, and Jean-Marc Ran Oppenheim. New York: Columbia University Press.

Harrison, Hubert
1914 "The Negro a Conservative: Christianity Still Enslaves the Minds of Those Whose Bodies It Long Held Bound." *Truth Seeker*, September 12, 1914.
1921 "The Brown Man Leads the Way." Review of *The New World of Islam* by Lothrop Stoddard. In Perry 2001.
1997 [1920] *When Africa Awakes.* Baltimore: Black Classic Press.

Higham, John
1955 *Strangers in the Land: Patterns of American Nativism (1860–1925).* New Brunswick, N.J.: Rutgers University Press.

Hourani, Albert
1983 [1962] *Arabic Thought in the Liberal Age, 1798–1939*. Cambridge, UK: Cambridge University Press.
James, Winston
1998 *Holding Aloft the Banner of Ethiopia: Caribbean Radicalism in Early Twentieth-Century America*. London: Verso.
Keddie, Nikki
1972 *Sayyid Jamal al-Din "al-Afghani": A Political Biography*. Berkeley: University of California Press.
1983 *An Islamic Response to Imperialism: Political and Religious Writings of Sayyid Jamal ad-Din "al-Afghani."* Berkeley: University of California Press.
Lauzière, Henri
2010 "The Construction of *Salafiyya*: Reconsidering Salafism from the Perspective of Conceptual History." *International Journal of Middle Eastern Studies* 42: 369–89.
League of Nations
1924 The Convenant of the League of Nations (Including Amendment Adopted to December, 1924), Article 22. http://avalon.law.yale.edu/20th_century/leagcov.asp#art22.
Malcolm X, and Alex Haley
1964 *The Autobiography of Malcolm X*. New York: Ballantine.
Muhammad, Elijah
1973 [1965] *Message to the Black Man in America*. Phoenix: Secretarius MEMPS Publications.
Perry, Jeffrey
2009 *Hubert Harrison: The Voice of Harlem Radicalism, 1883–1918*. New York: Columbia University Press.
Perry, Jeffrey, ed.
2001 *A Hubert H. Harrison Reader*. Middletown, Conn.: Wesleyan University Press.
Renan, Ernest
1883 "L'Islamisme et la science." *Journal de Débats*, March 29.
Spiro, Jonathan
2009 *Defending the Master Race: Conservation, Eugenics, and the Legacy of Madison Grant*. Lebanon, N.H.: University of Vermont Press.
Stoddard, Lothrop
1914 *The French Revolution in San Domingo*. New York: Houghton Mifflin.
1920 *The Rising Tide of Color against White World-Supremacy*. New York: Charles Scribner's Sons.
1921 *The New World of Islam*. New York: Charles Scribner's Sons.
Studard, Luthrub
1971 [1924] *Hadir al-Alam al-Islami*. Trans. Ajjaj Nuwayhid, ed. Al-Amir Shakib Arslan. 3rd ed. Beirut: Dar al-Fikr.
Tolbert, Emory
1975 "Outpost Garveyism and the UNIA Rank and File." *Journal of Black Studies* 5: 233–53.

Turner, Richard
1997 *Islam in the African American Experience*. Bloomington: Indiana University Press.
Wu, Frank
2002 *Yellow: Race in America beyond Black and White*. New York: Basic Books.
Young, Robert
1995 *Colonial Desire: Hybridity in Theory, Culture and Race*. London: Routledge.

6

Insha'Allah/Ojalá, Yes Yes Y'all

Puerto Ricans (Re)examining and (Re)imagining Their Identities through Islam and Hip Hop

OMAR RAMADAN-SANTIAGO

I had just arrived in Puerto Rico to start my summer research for my master's thesis in June 2010 when I found out that somewhere on the island in a few hours there was going to be an educational panel on Puerto Rican Muslims. I quickly informed my aunt and we made a few calls to figure out where it was and, more important, how to get there. The event turned out to be a few blocks away from my cousin's school, so we hopped in my aunt's van and made our way. Once there I witnessed how some Muslim Puerto Ricans are able to create their own identities, using cultural and religious influences to shape the persons they see themselves to be, despite being seemingly at odds with mainstream conceptions of what "Puerto Rican" means.

This apparent contradiction inspired my interest in the ways in which Puerto Ricans construct and choose to express their identity in the United States and in Puerto Rico and, in particular, in how this identity is shaped both by being Muslim and through their involvement in Hip Hop[1] art and culture. It is my hope that my work expands the narrow definitions of what it means to be Muslim as well as Puerto Rican in the United States and in the Caribbean by exploring how Puerto Rican Muslims make use of music, art (movement and visual), language, culture, religious doctrine, and self-education to rewrite their histories and create for themselves new identities that challenge existing stereotypes they refuse to fit.

In this essay I analyze how some Puerto Ricans consider themselves genuine members of Muslim and Hip Hop communities, often citing history as a means of validating their membership status. A growing literature is now focusing on the relatively recent attraction to Islam by various Latin American and Caribbean populations (e.g., Aidi 2009a; Martinez-Vazquez 2010; Smith 1999: 66–67). My focus is on Puerto Ricans because their status in the United States political arena, as well as in Hip Hop, is unique compared to that of other Latin American groups. As Juan Flores notes, Puerto Rican rappers have something that other Latino rappers do not: "a history in hip-hop" and an involvement in Hip Hop culture that has persisted since its birth in the Bronx in the 1970s (Flores 2000: 116). Islam has also been a large part of the Hip Hop scene through the participation of African American Muslims and such educational and religious organizations as the Universal Zulu Nation, Nation of Islam, and Nation of Gods and Earths. However, Muslim identity within Hip Hop, in fact, is not limited to the Americas but is a growing global phenomenon, demonstrated by the emergence of Hip Hop music among Senegalese Muslims, the prevalence of North African Muslim Hip Hop artists in France, and the popularization of Arab Hip Hop with such documentaries as *Slingshot Hip Hop* (Salloum 2009).

My fieldwork was centered on Puerto Rican Muslims involved in Hip Hop as DJs, MCs, aerosol/graffiti artists, and b-boys (each of these representing one of the four fundamental aspects of Hip Hop art and culture, to be discussed in fuller detail). It was conducted from the fall of 2009 to the summer of 2010, taking place on the north coast of Puerto Rico and in Pittsburgh, Pennsylvania, northern New Jersey, and New York City. All my interlocutors are male and living in either the United States or Puerto Rico and have embraced Islam later in life. In Puerto Rico, I interviewed MC Correa Cotto at a mosque and MC Profound in his home. I spoke with MC and aerosol artist Hamza Perez of the Mujahideen Team or M-Team (a music group consisting of his brother and himself and featured in his documentary *New Muslim Cool*) at his mosque in Pittsburgh. Finally, I conducted a telephone interview with David Muhammad, a Wisconsin-based DJ.

With the growing number of Latinos/Caribbeans/Latin Americans becoming Muslim, developing a more capacious understanding of the meanings of religious identity among Puerto Ricans is key to understanding the wider lived experiences of people of Latin American and Caribbean descent (Galvan 2008; Martinez-Vazquez 2010; Viscidi 2003). It is my hope that this project supplements popular and academic discourses addressing the rise of "many Islams" and religious identity transformations in the current post-9/11 moment in the Americas.[2] Predominantly Christian, and to a greater or lesser degree unfamiliar with or fearful of Muslims and Islam, these societies traffic in discourses about East and West, self and other, and traditional versus modern that homogenize identities and limit our understanding of the meaning and significance of religion as complex, context-contingent, and never entirely predictable. In this creative work of self-making, these individuals, along with their family networks and communities, are reexamining and reconstructing what it means to be Puerto Rican and Muslim. In recognizing the importance of music and culture in these formations, I explore how musical associations, religious affiliations, and cultural connections work together in the cultural translation of Islamic beliefs and practices and in the transformation of Muslim selves.

I explore the complex role that Islam plays in creating social boundaries that unite and differentiate, include and exclude, join and separate, among communities of practitioners who historically have roots in Christianity, particularly Catholicism, and I investigate the reasons why these transformations—conversions, syncretisms—are occurring in late twentieth-century and twenty-first-century contexts. I also examine how Hip Hop has been used as a force to spread knowledge and awareness about the said social boundaries and transformations. This is demonstrated by the use of Hip Hop as a form of *da'wah*, or a way to educate people about Islam, to be discussed later.

This project is in dialogue with scholarship focusing on authenticity and identity formation (Askew 2002; Bigenho 2002). It explores how history is utilized as a way to support the reworking of identities to create a newer, broader way of imagining the self in relation to various communities. The purpose is to explore how some Puerto Ricans see themselves as genuine members of communities in which they have not historically been positioned, such as the Hip Hop nation and Muslim *ummah* (referring to the global community of Muslims), due to stereotypes and misinformation, and how they may reimagine themselves, using historical evidence as reasoning, in order to claim authentic membership.

Authenticity/History

A theme throughout the essay is the concept of authenticity. Who has the right to claim something as their own? Puerto Ricans who are Muslim and identify as Hip Hop artists face questions from skeptical peers as to why they are involved with a religion or culture that assumedly is "not theirs." To combat these problematic stereotypes, my interlocutors partake in a historical excavation to show that Islam and Hip Hop are a part of their history as well, allowing them also to claim ownership and authenticity.

I must stress that this is not to say my interlocutors are on a constant mission to prove themselves genuine members of the Hip Hop and Muslim communities; that is not the case. While they have dealt with accusations that their loyalties have changed and that they are further marginalizing themselves by participating in communities that are "not theirs," they do not feel the need to remind others continually that they simultaneously belong to Puerto Rican, Muslim, and Hip Hop spaces. "Well, authenticity is important to everybody but I really don't think too much about it . . . I'm confident in myself" (Profound, interview). Their sense of authenticity is a quiet one; they are fully aware of their right to call themselves Puerto Rican, Muslim, and Hip Hop artists and feel no need to put this fact on display. "I think if you're genuine, and you're authentic, then you don't have to trip on trying to prove that" (Perez, interview). However, in the back of their minds they have the historical ammunition, ready to disprove any claims that Hip Hop or Islam is not theirs or that they in any way forfeited being Puerto Rican due to their choices.

My interlocutors claimed that becoming Muslim made them feel more strongly connected to Puerto Rican culture and identity. This is due to the discoveries they made during their research fueled by the desire to discover more about themselves and the communities to which they belong. Their "re-introduction" to Islam, as David Muhammad termed it, gave my interlocutors an opportunity to learn more about Puerto Rican history (Muhammad, interview). "When I became Muslim it made me go more to Puerto Rican culture and who I am as a Puerto Rican because Allah says in the Qur'an that He created us from different tribes so you can get to know one another. So before I can get to know somebody else's culture I have to get to know mine. So when I became Muslim, I started studying more about the struggles of Puerto Ricans, Lolita Lebrón, you know, Emeterio Betances, Pedro Albizu Campos, so it actually made me become more Puerto Rican" (Perez, interview). Many of the Hip Hop artists I interviewed conducted research on Islam in Puerto Rico, the greater Caribbean, and Latin America in order to refute the idea that one ceases to be Puerto Rican by becoming Muslim. As Correa Cotto pointed out, "El Catolicismo es de Roma. Él no deja de ser puertorriqueño porque vayas al iglesia, igual yo voy para la mezquita" (Catholicism is from Rome. One does not stop being Puerto Rican because you go to church, the same if I go to the mosque; Cotto, interview). According to this view, religious beliefs do not change one's cultural identity.

The importance of history to identity construction and validation is a crucial point. Demonstrating significant historical support can often prove authenticity and belonging. It is through their historical research and inquiry that my interlocutors have found their inherent right to be involved in and to redefine their role as members of the Hip Hop community and Muslim ummah, not to mention expanding definitions of what it means to be Puerto Rican.

Reverting/Going Back

Many Puerto Rican Muslims describe their embrace of Islam as "reverting," a term often used by "reverts" as well as other Muslims sensitive to the revert/convert debate, meaning a return to what they consider to be their original religion rather than "converting" or changing to a new religion. Profound commented that reverting is "going back to our original roots. Being Muslim is going back to where we all naturally belong" (Profound, interview). This idea of naturalness is important to unpack because it supports claims that Islam is not a foreign religion for Puerto Ricans, or anyone hailing from countries without a significant Muslim population for that matter, but is a religion they can authentically participate in and use as a guideline to life. Through a process of self-education via personal research in an effort to learn more about Puerto Rico, and Islam, Cotto found that his "raíces de verdad" (true roots) lie in Islam. This came with the discovery that in some way or another, Islam was already a part of his life before he was ever aware of it. He noted that Islam was part of his ancestry in Africa; in Andaluz, Spain; and perhaps even among the Taíno peoples of Borikén, the island that would later come to be known as Puerto Rico.[3] His statement affirms that Puerto Ricans can indeed claim Islam as their religion of choice. It is a challenge to anyone who questions whether a Puerto Rican can truly be Muslim. This questioning of authenticity has, unfortunately, been an issue for most of my interlocutors (including others I spoke with who are not involved in Hip Hop culture), who have heard that their culture prevents them from being "good" or "true" Muslims. This assessment came from other Puerto Ricans as well as individuals from countries where the majority of the population is Muslim.

This concept of "reverting" complements the idea presented to me by my interlocutors of "going back" when they discussed how they approach Hip Hop culture and music. Similar to how they feel they are going back to their original religion, I would argue that they also strive to return to what is referred to as "old-school" Hip Hop, avoiding the commercial and materialistic aspects that a significant number of mainstream and even underground Hip Hop artists have taken on today. To quote Profound, "When Hip Hop started it was revolutionary, it was talking about getting kids off the streets. It was talking about protecting yourself by all means and not letting people abuse you, and now it's bringing kids into the streets. Now it's bringing all kinds of negativity into our children's minds and that's what I'm against. I'm against that; I'm with the Hip Hop that started, the old-school" (Profound, interview). My interlocutors want to "go back" to the religion that is truly theirs, and to the Hip Hop culture that flourished in its early days. Part of this nostalgia has to do with how knowledge of one's history seems to be so crucial to identity formation.

The concept that the "original" or "pure" form of music or culture is the most authentic is not recent. This notion of going back to the "real" is central to Bigenho's analysis of how Bolivian musicians attempt to perform authenticity by striving for what is considered a "pure form" of the music (Bigenho 2002). Askew (2002) also focuses on how authenticity is constructed in relationship to what performers and audiences consider to be the most pure or static examples of their musical cultures. In these and other works, "purity" is a social construct for advancing claims to cultural authenticity and the various political projects that go with this (local, national, global). My Puerto Rican interlocutors' claims of "purity" are more related to the lyrical content of their work as well as to the cultural, societal, and political roles of Hip Hop, which are more easily defined and located. In this way, they have something more concrete to strive to "go back" to.

Imagined Communities/Ummahs/Nations

My interlocutors engage in the construction, assertion, and negotiation of the multidimensional expressions of being Puerto Rican, Muslim, and a Hip Hop artist. Part of this exploration of identity construction is concerned with how they see themselves within the context of the larger Latino and Caribbean communities, the Hip Hop nation, and the Muslim ummah. For the purpose of conceiving membership to these multiple communities, it is useful to view them as forming an "imagined community" (Anderson 1983). Benedict Anderson defines certain communities as "imagined" because all members will never know each other yet feel a bond over a shared group identity. They are a community because "the nation is always conceived as a deep, horizontal comradeship" despite the inequality and oppression that exists within it (Anderson 1983: 6–7). It is also important to acknowledge that the imagined community is imagined as limited because it does not encompass everyone worldwide (Anderson 1983: 7).

Anderson credits print capitalism as being the means in which a community can be imagined and can serve as a source of national consciousness and nationalism. Standard print language allows speakers of different vernaculars to have a shared language. Also, the circulation of novels and newspapers causes individuals to recognize other, unknown members as part of the same community. Together, these factors "created the possibility of a new form of imagined community" (Anderson 1983: 46). Anderson argues that a shared sacred text and language explain the imagined Islamic community, and his discussion of nationalism is relevant to the creation of an imagined Puerto Rican community. I believe it is media capitalism, instead of print, that fostered the imagining and development of a larger Hip Hop nation. It is imagined through shared visual and audio media (which, it could be argued, constitute a technologically more modern form of print capitalism). Tricia Rose (1994) examines how Hip Hop became a means for American youth to create for themselves "alternative local identities" usually attached to a group or "crew" and, I would add, eventually to the Hip Hop nation (Rose 1994: 34). When Samy Alim refers to the "transglobal hip hop umma" he is discussing a type of imagined community where membership is based on faith and culture instead of national borders (Alim 2005: 265).

Thomas Solomon focuses on how Turkish rappers are imagining their own personal identities using Islam and Hip Hop (Solomon 2011). It is this sense of "imagined" that allows my interlocutors to create an identity and therefore a community for themselves within which this identity fits. By imagining new identities and communities, they are contesting the identities and communities to which they have stereotypically been relegated.

The Islamic History of the Island of Borikén

While conducting my interviews, I gathered that my interlocutors had amassed a collection of narratives tracing Islam in Puerto Rico (or more accurately in Borikén, its original Taíno name) back to their African, Taíno, and/or Spanish ancestry. Multiple times during our conversations these accounts were raised in order to demonstrate the fundamental connections Puerto Ricans have historically had with Islam and Muslims. The actual history is not critical; the fundamental takeaway is that these histories are discursively used to support an ideology of the indigeneity of Islam in Puerto Rico and consequently the authentication of their identities as Boricuas (inhabitants of Borikén, a term still used today) who are Muslim. Since this information is often utilized in expressing Puerto Rican identity as a Muslim, we need to look at how Spanish colonizers, indigenous Taínos, and enslaved Africans have been tied to Islam in the New World.

On more than one occasion I was informed of the possibility that Muslims had had contact with the Caribbean well before Columbus set out on his voyages. I decided to explore this further and came across the work of Dr. Abdullah Hakim Quick. Quick provides a detailed examination of multiple sources supporting theories that Muslim explorers from Africa and the Middle East traveled across the Atlantic hundreds of years before European explorers and encountered the indigenous populations of what would later be regarded as the New World (Quick 1996).

Karoline P. Cook's dissertation research focuses on "Moriscos or Iberian Muslims" who were able to bypass unenforced Spanish laws prohibiting them from crossing the Atlantic to the Spanish Americas (Cook 2008: iii). She examines "approximately one hundred cases of individuals brought before the secular, ecclesiastical and inquisitorial courts during the sixteenth and seventeenth centuries, who were accused of practicing Islam or of being descendants of Muslims" (Cook 2008: 5).

The settlement of the New World also brought enslaved Muslims to Puerto Rico and the Spanish Americas. The numerous slaves of Iberia who spoke Spanish and had supposedly converted to Christianity (although Gomez argues that they were actually "undercover Muslims") were known as *ladinos* (Gomez 2005: 12). Of the ladinos, some were Arab or Berber and Muslim, while others were Hispanicized blacks who spoke Spanish and underwent a usually surface-deep conversion to Christianity (Rout 2003: xv). *Bozales* were slaves "brought directly to the New World from Africa and, therefore, neither Christianized nor Spanish speaking" (Rout 2003: xiv). Of the bozales, three ethnic groups are recognized as being almost entirely Muslim: the Jelofe/Gelofe/Wolof, the Mandingo/a, and the Fula/Fulani (Ortiz García 2006: 66–128). Puerto Rico's slave population included members from each of these groups. Throughout the sixteenth century the Spanish Crown consistently issued and reissued royal decrees attempting to hinder slaves who were Muslim or had ties to Islam in any way from entering the Americas.[4] This course of action indicates that the transport of Muslim Africans across the Atlantic was not so easily impeded.

The prohibition of Islam coupled with African Muslims' severance from their home countries and communities resulted in a steady decline in the number of Muslims in the New World. The next notable Muslim communities came from nineteenth- and twentieth-century immigration from South Asia and the Middle East, notably Syria, Lebanon, and Palestine. Due to the lack of documentation of enslaved Muslims and of colonizers, it has occasionally been assumed that these recent migrants were the first to introduce Islam to the Caribbean.

Utilizing Hip Hop

In Islam there is a concept called *da'wah*, meaning "to make an invitation," an invitation to learn about the religion and the worship of God. For my interlocutors Hip Hop is a vehicle of da'wah. But Hip Hop also serves as a means to express their identity as Puerto Ricans. I listened to their music, and besides spreading the message of Islam, in their verses I found references to social, political, and historical figures important to the Puerto Rican and African American movements in the Americas, such as Malcolm X, Lolita Lebrón, Pedro Albizu Campos, and Fidel Castro, and one even offered listeners his scathing review of Christopher Columbus. They discussed issues of education, police brutality and jails, the commercialization of Hip Hop, poverty, and drug and alcohol abuse. They had rhymes about blackness and their identification with Africa.

I discovered that to them, the message was more important than the money. Each MC offers samples, if not full albums, of their music online for free. For Cotto, if someone does not have the means to buy his music, then they can download it: "Si tu no tienes los chavos, pues bájalo" (If you do not have the money, well, download it). The important thing for these artists is to get their voices and messages heard.

I have encountered other Puerto Rican Muslims who do not consider music, and Hip Hop especially, as appropriate forms of da'wah. They find that Hip Hop praises materialism, sexual promiscuity, violence, and substance abuse and is therefore an inappropriate way to spread the teachings of Islam. Much of their stereotyping about Hip Hop music comes from commercial Hip Hop. I found no such themes in the music produced by the MCs I interviewed. In fact, they made a conscious effort not to be associated with the commercial mainstream Hip Hop deemed inappropriate among members of different Muslim communities: "But I made that real clear to him [the sheikh], I told him I'm not doing no commercial Hip Hop, I'm not going to have naked ladies in my videos, and I'm not going to be talking about nonsense, you know money and cars and all that materialistic stuff because that's what I got into Islam to get away from. I'm trying to shoo the devil away, I'm not trying to bring him in here" (Profound, interview). For my interlocutors, Hip Hop is an excellent method for da'wah in contemporary times, connecting the global phenomena of mature Islamic movements with the relatively young Hip Hop one.

Previous scholarship has addressed the use of Hip Hop, as well as other popular global art forms, as an emerging framework valuable in expressing various ideas, ideologies, and identities among Muslims (and non-Muslims) globally, especially among those considered marginal to their societies. However, often when examining Hip Hop among non–African American communities, the concern is with the appropriation of Hip Hop as a tool to (re)construct or, to quote Solomon, "revalorize" an identity or identities frequently regarded as socially and/or politically subaltern and thus analogous with African American experiences in the United States.

Tony Mitchell argues that this appropriation of Hip Hop outside the United States has gradually changed. Now that Hip Hop has "taken root, hip-hop scenes have rapidly developed from an adoption to an adaptation of U.S. musical forms and idioms. This has involved an increasing syncretism and incorporation of local linguistic and musical features" (Mitchell 2001: 11). With addition of personal and cultural elements, Hip Hop becomes a tool that can be utilized to reconstruct identities.

My work, although in dialogue with this literature, does not deal with the appropriation of Hip Hop. It does not involve a recent incorporation of Puerto Rican elements, because these elements were already included during the birth and development of Hip Hop in the South Bronx. This work is about a population that has been erased from the Hip Hop core reclaiming Hip Hop as a historically relevant instrument for Puerto Ricans to use in order to communicate their situations and rework their identities. There is no appropriation when Hip Hop is already theirs.

Remixed Histories

Afrika Bambaataa, widely recognized as the godfather of Hip Hop, defined what are known as the four elements or pillars of Hip Hop: DJing, MCing, graffiti, and b-boy/b-girling (with knowledge as a fifth pillar). I offer a brief history of these pillars through the journey of Clive Campbell, a.k.a. "DJ Kool Herc," commonly referred to as the father of Hip Hop due to his significant role in its development. In 1967, three years after he came to New York City from Jamaica, Clive Campbell adopted the tag name "CLYDE AS KOOL" and became an aerosol artist, a graffiti tagger, leaving his mark throughout the boroughs (Chang 2005: 75). In the 1960s graffiti became a way to combat the very real situation of living in an impoverished community and an attempt to gain a sense of control by putting one's personal mark on public property (Hoch 2006: 351). "Graffiti was a way of scarring the face of public memory with the incisions of black and brown presence" (Dyson 2007: 74). That is to say, while African Americans and Caribbeans may have been relegated to the subaltern, hidden from mainstream awareness, they forcibly made their presence known on public walls, stores, trains, and anything else that served as a canvas for their art.

Clive Campbell began to get noticed for his physical frame and attitude, earning him the nickname "Hercules," which he fused with his tagging name to create "Kool Herc" when he began to DJ. The fundamental qualities of the DJing technique "can be attributed to the dub and sound-system traditions from Jamaica, dating back to the 1950s" that were brought to New York City by Jamaican immigrants in the early 1970s (Hoch 2006: 352). Enormous speakers allowed the DJ to move from house parties to the block outside, enabling larger crowds to collect. The DJ would alter the sound, rhythm, instrumental breaks, and speed of the song—usually a disco, funk, soul, or R&B track—through a process of "scratching, looping, bumping, and mixing live" (Hoch 2006: 352).[5]

While DJing, Kool Herc began to notice how the dancers would wait for a moment in the record, called "the break," the instrumental section of the song. It was during the "break" that the dancers unleashed their best and most intense, complicated moves. Using a new technique, "the Merry-Go-Round," in which he played two copies of the same record simultaneously, Kool Herc was able to keep the break of the song playing for an unlimited amount of time, creating the "break beat" (Chang 2005: 15). The break was highlighted in order to get people excited (or hyped) so that they would dance. The dancing associated with Hip Hop culture came about through the adoption and transformation of various dance movements from West Africa, Puerto Rico, Cuba, and the Dominican Republic, and *capoeira* from Brazil, into the martial arts movement that was already popular in New York City due to kung fu movies being all the rage (Hoch 2006: 352). The result was the creation of an innovative dance form with movements centered on the breaks in the music emphasized by the DJ. Kool Herc began to call the dancers break boys and break girls, which became shortened to b-boys and b-girls.

As the party scene became more and more competitive, DJs were becoming increasingly "focused on developing technological prowess at the turntable," getting the crowd hyped with the refrains, "Yes, yes, y'all! To the beat, y'all!" and "Wave your hands in the air, wave 'em like you just don't care!" (Miyakawa 2005: 1). This call and response responsibility soon fell upon the masters of ceremony, the MCs, who would rap over the music the DJ was playing. Rapping comes from the oral traditions of "Afro-Cuban rumba, Puerto Rican plena, southern blues, and Jamaican toasting," from black and Latino political poetry of the 1970s, and surprisingly, according to Danny Hoch, from the limericks used in New York City schools to help children read (Hoch 2006: 353).[6] However, the main ancestor of rap is thought to hail from West Africa, where rhyming to a beat has been employed by storytellers and oral historians (Higgins 2009: 18–19). Today the MC has become the most visible, popular, and commercial aspect of Hip Hop culture (Erskine 2003).

Danny Hoch explains that "hip-hop's aesthetics lie foremost in the social context" from which it sprang (Hoch 2006: 350). He makes it clear that Hip Hop was developed through the interactions between African American and Caribbean peoples that were possible due to the social and cultural dynamic of New York City in the 1960s and 1970s. The period leading to Hip Hop is also crucial to explore. The civil rights movement was yielding center stage to militant political groups, such as the Black Panthers and Young Lords. Drugs and gangs were becoming an epidemic, as were what Hoch refers to as "the devastating effects of Reaganomics." Hip Hop culture arose as a strategic means to combat the urban reality and express the frustration of oppression (Rose 1994: 99). Rose explains how the four elements of the Hip Hop aesthetic were a way of taking back control: aerosol artists claimed public property by tagging; b-boys and b-girls turned the corner into their own stage; DJs were able to transform outdoor public space into a "community center"; and MCs used the microphone literally to make their voices heard (Rose 1994: 22). All this coupled with African and Caribbean forms of expression and art brought to New York City by African diasporic people resulted in the development of the cultural movement that would later be known as Hip Hop. It could not have happened anywhere else, at any other time.

A large part of why it could not have happened anywhere else was the constant interaction between African Americans, Jamaicans, and Puerto Ricans that was prevalent in the South Bronx. Even so, some modern consumers of Hip Hop would insist that the genre is a strictly African American creation, ignoring the latter two groups, especially Puerto Ricans, who sometimes do not fit preconceived notions of blackness. "Much too often the participation and contributions of New York Puerto Ricans to hip hop have been downplayed and even completely ignored. And when their presence has been acknowledged, frequently it has been misinterpreted as a defection from Puerto Rican culture and identity, into the African American camp" (Rivera 2003: 1–2). But the role Puerto Ricans played in Hip Hop's development is substantial, and knowing this history has influenced how my interlocutors consider their own involvement in Hip Hop culture.

How Puerto Rican Is Hip Hop?

Many Puerto Rican Hip Hop practitioners would find offensive the idea that Puerto Ricans have "adopted" Hip Hop, since this term ignores their role in its origins. Puerto Ricans have been its original members, early contributors, innovative participants, co-creators, initiators, and architects. Building on Juan Flores's work, I am investigating Puerto Ricans in Hip Hop in order to "defy the sense of instant amnesia that engulfs popular expression once it is caught up in the logic of commercial representation" (Flores 1996: 87). As Hip Hop became increasingly popular and commercially successful, with African Americans being the most visible group in the commercial Hip Hop world, Puerto Ricans were pushed aside, and their role was quickly forgotten. Raquel Rivera explains that "hip hop is ahistorically taken to be an exclusively African American expressive culture," which serves to exclude not only Puerto Ricans but other Caribbean groups as well, such as Jamaicans, from the "hip hop core" (Rivera 2003: 4).

Flores asserts that Hip Hop was a "cultural space shared by Puerto Ricans and blacks," much as the South Bronx and New York City in general were a physical place shared by Puerto Ricans and African Americans (Flores 1996: 103). Hip Hop has been referred to as a "ghetto phenomenon" that arose amid intense poverty, lack of job availability, and inaccessibility of educational opportunities. African Americans, Puerto Ricans, and other Caribbeans were part of adjacent if not the same neighborhoods. Therefore it is not surprising that a youth movement such as Hip Hop would foster intense "cultural interaction and hybridization" among African Americans, Puerto Ricans, and other Caribbean groups (Rivera 2003: 31).

As time passed and Hip Hop became more commercialized and widespread in the 1980s and 1990s, "Hip Hop" and "rap" came to be regarded as interchangeable, downplaying the other three Hip Hop elements and highlighting the mostly African American–dominated MC category (Rivera 2003: 79, 185). Since African Americans were much more visible as the "owners" of Hip Hop, new members of the Hip Hop nation (the community of participants in Hip Hop culture and its connoisseurs, artists, fans, educators, and producers) were not aware of its Puerto Rican legacy. The commercialization of Hip Hop meant giving it a strictly African American persona—Puerto Ricans were not considered by distributors of Hip Hop music as "black enough" to fit into this construction and were thus labeled as "a potential commercial liability" (Rivera 2003: 83). To put it bluntly, Puerto Ricans just did not sell.

The 1980s also signify a period in Hip Hop when black nationalism, Pan-Africanism, Afrocentricity, and Islamic themes became the focus of a number of artists, such as Public Enemy and Brand Nubian. As a result, Puerto Rican presence became further removed from the Hip Hop center (del Barco 1996: 69). In order to combat the fading Latino presence in Hip Hop, cousins Ricardo Rodriguez (a.k.a. Puerto Rock) and Anthony Boston (a.k.a. MC KT, or Krazy Taíno) formed the Latin Empire, infusing Spanish into their lyrics and not hesitating to celebrate being Puerto Rican and proud, as if to challenge the African American stereotype associated with Hip Hop. That is part of the reason why they chose the Latin Empire as their name—it was meant to arouse the same amount of strength and pride as Afrika Bambaataa's Zulu Nation. The Latin Empire was created in order to resituate Puerto Ricans back into Hip Hop history and current discourse.

Despite the Latin Empire's efforts, Puerto Ricans were still being dismissed by those who considered Hip Hop to be a "black thing" and were being elided from Hip Hop narratives with recommendations that they stick to "their own" music. Those who continued to be involved as MCs, DJs, aerosol artists, and b-boy/b-girls were mockingly labeled as "Porto Rocks" and were castigated by African Americans as well as fellow Puerto Ricans for trying to be someone they were not and for partaking in a culture that was not really "theirs." This is in large part due to Puerto Ricans being more visible and apparent in graffiti and b-boying/b-girling than in MCing or DJing (Rivera 2003: 67). Since rap was equated with Hip Hop, Puerto Ricans were assumed not to be a part of it by those who so quickly forgot, or never even knew, the role played by Puerto Ricans in the birth of Hip Hop culture (Flores 1996: 89).

So What's More Puerto Rican?

What makes certain musical genres more "suited" for Puerto Ricans? Simple, it would seem: whatever is in Spanish, namely salsa and reggaeton. Salsa takes much influence from the Spanish-speaking Caribbean, notably Cuba, while Hip Hop challenges "the Hispanocentric and island-bound definitions of Puerto Rican culture," since it creates a direct link to African Americans and the non-Spanish Caribbean islands connecting Caribbean Latinos to blackness (Rivera 2003: 42). Salsa does not form these connections but serves to separate Latinos from black Americans due to its Spanish language medium. Reggaeton, unlike Hip Hop, is considered an art form in which Puerto Ricans can participate because the lyrics are mainly in Spanish. The Spanish language, in this case, is seen as a direct reference to Latino culture, thus reaffirming the ostensible authenticity of Puerto Rican rights to participate in reggaeton. This assumption presumes, however, that all Puerto Ricans speak Spanish, alluding to the role that language plays in identity formation, and ignores the significant number of U.S.-born Puerto Ricans who are much more proficient in English.

As a result, the Hip Hop in which Puerto Ricans might authentically participate was "Latin Hip Hop," as long as it fulfilled the ethnic Latin requirements: much use of the Spanish language, samplings of Latin music, and/or references to "Latino" topics of interest (Rivera 2003: 95). Also this genre could be adopted by any Spanish-speaking Latino group, further marginalizing Puerto Ricans from Hip Hop's origins, since they were thrown in with other Latino groups who had not been part of the growth of Hip Hop in New York City. A number of Puerto Rican Hip Hop artists were disturbed by this genre as it meant a further severance from their African American counterparts. Also significant is how Latin Hip Hop had the possibly to make a number of Puerto Ricans question their *latinidad* if they did not speak Spanish, did not like the music, or did not identify with the topics addressed in the songs. Why is it that Puerto Ricans had to rap in Spanish to gain Hip Hop authenticity (as legitimate, unquestioned producers of Hip Hop, not poor imitators), especially in a genre considered to be an offshoot of "real Hip Hop" music?

The Muslim "Gimmick" in Hip Hop?

During our interview Correa Cotto remembered a time when people thought some Hip Hop artists were claiming to be Muslim in order to sell more records (Cotto, interview). Apparently being Muslim was seen, at least by some, as "a gimmick" to gain authenticity in the Hip Hop world and a following. He went on to explain that a Muslim MC has been considered the norm by producers and consumers of Hip Hop and elicits no special response (Cotto, interview). A reaction such as this is to be expected, considering the number of Hip Hop artists who infuse their lyrics with Islamic themes despite not publicly identifying as Muslim themselves. For example, Bronx-born MC Fat Joe's song entitled "300 Brolic" from his album *The Elephant in the Room* contains the lyric, "Poor righteous teacher I'm featured on Final Call" (Fat Joe 2008). Here he makes references to the Nation of Islam and Five Percent Nation using the phrase "poor righteous teacher," which refers to the 5 percent of the human population meant to educate others about Islam, and mentioning the Nation of Islam's newsletter *Final Call*. The next verse, "*Asalaam alaikum* and, yes yes y'all" connects the greeting of peace used among Muslims with a popular phrase from Hip Hop's early days (Fat Joe 2008). In a freestyle performed by Peedi Crakk that was posted on youtube.com in 2007, he inserts a common phrase used by Muslims, "all praise to Allah," amid lines about material excess and sexual braggadocio (Peedi Crakk 2007). Why have Fat Joe and Peedi Crakk (both of partial Puerto Rican descent) inserted references to Muslims and Islam into their verses? It could be why others such as New York City–raised MCs Jay-Z and Nicki Minaj have done the same, or why non-Spanish-speaking rappers throw in a line or two in Spanish. Islam and Puerto Rican identity are no strangers to Hip Hop. Using *asalaam alaikum* or *arroz con pollo* in a verse does not diminish anyone's street credibility, the preservation of which is a must in the commercial Hip Hop world. If anything, Islamic references in Hip Hop songs offer awareness of the close relationship Hip Hop has had with Muslims. Dare I say that it demonstrates knowledge about this history, possibly offering MCs who utilize it a bit more credibility in the Hip Hop world for knowing their roots?

Five Elements, Five Pillars

The perceived relationship between Hip Hop and Islam is far from a new concept. Islamic principles and Muslim voices were present in Hip Hop early on, if not from Hip Hop's inception, which is probably why journalist Harry Allen credits Islam as being the "official religion" of Hip Hop. When he was Clive Campbell, DJ Kool Herc "found himself hanging out with young Five Percenters [members of the Nation of Gods and Earths], absorbing their slang and science" after coming to the Bronx from Kingston, Jamaica (Chang 2005: 72). Even when Kool Herc took his parties from the house to the block, and thus from a private space to a public space inhabited by and accessible to members of rival gangs, he remembers groups of Five Percenters keeping the peace and thus allowing for the party to continue and Hip Hop to grow (Miyakawa 2005: 21). Phrases common in Hip Hop discourse, such as "What up, G?," "word is bond," and "droppin' science," are actually based on Five Percenter vocabulary. The "G" in the first phrase refers not to "gangster" but to "God," and the latter two are based on Five Percenter beliefs (Miyakawa 2005: 41). Other scholars, including Juan Floyd-Thomas (2003) and Richard Brent Turner (2009) have also acknowledged and discussed how Islamic themes and Muslim members have been present in Hip Hop throughout its development.

This information requires us to complicate even further the notion that due to their status as global phenomena, Hip Hop and Islam are considered to be compatible. The global status they share encourages a number of individuals in Muslim communities to appropriate Hip Hop as a modern and attuned way to create and express a new identity within oppressive societies. "It is perhaps not surprising that the long-standing world religion Islam and the more recently global musical genre of rap have intersected in various ways" (Solomon 2011: 27). In this sense, this magnetism between the Hip Hop and Islam is not necessarily a natural convergence but one constructed by those who find themselves a part of both communities and notice the harmony between the two as global movements that serve to empower.

But it is crucial to recognize the parallels between Islam and Hip Hop that allowed early Hip Hop artists to consider Hip Hop a proper conduit for an Islamic message. Probably the most significant point is the correlation between how Islam and later Hip Hop were spread. Afrika Bambaataa demonstrates this affinity, stating, "Rap has always been here in history. They say when God talked to the prophets, he was rappin' to them" (Fricke and Ahearn 2002: 76). The rhythmic nature of Hip Hop has been likened to that in the Holy Quran. Alim discusses the connections between Hip Hop lyricism and the manner in which the Quran was revealed to the Prophet and how this message in turn was spread worldwide: "The very means by which the Quran was revealed to the Prophet—that is, orally and, in large part, through rhymed prose—exhibits parallels to the linguistic and literary mode of delivery found in hip hop lyrical production" (Alim 2005: 266). The importance of the rhythmic nature to how Islam was spread is reflected in how Hip Hop came to be a global movement. "Rap's poetic force, its rearticulation of African-American oral practices, and its narrative strategies are central to rap" (Rose 1994: 85).

Islam and Hip Hop provided for many individuals a means of recognizing, realizing, and combating the harsh urban reality of oppression, marginalization, and inequality (Rose 1994: 21). It came to be that Islam bestowed some youth in the Hip Hop community with strength to stand up to forms of discrimination and to combat stereotypes imposed upon them by "the dominant culture" (Turner 2009: 145). Islam and Hip Hop have long been in dialogue, and together can be used to bring attention to and potentially combat the situation in which many black Americans, Caribbeans, and other marginalized peoples worldwide have found themselves.

Islamic teachings were spread through Hip Hop culture, exposing fans and aficionados alike to Muslim beliefs and ideologies. "Arabic, Islamic, or quasi Islamic motifs increasingly thread the colorful fabric that is hip-hop, such that for many inner-city and suburban youth, rap videos and lyrics provide a regular and intimate exposure to Islam" (Aidi 2009b: 292). In fact, for many, it was through Hip Hop that they first learned about Islam. Jorge "PopMaster Fabel" Pabón, vice president of the Rock Steady Crew, who identifies as Muslim and Boricua, explained to me:[7] "My first exposure to Islamic terminology was through certain Hip Hop raps/rhymes and sayings. As a member of the Universal Zulu Nation since 1981–82, I was taught to greet our sisters and brothers with, 'peace ahki' for the brothers and 'peace malika' for our sisters. These are Arabic terms for brother and sister. The legendary Hip Hop pioneer, Afrika Bambaataa was one of the founders of Zulu Nation. He compiled various kinds of information and called them 'Infinity Lessons.' These lessons included excerpts from the teachings of Nation of Islam and other Islamicly derived sources" (Pabón, 2013). This was also the case for each of my interlocutors. Listening to Hip Hop music (Public Enemy especially) or participating in Hip Hop culture exposed them to Islamic themes and terminology before they even thought of becoming Muslim.

Hip Hop has been recognized by religious leaders and Hip Hop artists alike as a vehicle for MCs to spread knowledge through their lyrics about Islam—and any other religion, for that matter. In fact, David Muhammad explained to me how Hip Hop introduced him to Islam. "If Christianity has gospel, Islam has Hip Hop. Islam was evangelized by Hip Hop. And so, I'm being acculturated into Islam . . . and loving it" (Muhammad, interview). Cotto shared these sentiments, telling me how it was Hip Hop that brought him the message of Islam, "El Hip Hop me trajo este mensaje . . ." (Cotto, interview). This belief in the power of Hip Hop as a vehicle for education is also exhibited by historian Michael Eric Dyson, who claims that "Hip-hop artists in many instances are the preachers of their generation" (Dyson 2001: 202). The Quran has been hailed by Islamic scholars as an inimitable, beautifully composed message from God to the Prophet Muhammad. They have described it as having perfectly selected word choice and incredible arrangement, unable to be replicated by human endeavor. In other words, it is "a miracle." Hip Hop music, which also involves careful (though not miraculous) word selection, is considered an appropriate conduit of Islamic education due to its rhythmic nature. "Muslim hip hop artists were making new connections between hip hop lyrical production and the method and means by which Allah revealed the Quran to the Prophet" (Alim 2005: 266). Utilizing a rhyming scheme is the cornerstone of the MCs' work; they create a flow between the lyrics and incite memorization. Therefore Muslim Hip Hop practitioners are able to use Hip Hop to educate people about Islam through their lyrics and fulfill a role as teachers.

Muslims in Hip Hop, at least in the United States, have been in some way affiliated, by themselves or their peers, with three main groups: Sunni Muslims, the Nation of Islam, or the Nation of Gods and Earths (the Five Percenters). Regardless of religious group affiliation, many Muslim MCs are considered to be doing what is called "conscious rap," especially during the "golden age of Hip Hop" from 1987 to 1993 (Dyson 2007: 64). This genre of Hip Hop is often viewed as being the opposite of commercial, materialistic rap. "This recent manifestation of the black Muslim presence in hip-hop has been positioned and marketed as a bulwark against the more facile, materialistic, and thuggish elements that tend to make the current state of mainstream rap music" (Floyd-Thomas 2003: 64). This ties in well with the idea of "going back" discussed earlier, to a "purer" Hip Hop much like that which originated in the South Bronx. The influence of Islam on Hip Hop during its golden age is demonstrated by Profound's own journey. "Now ever since I became a Muslim, yes, it has affected me because it changed my topics, of course. I started rapping about nonsense and now I'm rapping about consciousness. Now I'm rapping with a purpose" (Profound, interview). "Conscious rap" was socially aware and involved protest of political, social, economic, and educational conditions. Michael Eric Dyson credits "conscious rappers with being able not only to raise awareness among the people but also to influence the masses to stand up against injustice, verifying the inspirational quality Hip Hop can possess" (Dyson 2007: 70, 86).

My interlocutors, along with many other Hip Hop artists who are Muslim, have found that every core aspect of Hip Hop is compatible with Islamic doctrine. This has allowed them to continue to be a member in both the Hip Hop and Muslim communities. "I rap. Rap is rhythm and poetry. Y que es El Koran? El Koran es una gran poesía." (And what is the Quran? The Quran is great poetry; Cotto, interview). My interlocutors have also explained the b-boy/b-girl aspect of Hip Hop as a form of movement completely appropriate within Islamic doctrine, since it focuses on the individual and recalls the different dance cultures praised by the Prophet Muhammad. "And graffiti, that's basically our version of calligraphy in the streets" (Perez, interview). The fitting relationship between Hip Hop and Islam was commented on by David Muhammad during my interview with him: "You know, MCing, b-boying, DJing, knowledge, graf [graffiti], those are elements that don't have to exist in a criminal environment but they can be tools of expression for positive outcomes.... It's a tool. Muslims should use it as a tool" (Muhammad, interview).

Conclusion

The methods individuals use to reimagine and redefine themselves and the communities to which they belong are endless. My research focused on a small group of people who used history to authenticate their membership in communities where their status has been challenged. But what methods are available to individuals who are attempting to participate in communities with which they lack a history of affiliation? Do they still consider themselves to be authentic, and if so, according to what criteria? In what ways do they need to reimagine themselves in order to belong?

The Puerto Rican Muslim Hip Hop artists with whom I became acquainted are paving the way to make room for more Puerto Rican identities that challenge narrow definitions of what it means to be Boricua. In re-creating their identities they are disputing the incorrect notion that their Puerto Rican identity is inherently connected to Christianity and "Spanish" music.

Along with this is the creation of a new Puerto Rican Muslim community. John Voll's work on Muslims in the Caribbean focuses on immigrants from South Asia and the Syrian-Lebanese Levant (although he does acknowledge Afro-Caribbean converts). Due to their immigrant status and participation in their respective diasporas, he argues that Muslims in the Caribbean define themselves by their communal identity and not their religious one, indicating that there is no way to identify a "Caribbean Muslim" identity (Voll 2002: 266). I agree that this would be a rather arduous and unfeasible task. However, my work with Puerto Rican reverts, I would argue, has demonstrated that there is still a possibility for multiple Caribbean Muslim identities as opposed to a singular one; they are being created at this very moment. My interlocutors are practicing what Perez refers to as the "Puerto Rican flavor" of Islam (Perez, interview). This supports Manger's assertion that there are in fact "many Islams," and they are defined by how different Muslim groups practice them (Manger 1999: 17). This is not to say that there is not a universal Islam shared by all Muslims or that the "many Islams" are in any way disconnected. For this reason, I do not consider the notion of "many Islams" to contest Alim's assertion that the Prophet's message did not call for "Islamic Iraq" or "Muslim Senegal" (Alim 2005: 265). I would argue that the multiple Islams are still connected with one another due to a shared faith, together comprising the Muslim imagined community. What the notion of "many Islams" does is present how Islamic religious doctrine is incorporated into everyday life by different Muslims, in a way connecting it with cultural practice. "'Religious' identities go together with other identities that make up a total inventory of identities in a specific place" (Manger 1999: 17). My interlocutors' work is a way of demonstrating that this religio-cultural synthesis does not change their culture, their religion, or their identities as Puerto Ricans. Including Muslim as a possible way to identify, and Hip Hop as a possible means of da'wah, creates more encompassing examples of what it means to be Boricua for them. By illustrating how Puerto Ricans have a significant history in both Hip Hop and Islam, my interlocutors are able to demonstrate that their involvement in either community is not a denial of their roots but a celebration of them.

Notes

1. Although I am diverging from the conventional spelling often found in the literature, I write "Hip Hop" instead of "hip-hop" because my interlocutors prefer to see it capitalized. Their reasoning is that Hip Hop is a culture and must be respected as such.

2. For a discussion on "many Islams" see Manger 1999.

3. Some of the men I interviewed informed me about Abu Bakr II, uncle of Mansa Musa (also known as Kan Kan Musa), the king of Mali from 1312 to 1337, who is said to have introduced Islam to the Taínos before Columbus ever set foot on the island.

4. For more detailed accounts concerning the royal decrees issued by the Spanish Crown to hinder Muslim slaves from entering the Americas see Diaz Soler 1974: 179, 204; Gomez 2005: 12–13, 16; Majid 2009: 68–69; and Rout 2003: 21–24.

5. *Scratching*—using the hand to move a vinyl record back and forth on the turntable; *looping*—repeating a section of the record.

6. *Rumba*—Afro-Cuban rhythms and dances; *plena*—folkloric music native to Puerto Rico; *toasting*—talking or chanting over a melody.

7. Rock Steady Crew is a b-boying crew that was founded in the Bronx in 1977.

References Cited

Aidi, Hisham D.
2009a Let Us Be Moors: Race, Islam, and "Connected Histories." In *Black Routes to Islam*, ed. Manning Marable and Hisham D. Aidi, 121–40. New York: Palgrave Macmillan.
2009b "Jihadis in the Hood: Race, Urban Islam, and the War on Terror." In *Black Routes to Islam*, ed. Manning Marable and Hisham D. Aidi, 283–98. New York: Palgrave Macmillan.
Alim, H. Samy
2005 "A New Research Agenda: Exploring the Transglobal Hip Hop Umma." In *Muslim Networks from Hajj to Hip Hop*, ed. Miriam Cooke and Bruce B. Lawrence, 264–74. Chapel Hill: University of North Carolina Press.
Anderson, Benedict
1983 *Imagined Communities*. New York: Verso.

Askew, Kelly
2002 *Performing the Nation: Swahili Music and Cultural Politics in Tanzania*. Chicago: University of Chicago Press.

Bigenho, Michelle
2002 *Sounding Indigenous: Authenticity in Bolivian Music Performance*. New York: Palgrave Macmillan.

Chang, Jeff
2005 *Can't Stop Won't Stop: A History of the Hip-Hop Generation*. New York: Picador—St. Martin's Press.
2006 "Introduction: Hip-Hop Arts: Our Expanding Universe." In *Total Chaos: The Art and Aesthetics of Hip-Hop*, ed. Jeff Chang, ix–xv. New York: Basic Civitas Books-Perseus Books Group.

Cook, Karoline P.
2008 "Forbidden Crossings: Morisco Emigration to Spanish America, 1492–1650." PhD diss., Princeton University.

Cotto, Correa
2010 Interview by author, tape recorded July 16.

del Barco, Mandalit
1996 "Rap's Latino Sabor." In *Droppin' Science: Critical Essays on Rap Music and Hip Hop Culture*, ed. William Eric Perkins, 63–84. Philadelphia: Temple University Press.

Diaz Soler, Luis M.
1974 *Historia de la Esclavitud Negra en Puerto Rico*. San Juan, Puerto Rico: Editorial Universitaria.

Dyson, Michael Eric
2001 *Holler If You Hear Me: In Search of Tupac Shakur*. New York: Basic Civitas Books.
2007 *Know What I Mean? Reflections on Hip Hop*. New York: Basic Civitas Books.

Erskine, Noel Leo
2003 "Rap, Reggae, and Religion: Sounds of Cultural Dissonance." In *Noise and Spirit: The Religious and Spiritual Sensibilities of Rap Music*, ed. Anthony B. Pinn, 71–84. New York: New York University Press.

Fat Joe
2008 "300 Brolic." On *The Elephant in the Room* (compact disc). Virgin Records America 509995 1461 9 2.

Flores, Juan
1994 "Puerto Rican and Proud, Boyee! Rap, Roots and Amnesia." In *Microphone Fiends: Youth Music Youth Culture*, ed. Andrew Ross and Tricia Rose, 89–98. New York: Routledge.
1996 "Puerto Rocks: New York Ricans Stake Their Claim." In *Droppin' Science: Critical Essays on Rap Music and Hip Hop Culture*, ed. William Eric Perkins, 85–114. Philadelphia: Temple University Press.
2000 *From Bomba to Hip-Hop: Puerto Rican Culture and Latino Identity*. New York: Columbia University Press.

Floyd-Thomas, Juan M.
2003 "A Jihad of Words: The Evolution of African American Islam and Contemporary Hip-Hop." In *Noise and Spirit: The Religious and Spiritual Sensibilities of Rap Music*, ed. Anthony B. Pinn, 49–70. New York: New York University Press.

Fricke, Jim, and Charlie Ahearn
2002 *Yes Yes Y'all: The Experience Music Project; Oral History of Hip-Hop's First Decade*. Cambridge, Mass.: Da Capo Press.
Galvan, Juan
2008 "Who Are Latino Muslims?" *Islamic Horizons* 37(4): 26–30.
Gomez, Michael A.
2005 *Black Crescent: The Experience and Legacy of African Muslims in the Americas*. New York: Cambridge University Press.
Haddad, Yvonne Yazbeck, and John L. Esposito
1998 *Muslims on the Americanization Path?* Atlanta: Scholars Press.
Herc, DJ Kool
2005 "Introduction." In *Can't Stop Won't Stop: A History of the Hip-Hop Generation*, ed. Jeff Chang, xi–xiii. New York: Picador-St. Martin's Press.
Higgins, Dalton
2009 *Groundwork Guides: Hip Hop World*. Toronto: Groundwood Books, House of Anansi Press.
Hoch, Danny
2006 "Toward a Hip-Hop Aesthetic: A Manifesto for the Hip-Hop Arts Movement." In *Total Chaos: The Art and Aesthetics of Hip-Hop*, ed. Jeff Chang, 349–64. New York: Basic Civitas Books-Perseus Books Group.
Majid, Anouar
2009 *We Are All Moors: Ending Centuries of Crusades against Muslims and Other Minorities*. Minneapolis: University of Minnesota Press.
Manger, Leif
1999 "Muslim Diversity: Local Islam in Global Contexts." In *Muslim Diversity: Local Islam in Global Contexts*, ed. Leif Manger, 1–36. Richmond, Surrey, UK: Curzon Press.
Martinez-Vazquez, Hjamil A.
2010 *Latina/o y Musulmán: The Construction of Latina/o Identity among Latina/o Muslims in the United States*. Eugene, Ore.: Pickwick Publications.
Mitchell, Tony
2001 Another Root: Hip-Hop Outside the USA. In *Global Noise: Rap and Hip-Hop Outside the USA*, ed. Tony Mitchell, 1–38. Middletown, Conn.: Wesleyan University Press.
Miyakawa, Felicia M.
2005 *Five Percenter Rap: God Hop's Music, Message, and Black Muslim Mission*. Bloomington: Indiana University Press.
Muhammad, David
2010 Telephone interview by author, tape recorded November 27.
Ortiz García, Angel L.
2006 *Afropuertorriqueño(a)*. Río Piedras, Puerto Rico: Editorial Edil.
Pabón, Jorge "Popmaster Fabel"
2013 E-mail message to author, February 24, 2013.
Peedi Crakk
2007 Peedi Crakk and Elliot Ness Freestyle. YouTube video, 5:03. Posted by "Rapremixer," December 3, 2007. http://www.youtube.com/watch?v=wbyVpGbFZdQ.

Perez, Hamza
2010 Interview by author, tape recorded August 28.
Profound
2008 "Jewels for the Youth." On *Lost and Found* (compact disc). Borislam Productions.
2010 Interview by author, tape recorded July 20.
Quick, Abdullah Hakim
1996 *Deeper Roots: Muslims in the Americas and the Caribbean from Before Columbus to the Present*. London: Ta-Ha Publishers.
Rivera, Raquel Z.
2003 *New York Ricans from the Hip Hop Zone*. New York: Palgrave MacMillan.
Rose, Tricia
1994 *Black Noise: Rap Music and Black Culture in Contemporary America*. Middletown, Conn.: Wesleyan University Press.
Rout, Leslie B., Jr.
2003 *The African Experience in Spanish America*. Princeton, N.J.: Markus Wiener Publishers.
Salloum, Jackie Reem, director
2009 *Slingshot Hip Hop*. (DVD). New York: Fresh Booza Production.
Smith, Jane I.
1999 *Islam in America*. New York: Columbia University Press.
Solomon, Thomas
2011 "Hardcore Muslims: Islamic Themes in Turkish Rap between Diaspora and Homeland." In *Muslim Rap, Halal Soaps, and Revolutionary Theater: Artistic Developments in the Muslim World*, ed. Karin Van Nieuwkerk, 27–54. Austin: University of Texas Press.
Turner, Richard Brent
2009 "Constructing Masculinity: Interactions between Islam and African American Youth Since C. Eric Lincoln's 'The Black Muslims in America.'" In *Black Routes to Islam*, ed. Manning Marable and Hisham D. Aidi, 141–54. New York: Palgrave Macmillan.
van Nieuwkerk, Karin
2011 "Artistic Developments in the Muslim Cultural Sphere: Ethics, Aesthetics, and the Performing Arts." In *Muslim Rap, Halal Soaps, and Revolutionary Theater: Artistic Developments in the Muslim World*, ed. Karin van Nieuwkerk, 1–24. Austin: University of Texas Press.
Viscidi, Lisa
2003 "Latino Muslims a Growing Presence in America." Washington Report on Middle East Affairs, June. http://wrmea.org/wrmea-archives/251-washington-report-archives-2000-2005/june-2003/4624-latino-muslims-a-growing-presence-in-america.html.
Voll, John O.
2002 "Muslims in the Caribbean: Ethnic Sojourners and Citizens." In *Muslim Minorities in the West: Visible and Invisible*, ed. Yvonne Yazbeck Haddad and Jane I. Smith, 265–77. Walnut Creek, Calif.: Altamira Press.

II

CIRCULATION OF IDENTITIES, POLITICS OF BELONGING

7

Between Terror and Transcendence

Global Narratives of Islam and the Political Scripts
of Guadeloupe's Indianité

YARIMAR BONILLA

The events of September 11, 2001, marked the onset of a new "war on terror" that has been fought on the terrain of the imagination as much as on the battlefield. One of the consequences of this post-9/11 era has been the emergence of a new iconography of terror that shapes contemporary constructions of difference and "otherness" (see Engle 2007; Mitchell 2010; Puar 2007). Although the United States is taken to be the ground zero of this new war, the ramifications of these events are global. In the Francophone world the age of terror has merged with the discursive formation of a falsified "Islamic Other" that is placed in opposition to the core universalist values of the French Republic (see El-Tayeb 2011; Fernando 2009; Geisser 2003; Scott 2007; Silverstein 2004; Todorov 2010). Meanwhile certain images (most notably those of women wearing the hijab) have become both targets and symbols of this iconographic war.[1]

In this essay I consider one instance of this iconographic battle as it reverberated in the French Overseas Department of Guadeloupe. I examine a cartoon that appeared in the context of my fieldwork in which a local labor activist of East Indian descent was compared to Osama Bin Laden, the principal symbol of the global terrorist cell Al Qaeda. In what follows I explore how a labor activist with no affiliation to the religious or political movements of Osama Bin Laden came to be configured in this way, given both global narratives of terror and the particular place of labor activists and East Indians in the Guadeloupean political imagination.

Finding Osama in Guadeloupe

On October 24, 2004, Michel Madassamy, a well-known labor activist in Guadeloupe, was suddenly and dramatically arrested in a spectacular deployment of police force. Specialized police officers from France's elite counterterrorism unit, the Groupe d'Intervention de la Gendarmerie Nationale, were flown into the island from mainland France in order to secure his arrest. Over a dozen of these special unit officers, heavily armed in full riot gear and sporting black ski masks under the hot tropical sun, seized Madassamy at the Place de la Victoire—where he had stopped on his way home from work to buy a snack from one of the small food trucks that surround the colonial plaza. The officers reportedly grabbed him from the plaza, cuffed him, covered his head, and threw him into the back of a police van. He was then transported to the penitentiary in Baie-Mahault to begin serving a ten-month jail sentence for the "degradation of private property" (a charge related to his involvement in the labor demonstrations described later in this chapter).

Although his sentence had been issued several months prior, the timing of his imprisonment came as a surprise to both Madassamy and his lawyers since legal appeals were still in the works. Further, as his supporters contended, the conditions of his arrest were at odds with the nature of the charges against him. The use of a counterterrorism special unit police force sent from mainland France was particularly contentious. As an Overseas Department of France, Guadeloupe has been fully integrated into the French Republic since 1946, and its territory falls under the jurisdiction of the French police and army. However, despite formal integration, significant tensions remain around issues of policing, surveillance, military, and judicial affairs. Given that most military officers, jurists, and prosecutors are white *metrós* (the local term for residents of continental France), their actions are commonly read through the historical legacies of colonialism and slavery, particularly the legacies of legal institutions such as the *code noir* (which legally codified the slave economy), post-emancipation vagrancy laws (which often forced emancipated slaves to return to their former plantations against their will), and the deployment of police force to curtail labor strikes and pro-independence movements in the past.

In 2004 these colonial legacies converged with the emerging narratives of the global war on terror, and the show of force used to arrest Michel Madassamy became the object of much commentary and critique. In the satirical newspaper *Le Mot Phrasé*, Madassamy's arrest was parodied as a kind of Guadeloupean version of the "capture" of the notorious Osama Bin Laden.

Fig. 7.1. Cartoon depicting Madassamy's arrest and comparing him to Osama Bin Laden. From the newspaper *Le Mot Phrasé*.

The newspaper ran an editorial cartoon that depicted Madassamy wearing a union T-shirt (the standard "uniform" of Guadeloupean labor activists) being brought in to the central authorities by the heavily armed special unit police. In the drawing the police officers who executed the arrest are boasting about the fact that they captured him "ben" (presumably a play on *bien*, meaning that they "got him good," but also a reference to Osama *Bin* Laden) and that they had even beat the Americans to the punch. In the caption below the drawing Madassamy's name is rendered as Oussama Dassamy (again a play on Osama Bin Laden). The officer on the other side of the desk looks surprised, and the reader is left to speculate as to whether the counter-terrorist specialists had confused Madassamy for Bin Laden or simply felt their "catch" was equal in magnitude to the international man hunt that U.S. Special Forces were undertaking at the time.

This cartoon indexes how the figure of Osama Bin Laden circulates globally beyond areas directly involved in the U.S. war on terror. It also demonstrates how the deployment of imperial aggression—through the capture of an enemy of a state—is rallied as a positive signal of strength. Yet in order to unpack fully the political assemblages at work in this image, it is necessary to understand the social and political context in which it was produced. First, we must examine why and how a labor activist could be compared to an "enemy of the state." This requires an understanding of the role of labor unions in Guadeloupe and the place they occupy in the political imagination. In recent years labor activists (and in particular the UGTG union, of which Madassamy was a member) have emerged as important political actors in Guadeloupe, often held as symbols of the island's social and economic problems and lingering postcolonial relationships.[2] They have also become targets of legal intervention, facing numerous arrests and hefty fines for their actions. However, I would like to suggest that what led to this conflation of Madassamy with Osama Bin Laden was not just the fact that he was a member of the UGTG union but also the fact that he was an *Indien* (East Indian/South Asian).[3] Thus an examination of this image also requires an understanding of local politics of Indianité and of the ways in which Indo-Guadeloupean populations are represented through both local and globally circulating scripts of ethnic difference and political alterity.

The Boiling Pot Island

Guadeloupe's integration into the French system allowed the early legalization of syndical associations in 1884, and the local population quickly embraced French syndical institutions, combining them with local traditions of mutual aid throughout the post-emancipation period (Sainton 1993: 5). However, near the end of the twentieth century labor activism took a new turn as it became the site for a reinvigorated anti-colonial movement. In the early 1970s, as the "national liberation" model of the Cuban and Algerian revolutions lost favor, Guadeloupean anti-colonial militants found themselves reconceptualizing their movement as a workers' movement (UPLG 1983; Théodore 1991). These efforts eventually led to the creation of the Union des Travailleurs Agricoles (UTA, Union of Agricultural Workers) in 1970 and the Union des Paysans Pauvres de la Guadeloupe (UPG, Union of Impoverished Guadeloupean Peasants) in 1972. In 1973 the two merged into the Union Générale des Travailleurs de la Guadeloupe (UGTG, General Union of Guadeloupean Workers), which is at present the largest labor union in the French Antilles.

The move from an anti-colonial model of armed struggle to an emphasis on labor activism was not exclusive to Guadeloupe. Throughout the former French colonies (in Martinique, French Guyana, New Caledonia, Corsica, and Réunion) similar forms of postcolonial syndicalism developed that combined the tactical and ideological legacies of nationalist and anti-colonial struggles with the institutional strength of the French syndicalist tradition (see Andolfatto 2004). These movements were aided by the political climate of the Mitterrand government in France (1981–95) and its decentralization policies, which created fertile ground for social struggle. During the late 1990s and early 2000s, at a time when collective bargaining was thought to be on the wane throughout most of the industrial world, this new labor movement experienced a significant boom. By 2003 union density in Guadeloupe reached an all-time high of 18 percent—compared with 8 percent in mainland France (*France Antilles* 2003). The first decade of the new millennium saw an even greater expansion of labor activism as unions forged new alliances with other social, cultural, civic, and political actors, leading to a historic forty-four-day general strike that paralyzed the entire society in the early months of 2009 with as many as 100,000 people (25 percent of the population) participating in massive rallies (see Bonilla 2010).

Although labor has become an important rallying point throughout the overseas French territories, Guadeloupe is often cited as an especially contentious context. In 2002 the French magazine *L'Express* labeled Guadeloupe "l'île-chaudron" (the boiling pot island), and the French travel guide *Le Guide de Routard* warned tourists of radical labor activists endemic to the island (Perduran 2002). Within these narratives the enemy that looms large is the Union Générale des Travailleurs de la Guadeloupe.

The UGTG is the largest labor union in Guadeloupe, with more than six thousand members, and is responsible for over 70 percent of labor protests on the island (Direction du Travail 2002). The UGTG is also the only independent labor union—both in the sense that it is the sole labor union in Guadeloupe that is not a chapter of a French national union and also in the sense that it is the only labor union that favors Guadeloupe's political independence from France. Both of these distinctions are evident in the general tenor of UGTG practice, which is characterized by an emphasis on local cultural forms, including the use of Creole in public meetings and official negotiations, the presence of traditional *gwo ka* music at rallies and picket lines, and the emphasis placed on Guadeloupean history, particularly the history of slave revolts and the cultivation of what union leaders describe as the *esprit du neg mawón*, or the rebellious spirit of maroons (see Bonilla 2011).

In fact, Michel Madassamy's notoriety was initially rooted in his participation in the union's events to commemorate the abolition of slavery. In 1983 the French government, under François Mitterrand, designated May 27 as a commemorative holiday in Guadeloupe. However, despite being designated as a *jour férié*, Abolition Day was not recognized as a *jour chômée*, which meant that many private businesses and commercial venues continued to keep their doors open despite the holiday. In previous years, the UGTG had organized small marches and demonstrations on Abolition Day, but in 2001 they decided to escalate their initiatives—motivated in part by the passing of a new law in France (ratified on May 10, 2001) that designated slavery a crime against humanity. Thus in May 2001 UGTG members decided to shift from their usual symbolic demonstrations and declared a general strike. In particular, they demanded that local shop owners, whom they characterized as the *petit-fils* (grandchildren) of former slaveholders, release their workers, *fils d'esclaves* (sons of slaves) on this important day of remembrance, in order to "respect the memory of the 'freedom fighters' and the blood shed by the millions of victims of slavery, recently recognized by the French state as a crime against humanity." The demonstrations were focused around the commercial sector because, as one activist explained to me, "What was slavery if not the commerce of humanity?"

During the demonstrations on May 27, 2001, when union members marched through the streets of Pointe-à-Pitre demanding that employers release their workers, a violent confrontation ensued. Demonstrators vandalized several businesses, overturning shelves, smashing cash registers, and shattering store windows. Later, after union members returned to their headquarters, young residents from the surrounding neighborhoods followed in their wake, looting stores, vandalizing public property, destroying public phones, setting fire to trash dumpsters and parked cars, and firing shots into the air throughout the night in what the French newspaper *Le Monde* described as an "environment of civil war" (Nedeljkovic 2001).

Although numerous demonstrators were involved in the events, shop owners singled out Michel Madassamy as the main perpetrator, arguing that he was the only *tête* (head) they had recognized. At the time many speculated as to why an Indien would be involved in the commemoration of slavery, as this history is often imagined to be the exclusive property of Afro-Guadeloupeans. Further, the relationship of Indian communities to the commemoration of slavery is fraught, given how their history is entwined with the contested legacies of emancipation.

Liberté, Egalité, Indianité

Indians were brought to Guadeloupe as indentured laborers following France's final abolition of slavery in 1848. From 1854 to 1885 an estimated 45,000 Indian workers arrived in Guadeloupe (Schnepel 2004: 45). Initially these workers were recruited from French territories, particularly Pondichéry, Mahé, and Karaikal. However, when local planters deemed that a larger labor supply was needed, the French government petitioned England for permission to recruit workers from British territories in India. This arrangement was formalized in the Treaty of Paris signed on July 11, 1860.

Local planters who favored the recruitment of Indian workers often depicted them as the saviors of the sugar industry, arguing that they would allow sugar cultivation to survive the "labor crisis" of emancipation. Others, particularly the mulatto political elites and merchants, saw the use of contract labor as oppositional to a free economy and to the creation of improved work conditions for the newly emancipated slaves. The newly arrived Indian workers were often deployed by managers to break up strikes organized by Afro-Guadeloupean workers and were thus often seen as "scabs" (Adélaïde-Merlande 2000). As a result, labor unions at the time strongly opposed their recruitment (Sainton 1993).

As Munasinghe (2009) and others (Brereton 1981; Singh 1994; Wood 1968) have argued for the case of Trinidad, the narratives deployed by planters to justify the need for Indian labor tended to emphasize the differences between Indians and blacks, casting Indians as a "solution" to the "problem" of black labor (Munasinghe 2009: 174). In the case of the French Antilles, the cultural and linguistic differences between Indian and black workers were foregrounded as safeguards that would deter Indian laborers from finding common cause with Afro-Guadeloupean workers. For example, an opinion piece from 1855 in the newspaper *Moniteur de la Martinique* extolled the merits of Indian migration by stressing their outsider status:

> Overall we declare that Indian migration is the best.... The Indian is an element that can in no way be the object of fear. They will only ever arrive in Martinique as agricultural workers, they will be nothing outside of work, they will remain neutral even as their circle expands. Mutiny on the plantations or strikes will not be able to count on them. Outsiders to all, they are precious for all. Can we say the same of other immigrants? (cited in L'Étang 2000: 10)

The "other immigrants" referred to are Congolese workers, who were also brought early on as a supplementary labor force but were said to have integrated quickly into the population and to have participated in numerous labor uprisings. In contrast to the Congolese, who were figured as culturally and racially too similar to the local population, Indians were imagined as sufficiently distinct to avoid feelings of solidarity with the newly emancipated slaves. Their perceived difference was imagined to assure their "neutrality" to the point where they were granted no identity outside of work. As L'Étang suggests, the world *coolie* itself became metonymic with work, and the coolie was fashioned into a quasi-object: "he who works but does not speak" (L'Étang 2000: 16). As I discuss later, this trope of the Indian as a silent and "neutral" (or empty) symbol continues to shape contemporary understandings of the Indian population in the contemporary Antilles.

At present Guadeloupe has the fourth largest Indian community in the Caribbean, with nearly 50,000 residents of East Indian descent within a population of 420,000. In comparison to parts of the English-speaking Caribbean, where Indo- and Afro-Caribbean relationships have been characterized by histories of violence and antagonistic struggle over political power, the French Caribbean is thought to have more harmonious ethnic relationships. Some scholars have attributed this presumed harmony to the fact that the Indian community in the French Antilles is relatively small, it has integrated significantly in terms of outgroup marriages, and Indians have achieved substantial socioeconomic advancement within agriculture, industry, commerce, and public service (Schnepel 2004: 46).[4]

Others have suggested that Guadeloupe's lack of political independence eliminates disputes over who should inherit the reins of power from the colonizer (Outar 2013). Further, French principles of universalism, in which shared French civic identity assumes precedence over racial, ethnic, or cultural difference, and particularly the tenets of *laïcité*, which restrict religion to the private sphere, are also thought to have had a profound impact on Indian identity—transforming Hinduism into a cultural and civic practice (rather than a religious or political identity) that is easily celebrated as part of France's multicultural heritage (see Martín-i-Pardo 2011).[5] Last, it is worth mentioning that within the literary canon Indians have been celebrated as essential to the multicultural creole culture of the Antilles. In the *Éloge de la Créolité*— a literary manifesto, "In Praise of Creoleness," written by celebrated authors Jean Bernabé, Patrick Chamoiseau, and Raphaël Confiant—the Indian legacy is heralded as essential to the formation of Creole identity and part of what distinguishes a multicultural *créolité"* from a mulatto society (Bernabé et al. 1989).

Yet, aside from the celebration of Indianité in the *creoliste* texts, the figure of the Indian has for the most part been absent from public representations in the French Antilles. As Curtius (2010) argues, Indians in both Martinique and Guadeloupe alike have held a "silent" place in Antillean society. For example, important historic dates for the Indo-Guadeloupean population, such as the extension of French citizenship and voting rights to Indian immigrants and their descendants in 1923, do not enjoy public commemoration (Sahaï 2010: 139). In recent years activists within the Indo-Guadeloupean community have sought to counter these official silences—influenced in part by the broader turn toward historical politics that fueled the increased commemorations of slavery and the passage of the law designating it as a crime against humanity in 2001 (known as the Loi Taubira in honor of its author, Guyanese parliamentary deputy Christiane Taubira). This emphasis on the past, which has been described as a "memory boom" (Giraud 2004), was fueled in part by the critical dialogues that emerged around the Columbus Quincentennial in 1992, the commemoration of the 150th anniversary of France's abolition of slavery in 1998, and the bicentennial of the Haitian Revolution in 2004. During this time the idea of a *devoir de memoire,* a duty of memory, began to take hold in the Antilles, with numerous organizations addressing what were said to be previously silenced or obscured historical events (see Bonilla 2011).

Within the Indo-Guadeloupean community, this historical turn led to the formation of new traditions of commemoration focused around the theme of "Indian Arrival." The emphasis on arrival is due in part to the fact that given the historical entwinement of abolition and indenture, the 150th anniversary of abolition was quickly followed by the sesquicentennial of the beginning of Indian migration. However, the trope of arrival also speaks to the fact that Indo-Caribbean communities continue to be associated with discourses of movement and migration in ways that set them apart from the majority society (Khan 1997).

For its proponents, the celebration of Arrival Day was a way of recasting the arrival of indentured laborers as a positive event, in order to challenge the view of Indian workers as detrimental to the labor conditions of the Afro-Guadeloupean population. However, as celebratory commemorations of all kinds tend to do, both Indian Arrival and Abolition observances smoothed over the complex contradictions and painful realities of ethnic relations in Guadeloupe, abstracting instead a broadly positive message of triumph, settlement, and progress.⁶ Thus, much like celebrations of Abolition that focus on the eradication of slavery rather than on its lived experience, the celebration of Indian Arrival failed to address the lived reality of Indian communities in the Caribbean or their integration into the broader fabric of Guadeloupean society.

The monuments that were erected in celebration of the Indo-Guadeloupean presence during this period did not focus on local figures and communities but on abstract themes such as "arrival" and on global icons of Indian political subjectivity and identity, such as Mahatma Gandhi. In Guadeloupe a statue of Gandhi was placed in St. Francois, one of the towns with a highly visible Indian population.⁷ In Martinique, a bust of Gandhi was placed in a neighborhood that was populated in the 1940s by the descendants of indentured workers (see Curtius 2008, 2010). Both these monuments arrived as gifts from the Indian government, which in recent years has sought to create stronger ties to diasporic South Asian communities throughout the Americas.⁸ In addition to the Gandhi statues, a monument was also erected to commemorate the ship *Aurelie*, on which the first Indian immigrants were said to have arrived. The monument was made not by a local sculptor but by an Indian-born sculptor currently residing in France, Indrajeet Sahadev.

The emphasis on universal themes, foreign objects, and international icons of Indian identity speaks to the constraints placed on Indo-Guadeloupean identity in the context of French universalism, which stipulates that racial, ethnic, and religious allegiances must all take a back seat to a shared French nationality. This results in ambiguous and vacuous definitions of Indianité. For example, during an interview held on the occasion of the Arrival Day commemorations, Ernest Moutoussamy, the mayor of St. Francois and one of the most prominent figures of the Indo-Guadeloupean community, stated:

> "*Indianité* is not a philosophy, or an ideology. *Indianité* is a cultural fact, a historical fact: the Indian presence. I am of Indian origin physically, but I have no Indian practices. I don't play the music, I don't dance, I don't have the language, I don't have the cult, thus I am an Indian without Indianity." (Moutoussamy 2005)

Moutoussamy argues that he is an Indian without Indianity because he does not engage in cultural practices that can be traced back to the Indian subcontinent. In his comments he goes on to praise those Indo-Guadeloupeans who, unlike himself, did retain cultural practices from India, particularly culinary, musical, and religious practices. His words suggest that the true marks of an Indo-Guadeloupean identity are not locally specific—they are rooted in the Indian subcontinent. In fact, when asked what the difference is between Indians from Guadeloupe and Indians from India he deflects by contrasting Indo- and Afro-Guadeloupeans, suggesting that Afro-Guadeloupeans lost many of their African-based traditions due to the cultural stripping process of slavery, while Indo-Guadeloupeans managed to retain their original practices. Afro-Caribbean populations are thus imagined as "culture creators," while Indo-Caribbean populations are imagined as "culture bearers" (Munasinghe 1997). However, for someone like Moutoussamy—who does not see himself as having retained any Indian cultural traits—Indianity is reduced to physicality, an image stripped of content.

In what follows I examine how these constructions of Indianité came to the surface during the "Madassamy Affair." I argue that the way in which labor activists rallied around Madassamy's image during his solidarity campaign speaks to the place of Indians in Guadeloupe and to how these communities must navigate both local and international scripts of difference and alterity.

Who Is Michel Madassamy?

Looking back on Madassamy's arrest, Max, one of the union's principal leaders, explained that Madassamy was imprisoned not for what he did but for what he symbolized: "Any other militant would have received a suspended sentence, or community service . . . but he was arrested for what he represented, for his persona, and for the defiance that the union expresses through its personalities." As Max suggests, the "personalities" of the union are as important as the acts they commit, and Madassamy represented a very particular figure, partly because of the struggles he had been involved in but also because of his image—which over the years had become in and of itself an important icon of labor activism.

Madassamy was one of the founding members of the Union des Travailleurs des Produits Pétroliers—the UGTG subsidiary union for workers in the gasoline industry—created in 1994. He was initially the treasurer of the union but soon became its general secretary. As the head of the union he fought to establish a union contract for both gas station workers and truck drivers, in order to improve their working conditions, and to establish safety regulations for the transportation of hazardous materials. These syndical victories were won through multiple strikes involving hardline tactics that included acts of vandalism, the suspension of gasoline distribution, and the occupation of an oil refinery. During these struggles Madassamy emerged as a charismatic leader, but he also came to be known as a *"tête chaud"* (hothead) due to his involvement in some of the union's more aggressive actions. For example, in 2001, during stalled negotiations with the gas distribution company Société pour le Transport des Produits Pétroliers, the management hired replacement workers to ensure gasoline distribution during the strike. Madassamy was charged with "stealing" a gas tanker from one of the replacement workers. He seized the tanker and took it to the picket site, where it was held hostage until the end of the strike. In 2002 he was part of a large group of more than five hundred demonstrators who broke into the central oil refinery and distribution center in Guadeloupe, the Societé Anonyme de Raffinerie des Antilles. During a scuffle with gendarmes an oil valve was released (presumably by a demonstrator, though no one claimed responsibility), which led to a large gasoline spill and fueled rumors that the union had tried to blow up the entire island.

Along with these "hot-headed" syndical actions, Madassamy had also become widely known for his role in the 2001 battles over the commemoration of Abolition Day, as earlier discussed. Although numerous demonstrators were involved in the events, shop owners claimed Madassamy was the only *tête* (head) they had recognized. In the days following the demonstrations, the police held him without bail. Madassamy declared a hunger strike that in turn triggered a new wave of protests to demand his release, including a general strike among gas station workers that effectively shut down the entire system of gas distribution in Guadeloupe. During this time the UGTG union produced a series of documents with titles such as "Qui est Michel Madassamy?" (Who is Michel Madassamy?), "Vivre libre ou mourir" (Live free or die), and "Meurtre légal" (Legalized murder), in which they compared Madassamy to martyrs in Guadeloupe's past, most notably Louis Delgrès, who died during a protest against the reestablishment of slavery in 1802.[9] In press releases the UGTG accused the French state of sentencing Madassamy to death by refusing to release him.

After two weeks of candlelit vigils, public demonstrations, historical marches, and labor strikes, the government finally released Madassamy to await trial. His trial, held several months later, turned into a political circus. Union supporters filled the courtroom dressed in their Madassamy T-shirts, and when the judge called the court to order they responded with a revolutionary salute: simultaneously raising their left fists into the air.[10] When called to testify, union members spoke in Creole—forcing the court to secure a translator. During these proceedings the union called into question the authority of the courts and the rules of judicial procedure. While the prosecutors attempted to argue the facts of the case, union lawyers (who were noted figures in the anti-colonial movement) used the opportunity to decry the current colonial situation and the injustices of the legal system. In one of their statements the union described their defense lawyers as the "prosecutors of history," pleading a case against the injustices of the past.

In the end one of the charges against Madassamy was suspended, but he still received a three-month sentence for the degradation of private property. Despite this sentence the union declared his trial a victory and walked out of the courtroom triumphant, perhaps assuming that the sentence would never actually be enforced. The Madassamy Affair was thought to be behind them—that is, until Madassamy's sudden arrest in 2004.

This cluster of events—the demonstrations over Abolition Day, Madassamy's hunger strike and solidarity campaign, the gasoline strike, and his dramatic legal trial, which spanned May and June 2001—came to be known as (the original) Madassamy Affair, with his spectacular arrest in 2004 then constituting the sequel. The original Madassamy Affair was a watershed moment due to the diversity of symbolic elements it wove together: from the history of slavery and the politics of its memorialization to the rarely discussed role of Guadeloupe's Indian population, who are traditionally imagined as docile, weak, and lacking solidarity with Guadeloupe's black majority.

During this time Madassamy himself was consecrated as a multilayered symbol: an embodiment of the resistance, defiance, strength, and political success that the UGTG union represents in Guadeloupe. However, his construction as a charismatic figure hinged not on his "everyday man" persona but on his marked difference. He was not the embodiment of the average Guadeloupean common man but of the relatively uncommon Guadeloupean Indien.

During his solidarity campaign Madassamy's uncommon image took center stage. His picture was featured prominently in the union's press releases, and a series of union T-shirts was produced with a cropped picture of his face and long beard. At the rallies, press conferences, and demonstrations carried out in his name, his words or thoughts were rarely mentioned. His image, however, was ever present. Large poster boards with a cropped picture of his face hung behind protestors, were carried by demonstrators during protests, and were strewn about wherever union activities were being held, giving the impression that Madassamy was quietly observing the diverse events carried out in his name.

In discussing the case of Irish political prisoners' 1981 hunger strikes in the Maze prison, Allen Feldman argues that the mass production of iconographic photographs, paintings, and posters was part of the process of "sacralization" and "purification" through which hunger strikers were transformed from criminals into heroes and martyrs of the nation (Feldman 1991: 237). In the case of Madassamy, the mobilization of his static, lifeless image allowed him to be represented as a martyr, but it also served to transform his image from that of a person involved in acts of vandalism and sabotage to that of a person of conviction, principles, and political commitment. The image that circulated, with his long beard and serene stare, represented not a hotheaded activist but a serene and spiritual *Indien*. During this time he was often compared to Gandhi, and one of his lawyers (who was particularly prone to hyperbole) went so far as to call him the *fils de Gandhi* (son of Gandhi). On the one hand, the image of a nonviolent hunger protest served as a counterbalance to the otherwise hostile image of union struggle. At the same time, the connection rooted Madassamy in an ancestral homeland rather than in the local territory of Guadeloupe, thus representing him as a universal symbol of altruistic activism.

When I asked Max, one of the labor organizers centrally involved in Madassamy's solidarity campaign, what role Madassamy's ethnicity had played in the affair, Max argued that it had been "fundamental," particularly in regard to the Abolition Day demonstrations, "Because if he—who had not experienced slavery—was engaged, that gave the union another dimension—a more popular and general dimension. It became not a personal, particular struggle, but a political struggle."

In other words, Madassamy's Indianité served in part to detach him from the battle over the commemoration of slavery and to elevate that battle as a universal political struggle rather than an identitarian one. However, at the same time his particularity as an Indian was also key in his construction as a political icon. As Max explained, "The physical is very important in communication, in the diffusion of information. And in any case, he [Madassamy] has a very particular head [une tête particulière]."

As Max suggests, Madassamy's Indianité carried a deep communicative value, his "particular head" and his particular relationship to Guadeloupean history allowed him to become a polyvalent symbol of struggle and resistance, at once both particular and universal. The way in which he was represented during the solidarity campaign was deeply marked by this tension between his universality and particularity. For example, although he had written a letter "to his supporters" from prison, this letter was read only once, at one of the initial *mitins* (rallies) in the capital, Pointe-à-Pitre, and was not incorporated into the later rallies because, as Max explained, it was too general and universal.

The letter he wrote was very generic. What he wrote could have been written by anyone. 'I am in jail, I am on a hunger strike, I am writing to you. . . .' That has less appeal, less weight than what the flesh [*le chair*] can suggest. . . . Writing is limited, because you use words . . . which have particular connotations. . . . But here you have an individual who is invested in his person [*investi dans sa personne*]. There are no words for that.

Max further suggested, "From his image each person crafts their own critique and their own words, they each create their own story as well . . . each person creates their own narrative . . . that is the role of the imagination . . . of myth."

Madassamy's ambiguity thus allowed for him to be constructed as a multilayered symbol with which each person could identify in his or her own way. His image, disentangled from his own individual history and motivations, could thus circulate and give rise to further narratives. Through this process Madassamy was consecrated as a political symbol: a story to be told, a narrative to be created, and a script to be written—but not a voice to be heard.

In some ways this was not surprising, as Madassamy had always been a man of few words. Despite his seemingly charismatic persona he was not known for public statements. He never spoke at union rallies or press conferences, and throughout the initial Madassamy Affair he remained mostly silent, preferring to let the other union leaders speak on his behalf. When I asked him if he would grant me an interview, he declined, arguing that he wished to let his actions speak for themselves. At the time I was frustrated by his silence. However, I later came to appreciate how consistent it was with the silent role that he played in his own "affair."

Terror in the Streets

When Madassamy was originally imprisoned, the UGTG and its lawyers constructed a legal defense based on the "irregularities" of both his arrest and his incarceration, basically demanding that he be released on a technicality. However, as the days turned into weeks and Madassamy's hunger strike began to endanger his health, the union's legal team changed its strategy. Aided in part by a new legal consultant from Martinique, they began to rework Madassamy's case—dropping technical matters and recentering their efforts on a discourse of human rights. They reworked their claims and filed a motion for release based on article 720-1 of the French legal code, which states that the court can temporarily suspend the sentence of a prisoner requiring urgent medical care. The prosecutor responded by urging the court to ignore the claim, given that Madassamy's medical condition (starvation) was self-inflicted. He requested that the court dismiss the demands for release and order force-feeding instead.[11] As part of this new wave of legal proceedings, court-appointed doctors examined Madassamy and testified before the court that his health was indeed at risk, and that to end the hunger strike he would require medical assistance and a slow process of *"réanimation"* under the care of a specialized medical team.

For the prosecutor, the union's chaotic engagement with the legal system constituted a mockery of the legal order. He argued that their simultaneous and incompatible procedures, which included the use of hunger strikes, labor strikes, and public demonstrations in order to "pressure the court from the streets," represented an affront to the rule of law and order. With the political climate at peak intensity, the prefect called a press conference to condemn the union's tactics, particularly their "instrumentalization of the local youth," arguing that "in a legally constituted state, one can only contest a court decision through litigation." These comments echoed the usual allegations that the actions of labor activists constitute undemocratic acts of terror, bypassing legal channels by forcing change from the street.

On November 5, 2004, more than a month after Madassamy had begun his hunger strike, the sentencing court or Juge d'Application de Peines (JAP) was deliberating whether to release him for medical treatment. At the same time, a hearing was being held in the criminal courts concerning the original motion requesting Madassamy's release on the basis of legal technicalities. As both legal proceedings unfolded, union leaders and militants gathered in front of the union's headquarters for a demonstration. The turnout on this occasion was considerable; newspapers estimated 1,500–2,000 participants. It seemed clear that this would be the turning point in the Madassamy Affair.

The demonstrations began with a march from the union headquarters to the Centre Hospitalière Universitaire, where the JAP court was deliberating, and then moved toward Pointe-à-Pitre. The marchers were expected to head directly to the Palais de Justice, where Madassamy's lawyers were actively pleading his case. However, they instead detoured through the commercial streets of Pointe-à-Pitre, with both the press and the gendarmes anxiously following their path. Once again the energy was tense and confrontational, with what the press described as "virulent" slogans demanding Madassamy's release. In addition, marchers brandished a severed pig's head that was said to represent the centrally appointed prosecutor Patrick Vogt. It was the kind of pig head one could easily find at any butcher's market, but its presence struck a nerve with observers and police, and some viewed the act of marching with

Vogt's metonymic head on a stake through the streets of Pointe-à-Pitre as particularly aggressive.[12]

As demonstrators wove through Pointe-à-Pitre's commercial district with their virulent chants and impaled pig head, the prosecutor was stating his case against Madassamy at the courthouse. Several hours into the proceedings a faint noise began to penetrate into the courtroom. Soft but unmistakable, the sounds of the *ka* drums began to fill the air, and powerful chants began reverberating in the room: "Li-be-ré Ma-da! Li-be-ré Ma-da!" (Free Madassamy! Free Madassamy!). They eventually drowned out the lawyers' arguments, prompting the court to declare a recess.

Outside, the small plaza facing the courthouse was overflowing with union supporters and leaders who had set up a drumming circle near the court steps, where they were singing popular *gwo ka* protest songs accompanied by the sound of seashell horns. In the middle of the plaza, at the foot of a small statue to the nineteenth-century French admiral Jean-Baptiste-Marie-Augustin Gourbeyre, lay the controversial pig's head, which seemed to be quietly observing the developments.

The court reconvened after a short recess, but the session quickly came to an end. Rather than ruling on the Madassamy case, the court declared that another trial was needed to determine the competency of the court on the matter. However, at the same time the JAP court that had deliberated on Madassamy's medical state issued its ruling, stating that he should be released for two months in order to receive medical care. The only factor keeping Madassamy in jail at that point was the prosecutor, who could appeal the decision and drag out the affair. As the session drew to a close, the prosecutor exited the courtroom, never addressing or acknowledging the presence of the demonstrators or their pig head effigy. In the narrow hallway of the Palais de Justice he spoke to reporters and declared that he would not appeal the decision because he felt confident that the magistrates had reached a sound conclusion. He stated: "Magistrates don't rule to appease or to excite: they apply the law, nothing but the law, and all the law."

Once labor leaders received confirmation, they announced the decision to the crowd, which erupted into a loud roaring cheer. After a few statements on the part of the lawyers and leaders, they sang the union's revolutionary anthem and marched back to the union headquarters for an impromptu celebration, leaving behind at the foot of the statue the discarded pig's head, with a celebratory cigarette dangling from its mouth.

After sustaining his hunger strike for thirty-two days, Michel Madassamy was released into medical care. He slowly regained his strength and eventually made a full recovery. Since then he has appeared before the courts on multiple occasions. The charges against him were not dropped, but he has not been forced to serve his sentence. Due to his criminal record he lost his job as a truck driver, but with the help of the union he has started his own business: a small animal-feed store in his native town of Port-Louis. When I encountered him in 2007, three years after his hunger strike, he seemed at peace. His beard had grown and grayed, and although he still held a post in the union's Conseil Syndical, he had for the most part retreated from the public eye. I asked him once more if he would grant me an interview, but he simply smiled and walked away.

Conclusion: Navigating Terror and Transcendence

The episode known in Guadeloupe as the Madassamy Affair drew together a complicated and dense assemblage of both local and international scripts of political and cultural difference. On the one hand, it revealed the ways in which groups that pose challenges to the prevailing social order can be fashioned into antidemocratic "enemies" of the state through the deployment of globally circulating images of the war on terror. However, it also showed how these images function within a broader framework of counter-narratives. The result was an iconographic battle in which symbols of political terror were challenged by symbols of altruistic transcendence. In this case it appears as if Michel Madassamy was able to navigate these representations successfully to a somewhat felicitous outcome. Yet one can easily imagine how in other contexts the results could be more severe and worrisome. We thus need to think carefully about these politics of representation and the consequences of dissolving local histories and forms of difference into global tropes of terror that might not always be so readily transcended.

Notes

1. See Fernando (2009) on how symbolic battles over representation, such as those surrounding the headscarf ban, serve to shift focus away from the structural inequalities faced by these communities.

2. Similar tropes have been deployed in mainland France against immigrant workers from North Africa. In particular, during a strike at Renault/Citroën in the early 1980s anti-union campaigns in the media emphasized the threat that the "islamization" of syndicalism posed to the French principles of *laïcité* (secularism). For more, see Mouriaux and Wihtol (1987).

3. In the English-speaking Caribbean the term East Indian (as opposed to West Indian) is often used to refer to the descendants of indentured workers from India. In the French Antilles they are referred to simply as "Indiens."

4. The extent of their presumed integration should not be overstated here. Indian communities continue to be concentrated in certain geographic areas, they remain connected to the agriculture industry, and even their entrance into commerce is limited to certain sectors, particularly the construction industry and transport.

5. The constraints of French secularism have also placed significant limits on how the Indian community could rally around a shared religious identity, which as Aisha Khan (2004) and others have shown has been an essential element of Indian identity in the British Caribbean.

6. See Hesse (2002) for a similar argument about Abolition. For more on the politics of historical apologies see Trouillot (2000).

7. The visibility of St. Francois as a center of Indianité is due in large part to the role of local politician and poet Ernest Moutoussamy, who served as mayor of the commune from 1989 to 2008 and as a deputy for Guadeloupe in the French National Assembly from 1981 to 2002. Moutoussamy is also an accomplished poet, novelist, and essayist, who has written numerous works about the Indian presence in Guadeloupe; see, for example, Moutoussamy (1987, 2004).

8. See Rao (2011) on the iconicity of Gandhi's image (in statues and beyond) within India.

9. For more on the figure of Delgrès and the politics surrounding his memory see Dubois (2000).

10. For more details on the trial and the original Madassamy Affair see Crane (2002).

11. Ironically, the legal precedent for the force-feeding dated back to the French Algerian war, a fact that the union lawyers were quick to highlight at public meetings.

12. For a similar discussion of the "phenomenology of puppets" in direct action campaigns see Graeber (2007).

References Cited

Adélaïde-Merlande, Jacques
2000 *Les Origines du Mouvement Ouvrier en Martinique (1870–1900)*. Paris: Karthala.
Andolfatto, Dominique
2004 Le syndicalisme outre-mer et les tensions sociales. Les Etudes sociales et syndicales. Institut Supérieur du Travail. http://www.istravail.com/article219.html.
Bernabé, Jean, Patrick Chamoiseau, and Raphaël Confiant
1989 *Éloge de la Créolité*. Paris: Gallimard.
Bonilla, Yarimar
2010 "Guadeloupe Is Ours: The Prefigurative Politics of the Mass Strike in the French Antilles." *Interventions: International Journal of Postcolonial Studies* 12(1): 125–37.
2011 "The Past Is Made by Walking: Labor Activism and Historical Production in Postcolonial Guadeloupe." *Cultural Anthropology* 26(3): 313–39.

Brereton, Bridget
1981 *A History of Modern Trinidad, 1783–1962*. London: Heinemann.

Crane, Pascal
2002 "Des conflits sociaux nouveaux a la Guadeloupe: 'Les logiques d'action de l'UGTG en mouvement' (Etudes de cas: le conflit a la 'STTP' et l'affaire 'Madassamy Michel' autour du 27 mai 2001)." Diplôme d'études approfondies (DEA) no. 930393, Université des Antilles et de la Guyane.

Curtius, Anny Dominique
2008 "À fort-de-france les statues ne meurent pas." *International Journal of Francophone Studies* 11(1–2): 87–106.
2010 "Gandhi et au-béro, ou comment inscrire les traces d'une mémoire indienne dans une négritude martiniquaise." *L'Esprit Créateur* 50(2): 109–23.

Direction du Travail, de l'Emploi et de la Formation Professionnelle de la Guadeloupe (DTEFP)
2002 "Les Conflits Collectifs en 2002." DTEFP report.

Dubois, Laurent
2000 "Haunting Delgrès." *Radical History Review* 78: 166–77.

El-Tayeb, Fatima
2011 *European Others: Queering Ethnicity in Postnational Europe*. Minneapolis: University of Minnesota Press.

Engle, Karen
2007 "The Face of a Terrorist." *Cultural Studies—Critical Methodologies* 7(4): 397–424.

Feldman, Allen
1991 *Formations of Violence: The Narrative of the Body and Political Terror in Northern Ireland*. Chicago: University of Chicago Press.

Fernando, Mayanthi L.
2009 "Exceptional Citizens: Secular Muslim Women and the Politics of Difference in France." *Social Anthropology* 17(4): 379–92.

France Antilles
2003 "Le syndicalisme demure trés vivace." *France Antilles*, April 12, 2003.

Geisser, Vincent
2003 *La Nouvelle Islamophobie*. Paris: Découverte.

Giraud, Michel
2004 *Le passé comme blessure et le passé comme masque: La réparation de la traite négriére et de l'esclavage pour les peuples des départements français d'Outre-mer*. Cahiers D'Études Africaines XLIV (1–2), 173–74: 65–79.

Graeber, David
2007 *Possibilities: Essays on Hierarchy, Rebellion, and Desire*. Oakland, Calif.: AK Press.

Hesse, Barnor
2002 Forgotten Like a Bad Dream: Atlantic Slavery and the Ethics of Postcolonial Memory. In *Relocating Postcolonialism*, ed. David Theo Goldber and Ato Quayson, 143–73. London: Blackwell.

Khan, Aisha
1997 "Migration Narratives and Moral Imperatives: Local and Global in the Muslim Caribbean." *Comparative Studies of South Asia, Africa and the Middle East* 17(1): 127–44.

2004 *Callaloo Nation: Metaphors of Race and Religious Identity among South Asians in Trinidad.* Durham, N.C.: Duke University Press.

L'Étang, Gerry

2000 "Vini wé kouli-la: Anthropologie d'une chanson créole." In *Au visiteur lumineux: Des Îles Créoles aux sociétés plurielles, mélanges offerts à Jean Benoist*, ed. Jean-Luc Bonniol, Gerry L'Étang, Jean Barnabé, and Raphaël Confiant, 659–71. Petit-Bourg, Guadeloupe: Ibis Rouge.

Mitchell, William J. T.

2011 *Cloning Terror: The War of Images, 9/11 to the Present.* Chicago: University of Chicago Press.

Mouriaux, René, and Catherine Wihtol De Wenden

1987 "Syndicalisme français et islam." *Revue Française de Science Politique* 37(6): 794–819.

Moutoussamy, Ernest

1987 *La Guadeloupe et son Indianité.* Paris: Editions Caribéennes.

2004 *A la recherche de l'Inde perdue.* Paris: L'Harmattan.

2005 Interview by Stephanie Serac (in French). http://guadeloupe.rfo.fr/imprimer.php3?id_article=62. Accessed June 17, 2012.

Munasinghe, Viranjini

1997 "Culture Creators and Culture Bearers: The Interface between Race and Ethnicity in Trinidad. *Transforming Anthropology* 6 (1–2): 72–86.

2009 "Foretelling Ethnicity in Trinidad: The Post-Emancipation 'Labor Problem.'" In *Clio/Anthropos: Exploring the Boundaries between History and Anthropology*, ed. Andrew C. Willford and Eric Tagliacozzo, 139–86. Stanford: University of California Press.

Nedeljkovic, Eddy

2001 "La greve organisee par l'UGTG n'est pas parvenue a paralyser la Guadeloupe." *Le Monde,* June 9, 2001.

Outar, Lisa

2013 "L'Inde Perdue, L'Inde Retrouvée (India lost, India found): Representations of Francophone Indo-Caribbeans in Maryse Condé's *Crossing the Mangrove* and Ernest Moutoussamy's *A la recherché de l'Inde perdue*." *South Asian Diaspora* 6(1): 47–61.

Martín-i-Pardo, Meritxel

2011 "The Articulation of a French Civil Hinduism." *Journal of the American Academy of Religion* 79(2): 497–519.

Perduran, Hervé

2002 "Vivre dans les DOM en 2002: Guadeloupe l'île-chaudron." *L'Express,* April 18, 2002.

Puar, Jasbir K.

2007 *Terrorist Assemblages: Homonationalism in Queer Times.* Durham, N.C.: Duke University Press.

Rao, Vyjayanthi

2011 "Hindu Modern: Considering Gandhian Aesthetics." *Public Culture* 23(2): 377–94.

Sahaï, Jean S.

2010 "Aimé Césaire: Adagio pour la Da." *L'Esprit Créateur* 50(2): 135–56.

Sainton, Jean-Pierre
1993 "Aux origines du mouvement syndical guadeloupeen, 1889–1912." *Etudes Guadeloupéennes* 7: 141–59.
Schnepel, Ellen
2004 *In Search of a National Identity: Creole and Politics in Guadeloupe*. Hamburg: Helmut Buske Verlag.
Scott, Joan Wallach
2007 *The Politics of the Veil*. Princeton, N.J.: Princeton University Press.
Silverstein, Paul
2004 *Algeria in France: Transpolitics, Race, and Nation*. Bloomington: Indiana University Press.
Singh, Kelvin
1994 *Race and Class Struggles in a Colonial State: Trinidad 1917–1945*. Mona, Jamaica: University of the West Indies Press.
Théodore, Louis
1991 "De l'ombre à la lumière: Vers une nouvelle initiative historique." Interview with Georges Combe, L. R. Danquin, and Cyrille Serva. *Etudes Guadeloupéennes* 4: 26–81.
Todorov, Tzvetan
2010 *The Fear of Barbarians: Beyond the Clash of Civilizations*. Chicago: University of Chicago Press.
Trouillot, Michel-Rolph
2000 "Abortive Rituals: Historical Apologies in the Global Era." *Interventions* 2: 171–86.
Union Populaire pour la Libération de la Guadeloupe (UPLG)
1983 "La situation politique en Guadeloupe depuis le 10 mai." *Le temps modernes* 39(441–42): 1961–73.
Wood, Donald
1968 *Trinidad in Transition: The Years after Slavery*. Oxford, UK: Oxford University Press.

8

The Politics of Conversion to Islam in Southern Mexico

SANDRA CAÑAS CUEVAS

The conversion to Islam among Mayas in southern Mexico is best understood against the backdrop of larger processes taking place in Latin America and more specifically in Mexico—namely, the crisis facing the Catholic Church and the increasing religious diversification of the population.[1] In 1950 Catholics represented 98.2 percent of the population. By the year 2000 the percentage of Catholics in the country dropped 10.2 points, representing a total of 88 percent of the population. The last census carried out during the second half of 2010 reports that Catholics represent 83.9 percent, Evangelicals 7.6 percent, and other religions 2.5 percent, showing a considerable decline of 14.3 points in the number of Catholics over the course of sixty years. As official statistics reveal, this decline has remained constant for the last sixty years. At the same time, the statistics show a remarkable growth in other religions, such as Jehovah's Witnesses, Pentecostals, Mormons, and several other Christian churches. In addition, more people reported practicing "no religion" (4.6 percent compared to 0.60 percent reported in 1960). Interestingly, the rise in people reporting no religion, the diversification and growth of non-Catholic churches, and the decline of Catholics are more significant in the southern part of Mexico, including the state of Chiapas. While the most recent census does not show the presence of Muslims in Mexico, religious diversification taking place in the country includes the increase of Muslim converts.[2]

Origins of Islam in Southern Mexico

Conversion to Islam among Mayas settling in the rural-urban fringes of San Cristóbal de Las Casas, Chiapas, began in 1995, with the arrival of a group of

Spanish Muslim converts from Andalucía. The Zapatista uprising on January 1, 1994, was the starting point for the encounter between Mayas and Spanish Muslim converts. The converts belong to the Murabitun Movement, a *da'wah* (proselytizing, an invitation to Islam) movement originating in England in the 1980s.[3]

Interested in the Zapatista struggle, Spanish Muslim converts attempted, albeit unsuccessfully, to spread the message of Prophet Muhammad among Zapatista-affiliated Maya communities. The Spanish Muslim converts believed that the Zapatista agenda shared important similarities with their own politico-religious agenda, namely, liberation from market and state oppression. However, for the Spanish Muslim converts this project could only be possible through Islam (Morquecho 2004). Despite this initial failure, Spanish Muslim converts were determined to continue their missionary project and settled at the rural-urban fringes of the city of San Cristóbal de Las Casas.

This area has witnessed the development of several shantytowns predominantly inhabited by impoverished landless Maya peasants expelled from their original communities due to political and religious conflicts. These conflicts began in the early 1970s, when the lack of arable lands and paid jobs paved the way for increasing social differentiation within Maya communities, only to be aggravated by the presence of local corrupt leaders, known as *caciques*. The arrival of evangelical religions in the region played an important role in this context, becoming a means for Mayas to express their opposition to local leaders. However, in order to quell rising tides of social discontent, the caciques expelled Maya evangelical converts from their lands (Morquecho 1992; Robledo 1997).

Spanish Muslim converts had more success among Mayas inhabiting these shantytowns, resulting in the conversion to Islam of approximately six hundred people in 1995 (Morquecho 2004). This conversion process to Islam took place amid the reproduction of "the old ways"; that is, the emergence of new corrupt religious and political leaders or caciques within the shantytowns, often tied to local evangelical churches. The majority of Mayas who converted to Islam did so more than fifteen years ago, in 1995, this being their second or third religious conversion experience. Before converting to Islam, they had belonged to the Presbyterian and Seventh-day Adventist Churches, respectively. Serial conversions are a common experience in the region. Throughout the centuries Mayas have organized to resist domination. In this process religion becomes an important source of support and a means to resist and contest oppression and marginalization (Reifler 1979).

This conversion process took place in a national context characterized by

Mexico's constitutional recognition in 1992 as a multicultural country, a constitutional change that recognizes the presence of ethnic groups with their own distinct cultural rights. At the same time, however, it made possible the implementation of structural reforms aimed at strengthening of the neoliberal project in Mexico. One of the most significant reforms privatized landed property, and as mentioned at the start of this chapter, the Zapatista uprising unfolded as a response to these structural shifts, marking the beginning of struggles that would come to connect a multiplicity of indigenous nations not only in Mexico but across the globe.

In a context characterized by historical dispossession and increasing economic and sociopolitical marginalization, Maya Muslims struggle on a daily basis to reshape their lives and reestablish community relations at the rural-urban fringes of the city of San Cristóbal de Las Casas. This effort includes not only building a strong Muslim community among themselves but also building relations with Mayas from different regions and municipalities who were likewise expelled from their original lands and, in the process, overcoming political divisions that originated with the land struggles.

One of the most acute problems they face is land regularization. A central aspect of the Zapatista agenda was land claims. Within this context, several Maya organizations took idle lands located at the urban-rural fringes of San Cristóbal de Las Casas. Some of these areas became shantytowns consisting mainly of Maya people. It is important to mention that the majority of these settlements have succeeded in their land regularization struggles and eventually obtained their land titles. However, this is not the case for the Maya Muslim converts discussed in this chapter. Lack of access to land makes Maya Muslims vulnerable to eviction and arbitrary detention by local authorities, who often see indigenous people as illegal invaders.

Even if Maya Muslims have found in Islam an important means for restructuring community, their conversion experience is not without challenges and difficulties. The initial relationship established between Mayas and Spanish Muslim converts was marked by conflicts and tensions, resulting in approximately thirty Maya extended families separating from the Spanish Muslim community between 2004 and 2007. Among the causes that led to the separation are the open ethnocentrism of Spanish Muslim converts, reflected in their rejection of Maya converts' mother tongue as well as their cultural practices and traditions concerning food and dress.[4] Maize is a central aspect of Maya culture and identity. Maya Muslims are very proud of their mother tongue and want to transmit it to younger generations, and Maya women wear traditional clothes as a means to affirm their ethnic identities.[5] Moreover, the

Spanish leaders, intending to build a strictly Muslim community, pressured indigenous people to stop associating with non-Muslims. In a context of growing indigenous presence within the city, such changes would have produced results contrary to their interests, essentially requiring abandonment of the social network key to their survival.

Other important disagreements between Maya Muslim converts and Spanish Muslims are directly related to religious doctrine and the practice of Islam, particularly polygamy and veiling, both discussed later. However, despite their separation from the Spanish Muslim group, these indigenous Maya Muslim families decided to continue practicing Islam on their own. Some time after the separation, Maya Muslims chose to affiliate with a different Muslim organization, based in Mexico City.[6] The Islamic Cultural Center (CCI) is one of the most important Muslim organizations in Mexico, and while it welcomed the affiliation of Maya Muslims, the relationship between them is far from strong. This is due not only to the geographical distance between the state of Chiapas and Mexico City but also to Maya Muslims' lack of resources; traveling to Mexico City is expensive. However, at least twice a year, the CCI sends some of its members to visit the Maya Muslims.

Focusing on the particular conversion experience of Maya Muslims in San Cristóbal de Las Casas, this chapter describes the key role Maya Muslim women are playing in selectively appropriating a new religious language and the ways in which they transform Islam into a more inclusive religion. This understanding of conversion involves not only religious change but also broader social and political processes taking place along with it (Clearly and Steigenga 2004).

In a broader sense, I also call into question some of the most common stereotypes about Islam and Muslims. Conversion to Islam among the Mayas challenges many inherited ideas about Islam, ideas often reinforced by feminist scholarship, depicting Muslim women as victims and Muslim men as oppressors. Finally, I show how Maya ethnic identities are redefined in relation to Islam, and I argue that conversion to Islam among Mayas does not undermine their ethnic identities and that it is possible to be both Muslim and Maya at the same time.

Gender Dynamics and Teachings at the Mosque

On Fridays Maya Muslims get together to pray and listen to a sermon at the mosque. The mosque is a modest room made of concrete located at the end of the main unpaved road in the shantytown. Maya Muslim men tend to arrive earlier to straighten up the place; they usually dust and sweep the floor. After cleaning up the room they discuss the topic to be addressed during the sermon. Before the sermon or *jutba* begins, one of the men, the *muezzin*, recites the *adhan* or call for prayer, a practice exclusive to Muslim men.[7] Around twenty Maya Muslim families gather for the occasion. Children are not excluded, and the youngest enjoy the time playing both inside and outside the mosque. The oldest children are taught to perform ablution or purification by the adults before entering the mosque. Their parents patiently teach them how to perform *wudu*; that is, how to clean their faces, hair, ears, arms, and feet before prayer. According to the Hadith, children are expected to learn prayer at the age of seven.[8] Infants are carried by their mothers, held closely to their backs with the help of a shawl. Single women are allowed to attend the mosque; however, they rarely attend Friday prayers, preferring instead to stay at their parents' homes, performing routine household chores.

In a number of Muslim and non-Muslim countries, mosques are mainly male spaces, and women are discouraged or even forbidden from visiting them. This is not the case among Maya Muslims in southern Mexico, where the mosque is a space open to all Muslims. However, inside the mosque a curtain separates women from men. Women have their place on the right side of the mosque, while men remain on the left. Everyone must enter the mosque barefoot and with head and body covered. Due to a lack of access to proper covering clothes or *hijab*, indigenous women cover their heads with pieces of fabric they have turned into veils for the occasion. Men may or may not cover their heads, depending on their access to Islamic clothing. When other Muslim converts from Mexico City visit the Maya Muslim community, the visitors occasionally bring Islamic clothing as presents. However, the number of items is limited and does not fulfill the needs of the entire Maya Muslim community.

Once the *jutba* begins, a man—preferably one who is considered the most knowledgeable by the rest of the community (and the same individual most of the time)—reads a *sura* (chapter) from the Quran or Hadith, Islamic sacred texts. The reading takes place in Spanish, followed by comments and discussions in both Spanish and Tsotsil.[9] However, discussions in both languages are often mixed with isolated words in Arabic.[10]

More than once I witnessed how the curtain separating women from men disappeared when women interrupted men's comments on the sermon. Interruptions were made to correct or share a thought or opinion about a specific interpretation of the sacred texts. While this dynamic was surprising to me, Maya Muslim converts see it as a common practice in which everyone engages.

Access to sacred texts is not exclusive to men, as women also read and discuss them, not only among themselves but also with the men. As several Maya Muslims have expressed, this experience contrasts with their previous conversions to evangelical religions, when only religious leaders had access to the Bible. Maya Muslims greatly value the possibility of directly engaging with and interpreting Islamic sacred texts. Once the sermon and discussion come to an end, Maya Muslim converts prepare for the collective prayer. Men and women stand up in parallel rows, facing Mecca, to perform the *salat* or prayer.[11]

The man responsible for the sermon also guides the collective prayer, which is followed by the rest of the attendees. Men's voices are deliberately louder than women's voices, which can barely be distinguished. Women are aware that men are the only ones allowed to guide the collective prayer and lead the sermon, or at least this is what they have been told. However, they are not completely sure this is a religious mandate, and they still hope that one day they will find a different prescription in the sacred texts. They are only willing to accept this prescription because they have not found evidence stating the contrary, and they will continue studying the sacred scriptures to make sure this is the case. Maya Muslim women hold informal study groups when their daily chores allow them some spare time. However, this is more the exception than the rule.

After the collective prayer is over the mosque transforms into a more informal socializing space. Maya women take advantage of this moment to read and comment on the Hadith and to chat with other women about matters not necessarily related to religion. Some women also use this time to rest for a while from their everyday responsibilities and activities. Based on their readings, literate Maya women share their religious knowledge and interpretations with illiterate women. The majority of Maya women are illiterate and monolingual, speaking only Tsotsil, their mother tongue. Meanwhile, on the other side of the curtain, one can listen to the men engaging in different discussions and conversations.[12] Gender segregation within the mosque is not different from Maya life outside it. In this sense Maya gender precepts overlap with Islamic rules.

To a greater or lesser extent Maya women are interested in learning more about their religion. In particular, some are very interested in learning about Prophet Muhammad's life and daily practices. Maya women attempt to incorporate Muslim practices and customs gradually into their everyday lives. Besides performing the mandatory five daily prayers, considered as the most important pillar within Islam, Maya women actively seek to practice what they learn from the religious scriptures, particularly from the Hadith. Among other things, the teachings Maya Muslim women put into practice are related to the proper ways to relate and interact with other Muslims and non-Muslims. These teachings seek to promote hospitality and kindness, both of which are considered to be virtues highly regarded and rewarded by Allah.

The Maya Muslim community has slowly incorporated certain religious practices that involve the use of the Arabic language, such as salutations between themselves and praising and recalling Allah in specific situations—for example, before a meal or after someone sneezes. They have also gone through more personal transformations. In the case of younger women, they have stopped using makeup and perfume and have replaced ornaments and colorful clothes with more modest and discreet accessories. Despite these changes, Maya women still wear their traditional clothes. This was a conscious choice, since, as they explain it, the Prophet taught that Muslim women should be modest and simple. As Muslims they are particularly cautious with their personal hygiene and strictly follow the religious prescription of not attending the collective prayers at the mosque when they are menstruating. In this respect they emphasize that Muslim men have a greater obligation to attend the collective prayer at the mosque because they are not constrained by physiological limitations as are women, who may miss collective prayer at the mosque but not skip the daily prayers, which they are expected to perform at home.

Another important teaching they have learned from religious scriptures and incorporated into their everyday lives is a growing concern for preserving their natural resources. I witnessed several discussions taking place about where and how to best build a new house without affecting trees, plants, the nearby stream, beehives, and anthills. A constant major concern is related to the threat of fires in the natural reserve near the shantytown. Beyond the political conflicts derived from the land regularization struggles taking place within the shantytown, Maya Muslims have organized among themselves and with non-Muslim inhabitants to protect the reserve from fires. Indigenous Muslim women's interest in learning about their religion in order to incorporate the teachings into their daily lives may seem to suggest a conservative worldview. However, indigenous Muslim women are challenging the foundations of a patriarchal religion, democratizing it, even if not without difficulties and contradictions.

The mosque is not only a ritual and religious space where sermons and collective prayers take place. It is also a space where Maya Muslims discuss current local politics, in particular the land regularization struggle they have faced for the past fifteen years. Despite the fact that the call for prayer and the sermon are exclusive male activities, when it comes to the discussion of current politics, women participate on a par with men. The reading of excerpts from the sacred texts is often related to the land regularization problem facing the shantytown.

In this context Maya Muslims often make reference to the life of persecution lived by the Prophet, comparing his life with their own experience. As mentioned, Maya Muslims were expelled from their original communities and are constantly threatened by local authorities, who see them as "illegal" invaders: "We thank Allah for making us stronger and keeping us together in moments of suffering, pain and persecution. Like the Prophet who also experienced persecution, so we experience it. They want to expel us from our lands, but now with Islam we are stronger and have confidence. We are poor, but we never feel hunger and we are able to provide our children with shelter. Allah provides. Now we have confidence, because this is the last revelation, it speaks about one god, unlike the Christians or Evangelicals; we finally have confidence."[13]

In a context infused by increasing marginalization, conversion to Islam among Mayas is playing a key role in providing them with a means to remake their community and, more important, to interpret everyday life problems, thus becoming a key source of strength and community building. Drawing upon their interpretation of the sacred scriptures, Maya Muslims have been able to put an end to many of the divisions within the shantytown that originated with the land regularization struggle.

At the rural-urban margins of San Cristóbal de Las Casas, the mosque becomes a crucial space where gender roles are redefined and are becoming more horizontal. The modest concrete room that constitutes the mosque is appropriated by Maya women interested in learning about and practicing their religion, and in the process they redefine it, along with Maya Muslim men, in more inclusive forms. At the same time the mosque is a space where already existing gender roles and arrangements are reinforced. According to these roles and arrangements Maya women have full rights to participate in discussion and decision-making processes related to local politics that go beyond the Muslim community. As this conversion experience shows, Islam is far from constraining indigenous women's active participation in local politics and religious affairs within the community.

Veiling Politics

The veil has been a subject of much heated debate in feminist theory. Both so-called Western and non-Western feminist approaches tend to portray this piece of fabric as a symbol of Muslim women's oppression. From this view, women wearing a veil are represented as passive victims of a patriarchal religious system (El Saadawi 1997; Moghissi 2009). These representations not only ignore Muslim women's thoughts on the matter but also generate simplified and homogenous ideas of what a Muslim woman is obliterating, namely, cultural and historical differences that complicate veiling politics. As Homa Hoodfar argues, "the imaginary veil that comes to the minds of most Westerners is an awkward black cloak that covers the whole body, including the face, and is designed to prevent women's mobility" (2001: 424). The veil conveys different meanings depending on sociohistorical and cultural conditions that crosscut women's lives and cannot be reduced to a simple, unattractive cover.

Feminists with Muslim origins have shown the diverse meanings the veil has in different Muslim societies, depending on the historical moment women are facing, their class, and cultural background (Abu Lughod 1986; Ahmed 1992; Hoodfar 2001; Mahmood 2005; Mernissi 1987). In their work they show that Muslim women choose to veil not only for religious motivations but also as part of their identity politics or even as a symbol of political opposition and resistance. In this sense Maya Muslim women are appropriating an apparently uniform Muslim practice, modifying it according to their particular cultural context. In the gradual process of incorporating the veil into their everyday lives and routines Maya Muslim women, like many other Muslim women elsewhere, are calling into question oversimplified ideas of the veil, showing its diversity and complexity.

While still belonging to the Spanish Muslim community (that is, before the separation in 2004), Maya Muslim women were forced by Spanish Muslim leaders to wear the veil all the time, both outside and inside their homes. The only moment when they were allowed to take off their veils was in the company of other Muslim women. Maya Muslim women expressed their discomfort about wearing the veil all day long and felt this requirement to be unnecessary and an imposition. Moreover, as recent converts, they felt somewhat embarrassed in public places, fearing other people would stare and make fun of them. However, they agreed to wear the veil because they did not want to be singled out as contradicting the tenets of their new religion. Spanish Muslim converts also pressured Maya Muslim women to stop using their traditional clothes, arguing that they were not appropriate clothing for Muslims. Other constant pressures included rejecting the use of their mother tongue and discouraging the consumption of tortillas made of corn. Spanish Muslim converts regarded corn tortillas and maize in general as poor-quality food and unworthy of Islam.

> When we still belonged to the Spanish Muslim community they did not like my traditional clothes, and they would say that I look prettier with a regular skirt. This is why I stopped using my traditional clothes, because they told me to. Also, they did not want me to speak Tsotsil. Now, after the separation, I am wearing my traditional clothes again and I speak Tsotsil all the time, and teach my children to speak our mother tongue.[14]

The criticism against core cultural values defining Mayas' ethnic identities was one of the main factors that provoked the separation of Maya Muslim families from the community of Spanish Muslim converts. Now that they no longer belong to the Spanish Muslim convert community, Maya Muslim women wear the veil only to attend collective prayers at the mosque and when they pray individually at their homes. For them, it is important to learn more about their religion before they feel prepared to wear the veil all the time. A more thorough knowledge of Islam will enable a state of mind where they will feel sufficiently confident to appear veiled in public, without experiencing discomfort or feeling threatened. This idea corresponds with their belief that conversion to Islam is a gradual learning process and that no one becomes a Muslim in the blink of an eye. The majority of Muslim women expressed the idea that they will not wear the veil at all times until they achieve a higher degree of religiosity; that is, until their *iman*, or faith, becomes stronger.

Challenging Polygamy

Islam has precise stipulations with regard to polygamy. This practice has long been the focus of much debate. Like other Muslim women who have actively questioned the current validity of this practice, Maya Muslim women also challenged and rejected it. Indeed, polygamy became one of the main reasons for the separation of Maya Muslim families from the Spanish Muslim community.

Within the Maya Muslim community, women and men are entitled to the same rights and should therefore be equally punished if they commit adultery or abuse their partners. While still part of the Spanish Muslim community, married Maya Muslim men were constantly pressured to seek a second wife, without even considering their partners' opinions. According to some of the testimonies shared, Spanish Muslims insisted on promoting second marriages in an effort to expand their community more rapidly. However, these efforts proved unsuccessful. Maya Muslims sought out opinions from other Muslims, finding that polygamy is not an obligation for Muslims, as the Spanish Muslims tried to make them believe: "They would say that women do not have rights and should not speak their word, that our job is to obey our husbands and remain silent. They would also say that we have to accept our husbands taking a second wife because it would secure us a place in Paradise. This is when we stopped agreeing, because a lot of suffering is caused when a man takes a second wife. The most important thing to win a place in Paradise is not accepting your husband's decision to take a second wife, but performing your *salat*."[15] Maya Muslim women are not willing to accept that their husbands, or in the case of single women their fiancés, marry a second wife. Moreover, they have learned from other Muslims' experiences that polygamy is a practice subjected to specific rules and contexts, such as considering the opinion of the first wife.

Polygamy has also been a common practice within Maya communities. However, research among Tsotsil-speaking Maya shows that taking a second wife is actually disapproved of by the rest of the community; it is a source of tension between husband and wife and an ideal for men that is rarely met. Moreover, the community condemns men who look for a second wife. As Brenda Rosenbaum argues in her research on Mayas in the municipality of San Juan Chamula, Chiapas, "Female public opinion, in particular, expresses sympathy for the first wife since any woman could find herself in the same predicament" (1993: 58). Therefore monogamy remains the preferred model to follow.

Conversion to different religions among Mayas in the highlands of Chiapas in the last four decades, starting with conversion to evangelical religions, led to the rejection of polygamy and the reinforcement of monogamy as the ideal model to follow. In this respect research shows that gender relations, particularly among Maya women, have benefited from conversion to evangelical religions (Gil 1999; Robledo 2004). However, when local anthropologists and activists found out about Maya conversion to Islam, many were concerned about the implications of this experience for the Maya community in general and Maya women in particular.[16] Some of the old prejudices and concerns generated during the 1970s with respect to conversion to evangelical religions reemerged in the context of the more recent process of conversion to Islam (Medina Hernández 1991; Stoll 1984). Some of those concerns were about the undermining of Maya culture and Maya ethnic identities through indoctrination. For their part, feminists were concerned that evangelical religions would contribute to reinforcing Maya women's subordination (Barrios and Pons 1995). In this context evangelical religions were perceived as a conservative discourse hindering Maya women's liberation processes.

At the center of this reemergence was the sense among local scholars and activists that Islam is a foreign religion, unlike evangelical options directly related to Christianity and therefore more familiar. Interestingly, the historical connections of Islam and Christianity were completely overlooked.

For Muslim Maya women conversion to Islam has become, among other things, the means to secure their partners' fidelity. Maya women and men alike disapprove of infidelity, especially when it is practiced by their relatives, whether Muslim or non-Muslim. Not only is monogamy reinforced with the appropriation of Islam—it also brings the rejection of alcohol among Maya Muslim men. These processes point to the continuity of an already existent improvement of marital relations achieved through previous conversion processes to evangelical religions, such as Presbyterianism or becoming Seventh-day Adventists. Conversion to evangelical religions paved the way for the rejection of alcohol, making possible a life without domestic violence and with improved household finances; conversion to Islam has further strengthened this rejection.

Building New Marriage Arrangements

Research on the transformations in gender relations experienced through conversion to evangelical religions describes how apparently conservative religious discourses give rise to positive changes in Maya women's lives. As noted, these transformations include men's renunciation of alcohol, improvement of household finances, and more harmonious marital relations. This research has also emphasized women's increasing participation in decision-making processes within their households, communities, and religious groups (Eber and Kovic 2003; Gil 1999; Robledo 2004).

The case of Maya Muslim converts is not an exception, and their conversion experience has generally resulted in increasing participation of women in decisions within their households and also in the public sphere. Increased participation is noticeable in community assemblies. As some women have expressed, "Now we are no longer afraid to speak our word, now we defend our right to participate in the decision-making processes affecting the shantytown. Before Islam we attended the meetings but we remained in silence, only watching what others said."[17] Nevertheless, this participation is not without its limitations and contradictions, making it difficult to formulate a general assessment claiming only positive aspects in the conversion process.

The case of unmarried Maya Muslim women best exemplifies these contradictions and limitations. Being under parental tutelage, specifically under maternal authority, makes it rather difficult for unmarried women to make any decisions of their own. Unmarried Maya Muslim women are the ones who attend the mosque the least because they are expected to remain at home helping with chores. The majority of them have completed elementary school but have not continued their studies, partly due to scarce economic resources. Many of these women are sixteen years old or older and have received marriage proposals, which they have rejected, which often goes against their parents' opinions and wishes. However, parents are increasingly considering their daughters' opinions in these matters. This is an important difference, since women from older generations rarely had a say when men proposed marriage.

As part of a larger religious community, unmarried women have received marriage proposals from non-Maya Muslims. While insisting that they would prefer to marry a Muslim man even if this man is not Maya, until very recently few women have done so. It would seem that Islam becomes particularly relevant when considering marriage. This ideal suggests that ethnic identities are not fixed but, rather, are constantly negotiated and redefined. Choosing a spouse is slightly different for Muslim men. As they expressed it, it is easier for a non-Muslim woman to accept converting to Islam than it would be for a non-Muslim man.

Religious adherence to Islam is not the only aspect to be considered when a woman entertains marriage, as Maya women also express the importance of men being hard workers as well as home and/or land owners. The desire for their children to improve their standard of living and to have more opportunities than their parents and grandparents has also been reported among Maya groups undergoing conversion processes to progressive Catholicism such as Liberation Theology (Gil 1999: 171). It is important to underline that the appropriation of different religious discourses tends to have similar implications and outcomes, such as the desire for a better future and the improvement of family relations. Even if indigenous peoples are convinced that the deprivation they have experienced secures them a place in Paradise, they seek to transform their situation in the present, hoping for better life conditions for their offspring.[18]

As we shall see, both men and women work equally hard to escape from poverty. Men have organized a carpentry workshop and women are working to put together a food stand and a sewing workshop, to list some examples. The new religious discourse has played an important role in instilling a sense of betterment at both personal and collective levels. This experience contrasts with previous religious conversions, where religious doctrines suggested a more passive approach to poverty and deprivation.

Due to religious restrictions I was unable to interact as much with Maya Muslim men, making it difficult to account for their thoughts and actions. Despite the limitations, I noticed that younger Maya men are expected to help their fathers with the toughest tasks, such as cutting firewood, building houses, and working in the cornfield. They are also expected to help their mothers running errands and babysitting their younger siblings. These Maya youths are less than fifteen years old, and none of them had completed elementary school. Female unmarried youth outnumber males, yet this expectation of cooperative contribution from both genders is due to a combination of Maya and Islamic traditions, each placing a premium on collective work and subsistence.

Like their female counterparts, unmarried Maya men are also subject to parental authority, but unlike indigenous women, they enjoy a considerable degree of freedom. Their increased freedom translates into more opportunities to spend time outside the household without this representing a threat to their families' reputation. Early age boundaries are established that clearly divide female and male spaces. Only after women get married can they safely cross these boundaries without being criticized by the rest of the community. Before getting married, both Maya men and women are expected to remain within the spaces approved by religious as well as indigenous tradition. In this respect the segregation between women and men has an important role both in Islam and in Maya social organization.

In fact, Islam and indigenous tradition share several important commonalities with respect to social arrangements. Indigenous tradition has stringent gender rules. These regulations pertain particularly to unmarried women, who are forbidden from establishing any type of contact with a man. Friendship is hardly an option between Maya women and men.[19] If friendship is discouraged, courtship is completely forbidden. Notwithstanding gender prescriptions, Muslim Maya women are increasingly undermining traditional rules and engage in secret courtship relations before getting married. Interestingly, Maya women who had male "friends" before marrying them had lived outside San Cristóbal de Las Casas for long periods, away from their families, while selling handicrafts to tourists in other cities. These trips have become a common means to make a living among Maya people living in the rural-urban fringes.

It is noteworthy that the Spanish Muslim community played an important role in facilitating the establishment of friendship and courtship relations, a practically nonexistent practice among Maya people before conversion. These relations almost always developed into marriages sanctioned by the entire religious community. Providing a sanctioned space for interacting with the opposite sex meant that indigenous women in particular had a greater degree of freedom to choose a partner as well as the opportunity for knowing him better before considering marriage.

One of the Maya Muslim women went beyond friendship and secretly agreed to date a Muslim man. When her parents found out about it they attempted to forbid her to continue the relationship. She argued that her boyfriend had honest intentions and wanted to marry her. After some time, her parents finally accepted their relationship, and a year later the young man appeared at her parents' home formally requesting their daughter's hand in marriage. The petitioning did not follow what indigenous tradition usually dictates. Several key traditional elements were absent: the groom's family did not offer any presents, the godparents did not accompany them, and the ritual drink called *posh* was completely missing.[20] Despite these transformations in the proposal ritual, the importance of considering the bride's parents' views in the matter remains. In this respect Rosenbaum argues that paying respect to the bride's parents is important in making it possible for the newlyweds, especially the woman, to preserve family support (Rosenbaum 1993).

In general terms, marriage allows for a significantly higher degree of autonomy and status for the majority of Maya Muslim women. It becomes the means for breaking away from parental tutelage and authority and for being able to make their own decisions freely. As several Maya Muslim women expressed, it means "being in charge."

Some Maya women converted to Islam before getting married while others did so afterward. The former were petitioned according to indigenous tradition and did not have the opportunity to get to know their partners. Younger Maya women who married after conversion to Islam had a different experience. Maya women married before conversion decided to convert largely because their spouses had already converted to Islam. As mentioned, contrary to general expectations, conversion to Islam has meant increasing improvement within marital relations or, at least, previous achievements have been sustained through processes of conversion to evangelical religions. Several women expressed that their spouses tend to help them a lot more with household chores, such as tending their small stores and taking care of the children. There are some cases where a few Maya Muslim men get even more involved, attending to meal preparation and house cleaning: "My husband is very kind, he does help me. If I am away from home running errands, he prepares his own meals. If I get sick, he cooks for me and for the children, and he even washes the clothes."[21] Other women confided that since they converted to Islam, indigenous men treat them better, more respectfully, and avoid screaming and scolding.

The new religious doctrine makes possible the establishment of solidarity networks among Maya women belonging to different generations and kinship. These solidarity networks go beyond the Maya Muslim community supporting other non-Muslim women who lack support, especially single mothers who live within the shantytown. Drawing upon Islamic ideas of kindness and community, Maya Muslim women are actively contributing to overcome divisions within the shantytown, instead promoting solidarity and in the process re-creating a larger community that includes both Muslims and non-Muslim Mayas.

Making Ends Meet

Among Maya Muslims both men and women contribute to household maintenance. Islam has not limited women's participation in this respect. Long before getting married both men and women play an important role in sustaining the family with their earnings. It is a common practice for Maya women to sell handicrafts and groceries at the local markets and even travel to other cities looking for better selling opportunities, as earlier noted. These temporary trips away from their families translate into more independence and also learning new subsistence strategies. Maya women under fifteen years old weave bracelets and belts that they usually sell to market-stand owners or to their relatives leaving for other cities. Another subsistence activity among Maya women is raising and herding sheep, from which to obtain wool that they can later sell. This activity is mostly carried out by unmarried and widowed Maya women, since it requires long periods away from the household.

Marriage does not prevent women from providing income to their households, as they continue selling groceries and handicrafts, often along with their spouses, for whom it is becoming increasingly difficult to find stable jobs. This dynamic pertains until Maya women have their first child, which makes it more difficult for them to travel to other cities to sell their handicrafts. In these circumstances Maya women seek alternative sources of income and strategies to earn money. One of the most common strategies is installing a small store at their homes, where they sell such basic goods as salt, sugar, candies, and soft drinks. Another strategy consists of going back to weaving bracelets and belts and asking someone else to sell them at the local squares and markets, or sending them for future sale by a relative residing in a different city. Women themselves are in charge of their small stores and decide how to use the money they earn. Most of the time they use the money to complement their spouse's limited income. However, recent years have seen a growing unemployment rate among Maya men, a situation that forces women to cover expenses and sustain their households, effectively becoming the breadwinners. For their part, Maya men struggle to find jobs as baggers at the local markets, taxi drivers, and laborers at construction sites. At the same time they still grow corn in their reduced cornfields. However, this activity is being severely undermined by rapid growth of the city reducing of cultivable lands.

Both men and women living in the rural-urban fringes constantly seek new opportunities to overcome their precarious situation. Maya Muslim women are saving money to buy sewing machines as part of a bigger project that will involve other women to produce blouses at a lower cost, as demand for blouses is high. Maya Muslim men are opening carpentry shops, slowly buying tools and necessary equipment. As a religious community, their main goal is to become a self-sustaining community. However, this is a long process yet to be realized. As conditions worsen, some men migrate to the United States, leaving their families behind to search for better opportunities.

The experience of the Maya Muslim community is far from unique. Thousands of indigenous people in Chiapas, as elsewhere in Mexico, have long been undergoing transition from a subsistence economy to a monetized economy. One of the key causes is the intensifying scarcity of arable land in the region, forcing large numbers of indigenous people to migrate from their communities in search of jobs. Until recently migration among indigenous peoples was a domestic, intra-national affair. Currently, increasing numbers of men are choosing to migrate beyond national borders to the United States. This transition from a subsistence regime to a monetized economy is crosscut by gender politics. Nonetheless, indigenous women, on a par with indigenous men, are actively and increasingly searching for new options and strategies to make ends meet. In the context of complementary economic and religious processes, they are redefining traditional gender roles.

Concluding Remarks

The experience of conversion to Islam among Maya in southern Mexico shows that religious discourse is not imposed on converts. Both Maya men and women are selectively appropriating certain religious prescriptions that they consider most meaningful to their everyday lives and communal development. At the same time, they are rejecting or reformulating religious discourse when they interpret it as abrading their interests as a community.

In this active process, Maya Muslim women are playing an important role. Not only are they appropriating a ritual space such as the mosque; they are also gaining increasing access to sacred texts and critically discussing them. They resort to religious scripture only when it does not go against their traditional ideas about well-being, as exemplified by their rejection of polygamy and their reformulation of veiling practices. In this sense they are transforming Islam according to their own cultural logic, viewing veiling, on the one hand, as a gradual practice directly related to a more complete command of their religion and, on the other, as the result of a stronger faith, or *iman*. Moreover, this conversion experience shows that veiling practices do not necessarily mean doing away with ethnic-indigenous traditional dress. In the same vein, learning Arabic in order to be able to read the Quran does not necessarily mean forgetting or rejecting one's mother tongue. In the case of Maya conversion to Islam, the new religious identities are not supplanting ethno-linguistic identities. They are showing how it is possible to be both Muslim and Maya at the same time.

In general terms, Islam is bringing positive outcomes to gender relations among Maya converts, favoring more harmonious and equal relations. Besides these positive transformations, Islam becomes the means for reinforcing men's renunciation of alcohol, giving continuity to improvements achieved under previous conversion processes, notably evangelical Christianity. Conversion to Islam also favors the continuation of women's participation in land regularization struggles within the shantytown as well as in the generation of income. In this sense Islam need not be an obstacle in the improvement of women's lives, Maya or otherwise, as is still often thought to be the case.

However, these transformations are not without limits and contradictions. Some of the limits are directly related to the fact that the Maya Muslim community is not large enough and does not have strong support from larger and more consolidated communities established in Mexico City. This lack of guidance and support restricts Maya Muslims' ability to expand their social networks and thus the boundaries of the community. Maya Muslim women are the most affected by these precarious connections. Until now only Maya men have attended retreats and workshops organized by Muslim organizations based in Mexico City where they had the opportunity to meet other Muslims and interact with them. Married Maya women are at a disadvantage since they are the ones who stay at home taking care of domestic duties, and unmarried women are considered too young to travel by themselves.

It is important to note that these contradictions and limitations are not the direct result of religious discourse and practice but rather the result of specific existing gender arrangements related to maternity and women's civil status that tend to justify their exclusion. In this respect married Maya women enjoy greater status within the community and a considerable degree of autonomy. However, their relative degree of autonomy tends to diminish when Maya women have children. Unmarried Maya women's voices and opinions are now increasingly being taken into consideration with respect to marriage decision making, but at the same time they remain under paternal authority that constrains their mobility considerably.

Beyond contradictions and limitations, conversion to Islam among the Maya of southern Mexico calls into question misconceptions about Islam that portray this religion as uniformly patriarchal, rigid, antithetical to modernity, and incapable of beneficial transformation synchronously with contemporary currents. Maya Muslim women's active participation in the selective appropriation of Islamic religious discourse challenges some of the most problematic tenets of feminist scholarship. Within this scholarship, "Third World Women as a group or category are automatically and necessarily defined as religious (read: not progressive), family oriented (read: traditional), legally unsophisticated (read: they are still not conscious of their rights), illiterate (read: ignorant), domestic (read: backward), and sometimes revolutionary (read: their country is in a state of war; they must fight!). This is how the 'Third World difference' is produced" (Mohanty 2003: 40).

In any case, as this conversion experience shows, Maya Muslim women are religious by their own choice, and this does not mean being conservative or going against their rights and desires. In fact, the ways they are choosing to practice Islam result in some positive transformations in their lives. What at first glance might appear a conservative process is actually giving rise to unexpected outcomes.

This conversion experience is also relevant to the extent that it undermines generalized assumptions about "foreign" religions and their negative implications for the persistence of indigenous cultures and ethnic identities. Maya conversion to Islam shows the ways in which and extent to which people are reshaping their ethnic identities in relation to Islam. As described, there are several key aspects of Maya ethnic identities that are non-negotiable, among them the Tsotsil tongue, daily consumption of maize, and use of traditional clothes. At the same time, however, there are other aspects that may be negotiated, such as marriage arrangements and rituals. Overall, this conversion experience shows that the selective appropriation of Islamic doctrine by these Maya communities need not pose a threat to their identities and culture.

Finally, as Charles Hirschkind and Saba Mahmood argue, "We tend to forget that the particular set of desires, needs, hopes, and pleasures that liberals and progressives embrace do not *necessarily* exhaust the possibilities of human flourishing" (2002: 353). In this respect Maya Muslims' religious practice dislocates liberal understandings of freedom and submission, infusing and expanding them with culturally specific meaning. The lives of indigenous peoples have never been fully molded by liberal traditions. And conversion to Islam should not be perceived as leading to a condition that requires recuperation by presumably progressive notions of either freedom or submission.

Notes

1. This chapter is based on extended fieldwork in the region since 1997. Although I have conducted research among the Zapatistas since 1997, my attention shifted to the conversion experience discussed here in 2001, when I first found out about the Maya Muslim converts through a journalist friend.

2. The Islamic Cultural Center (CCI), one of the most important Muslim organizations in Mexico, estimates the number of Muslims in Mexico to be 2,000 to 3,000. This number includes both Mexican converts to Islam and people born Muslims. The latter category includes migrants from Muslim countries and their descendants. For more information see also http://www.islam.com.mx.

3. According to its leader, Shaykh Dr. Abdalqadir as-Sufi, a convert himself, the movement has presence in several different countries, including England, Australia, France, Denmark, Turkey, Germany, Spain, Nigeria, and Malaysia. One of the movement's main objectives is to create a new Islamic society emulating the first *ummah* founded by Prophet Muhammad (Morquecho 2004). Unfortunately there is not much information available on the Murabitun Movement. They had a Web site, but it is no longer online.

4. The mother tongue is Tsotsil (or Tzotzil), an indigenous language in the Mayan language family and spoken in Chiapas.

5. Women's traditional dress consists of a wool hand-made black skirt, attached to the waist by a belt, and a bright embroidered blouse.

6. For further analysis and description see Cañas Cuevas 2006.

7. In Islam, the official who proclaims the call to prayer.

8. The Hadith are short narratives about Muhammad and his companions and contemporaries collected into written form three or four centuries after Muhammad died.

9. Sacred texts are in Arabic, but Maya Muslims have versions in Spanish provided by the organization to which they belong.

10. Indigenous people started learning rudimentary Arabic with Spanish converts in informal settings, but they have a rather basic knowledge of it.

11. Muslims are expected to perform prayers five times a day at specific times: dawn, noon, midafternoon, sunset, and nightfall.

12. Due to gender segregation rules I was unable to observe and register interactions among men at the mosque.

13. Excerpt from field notes.

14. Excerpt from field notes.

15. Excerpt from field notes.

16. During two different conferences, both organized in 2004 in San Cristóbal de Las Casas, I witnessed these responses.

17. Excerpt from field notes.

18. The idea of Paradise is not part of Maya cosmology; instead, it is an idea appropriated through conversion to evangelical religions.

19. In this context friendship is understood as a cordial relationship between a woman and a man. However, unmarried women and men are expected to spend time together under the supervision of adults.

20. Traditional fermented drink made of corn.

21. Excerpt from field notes.

References Cited

Abu Lughod, Lila
1986 *Veiled Sentiments: Honor and Poetry in a Bedouin Society*. Berkeley: University of California Press.
Ahmed, Leila
1992 *Women and Gender in Islam*. New Haven, Conn.: Yale University Press.
Barrios Ruiz, Walda E., and Leticia Pons Bonals
1995 *Sexualidad y Religión en los Altos de Chiapas*. Chiapas, México: UNACH.
Cañas Cuevas, Sandra
2006 "Koliyal Allah Tsotsunkotik, Gracias a Allah que somos más Fuertes: Identidades étnicas y relaciones de género entre los sunníes en San Cristóbal de Las Casas, Chiapas." Master's thesis, Centro de Investigaciones y Estudios Superiores en Antropología Social (CIESAS), México, D.F.
Clearly, Edward L., and Timothy J. Steigenga (eds.)
2004 *Resurgent Voices in Latin America: Indigenous Peoples, Political Mobilization, and Religious Change*. New Brunswick, N.J.: Rutgers University Press.
Eber, Christine, and Christine Kovic (eds.)
2003 *Women of Chiapas: Making History in Times of Struggle and Hope*. New York: Routledge.
El Saadawi, Nawal
1997 *The Nawal El Saadawi Reader*. New York: Zed Books.

Gil Tébar, Pilar R.

1999 *Caminando en un solo corazón: Las mujeres indígenas de Chiapas*. Serie Atenea estudios sobre la mujer. Málaga, España: Universidad de Málaga.

Hirschkind, Charles, and Saba Mahmood

2002 "Feminism, the Taliban and Politics of Counter-Insurgence." *Anthropological Quarterly* 75(2): 339–54.

Hoodfar, Homa

2001 "The Veil in Their Minds and on Our Heads: Veiling Practices and Muslim Women." In *Women, Gender, Religion: A Reader,* ed. Elizabeth A. Castelli, 420–46. New York: Palgrave.

Mahmood, Saba

2005 *Politics of Piety: The Islamic Revival and the Feminist Subject*. Princeton, N.J.: Princeton University Press.

Medina Hernández, Andrés

1991 [1967] "Comentario Previo." In Gonzalo Aguirre Beltrán, *Obra Antropológica IX, Regiones de Refugio: El desarrollo de la comunidad y el proceso dominical en Mestizoamérica,* 7–24. Veracruz, México: Universidad Veracruzana, INI, FCE.

Mernissi, Fatima

1987 *Beyond the Veil: Male-Female Dynamics in Modern Muslim Society*. Bloomington: Indiana University Press.

Moghissi, Haideh

2009 *Feminism and Islamic Fundamentalism: The Limits of Postmodern Analysis*. New York: Zed Books.

Mohanty, Chandra T.

2003 *Feminism without Borders: Decolonizing Theory, Practicing Solidarity*. Durham, N.C.: Duke University Press.

Morquecho Escamilla, Gaspar

1992 *Los indios en un proceso de organización: La Organización Indígena de los Altos de Chiapas (ORIACH)*. Tesis de licenciatura en Antropología Social, Universidad Autónoma de Chiapas, San Cristóbal de Las Casas, Chiapas, México.

2004 *Bajo la bandera del islam: Un acercamiento a la identidad política y religiosa de los musulmanes en San Cristóbal de Las Casas*. San Cristóbal de Las Casas, Chiapas, México: Ediciones Pirata.

Reifler De Bricker, Victoria

1979 "Movimientos religiosos indígenas en los Altos de Chiapas." *América Indígena* (Instituto Americano Indigenista) 39(1): 17–45.

Robledo Hernández, Gabriela

2004 "Cambio religioso y transformación de identidades de género en Los Altos de Chiapas." Ponencia presentada en el X Congreso Latinoamericano sobre Religión y Etnicidad, Pluralismo y transformaciones sociales, San Cristóbal de Las Casas, Chiapas, México, July 5–9.

1997 *Disidencia y religión: Los expulsados de San Juan Chamula*. Universidad Autónoma de Chiapas, Facultad de Ciencias Sociales, Asociación Mexicana de Población, Tuxtla Gutiérrez, Chiapas, México.

Rosenbaum, Brenda
1993 *With Our Heads Bowed: The Dynamics of Gender in a Maya Community.* Austin: University of Texas Press.

Stoll, David
1984 "¿Con qué derecho adoctrinan ustedes a nuestros indígenas?: La polémica en torno al Instituto Lingüístico de Verano." *América Indígena* (Instituto Americano Indigenista) 44(1): 9–24.

9

Bahamian and Brazilian Muslimahs

Struggle for Identity and Belonging

JERUSA ALI

The Bahamas and Brazil share very little in terms of demography, language, or cultural heritage, yet like other countries in the Americas, both have growing Muslim communities who must confront many of the same obstacles to practicing their faith and maintaining their unique cultural and Islamic identities.[1] In the Americas there are diverse subgroups of local Muslim communities that are largely underrepresented in scholarly literatures otherwise replete with ethnographic research on immigrant diasporas.[2] This chapter concerns Muslim women who self-identify with their country of origin as "Bahamian" and "Brazilian" and whose ethnic heritages are drawn from African, European, South Asian, and Amerindian backgrounds, differentiating them from first, second, and third generation Arab and South Asian diasporic communities. The women in these "mixed" Muslim minority communities in the Americas thus possess only a degree of indivisibility within the *ummah* (global Muslim community). The aim of this chapter is to offer a preliminary exploration of the historical, cultural, and religious dimensions of identity in the Bahamas and Brazil for Muslimahs (Muslim women).[3] It begins with an overview of the histories and contexts of the growth of Islam and the presence of Muslims in the Bahamas and Brazil from the colonial period to the present day, followed by an analysis of Bahamian and Brazilian Muslimahs' struggle for identity and belonging.

Muslim minority women face difficult and complex challenges to their minority existence and at the same time struggle to maintain their Islamic identity. In an attempt to explore how Bahamian and Brazilian Muslim women construct their identities, live their lives, and negotiate the norms of the societies and Muslim communities in which they live, and to understand what it means for them to be modern Muslim women in these two countries, this multi-site ethnographic research included informal, semi-structured interviews conducted in 2011 with Muslim women from Nassau, New Providence, in the Bahamas and São Bernardo do Campo, São Paulo, in Brazil. Most of the women interviewed were either converts to Islam or their parents had converted to Islam. These women represent a variety of socioeconomic backgrounds and have been influenced by a number of Islamic schools of thought and sects, including but not limited to Sunni, Hanafi, Salafi, and Sufi. Pseudonyms have been used for names and places in order to protect the identities of the participants. Muslimahs interviewed were asked questions relating to what it means to be Muslim in Brazil and the Bahamas, and their responses give a sense of their religious beliefs and practices, their individual struggles for identity and belonging, and how they perceive their place within the ummah in a local and global setting. Common themes are identified in their personal stories, including the influence of "predatory Islamist ideology" (Abd-Allah 2006: 2) from abroad and a critique of how non-Muslims and immigrant Muslims perceive the Muslimahs' presence in their unique cultural spaces.

The intent of this research is neither to construct and produce the Muslimah in the Americas as a singular monolithic subject nor to treat the women as a unified group and therefore deny the specificity of their existence. The meanings and interpretations generated by the Muslimahs' personal narratives will no doubt be influenced by different readings of this chapter. Interviews were conducted in such a way as to avoid producing, "appropriating and colonizing the constitutive complexities which characterize the lives of women" (Mohanty 2003: 51). Religious and cultural identity should not be reduced in an essentialist way to a "theoretical homogenization, abstraction and reductionism," because such a perspective misses out on "the diversity, complexity and open-endedness" of the lived experience (Modood 2007: 110). Islamic cultural coherence is a fundamental value espoused by all the interviewees, and the repetition of this theme should not be interpreted as being reductionist. The Muslimahs are independent, educated, multilingual, multiracial, faithful, mothers, daughters, sisters, and hajjahs whose personal narratives yield the important emergent themes: cultural identity as the "moving vehicle" of difference; righteousness and resilience in the ideal Muslimah; and the ummah as a context transcending cultural space.

A History of Islam in the Bahamas and Brazil

Islam first arrived in Brazil and the Bahamas during slavery when enslaved peoples, primarily from West Africa, were brought to work as field laborers on the plantation settlements.[4] According to Sylviane Diouf (1998: 83), African Muslims made up at least 10 percent of the more than 10 million slaves imported to the Americas between the 1500s and the 1800s. In the Bahamas slaves labored in harvesting cotton, lumber, and salt; a minority of them were employed as skilled craftsmen and stevedores. In Brazil slaves labored in the sugar and coffee industries as well as the mining sector and other skilled labor positions. The exact number of slaves and percentage of Muslims among them cannot be established with great certainty because information such as ethnic origin and religion were not included in the slave registers. In the Bahamas, for example, slaves was counted as property and described in terms of numbers of slaves per square mile, and initially slave registers kept only the details of the number of slaves being exported to other colonies (Higman 1995). Slavery reached its peak in the late eighteenth and early nineteenth centuries, and the official period of slavery ended in the Bahamas with the British Abolition of Slavery Act (1833) and in Brazil with the Golden Law (1888).[5] Slavery was a brutal period of cultural and religious repression and oppression for African Muslims. Islam, as a cohesive religious doctrine and practice, did not survive beyond that era.

During the colonial period of slavery there is evidence that slaves strived to maintain a connection to their Islamic heritage through religious rituals, teaching Arabic, passing on knowledge of the Quran, giving Muslim names to their kin and in rebellion against their Christian masters. Nadia Elia describes the giving of charity (*saraka* or *sadaqa*) during Ramadan and on the day of Eid ul Fitr as one of the religious rituals common to slaves in the Bahamas. She explains that during Ramadan in the early 1800s, a Bahamian-born slave, daughter of an African-born slave named Bilali Mohamed, was known to have worn a white cloth thrown over her head like a veil and to have prepared saraka cakes around the time of Ramadan (Elia 2003: 186–87). Similar rituals were observed among Brazilian slaves (Reis 2005). For example, in the mid-1800s in Bahia, Brazil, in the aftermath of the Malê slave rebellion the police found amulets containing written *suras* (chapters) from the Quran, papers containing the opening verses of the Quran used in prayer, and as evidence of private religious schools or *jama'a* (Reis 2005: 93–111). The practice of wearing amulets has continued among some Muslims who believe in the healing powers of the profession of faith (*shahada*) and the opening verse sura al

Fatiha. Following the 1835 rebellion, and fearful of the growth and ideological influence of the Islamic community in Bahia, the Brazilian government gave slave masters six months to baptize their slaves into Christianity and provide them with a basic religious education (Diouf 1998: 53). The practice of forced conversion of slaves and the assigning of Christian names also occurred in the Bahamas, where although slavery was officially abolished in 1833, apprenticed labor and voluntary slavery (also known as free labor in the West Indies) continued into the late 1800s, when subjects were similarly forced to convert (Gomez 2005; Powles 1996 [1888]). According to Craton and Saunders (1992: 130), Bahamian slave "masters and mistresses were enjoined to set an example and discourage 'oaths and unseemly discourses' among their slaves." Letters written in Arabic, the lingua franca of all Muslims and the language of educated Muslims of this period, were collected from a liberated slave and apprentice named Abdul Keli in the Bahamas (Rashad 2009; Turner 2007). Slaves born in the Caribbean were also generally given Christian names, and rarely were their original names listed in the slave registers (Sheridan and McDonald 1996: 190). An examination of several nineteenth-century slave registers for the Bahama Islands reveal black African-born and Creole Bahamian-born slaves (named racial categories in the registers) with names common to African Muslims of that period, such as Mahomet (Muhammad), Fatima, Mimbo, Mamaya (Amaya), Satira, Juba, and Affy (Slave Registers 1812–34). Bahamian and Brazilian Muslimahs interviewed had little knowledge of this period of history from a religious perspective; however, particularly for Muslimahs of African descent, there was a sense of pride when referring to what they perceived as their "West African" Islamic heritage.

The second introduction of Islam to the Bahamas and Brazil came with Arab, South Asian, and African immigration to the Americas. Arab migrants fleeing the Ottoman Empire in the Levant began settling in Brazil in the late 1800s, again in the 1920s, and in a third diaspora in the post–World War II period. Arab immigrants, largely Christian but including some Muslims as well, were drawn to better merchant opportunities in the Americas, opportunities not available during and after Turkish occupation. Muslim communities in Brazil were therefore influenced by the cultural practices of Arab immigrants. Lebanese and Syrian migrants also settled in the Bahamas during the same periods; however, none were known to be practicing Muslims, and they were more likely to have been part of the Christian communities in diaspora. Bahamians, unlike Brazilians, displayed outright xenophobia and were "actively" antipathetic toward Lebanese and other immigrants from the 1930s onward (Craton and Saunders 1998: 257). The Owade (Baker), Armaly, Moses, and

Amoury families, who gained a profit share of the Bahamian sponge and dry goods market in the late 1800s benefiting from the extended Lebanese family networks that stretched from New York to Brazil, were an exception (Craton and Saunders 1998: 258).

Neither the Bahamas nor Brazil experienced a large influx of South Asian indentured laborers after the abolition of slavery, as, for example, did the British West Indies from 1838 to 1917 (Kale 1998). There was also no large influx of Muslim Indian or Javanese laborers, as occurred in the Dutch colony of Suriname (Hoefte 1987). After Bahamian independence in 1973, migrants fleeing the economic malaise of postcolonial statehood were recruited to the Bahamas from Commonwealth countries, such as India and Nigeria, to practice medicine and other professions (Ansari 2000; Rashad 2009). In Brazil, according to the Indian government, a small number of Indians from Goa, Sind, and the former Portuguese colony of Mozambique settled as merchants and university professors in the 1960s and 1970s (Ministry of External Affairs, India 2000).

Bahamian and Brazilian immigrant communities, dissimilar in many respects, are similar in that their immigrants migrated to the Americas for economic reasons. There is inherent tension between the immigrant and local communities as well as a sense that the immigrant communities have failed to live up to the *da'wah* (proselytization, invitation to Islam) expectations of the local settled communities and have instead preferred to focus on commercial endeavors. Both Bahamians and Brazilian Muslim women interviewed still speak with ambivalence about the cultural and religious legacy of immigrant Muslims and critique their experience with the immigrants in public and private gatherings. "The problem is that the Lebanese-Syrian Muslim . . . families didn't come to Brazil to give da'wah . . . they came to Brazil to make money," asserts Jandira, 26, a Brazilian Muslim of Portuguese descent, who has sought religious education from sources other than the "Arab" mosques and cultural clubs. Mona, 42, who considers herself part of the first generation of Bahamian Muslims, explains: "I don't think they [immigrant Muslims] respect us. The reason why I say that . . . when we have functions, they don't participate or show up. They don't show up for Eid or separate functions. Here in the Bahamas, I have had negative experiences with non-Bahamian Muslims." For Muslim minorities in the Americas, Eid ul Fitr (the festival marking the end of Ramadan) and Eid ul Adha (also called Qurbani or Bakra Eid, the festival of sacrifice held after the Hajj period) are not only significant religious festivals with required observance (*wajib*) but are family and community-oriented events. Arab immigrants in Brazil generally do not mix with local

Muslims, and "diasporic marriage arrangements" have been the norm in these communities (Karam 2007: 98). These types of endogamous arrangements were confirmed by Muslimahs interviewed in both countries. Umm Qasim, a self-described black Bahamian, told of similar arrangements among Indians, Pakistanis, and Bangladeshis in the Bahamas. According to Umm, one of the South Asian sisters created a listing on an online Muslim matrimonial site for her children in order that they marry someone "from our community," as was written in her profile. She was careful to distinguish immigrant communities who came from South Asia from the Indo-Trinidadian and Guyanese Muslims who regularly mixed with and married local Bahamians. Despite the closed nature of the first generation immigrant communities, according to the participants, some of the second and third generation immigrants in the Bahamas and Brazil married locally and adopted the culture of their birthplace.

The third introduction of Islam to Brazil and the Bahamas came through da'wah activities of foreigners in the 1970s–1980s that paralleled da'wah activities in other Muslim minority areas. There was an effort to link Islam to a local Muslim identity for the purposes of proselytization and propagation. International and regional Islamic da'wah bodies formed a presence in the Americas, assisted by the financial resources of the government and charitable trusts of the Kingdom of Saudi Arabia. Shi'a-oriented religious organizations in Brazil received funding from other governments, such as Iran, and from charitable trusts in Lebanon. Ali Kettani acknowledges that in the case of Brazil, the activities of Muslim countries in non-Muslim countries were sometimes used to promote political advantage and not necessarily to benefit the growth of the ummah (Kettani 1990: 226–23).

During this da'wah period, foreign cultural Islam was replaced by a genuine effort to encourage Muslims to seek religious knowledge and foster a Muslim identity based on religious values instead of local cultural practices. Various study groups, Islamic organizations, and movements were formed by Brazilian Muslims who had traveled abroad for education in Saudi Arabia and who established themselves by offering scholarships, training, and guidance to Muslims in the Americas in their native languages of English, Portuguese, and Spanish. Private charitable grants were given to local Muslim organizations by members of the royal family of Saudi Arabia and Kuwait. Organizations that established a presence included the Muslim World League (Makkah), World Assembly of Muslim Youth (Riyadh), Darul Iftaa (Riyadh), Organization of Islamic Conference (Jeddah), International Islamic Federation of Student Organizations (Kuwait), Qur'an and Sunnah Society (North America), and Organización Islámica Para América Latina (Buenos Aires, Argentina). Many of them are still active in the Caribbean and South America. In Brazil second generation Arabs began forming Muslim benefit societies focused on religious education rather than the ethnic associations that were prevalent in the past. In the 1980s the first Brazilian-born Muslims were sent to Saudi Arabia to study to become sheikhs at the University of Medina (Peres de Oliveira 2006; Pinto 2011). In 1979 the Federação das Associações Muçulmanas do Brasil (FAMBRAS), one of the largest umbrella Muslim organizations in Brazil, which describes itself as an "Arab-Muslim Brazilian umbrella organization," was established (FAMBRAS 2012). The first Bahamian Muslim organization, Jamaat-ul-Islam (known in English as the Revolutionary Islamic Movement in the Bahamas), was formed in the 1970s (Rashad 2009). The founding members included Mustafa Khalil Khalfani, Dr. Munir Ahmad Rashad, Bashan Saladdin, Zubair Ali, and Fareed Abdullah. The da'wah movement of the Tabligihi Jamaat (Mewat, India) also briefly established itself during this period, sending three Bahamians on a study tour, but it was soon overshadowed by the Salafi da'wah, which led to the establishment of the Jama 'Ahlus Sunnah in the late 1990s (Rashad 2009).

For those Bahamian and Brazilian Muslims sent abroad to study, this was an era that heralded hope and Islamic revivalism, yet it was also a time of social alienation. After adopting a new religion, many of the first converts felt alienated from their own families at home and felt cultural and linguistic alienation from the Muslim majority host communities. Islamic revivalism took on a foreign cultural expression promoted as puritanical Islam and was considered different from the original cultural Islam of first generation immigrants, which was now viewed as being imbued with innovations (*bid'a*), religious syncretism, and morally corrupt cultural practices. In Brazil, Islamic revivalism reflected Lebanese-Syrian-Arab culture that was expressed through an increased focus on teaching Arabic in religious schools and universities in São Paulo and on translating Arabic sermons and religious texts into Portuguese. It was also reflected in the manner of dress and behavior of Brazilian Muslims, who in urban areas like Rio de Janeiro and Brasília began adopting the traditional dress of the Arabian Peninsula (*abaya, thobe, ghutra*). In the Bahamas the hallmark of Islamic revivalism took the form of an overemphasis on the purity of faith that was expressed through Arab-Sunni cultural practices (as in Egypt, Saudi, Yemen, and the Arabian Peninsula), such as the wearing of the abaya, *khimar,* and *niqab* among sisters, and the now commonplace use of *kunyas* (teknonyms)—"Umm," mother of, "Abu," father of—to address fellow Muslims. The use of kunyas in the Arab and Muslim world has both cultural and religious significance and is generally considered a prefix of reverence and respect. In the Americas the use of *kunyas* and *nasabs* (patronymics, heritage) can be seen as a marker of religiosity.

The divide between revivalism and alienation is not only a geographic and cultural divide; it is also a divide based on gender for Muslims in the Americas. The Muslimahs interviewed were born between 1970 and 1988, and their identities have been impacted by the gender division within their communities. Some have positive nostalgic memories of educative gatherings such as attending conferences in North America during Christmas and Easter (Bahamians) and religious retreats during carnival (Brazil), yet many women grew up feeling largely excluded from public discourse and official da'wah activities. They were not sent abroad to study, and they were not given public leadership roles in the community. Although they benefited through private *'aqidah* classes and the knowledge gained from books donated by da'wah organizations and charitable trusts, they also experienced marginalization in the ideological discourse influenced by Saudi-funded, restrictionist interpretations of Islam. The restrictionist ideology is more prevalent in the Bahamas, where the weekly community newsletter called the *Reminder* is essentially a cut-and-paste distribution of religious knowledge and manners from various Salafi Web sites and scholarly works such as that of Dr. Saleh As-Saleh (a student of Shaykh Ibnul-Uthaymeen). In both the Bahamian and Brazilian Muslim communities women describe themselves as the visible bearers of Islamic identity with the expectation that they should model the ideal Muslimah in speech, dress, and actions. The *Ideal Muslimah* is also the title of a text written by Dr. Muhammad Ali al-Hashimi (1996), translated into many languages, including English and Portuguese, and distributed as part of da'wah packages in Muslim minority countries. In this text the ideal Muslimah is encouraged to stay at home and to examine her behavior to ensure that her actions are not influenced by modern *bid'a* or pre-Islamic *jahili* customs (al-Hashimi 1996). Muslimahs reacted in two distinct ways to the challenges of their Bahamian and Brazilian Muslim identity: some women completely rejected the Arabization of Islamic identity, and others adopted some of the manners of the ideal Muslimah. The concept and challenge of becoming the ideal Muslimah appeared as a recurring theme during the interviews and is discussed in greater depth later in the chapter.

Cultural Identity as the "Moving Vehicle" of Difference

The tension between immigrant Muslims and their descendants and Brazilian and Bahamian Muslims is apparent from the experiences already described.

Even more apparent is the cultural divide between Muslims and non-Muslims and the persistence of negative stereotypical portrayals of Muslims in the media, or the exclusion of images of local Muslims in popular culture. In Brazil some non-Muslims associate Muslims with the popular telenovela *O Clone* (Globo Network Brasil), the story of a young Arab Muslim girl caught between her Brazilian cultural identity and Islamic/Moroccan religious identity. The telenovela, which has recently been re-produced in Spanish as *El Clon* by Telemundo for the Americas market, depicts a cultural, racial, and religious hierarchy headed by an Arab Muslim patriarch (Muslimah Media Watch 2010). In the Bahamas, Muslims have repeatedly complained of negative portrayals of Muslims in the media. For example, in an article about a local development project in Mayaguana, critics claimed that islanders "fear [that] terrorism, spurred by Islamic fundamentalism, could make its way to the island" because some of the workers are Muslim (Kongwa 2006).

The relationship with non-Muslims is a painful subject exemplified by the rejection and othering of Muslims. The apex of cultural insecurity and representational struggle is the public perception that Islam is an all-encompassing ethnicity and that Muslims simply cannot be Brazilian or Bahamian. This perception creates boundaries between Muslims and non-Muslims who live in the same cultural space and discourages avenues of positive cultural and religious self-representation. Brazilian Muslimahs, often perceived by their peers as Arabs, "Turcos," or foreigners, feel alienation in their own communities. When asked about how Brazilians view her Islamic attire, Hanan, a 24-year-old self-described *niqabi*, comments: "Some Brazilians stop to take a picture of me and my friends, especially when we are outside the city. Some of them are bold and run past us and have their friend take a picture ... they think they got a picture of a real Arab!" In speaking with Maisa, 23, a graduate student of European and indigenous descent, it became clear that being perceived as both Muslim and Brazilian was central to her identity. Maisa, who wears a *hijab*, struggles with being mistaken for an Arab: "There are some ignorant people in Brazilian society who make bad jokes about women, about Muslims as terrorists, and use other pejorative terms. This does not affect my identity. For me, this is less of a problem than the issue of not being recognized as *Brazilian*. Most people who see me on the street covered think that I'm Arabic ... unless they hear me speak Portuguese." All forms of Islamic attire and speech are associated with foreigners.

Yasmeen, 28, explains that Bahamians are largely ignorant of the existence of Muslims: "As a Muslim woman in the Bahamas you are a visible minority ... [you] live your life in the exterior of Bahamian society ... whenever you walk into a room people see you as different.... They see you as essentially this moving vehicle of differentness. I have lived in this country for twenty odd years and [yet] this country has rejected me at every turn.... I don't feel Bahamian because when people see me they see 'Other.'" But despite being viewed as a foreigner by her peers, Mona, a Bahamian mother and business owner, expresses pride in her Muslim identity: "I'm proud to be a Bahamian Muslim. Sometimes it's difficult, but generally I'm proud to be a Bahamian Muslim. I'm proud when persons come and say 'I didn't know that Bahamians were Muslims... I thought only foreigners were at that white building [referring to the Carmichael Road Mosque]!' I'm proud to tell them that there are Bahamian Muslims. I am proud." Both women complain that the Bahamian education system has failed to expose children to cultural and religious diversity and that the education system in general is Christian centered, leading to misinformation about Islam and the very existence of Bahamian Muslims.

The relationship between race and cultural identity in the Bahamas and Brazil is complicated by the legacy of slavery and the history of race relations in these two countries, one a black majority society and the other with a significant black population. For example, São Paulo, by all accounts, is distinct from other areas in Brazil. Edward Telles, a sociologist who has lived in several cities in Brazil, confirms that "as the primary destination of mass European immigration, São Paulo had become an ethnic mosaic, and blacks [are] a stigmatized minority" (Telles 2004: 8). Zahra, 26, an Afro-Brazilian, speaks of the problem of being a Brazilian Muslim of African descent living in an area like São Paulo in southern Brazil: "I can't explain it, but I know that if I were to walk into the *masjid* [mosque], they would think less of me.... Some of the Afro-Brazilian brothers meet in their homes. São Paulo is not like Rio, there is not such a black [consciousness].... I prefer to go online for religious study." Online religious study is also becoming a trend among Muslims in the Bahamas and other Muslim minority countries. Gary Bunt observes that the "Muslim online discourses are part of the contemporary discussion about Islamic identities. The Internet has not superseded traditional forms... but is a means through which conventional boundaries and barriers can be transcended" (Bunt 2003: 11). Wilna Meijer explains that for European Muslim minorities Internet Islam "rejects the entire intellectual history of Islam, and simply wishes to base itself on the Qur'an and the hadith" (Meijer 2009: 14). There are fewer scholarly sources in Portuguese (English, French, and Spanish are dominant), and some Muslimahs in Brazil indicated that they follow Islamic blogs written by Portuguese-speaking Muslims in Brazil, Portugal, Egypt, and the United Arab Emirates, among other places. These sites, as well as Islamic chat sites marketed to Muslim minorities, are a source of both knowledge and sisterhood; they also offer future research opportunities to assess the impact the sites have on religious ideology and identity.

During the interview process it became clear that many Muslims in Brazil and the Bahamas have not been exposed to historical knowledge of their rich African heritage. The Mali, Songhay, Kanem-Bornu, and Hausa-Fulani empires and the twelfth-century university at Timbuktu were simply not part of their school curriculum. Not until 2003 did Brazil introduce a law obliging primary and secondary schools to include African and Afro-descendant history and culture in the curriculum (see Paixão 2008). The subject of race is a highly sensitive topic for Brazilians, who when interviewed emphasized the belief that Islamic identity ought to transcend racial categories.

The Bahamian government did little in the way of teaching African history or Afro-Bahamian history until quite recently, although the Bahamas is a country with a predominantly black population. The curriculum remains Anglo-European and Christian-centric. After national independence in 1973 the government was more concerned with hiring Bahamian teachers to replace expatriates than with revising curricular materials (Ministry of Education 1973). The "Bahamianization" policy that spoke of "the pursuit of social justice for all, national pride and loyalty, self-discipline and integrity based on Christian principles" made no mention of race or ethnicity.[6] Deena, 32, a Bahamian of European descent who feels that her Muslim identity has distanced her from being negatively associated with the "Bay Street Boys" (a colloquial term referring to the white oligarchy of merchants), remembers growing up in the 1980s: "When I was in primary school race taught during history class was diluted to 'I'm black and I was a slave and you're white and you were a slave master' without any explanation or analysis." She went on to warn, "I don't ever want my child to experience what I experienced." The lack of sensitivity to race and racial history is compounded by the problem that the goal of the past and present Religious Studies curriculum in the Bahamas is to "examine the basic beliefs and teaching of Christianity" (Ministry of Education 2010). In 2007 Latif Johnson and Khalil Mustapha Khalfani accused the government of forcing Muslim children to accept Christian religious instruction and therefore violating the Bahamian constitutional provisions for religious freedom (*Nassau Guardian* 2007). When asked about the incident, Khalfani explained that his family had made the painful decision to leave the Bahamas permanently. In order to provide his children with the best Islamic education and to instill in them a sense of racial and ethnic pride, the family moved to Senegal.

One of the defining moments for Muslims living in the Bahamas, Brazil, and other Muslim minority countries was the effect of the post–9/11 environment and the anti-Muslim discourse of the "War on Terror." In that atmosphere of suspicion and condemnation the negative perceptions of Bahamian and Brazilian Muslims by non-Muslims in their community were cemented. Muslims became unwillingly associated with terrorists, Islamists, and jihadists, and they were assumed to be sympathetic to organizations like Al Qaeda, Hezbollah, Hamas, or the Taliban. Bahamian Muslims experienced being the subject of classified U.S. Embassy reports published by Wikileaks. According to Amir Faisal Hepburn, Bahamian Muslims were "deeply offended" by the Security and Environment Profile Questionnaire completed by embassy officials, which described Bahamian Muslims as "sympathetic toward foreign terrorist groups" (McCartney 2011).

Muslimahs in the Bahamas made a clear distinction between what they saw as ignorant people stereotyping them versus their experiences of real prejudice, hate, and discrimination. Sara, a Bahamian who does not wish any of her personal details to be disclosed, described her experience after 9/11: "It is one thing to be called a terrorist by someone on the street, but it is another thing to have the U.S. Embassy call and say that your visa has been revoked.... We as Muslims must recognize that we live in a post-9/11 environment of prejudice and misunderstanding." In a distressed voice, Umm Qasim, a black Bahamian niqabi, laments: "We rarely go to the beach as a family. I don't want my children to have their memory of the beach be of someone calling their mother 'Bin Laden's wife' or telling their father to 'go home to Arabia.' I don't want my children to hear people saying that 'your family is a family of terrorists.'" In response to the hegemonic post-9/11 objectification of Muslims, Nabeela reappropriated the highly charged political term Taliban: "Some people call me Taliban... [but] it depends on the context.... [When] people who are ignorant say it—you have to correct them. At work, they know I'm *not* Taliban, but because of my forceful personality my nickname is Taliban [laughter]. It doesn't bother me."

For Muslims in Brazil, daily acts of religious expression, such as prayer, covering, and reciting in Arabic, have been reinscribed as suspicious and associated with the acts of terrorists, a perspective reified by the media. Maisa, 23, thinks "Brazil needs a real and effective way of spreading religion through da'wah and demystifying what is said about us in the media.... People who are influenced by the media really believe we are terrorists." Brazilian Maria, 34, who was raised a Catholic, described being confronted with social prejudice against Muslims: "My relatives think that I've become a terrorist. They began thinking this when I started covering. They are uncomfortable when I pray, when I use Arabic words like saying *halal* [lawful] or *haram* [unlawful] and say Allah (SWT) instead of God." Hanan, 24, explains that "Arabs see us Brazilian Muslims as crazy; non-Muslim Brazilians see us as completely crazy [laughter].... For me, wearing the niqab is a tricky thing.... [People think] is she a terrorist or a witch or a nun? They may call you anything or even assault you." These three examples should not be read as supporting the assumption that all Brazilian Muslims face rejection by their families. Rana, 24, a student of Portuguese descent, explains that this negative perception is not universal: "Some people automatically assume that because I reverted [converted] to Islam, my family had rejected me. On the contrary, my family supports me and my father especially defends my rights when we are in public. To those Christians who ask about my hijab, he says, 'Why don't you read Genesis and Corinthians and then decide about the practice of veiling?' It's true that veiling was an important part of Brazilian culture until the Catholic Church became 'modern.' ... Wearing the abaya can be compared to the mantilla of Paulistanas [a historical reference to the Catholic inhabitants of São Paulo]." None of the Muslimahs interviewed chose to or were pressured to uncover or to modify their religious practices because of growing discrimination.

Righteousness and Resilience: The Ideal Muslimah

Complex cultural and religious identities are simplified into unified ideological constructs such as the "ideal Muslimah" promoted by the patriarchal discourse among conservative religious leaders and visiting scholars from Muslim minority countries. The status quo ideal Muslimah derives from the monolithic representation of the Quranic ideal, a "woman whose examples to follow are the female-companions of the Messenger (SAWS) ... [and] the wives of the Messenger (SAWS)" (al-Hashimi 1996; see SAWS in glossary). There is the presumption of subservience in the social construction of Islamic identity in the Bahamas and Brazil, as in the ideal Muslimah. Local and political analyses reveal the effect of the historically and culturally patriarchal hierarchies of mosques and Islamic organizations and how the Muslimahs are situated within these contexts.

The expectation that Muslimahs ought to strive toward being the ideal Muslim woman is echoed in the experiences of both Bahamian and Brazilian women who were born into or converted to Islam. For most, the ideal is viewed as an admirable aim, yet a difficult if not unattainable spiritual goal. In the Bahamas the ideal Muslimah is constructed on the precepts of conservative Salafi ideology that has been endorsed by community leaders. Nabeela,

24, who describes herself as second generation Bahamian Muslim, comments on the women in the community who continue to "perpetuate [the] unattainable goal of being the perfect Muslimah.... In the Bahamas they get into wars over what is bid'a like prayer rugs, prayer clothes ... and foolishness like that." Yasmeen, 28, who has rejected the conservative ideology and identifies herself as "just a Muslim," explains what it was like growing up in the Bahamas in the 1990s, when the Bahamian Muslim community embraced the Salafi ideology with its prescriptive definition of the ideal Muslimah. She recalls that "in the 1990s [the leadership] went to the Qur'an and Sunnah Society Conference and embraced the Salafism. That whole way of Salafism peaked in 2000–2001. Every woman was wearing niqab and gloves! That kind of faded away a little bit, but the community still follows Salafism." Her negative experiences led her to leave the community, to which she later returned. Mona, 42, describes the experience of a close Muslim friend whose need to work away from the home precluded her ability to conform to gender roles prescribed by conservative ideology: "Khadija became Muslim, but as a single professional woman, she couldn't wear a khimar or niqab, she couldn't stay at home. She had children to feed and bills to pay. That's the problem with the way some Bahamians practice Islam ... they understand Islam in a book and cannot apply it to life in the Bahamas."

When these women discussed their location in society, fault lines began to appear in their thinking that contradicted their seemingly subservient relationship to the hierarchy of religious institutions. For example, although many reluctantly accept their subordinate positions within local religious institutions, some women are becoming adept at developing effective strategies to resist, challenge, or even subvert conservative, foreign-influenced religious ideologies.

Bahamian Muslims were heavily influenced by the charismatic personalities of leaders from the "largest most vibrant da'wah group"—the Salafi movement of African Americans in the United States in the 1990s (El Masry 2010: 217). In 1992 Dr. Abdullah Hakim Quick, a graduate of University of Medina (1979) and a key figure of the Salafi movement, gave a symposium at the College of the Bahamas on the "Deeper Roots of Islam in the Caribbean"(Rashad 2009). The community at the time was led by Imam Daud Abdul Haqq, a Barbadian who had also studied in Saudi Arabia.[7] Maryam, 25, a Bahamian graduate student, speaks about the rise in community conservatism: "As I have grown up I have watched the community become more conservative. For example, regarding Eid celebrations. I wanted to do a play.... But there are some voices—rigid people in the community—that do not want little boys and girls to mix. Some of the older men in the community take purdah to the extreme."

The conservative image of the ideal Muslimah in Salafi da'wah does not translate neatly into the Brazilian context. In Brazil there are multiple Islamic traditions, *madhabs* (schools of thought), and ideologies (Pinto 2011) compared to the Bahamas, where there is one dominant Islamic ideology. It should be noted that although the experiences of Muslimahs from São Bernardo do Campo—the base of the first Brazilian sheikhs and the current headquarters of the Brazilian branch of the Saudi organization World Assembly of Muslim Youth (Peres de Oliveira 2006)—differ from those of their Bahamian sisters, some of the Brazilian women share a similar understanding of the ideal Muslimah. Umm Zeinab, 35, who does not regularly attend a masjid and describes herself as Salafi, embraces the traditional definition of the ideal Muslimah: "I think there should be a strong focus on character building.... There are many hadith to support this in the Muslim and Bukhari texts. As a Muslim woman, I try to improve my character and manners on a daily basis. 'Aisha Radiya Allahu 'anho is my example." According to religious tradition, many blessings distinguish the Umm al Mu'minin (Mother of the believers) and third wife of the Prophet Muhammad (SAWS), 'Aisha bint Abu Bakar As-Siddiq, who is greatly revered by Sunni Muslims. In her lifetime she was responsible for recording numerous hadith, and she was known for establishing the first religious school for women. Aisha Geissinger explains: "The Qur'an imputes a level of religious authority to the wives of the Prophet as a group, directing them to remember Muhammad's revelations. However, Muslim tradition singles out 'Aisha as the pre-eminent female source of legal rulings, hadiths, and also Qur'anic variant readings" (Geissinger 2011: 45). Fatima, 33, who converted to Islam from Catholicism, describes herself as a Sunni who was influenced by the 'aqidah books she received from her local masjid. Called to Islam, she abandoned her "life in Brazil and made *hijra* [flight, departure] to a Muslim country for several years to learn about how to make Islam a reality" in her life. According to Fatima, "Islam should be based on the Qur'an and the Sunnah and never be tied to cultural practices and customs."

An oft-quoted hadith is that marriage is considered half of the *deen* (way of life) of Islam and young women often feel pressure to find a spouse.[8] Bahamian and Brazilian Muslimahs are confronted with a serious dilemma: how to find the ideal Muslim man. Muslimahs not born of Arab or South Asian diasporic communities face ethnic barriers that limit their opportunities of finding a spouse. According to Aminah McCloud, "Authenticity (being born in an ethnically recognized Muslim tradition) is often used as an indicator of social status and as a guide in the Muslim world for access and privilege including marriage alliances in a variety of settings" (McCloud 2010: 544; see also Karim 2006). In Brazil, the assumption that Arabs are the only authentic Muslims is taken for granted, but young Brazilian Muslims challenge this assumption. Zahra, 26, an Afro-Brazilian, explains: "I would never be able to marry a Lebanese-Brazilian Muslim. The white Brazilians marry their own people. My best chance at finding a husband is to marry a student from Africa. Another consideration for me is that my ideal husband must be a practicing Muslim [with] knowledge of the deen... to me the Lebanese don't really practice Islam." Having their daughters marry a believing Muslim is considered a priority for Bahamian parents such as 'Aisha, 42, a Bahamian mother of three girls who worries about the scarcity of Muslim men of good character: "When it comes to my daughters, I would understand if they did not want to marry a Bahamian Muslim.... I have taught them that it is important to be educated, but more importantly to be of *good* character... and these brothers become Muslim... [and] don't even attempt to improve their character.... How could I let my daughter marry somebody... like that?"

There is a double standard of behavior for men and women in religious practice and in the expression of their sexuality. Contradictions are reflected in the lived experiences of Bahamian Muslimahs at home and abroad. Salma, 41, a Bahamian who married a Southeast Asian Muslim, describes her disappointment with the hypocrisy and inequality she experienced in Muslim married life: "I fell in love and married a Muslim man from Southeast Asia. I willingly converted to Islam, I moved to his country, I learned his language, I took classes on Islam.... I tried my best to pray and fast... according to the expectations of my in-laws [but] my husband rarely prayed or fasted unless we had guests at the house.... Our marriage wasn't what I expected." Nabeela, an outspoken and well-educated single Muslimah, is aware of different sexual standards for men and women: "There are aspects of Bahamian culture that are condoned... or just accepted by the community. For example, a man [who converted to Islam] had several children outside of marriage and it was accepted because of Bahamian society. They will say, 'You know he had a bunch of children.' No matter how much a person puts on a thobe or abaya our culture is ingrained in us... there is a double standard." For men, having children out of wedlock does not have the same negative social stigma in the Caribbean as it does in other regions. Nabeela contends that people in her community have little understanding of male and female sexuality in Islam and are unaware that during the time of Prophet Muhammad (SAWS) women had the right to choose and repudiate men according to their own sexual desires (Mernissi 1987: 53).

The Ummah: Transcending Cultural Space

In speaking with Muslimahs from both countries, the centrality of the concept of the ummah was revealed with their reference to two *ayat* in the Quran: the religious sense of belonging, "And hold firmly to the rope of Allah together and do not become divided" (Quran 3:103); and the philosophical sense of belonging to and being accepted by all of humankind, "We have created you from male and female and made you peoples and tribes that you may know one another" (Quran 49:13, Saheeh International 1997 translation). Abdullah al-Ahasan (1986: 606–16) provides an etymology of the term *ummah* from a Quranic perspective: the term *ummah* can be associated with a single source (*umm*), a creature (*umam*), a mother (*umm/ummi*), one community (*ummatan wahidatan*), a balanced community (*umatan wasatan*), the best community (*khaira ummatin*), the community of believers (*ummat al-mu'minin*), and those associated with the community of believers (*ummah m'a al-Muslimin*). Yet ummah is more than a religious and philosophical concept; it is the binding source of identity for Muslim minorities living in the Americas. Sultana Afroz observes this principle in Jamaica: "The splendorous past of the Muslim ummah serves as a source of spiritual inspiration to maintain [their] Islamic identity in [this] multicultural and religiously diverse society" (Afroz 2003: 211–12). The bond with the ummah provides a sense of cultural and religious authenticity for Muslimahs that transcends race and ethnicity.

The concept of the ummah in the Americas is not a source of political mobilization as it is in Arab and South Asian political discourse (Deviji 2011; Fatima 2011). However, it is an important source of religious deterritorialization of Islamic identity (Appadurai 2003: 38). Nikos Papastergiadis explains that "the deterritorialization of culture refers to the ways in which people now feel they belong to various communities despite the fact that they do not share a common territory.... The authenticity of a cultural formation is no longer singularly linked to its physical proximity to a given cultural center" (Papastergiadis 2000: 115–16). Muslim women in the Bahamas and Brazil have developed a Muslim cultural identity that transcends race (black, white, South Asian, Southeast Asian), ethnicity (African, Portuguese, English, Amerindian, Indigenous Brazilian, Malay), language (English, Portuguese, Spanish, Arabic), and territory (Americas). Strengthened by their resolve to view Islam as a broad source of religious knowledge, they are nomadic (Deleuze et al. 2004), not restricted by territory, race, ethnicity, gender, or the patriarchal if not hostile environments they may encounter on their spiritual journeys; they inhabit a "third space" of hybrid identities (Khan 2002).

In the Americas, Muslim immigrant communities that practice cultural interpretations of Islam rooted in particular madhab have been a catalyst for promoting a more transcendent religious identity for indigenous Muslims. The Muslimah participants in my research speak with pride about their unique religious and philosophical differences and the depth of their knowledge of Islam, which in some cases surpasses that of their first generation immigrant Muslim counterparts. Many of these Muslimahs resist being identified as Sunni or Shi'a, Hanafi or Ja'fari. They are adamant that being Arab or speaking Arabic does not make one a more legitimate or authentic Muslim. They choose not to follow a particular madhab or cultural practice in Islam and instead self-identify as Muslim and as being part of a deterritorialized global ummah that is no longer attached to an ethnic homeland. They are passionate about how they have helped shape their ummah and about their vision for the future of the ummah.

For Mona, 42, her Bahamian ummah is not Arabia: "My point, when I have the chance to talk to sisters . . . I tell the sisters, once your culture is not dealing with *shirk* [idolatry], it is not haram [unlawful]. I tell people outright—I am *not* an Arab, I am not going to dress like an Arab. But I see it happening around me." Yasmeen explains that because the language of religious instruction is English in the Bahamas, people in her community do not "feel awkward because the *juma khutbah* [sermon to the congregation] is read in English and Arabic." Nabeela confirms that her community is accepting of ethnic difference: "We are very open-minded. When I have been abroad in an Arab community—they do not accept non-Arabic speaking Muslims . . . they could not accept that. They feel that if you didn't speak Arabic, you were a deficient Muslim in some way. . . . The Bahamas is the opposite . . . we grew up as a mongrel pot. . . . If this person is Trini or Guyanese or South African or Swedish it doesn't matter . . . we despise *assabiyah* [prejudice]."

Brazilian Muslimahs also seek an inclusive ummah that is not bound by culture or language, and the importance of deterritorialized space is a dominant theme in the voices of Brazilian Muslimahs. Maisa, 23, complains about exclusive, privileged Arab culture in her community: "There is little distinction in Brazil of what belongs to Islamic culture and what belongs to Arab culture, most likely because the community itself has an Arab majority.... As Brazilians we can also be legitimate Muslims." Fatima, 33, who has spent time abroad, does not want her spiritual community to "practic[e] a religion that has been hijacked by the Lebanese who immigrated to Brazil." According to Jandira, 26, converts to Islam will help define the future of the Brazilian ummah: "The Brazilians who were born Muslim and had parents who were from Muslim countries are only concerned with their culture.... The masjids in Brazil are a reflection of Arab and Persian culture and there is a lot of discrimination against non-Arabs.... Claiming a new Brazilian Muslim identity is only possible with reverts [converts] to Islam."

Another dominant theme for both Bahamian and Brazilian communities is the importance of religious education based on legitimate textual sources. Maryam, 25, explains with pride that in her ummah, "The source of knowledge comes directly from the Qur'an and Sunnah.... Sisters row up ankle to ankle, shoulder to shoulder for *salat* [prayer] ... [and] give each other salaams *always*, no matter what your background." Living in a predominantly Arab community in Brazil, Maisa, 23, emphasizes: "My religious belief was not influenced by my community ... [but] derived from researching Islamic texts." Hanan, 24, also emphasizes the role of education: "My belief stems from the discovery of the falsehood for which I was raised.... People are still ignorant—even other Muslims ... they need to read—[in Arabic] 'read in the name of your Lord' ... and they need to avoid what is between the halal and the haram" (Quran 96:1; Hadith of An-Nawawi).

The central unifying theme in the narratives of these women is that their ummah should be open-minded, transformative, and further deterritorialized. In her ummah, Bahamian Nabeela explains that gender segregation in the public space should be kept to a minimum: "I believe men and women should intermingle; encouraging gender segregation stops the free flow of ideas ... and you end up with people who are emotionally stunted." Deena, 32, argues that "Islam is supposed to transform. We are supposed to be investing in our community first and growing as part of a global *ummah*. We should be sending young Muslims to college and technical training in the Bahamas.... We need economic and social development in order to foster spiritual development." Maisa, 23, agrees with the focus on education and deterritorialization: "I would like to learn more about Muslims in the Americas, whether through the Internet or through visiting other countries.... Muslim sisters can be a source of knowledge for each other. Where we live doesn't matter because we are all part of this global ummah."

Conclusion

Muslimahs are constituted within a changing network of power relations including the ideological practices of Islam and the social construction of the ideal Muslimahs in various cultural contexts. In this chapter Islam is treated as a religion and as a discourse, which includes rules for social and power relations within society. Islam is also defined as a personal ideology. Personal ideologies provide a "'symbolic outlet' for emotional disturbances generated by social disequilibrium. . . . Reactions to the disturbances will be similar, a similarity only reinforced by presumed commonalities . . . among members of a particular culture" (Geertz 1973: 204). The women self-identify as Bahamian and Brazilian, yet they are ultimately represented as Muslimahs through the complex interaction of culture, religion, class, and other ideological frameworks. Islam is a cultural marker and a boundary to local cultural cohesiveness, yet as a worldview it provides the foundation of their identity and belonging.

Local and political analysis of the Bahamian and Brazilian contexts reveals the effect of the historically and culturally patriarchal hierarchies of mosques and Islamic organizations and how the Muslimahs are situated in these contexts. The presumption of subservience in the social construction of Islamic identity in the Bahamas and Brazil in line with the ideal Muslimah model is discredited. The public perception that Islam is an ethnicity defines the women's cultural insecurity and creates boundaries between Muslims and non-Muslims. The courageous women who participated in this research identify with the global Muslim ummah, and they are proud of their local roots. Most important, they are committed to improving the ummah on a local and global scale. The ideal Bahamian and Brazilian Muslimah in her struggle against a politicized identity is righteous and resilient and determined to promote positive cultural and religious self-representations. The voices of Muslimahs from the Bahamas and Brazil contribute to the definition of the ummah in the Americas. It is hoped that this small snapshot of their struggles for identity and belonging will inspire Muslims in other Muslim minority countries to embrace their local Muslim identities and to build bridges with other women in the Americas. Is this not, after all, the meaning of ummah?

Glossary of Islamic Terms

The terms that follow are transliterated according to common usage in the Bahamas and Brazil (translations from Portuguese).

Abu/aboo *n.* Father, also used for the nickname (see *kunya*).
Allah/Allaah *n.* God.

'Aqidah/'aqeedah *n.* Creed; foundation of belief and practice; school of theology (see *madhab*).

Ashura *n.* Ashura is the tenth day of Muharram (in the Islamic calendar) and is celebrated by Shi'a Muslims as a day of mourning of the martyrdom of Hussein ibn Ali and by the Sunni Muslims as a day of fasting.

'Assabiyah/'assabiyaah *n.* Prejudice, often in the form of tribalism, ethnocentrism, racism, caste discrimination, or nationalism. It also describes the hegemonic ideology of misguided Islamic scholars and intellectuals.

Bid'a/bid'ah *n.* An innovation in religious practice.

Da'wah *n.* The invitation of non-Muslims to Islam; the summoning of Muslims of weak faith back to Islam. Da'wah is an act of *ibadah/ibada* (worship).

Deen/Dīn *n.* Way of life in Islam.

Eid *n.* Festival or holiday in Islam. Two main holidays in Sunni Islam are Eid ul Adha, also known as Bakra Eid, Qurbani Eid, or Kurban Bayram (festival of sacrifice held after the pilgrimage) and Eid ul Fitr, also known as Hari Raya Aidilfitri (festival at the end of the month of fasting). Shi'a Muslims also celebrate Eid in addition to other holidays, such as Ashura.

Hadith/hadeeth *n.* Narrations and actions of the Prophet Muhammad (SAWS); collected in the books of Sahih Bukhari and Muslim and the Sunan of an-Nasa'ii, Abu Dawud, at-Tirmidhi and ibn Majah.

Hajj *n.* Pilgrimage; one of the Five Pillars of Islam.

Halal *a., n.* That which is lawful and permissible in Islam. This may refer to actions and objects. *Haram* is the opposite of halal and refers to that which is unlawful and forbidden.

Imam/Imaam *n.* Religious scholar; leader of the state; leader of the community; leader of the prayer.

Islam/Islaam *n.* Submission to the will of God; the religious belief system of the Muslims explained in terms of the Five Pillars: faith (*shahada*), meaning belief in one God and the Prophet Muhammad (SAWS), prayer (*salat*), fasting (*sawm*), charity (*zakat*), and pilgrimage (*hajj*).

Jamaat/jama'at/jama'a *n.* An Islamic movement or organization; can also refer to a congregation or community.

Juma/jummah/juma'a *n.* Friday. The day of congregation worship for Muslims. A sermon (see *khutbah*) is given during *juma salat*.

Khimaar/hijab *n.* Head covering for women reflecting the concept of modesty; mentioned in the Quran 24:31. Other forms of covering include scarf, shayla, shawl, and amira.

Khutbah *n.* Sermon given during congregational prayers on Friday.

Kunya/Kunyah *n.* The honorific nickname of an Arab or Muslim adult derived from the person's offspring (e.g., Hameeda, mother of Yahya, becomes Umm Yahya; Umar, father of Fareed, becomes Abu Fareed).

Madhab/mazhab/madh'hab *n.* School of religious jurisprudence. The main Sunni madhabs are Hanafi, Maliki, Shafi'i, and Hanbali. The main Shi'a madhabs are Ja'fari, Ismaili, Ibadi, and Zahiris. There are many other subsects that are considered cultural or mystical expressions of Islam (e.g., Dawoodi Bohra—South Asia; Tijaniya Sufi—West Africa).

Masjid/jamia *n.* Mosque (Portuguese *mesquita*); place of worship; place of prostration. In non-Muslim countries the masjid is an important place for education and community life. *Jamia* is another word for a place of gathering or congregating.

Muslimah/Muslima *n.* Female Muslim. Muhajabah is a Muslim woman who wears the hijab. Hajjah is a Muslim woman who has been to hajj.

Niqab/Niqaab *n.* Veil covering the face. A person who wears a niqab is sometimes called a *niqabi*, just as a person who wears a hijab is sometimes called a *hijabi*.

Purdah *n.* Segregation of the sexes; the seclusion of women to the home; a requirement for women to "draw a curtain" between herself and any males not her relatives; a requirement to wear clothing that covers the whole body, including the face.

Radiya Allahu 'anho *phr.* May Allah be pleased with. Follows the name of an Islamic scholar or a companion of the Prophet (SAWS).

Ramadan/Ramadhan *n.* In the Islamic lunar calendar, the month the Quran was revealed; the period of ritual fasting.

Sahih/saheeh *n.* An authentic hadith.

Salat/salaah/namaaz *v., n.* Prayer performed five times a day (morning, noon, afternoon, evening, and night) and in congregation on Fridays.

Salaf *n.* The early Muslims; the companions of the Prophet (SAWS); the first three generations of Muslims.

Salafi/Salafiyyah/'Ahl-us-Sunnah/'Ahl al Sunnah wa Jama'ah *n.* A traditional conservative movement in Islam in which believers follow the Salaf al-Saalih (pious predecessors) of the Prophet Muhammad (SAWS). The movement has roots in Saudi Arabia and the Wahabi movement (Ibn 'Abd al-Wahab), which was inspired by the scholarship in the 1300s of Ibn Taymiyya, Ibn Qayyim al Jawziyya.

SAWS, *n.* Abbreviation of "Sallalahu 'alayhi wa sallam" (May the peace and blessing of God be upon him).

Sheikh/shaikh *n.* Scholar of Islam.

Shi'a/Shi'ah/Shiite *n.* From the followers of 'Ali. Shi'a and Sunni Islam share some of the same basic belief system but differ on matters concerning succession, leadership (imamate), and practice. Shi'a Islam is represented in the Caribbean and Latin America in the descendants of Lebanese, Syrian, and South Asian Muslim immigrants and, to a lesser extent, Persians (Iranians).

Shirk *n.* Idolatry; associating partners with Allah (SWT).

Sunni *n.* Followers of the sayings, habits, and practices of the Prophet Muhammad (SAWS). The Sunnis accept the guidance of the Quran and the hadith. Sunni and Shi'a Islam share some of the same basic belief system but differ on matters concerning succession, leadership, and practice.

SWT, *n.* Abbreviation of "Subhana wa ta'ala" (Be glorified and exalted).

Thobe, kufi, keffiyeh/ghutrah *n.* Garments commonly worn by Muslim men, especially in the Arabian Peninsula. The thobe is a long kaftan. The kufi is a small cap or hat. The keffiyeh or ghutrah is a square cotton scarf commonly associated with Palestinians but also popular with Muslims and non-Muslims alike.

Taliban *n.* Persons in Afghanistan whose religious fundamentalist doctrine is influenced by the Sunni schools of thought Deobani (India), Wahabi (Saudi Arabia), and Hanafi (South Asia). Also used as a derogatory term toward Muslims. The root of the word is *talib* (student).

Umm *n.* Mother. Also used as a nickname (see *kunya*).
Ummah/ummat al-mu'minin *n.* A Muslim community; the community of believers; the Muslim world.
Wajib *n.* Required religious observance. The synonym *fard* denotes a required religious duty; *mustahabb* are recommended observances.

Notes

1. I am extremely grateful to Letícia Rodrigues Cavalcante (Safiya Ishaq) for facilitating interviews in Brazil and to Maria Eduarda Yurgel for assisting with translations. The actual population figure is contested in both countries, and there is no survey that differentiates between settled immigrant populations and indigenous Muslims. Brazilian Muslims claim to represent a total population of over 700,000, but official statistics list only 27,239 Muslims in a total population of 190.7 million (Brazilian Government Census 2010). John Tofik Karam asserts that the numbers of persons of Syrian and Lebanese descent in Brazil, for example, have been greatly exaggerated for political gain (Karam 2007: 11). Bahamian Muslims claim to represent 200–350 persons in a total population of 353,658 (Department of Statistics, Bahamas: 2010, Carmichael Road Masjid records).

2. The term *indigenous* Muslim has been adopted by scholars of Islam in the United States as a means of cultural differentiation between communities of Muslims born in America and immigrant diasporic communities (Jackson 2005; Abd-Allah 2006). I have opted not to employ *indigenous* because the term is embedded with a complex cultural meaning in the Caribbean and South America. Also, the indigenous/immigrant binary defines the controversial and antagonistic relationship that exists in religious discourse in the North American public sphere (Webb 2009).

3. See glossary later in this essay for definitions of Arabic words used. It is common practice for Muslims to use Arabic words in everyday parlance. Arabic words appear throughout the essay, reflecting this practice.

4. See also Quick 1996: in this controversial book Quick argues that Muslims traveled to the Americas prior to the Europeans and made contact with the Caribs, as evidenced by their cultural practices.

5. An Act for the Abolition of Slavery throughout the British Colonies; for promoting the Industry of the manumitted Slaves; and for compensating the Persons hitherto entitled to the Services of such Slaves (August 28, 1833) and the Lei Áurea (Golden Law), Signed by Princess Isabel on behalf of her father Emperor Pedro II (May 13, 1888).

6. See Ministry of Education (1973). The white paper spoke of the policy of Bahamianization: "The security of its people, resources and the environment, restoring a sense of dignity to labour, the pursuit of social justice for all, national pride and loyalty, self-discipline and integrity based on Christian principles" (7); and yet it was acknowledged throughout that as a result of economic constraints, the curriculum would be borrowed from the Commonwealth.

7. Daud Abdul Haqq is now the imam of the National Islamic Association, a Caribbean majority congregation in Newark, New Jersey.

8. Reported in various hadith and emphasized in the Quran: "And of His signs is that He created for you from yourselves mates that you may find tranquillity in them; and He placed between you affection and mercy. Indeed in that are signs for a people who give thought" (Saheeh International 1997: 30.21).

References Cited

Abd-Allah, Umar Faruq
2006 "Islam and the Cultural Imperative." *Cross Currents* (New York: Association for Religion and Intellectual Life), 1–14.

Abolition of Slavery Act
1833 An Act for the Abolition of Slavery throughout the British Colonies; for promoting the Industry of the manumitted Slaves; and for compensating the Persons hitherto entitled to the Services of such Slaves. http://www.pdavis.nl/Legis_07.htm.

Afroz, Sultana
2003 "Invisible Yet Invincible: The Muslim *Ummah* in Jamaica." *Journal of Muslim Minority Affairs* 23(1): 211–22.

al-Ahasan, Abdullah
1986 "The Quranic Concept of Ummah." *Journal of the Institute of Muslim Minority Affairs* 7(2): 606–16.

al-Hashimi, Muhammad Ali
1996 *The Ideal Muslimah*. Trans. International Islamic Publishing House. 15th Shawwal 1416 (Islamic calendar). Riyadh, Saudi Arabia: International Islamic Publishing House.

Ansari, Anis
2010 "Islam in the Bahamas: Islamic Movement." *Radiance Views Weekly*. http://www.radianceweekly.com/199/5243/suicide-by-a-naxalite-will-maoists-live-long/2010-04-04/islamic-movement/story-detail/islam-in-the-bahamas.html.

Appadurai, Arjun
2003 [1996] *Modernity at Large: Cultural Dimensions of Globalization*. Minneapolis: University of Minnesota Press.

Braziel, Jana E., and Anita Mannur
2003 *Theorizing Diaspora: A Reader*. Oxford, UK: Wiley Blackwell.

Brazilian Government Census
2010 Brazil Brazilian Institute of Geography and Statistics (IBGE). http://www.censo2010.ibge.gov.br/.

Bunt, Gary R.
2003 *Islam in the Digital Age: E-Jihad, Online Fatwas and Cyber Islamic Environments*. London: Pluto Press.

Craton, Michael, and Gail Saunders
1992 *Islanders in the Stream: A History of the Bahamian People*. Vol. 1: *From Aboriginal Times to the End of Slavery*. Athens: University of Georgia Press.

1998 *Islanders in the Stream: A History of the Bahamian People*. Vol. 2: *From the Ending of Slavery to the Twenty-First Century*. Athens: University of Georgia Press.

Deleuze, Gilles, Félix Guattari, and Brian Massumi
1987 *A Thousand Plateaus: Capitalism and Schizophrenia*. Minneapolis: University of Minnesota Press; repr. London: Continuum International Publishing Group, 2004.

Department of Statistics, Bahamas
2010 Preliminary Population and Housing Count by Island and Supervisory District (2010 All Bahamas Census). Department of Statistics of the Bahamas, May 9.

Deviji, Faisal
2011 "Muslim Universality." *Postcolonial Studies* 14(2): 231–41.

Diouf, Sylviane A.
1998 *Servants of Allah: African Muslims Enslaved in the Americas*. New York: New York University Press.

Elia, Nadia
2003 "'Kum Buba Yali Kum Buba Tambe, Ameen, Ameen, Ameen': Did Some Flying Africans Bow to Allah?" *Callaloo* 26(1): 182–202.

El Masry, Shadee
2010 "The Salafis in America: The Rise, Decline and Prospects for a Sunni Muslim Movement among African Americans." *Journal of Muslim Minority Affairs* 30(2): 217–36.

Fatima, Saba
2011 "Who Counts as Muslim? Identity, Multiplicity and Politics." *Journal of Muslim Minority Affairs* 31(3): 339–53.

Federação das Associações Muçulmanas do Brasil (FAMBRAS)
2012 FAMBRAS website. http://www.fambras.org.br/.

Geertz, Clifford
1973 *The Interpretation of Cultures: Selected Essays*. New York: Basic Books.

Geissinger, Aisha
2011 "'Aisha bint Abi Bakr and her Contributions to the Formation of the Islamic Tradition." *Religion Compass* 5: 37–49.

Gomez, Michael Angelo
2005 *Reversing Sail: A History of the African Diaspora*. Cambridge, UK: Cambridge University Press.

Higman, Barry W.
1995 [1984] *Slave Populations of the British Caribbean, 1807–1834*. Kingston, Jamaica: University of the West Indies Press.

Hoefte, Rosemarijin
1987 "The Position of Female British Indian and Javanese Contract Laborers in Suriname: A Last Word." *Boletín de Estudios Latinoamericanos y del Caribe* 43: 121–23.

Jackson, Sherman A.
2005 *Islam and the Blackamerican: Looking toward the Third Resurrection*. New York: Oxford University Press.

Kale, Madhavi
1998 *Fragments of Empire: Capital, Slavery, and Indian Indentured Labor Migration in the British Caribbean*. Pittsburgh: University of Pennsylvania Press.

Karam, John Tofik
2007 *Another Arabesque: Syrian-Lebanese Ethnicity in Neoliberal Brazil.* Philadelphia: Temple University Press.

Karim, Jamillah A.
2006 "To Be Black, Female, and Muslim: A Candid Conversation about Race in the American *Ummah.*" *Journal of Muslim Minority Affairs* 26(2): 225–33.

Kettani, M. Ali
1990 "Muslims in non-Muslim Societies: Challenges and Opportunities." *Journal of the Institute of Muslim Minority Affairs* 11(2): 226–23.

Khan, Shanaz
2002 *Aversion and Desire: Negotiating Muslim Female Identity in the Diaspora.* Toronto, Ontario: Women's Press.

Kongwa, Raymond
2006 "A Bahamian Boom." *Nassau Guardian,* September 29, A4.

Lei Áurea [Golden Law]
1888 Signed by Princess Isabel on behalf of her father Emperor Pedro II, Brazil, 13th May. http://newsgroups.derkeiler.com/Archive/Alt/alt.talk.royalty/2006-01/msg 00432.html.

McCartney, Juan
2011 "U.S.: Local Terror Ties Suspected, Muslim Leaders Claim They are Being 'Harassed' by Embassy Officials." *Nassau Guardian,* 12 June. http://www.thenassauguardian .com/index.php?option=com_content&view=article&id=10797&Itemid=27.

McCloud, Aminah B.
2010 "African American Islam: A Reflection." *Religion Compass,* 4: 538–50.

Meijer, Wilna A.
2009 "Tradition and Future of Islamic Education." In *Religious Diversity and Education in Europe,* vol. 10. Munster, Germany: Waxman Verlag GmbH.

Mernissi, Fátima
1987 *Beyond the Veil: Male-Female Dynamics in Modern Muslim Society.* Bloomington: Indiana University Press.

Ministry of Education, Bahamas
1973 *Focus on the Future.* White paper on education, based on Progressive Liberal Party education platform. Nassau, New Providence: Government of the Bahamas.
2010 Religious Studies Scope and Sequence Chart, Curriculum. http://www.bahamase-ducation.com/curriculum.asp.

Ministry of External Affairs, India
2000 "Other Countries of Central and South America." Ch. 19, Report of the High Level Committee on the Indian Diaspora. Ministry of External Affairs, Foreign Secretary's Office, Government of India. http://indiandiaspora.nic.in/diasporapdf/chapter19.pdf.

Modood, Tariq
2007 *Multiculturalism: A Civic Idea,* Cambridge, UK: Polity Press.

Mohanty, Chandra Talpade
2003 "Under Western Ideas: Feminist Scholarship and Colonial Discourses." In *Feminist Postcolonial Theory,* ed. Reina Lewis and Sara Mills, 49–74. New York: Routledge.

Moxley Rouse, Carolyn
2004 *Engaged Surrender: African American Women and Islam.* Berkeley: University of California Press.
Muslimah Media Watch
2010 "*Cómo Orientalistas*: Telemundo's El Clon, Part 1." Muslim Media Watch Blog, Diana, April 21, 2010. http://www.patheos.com/blogs/mmw/2010/04/como-orientalista-telemundos-el-clon-part-i/.
Nassau Guardian
2007 "Muslims Complaining about Discrimination on the Grounds of Religion." *Nassau Guardian*, November 15.
Paixão, Marcelo
2008 "Brazilian Experience in the Fight against Racism and in Promoting Racial Equality: Policies, Trends and Limits" (with reference to law 10.639). Paper presented to Human Rights Council, 7th session, Working Group of Experts on People of African Descent, Geneva, January 14–18, 2008. A/HRC/7/AC.3/BP/6.
Papastergiadis, Nikos
2000 *The Turbulence of Migration.* Cambridge, UK: Polity Press.
Peres de Oliveira, Vitória
2006 "O Islã no Brasil ou o Islã do Brasil?" *Religiao e Sociedade* 26(1): 83–114.
Pinto, Paulo
2011 "Arab Ethnicity and Diasporic Islam: A Comparative Approach to Process of Identity Formation and Religious Codification in the Muslim Communities of Brazil." *Comparative Studies of South Asia, African and the Middle East* 31(2): 312–30.
Powles, Louis Diston
1996 [1888] *The Land of the Pink Pearl: Recollections of Life in the Bahamas.* Nassau: Media Publishing.
Quick, Abdullah Hakim
1996 *Deeper Roots: Muslims in the Americas and the Caribbean Before Columbus,* 2nd ed. London: Ta-Ha Publications.
Rashad, Munir Ahmad
2009 "The History of Islam in the Bahamas." Lecture presented to the Bahamas Historical Society, January 22, 2009.
Reis, João José
2005 *Slave Rebellion in Brazil: The Muslim Uprising of 1835 in Bahia.* Baltimore: Johns Hopkins University Press.
Saheeh International
1997 *Translation of the Holy Qur'an.* Riyadh, Saudi Arabia: Abdul Qasim Publishing House (Al-Muntada Al Islami).
Sheridan, Richard B., and Roderick A. McDonald
1996 *West Indies Accounts: Essays on the History of the British Caribbean and the Atlantic Economy in Honour of Richard Sheridan.* Kingston, Jamaica: University of the West Indies Press.
Slave Registers
1812–1834 Microfilm Publication of Slave Registers of Former British Colonial Dependencies. Office of Registry of Colonial Slaves and Slave Compensation Commission

(Records created and inherited by Her Majesty's Treasury, Kew, Surrey, England). National Archives of the United Kingdom.

Telles, Edward E.

2004 *Race in Another America: The Significance of Skin Color in Brazil.* Princeton, N.J.: Princeton University Press.

Turner, Grace

2007 In His Own Words: Abdul Keli, a Liberated African Apprentice. *Journal of the Bahamas Historical Society* 29: 27–31.

Webb, Suhaib

2009 "Framing the Discussion on Culture and the Fitna of the Immigrant/Indigenous Dichotomy" Lecture. http://www.suhaibwebb.com/islam-studies/the-tarbiyyah-imperative-framing-the-discussion-on-culture-and-the-fitnah-of-the-immigrant-indigenous-dichotomy/.

III

SPATIAL PRACTICES AND THE TRINIDADIAN LANDSCAPE

10

"Up Against a Wall"

Muslim Women's Struggle to Reclaim Masjid Space
in Trinidad and Tobago

RHODA REDDOCK

When in the first decade of this century the women of the San Juan Muslim Ladies Organization began their resistance against efforts to curtail and circumscribe their attendance at and use of masjid space at the Nur E Islam masjid in El Socorro, San Juan, Trinidad and Tobago, they were possibly unaware of the global movement of Islamic women to reclaim masjid space for congregational worship and other activities.[1] This was also true for Feroza "Rose" Mohammed when, in shock at Eid Prayers (*salaah*) in 2007, she stormed the recently installed barriers at the Trinidad Muslim League, or Jinnah Memorial Masjid, in St. Joseph.[2] Taking a historical perspective, in this essay I explore the changing position of women in Islamic religious practice in Trinidad and Tobago with specific emphasis on their use of masjid (mosque) space. I also explore the critical role of religious reformer Moulvi Ameer Ali in the transformation of women's religious and mosque practice in Trinidad and Tobago in the early twentieth century and provide three case studies of recent and ongoing negotiations and struggles over access to masjid space.

Women's mosque movements have a history over many years but took on new significance in the early twentieth century as part of the anti-colonial and first wave feminist movements of that period. Margot Badran refers to the period in 1911 when Egyptian anti-colonial writer, educator, activist, and feminist Malak Hifni Nasif took the opportunity to "demand that women regain the right to participate in congregational prayer in the mosque that, as she pointed out, they had enjoyed in Mecca and Medina in the early days of Islam" (Badran 2006: 1).[3] Although for some this would be seen as a religious demand, it was also a demand for their human rights as women.

Not surprisingly, most of the recent international media focus has been on the mosque movements in North America. Attention has been drawn to African American Muslim professor and theologian Amina Wadud, author of *Qur'an and Woman: Re-reading the Sacred Text from a Woman's Perspective*, who delivered the *khutbah* (sermon) and led *juma* prayers in New York on Friday, March 18, 2005.[4] But already in August 1994 Wadud had delivered the *khutbah* at the Friday prayers at the Claremont Main Road Mosque in Cape Town, South Africa, the first time a woman was invited to do so (Badran 2006: 3).[5]

In addition, the spotlight has been focused on Asma Nomani's *Standing Alone in Mecca*, where among other things she discusses women's efforts to claim their space at the Morgantown mosque in West Virginia by walking through the front door (cited in Badran 2006: 3). The exclusion of women from masjids has been a common practice in many parts of the world. Justification for these practices is usually drawn from interpretations of certain *hadiths*—sayings and approvals of the Prophet Muhammad (SAWS).[6] Those who support this exclusion refer to sayings like the following: "It is more excellent for a woman to pray in her house than in her courtyard, and more excellent for her to pray in her private chamber than in her house" (Sunan Abu Dawood translation, vol. 1, ch. 204, hadith no. 570). Or the statement by the Prophet's wife Ayesha (may Allah be pleased with her) when she said sometime after his death, "If the Prophet (peace and blessings be upon him) would have seen what the women do now, he would have stopped them from coming to Mosques."

Those who challenge this position, however, have equally strong justification for their position. They cite the words of the Prophet: "Do not prevent the she-servants of Allah from Allah's mosques" (Sahih Muslim, vol. 1, ch. 177, hadith no. 886).[7] They also note that in the time of the Prophet women and men both offered prayers, a practice that continues in Mecca and Medina today.[8] These prayers could take place anywhere; sometimes even in Christian churches not in use at the time. This sentiment is summarized in the following hadith: "The Earth has been made a place of prayer (Masjid) for me, and pure. Therefore, anyone from my community who is overtaken by the time of prayer let them pray [wherever they may be]" (Bukhari, vol. 1, book 7). In some countries this exclusion is widespread, while in others women have been allowed varying degrees of involvement and participation. Where women are allowed to pray in masjids they usually pray behind the men, separated from them by a partition or a wall, or in a basement, or on a balcony—that is, in a separate space altogether. There is normally also a separate women's entrance, often at the back or the side of the masjid.[9] Among concerned women the issues have normally involved not only the separation but also the quality of the space. In many instances the space is perceived as inferior as they are unable to see or, at times, to hear the imam give the *khutbah* (sermon).

Women's Mosque Movements in Global Context

Badran dates the emergence of the contemporary global women's mosque movement with the 1994 invitation by the Claremont Main Road Mosque in Cape Town, South Africa, to U.S. Islamic feminist Amina Wadud to give the *khutbah* at Friday prayers.[10] South Africans, however see an earlier emergence, linked to the women's movements that emerged alongside the anti-apartheid struggles in South Africa. While the Claremont Main Road Mosque has become synonymous with mosque struggles in that country and internationally, according to Ilham Rawoot (2010) Muslim women activists and the Muslim youth movement fought from the late 1970s for both an equal amount of space *and* equal quality of space for women and men in South Africa. Today at the Claremont mosque women and men pray side by side, and women can read the *khutbah* at Friday prayers, something still unthinkable in most parts of the world. In the 1990s in Johannesburg sit-ins were organized at mosques that had no space for women, and "The 23rd Street Mosque became the first Indian-run mosque in Johannesburg to accept women (Rawoot 1.4.2010)" (Gamieldien 2004).

In a recent article Rawoot (2010) cites religious scholars who argue that in South Africa the mosques influenced by the Indian subcontinent tend to be more conservative than others, whereas in the Western Cape, characterized by a diversity of traditions—Indian, Malay, and African—there is a diversity of practices related to women's access to mosque space (Rawoot 2010). On the Indian subcontinent, from which the vast majority of Trinidadian Muslims originated in the mid- to late nineteenth century, women of the dominant Hanafi 'ulama legal school of the Sunni tradition are discouraged from attending the mosque (Islamic Research Foundation International 2010). As late as 2010, a women's movement Web site in India was requesting donations to assist a Muslim woman member, Daud Sharifa Khanam, to build a mosque for women in her village. To support her plea she complained,

> The idea of a women's mosque was born out of mounting frustrations with the rulings of the jamat—the group of Islamic male elders who decide on family issues such as marriage, dowry, divorce, domestic violence, custody, and child abuse.

> If women go to the police for help with such cases, most often the matter is referred to the jamat. But there is one big problem with this: the jamat sit in the mosque—a place where women are not allowed to enter. In India, Muslim women mostly pray in adjoining buildings.
>
> So women cannot give their side of the story or hear judgments in cases that intimately involve them. As Daud Sharifa puts it: "They are dealing with my case without me. They are talking about me without me. And they are also passing judgment without me." (Khanam 2010)

Fatima Mernissi identifies the creation of spatial boundaries between women and men as a central component of Islamic thought and practice. She notes that whereas in Christianity sexuality is perceived as a threat to order and civilization and therefore in need of control, in Islam it is women who are perceived thus. In Christianity, she explains, "The individual was split into two antithetical selves; the spirit and the flesh, the ego and the id. The triumph of civilization implied the triumph of soul over flesh, of ego over id, of the controlled over the uncontrolled, of spirit over sex" (Mernissi 1987: 44).

In Islam sexuality is accepted as having important social functions; rather, it is woman who poses a threat and who is "the symbol of disorder. The woman is *fitna*, the epitome of the uncontrollable; a living representative of the dangers of sexuality and its rampant disruptive potential.... Sexuality per se is not a danger (Mernissi 1987: 44)." As a result of this, Mernissi argues, Islam is territorial and organizes itself on the basis of strict segregation of the sexes. Transgression of these spatial and social boundaries is perceived as a danger to social order (Mernissi 1987: 137–38).

Nevertheless, the exclusion of women from masjids in various parts of the world contrasts, as mentioned earlier, with the situation today at Mecca and Medina, the most important sites of Islam. Not surprisingly, therefore, women mosque activists throughout the world "figuratively and literally" look to Mecca for inspiration in this struggle (Badran 2006: 1). Consequently, in August 2005 when news spread that plans were in train to curtail their movement and the space allowed women at these holy sites, a worldwide campaign led by sisters in Saudi Arabia resulted, which successfully ended this plan:

> Alerted by Saudi women, news of the proposed restrictions sent out shock-waves among Muslim women world-wide. Aisha Schwartz, founder-director of the Muslimah Women's Alliance in Washington, immediately set up the Grand Masjid Equal Access for Women Project that circulated a petition protesting the restrictions. Very quickly a thousand signatures were collected. Women inside Saudi Arabia and around

the world, meanwhile, carried on protesting in the media. It was the most striking example to date of concerted Islamic feminist global protest and one that authorities could not ignore. (Badran 2006: 2)

These movements are taking place within a context of a global Islamic revival and what has been described by some as a process of Islamization. According to Salma Nageeb, writing on the Sudan, this "involves the process of cultural homogenization guided by the notion of (the) Islamic society and its way of life. Islamization is the claiming of an authentic Islam, or the juxtapositioning of the 'correct Islam' with ordinary everyday life as lived by Muslims in Sudan" (Nageeb 2007: 9). As a result, Nageeb argues, there is "a process of acculturation and social restructuration which creates distance between local 'traditions' viewed as not Islamic enough. At the same time it promises a secure way of mastering modernization in order not to lose identity" (Nageeb 2007: 9). Nageeb observes further that as with other similar situations, "the success of the Islamization project depends on the participation of women, thus the contentious question of what the position of women should be and how they should live is at present one of the most relevant issues not only for discourse but also for everyday life in Sudan" (Nageeb 2007: 9).

Women's Mosques

What is seen as audacious and revolutionary in twenty-first-century India has a longer history in other parts of the world. Another response to women's exclusion from mosque space has been the emergence of women-only mosques. While this is a new response in some parts of the world, seen as an acceptable response to the Islamic practice of sex segregation and the needs of women for congregational worship, in other places this response is part of an older tradition that is now under threat. In their work *The History of Women's Mosques in Chinese Islam: A Mosque of Her Own*, Maria Jaschok and Shui Jingjun (2000) note that although the majority of women's mosques were invisible until 1993 and 1995, or not counted because they are attached or semi-attached to men's, "women's mosques constitute at least one seventh of *nansi* (men's mosques) with Henan [Province] listing a total of 91 women's mosques," four being fully independent. They also note a trend toward an increase in *nusi* (women's mosques; Jaschok and Shui 2000: 15).

The authors document the emergence of women's mosques in China in the nineteenth century as a culmination of the development of female-led segregated sites of religious life, such as women's Quranic schools. These *nusi* were led by female *ahong* (religious leaders) whose duties included "religious instruction and consolation, sexual education, knowledge of hygiene and sanitation," providing knowledge that although gendered was not available to non-Muslim women (Jaschok and Shui 2000: 18).

Today these women's mosques are under threat from different directions. On the one hand they are facing a new illegitimacy from the new orthodoxy of Islamic revivalism and the Islamization process affecting China along with other parts of the world since the 1980s. These approaches seek to purify Islamic practices from polluting local influences—in the case of China, Confucianism as well as other indigenous incursions.

> The third wave of Islamic revivalism has been sweeping parts of Southwest and Northwest China since the 1980s. [It is] pressing for criticism of all preceding traditions as over written by non-Islamic values and practices, and leading the way to a more modern scientific religious praxis through a modernized education which combines thorough religious understanding with secular knowledge, to be taught to both women and men....
>
> Supported by the wealth of Saudi Arabia, these new approaches are modernist in that they seek education for women and men but orthodox in their insistence on segregation and on the subordination of women to men." In this new context these women's mosques are struggling to maintain their raison d'être as they lack financial resources to survive in a neoliberal China and are unable to attract funds from international sources such as Saudi Arabia which do not support their existence. (Jaschok and Shui 2000: 18, 24)

The authors observe that "the continuing conflict over legitimacy of continuing women's mosques, their disappearance in some regions and controversies where the trend is rising, the current tensions between women's mosques striving for independence and Islamic patriarchal leadership requesting their curtailment if not closure, are indicative of an on-going strain in relations between women and men over definitions and realization of contested terrains of social and sexual equality and their place in the religious sphere" (Jaschok and Shui 2000: 26). More recently in other parts of the world other attempts to form women's mosques are emerging with varying degrees of success.

For Margot Badran and others, women's mosque movements are one manifestation of Islamic feminist activism. This feminism, she suggests, emerges when women are prevented from praying in the central masjid space and from exercising their faith by the patriarchs of the faith, usually imams and mosque boards, although some women also defend this practice. Their actions result in a challenge to male power in order to defend their right to congregational worship (Margot Badran, personal communication, New Delhi, December 2004). For others this may be going too far. Still others suggest that these movements, as well as the movement to create women's mosque groups, can be perceived as some form of agency or resistance (Mahmood 2005; Nageeb 2007). Mahmood, for example, argues:

> Even in instances where an explicit feminist agency is difficult to locate, there is a tendency among scholars to look for expressions and moments of resistance that may suggest a challenge to male domination. When women's actions seem to reinscribe what appear to be "instruments of their own oppression," the social analyst can point to moments of disruption of and articulation of points of opposition to male authority—moments that are located either in the interstices of a woman's consciousness or ... in the objective effects of women's actions, however unintended they may be. (Mahmood 2005: 8)

Whereas the women's mosques in China are under threat from the new Islamic revivalism, Salma Nageeb (2007) documents the emergence of women's mosque groups in Sudan in the wake of Islamization processes, which intensified after 1989. Following Saba Mahmood's (2005) work on the women's mosque groups in Cairo (based on 1995 fieldwork), Nageeb notes the emergence of these self-organized groups of women, meeting in the mosque to read and interpret the Quran for themselves. For Mahmood these groups represent a form of women's agency. Hence while the mosque groups that emerge within the context of Islamization "provide women with a socially and politically legitimate ground on which to challenge traditional social and religious authorities," they also facilitate the internalization and integration of the new "authentic" norms of Islamic practice (Nageeb 2007: 12–13).

The Significance of Masjid Worship

But why is masjid worship so important? And how are we to understand these movements? Jaschok and Shui note that while a mosque for women can become an important social space, it is also an important spiritual space:

> Regardless of whether the mosque is built for the use of men or women, the project contributes to the Islamic cause of enlarging the religious culture and obtaining Allah's mercy. In Chen Keli's translation of the

Hadiths, it is written that "Whoever builds a mosque for the pleasure of Allah, Allah will build him in paradise such a mosque" (Chen Keli 1994: 135). It is thus a common sight to behold Muslim women and men work as one in constructing or enlarging a mosque, might it be for the use of men or of women. (Jaschok and Shui 2000: 26)

They note therefore that even where women's mosques are established, or where women seek access to mosque space—"although fulfilling multiple service functions and women's congregations' social needs, from family blessings to funereal rites"—the main reason for Muslim women's fight for these spaces is not for secular rights, but for religious rights, as "these sites are expressions of yearning for Allah and for a place in Heaven" (Jaschok and Shui 2000: 26).

Islam and Women in Trinidad and Tobago

The introduction of Islam into Trinidad and Tobago is usually identified with the introduction of African Muslims during the nineteenth century, mainly from the Senegambia region in West Africa. The 1813 slave registration returns note the existence of 187 male and 100 female slaves, usually referred to as "Mandingos," who would most likely have been Muslim. Bridget Brereton (1981) notes the existence of one group of Mandingo ex-slaves who lived in a community in Port of Spain. Led by Jonas Mohammed Bath, a Muslim religious leader who arrived in Trinidad as a slave in 1804–1805 and who eventually bought his freedom, this community pooled its resources to purchase the freedom of other enslaved Mandingos (Brereton 1981: 67).

The group was augmented by the arrival of liberated Africans with indenture contracts in the period after the abolition of the British slave trade in the early nineteenth century.[11] Some settled in the Montserrat Hills area of South Trinidad. A number of the African-born ex-soldiers of the West India Regiment who settled in northeast Trinidad (e.g. Valencia) were known to be Muslim and were reported to have converted Christian settlers to Islam in this then remote region of the island (Brereton 1981: 69).[12] The continuity of this earlier Islamic tradition, however, was eventually lost.

According to David Trotman and Paul Lovejoy (2004), the Mandingos, more than any other African group, sought repatriation to Africa, and some did succeed. Additionally, males were much more predominant among Muslim slaves than among other African groups. Not surprisingly, therefore, despite their efforts at community formation, their survival was affected by this skewed sex ratio (Trotman and Lovejoy 2004: 224), along with the challenges and hardships of the colonial environment. Members of the Muslim settlement established by Mohammed Bath in the early nineteenth century, through self-help activities, engaged in trade, money lending, and agricultural production. They owned cocoa estates, slaves (along the lines of traditional African slave systems), and such property as houses. Apparently they also retained their African identity and Muslim names, and some members were able to find their way back to Africa on their own (Brereton 1981: 67–68). Nonetheless, they were unsuccessful in creating a permanent and continuous presence in Trinidad (Samaroo 1988).

The second and much more significant wave of Islam came during the period of indentured Indian immigration (1845–1917).[13] While the majority of immigrants was Hindu, a significant minority (approximately 13.44 percent in 1893; Jha 1985: 4) was Muslim, with a minuscule number of Christians. The Muslim majority was Sunni, of the Hanafi school of thought, while a minority was Shiite, with a smaller number of Wahabi (Kassim 2002). According to Halima-Sa'adia Kassim (2002), although distinct, Islam as practiced by the migrants was strongly influenced by the interactions with Hinduism on the Indian subcontinent. Frank Korom, among others, argues that their religious development can be understood as a "regional [South Asian] variation" of the centuries-old habit of "cultural borrowing" (Korom 2003: 53). One such illustration is the early notion of ideal womanhood for Muslim women in early 1900s Trinidad. In interviews conducted by Halima Kassim with elderly Muslim women who experienced Islam in the early 1900s, they admitted to not knowing about key female figures in Islamic history, such as 'Aisha/Ayesha. However, their understanding of an ideal woman was the historical Hindu figure Sita, who symbolized purity and virtue (Kassim 1999: 47–48). Writing over one hundred years later, visiting Indian historian J. C. Jha commented:

> The Indian Muslims brought to Trinidad their scripture, the Quran ("Recital"), the infallible word of Allah (God), containing the creed and the proper way of life, believed to have been revealed to the Prophet Muhammad. Even now the reading of the *Quran* and offering of *namaj* (prayer) is imperative for Muslims of Trinidad. Islam is a brotherhood of all the faithful being equal before God. But in Indian conditions a sort of social hierarchy had been created in Muslim society also, and such a social stratification with the *Shaikhs* at the top and *Momins* and *Dhunias* at the bottom presumably came to Trinidad. (Jha 1985: 4)[14]

Early mosques were built on estates. They were simple structures, "bamboo sheds near to the barracks" (Kassim 2002: 4). By the 1860s the Reverend

John Morton, Canadian Presbyterian missionary to Trinidad, recorded the existence of a "Mohammedan house of worship—a nice little building with galvanized roof" (cited in Kassim 2002: 5). As villages developed, mosques were built; as the former indentured workers acquired money and property, they built mosques.

While local Islamic leaders emerged among the population, there was much dependence on missionaries in the absence of learned Islamic scholars. As early as 1888, thirteen-year-old Yacoob Ali was sent to India to train as a *hafiz*; he returned in 1898.[15] In 1923, under the influence of Punjabi missionary Maulana Duranni of the Muslim League in Woking, England, young Moulvi Ameer Ali left for Lahore to study Islamic theology at the Ahmadiyya Anjuman Ishaat-e-Islam Institute. In January 1925 the first Muslim organization, the nonsectarian Tackveeyatul Islamia Association (TIA), was formed at Crescent Hall, St. Joseph, in northern Trinidad.[16] On his return in 1931 Ameer Ali would be made president for life, although this was not to be.

Over the twentieth century and especially during the last three decades, the number of Afro-Trinidadian Muslims increased through conversions, primarily through African American Islamic influences. While there are a few masjids with a predominantly Afro-Trinidadian membership, this varies with geographic location and the specific history of each mosque.

These new Muslims were among the first to introduce the more conservative practices related to women, such as veiling and heightened segregation. Nasser Mustapha mentioned the role of the new young Muslim radicals, including a significant proportion of African Muslims who influenced his renewed commitment to Islam in the 1980s (Mustapha, interview).

Moulvi Ameer Ali and the Emancipation of Islamic Women in Trinidad and Tobago

In her book *Feminism and Nationalism in the Third World*, Kumari Jayawardena describes a period of early twentieth-century Islam so different from today. She chronicles the anti-colonial movements for independence and greater self-government in Asia and the Middle East and the parallel emergence of movements for women's emancipation. She also identifies the role of male reformers, politically progressive men who saw transformations in women's status as part and parcel of the process of social change and modernization. But by harking back to earlier periods of emancipated womanhood in their traditions, these assertions were closely linked to national and religious identity (Jayawardena 1986: 14). It was at this period that the Egyptian call to which Badran refers was made, pressing for women's access to mosques for congregational worship. This development could be located at the interstices of larger social and revolutionary movements, which often provide a space for women's movements to emerge.[17] Scholars of the history of women's movements have noted that they have usually emerged in a context of other social movements, such as the anti-slavery movements of the late nineteenth century, the anti-colonial movements of the early twentieth century, and the Black Power and civil rights movement of the 1960s and 1970s (Jayarwardena 1985; Wieringa 1995).

In Trinidad and Tobago Moulvi Ameer Ali was one such reformer. Born in 1898 in Pointe à Pierre in South Trinidad, he was educated up to primary level but continued his education through reading on his own. Prior to returning home from Lahore, he continued his studies at Al-Azhar University in Cairo, Egypt, and was able to travel in North Africa and the Middle East, thus gaining a wider understanding of the diverse experiences of Islam in different parts of the world (Zaffar Ali, interview).[18] In Trinidad and Tobago his influence would be significant, although his name is virtually unknown outside the Indo-Trinidadian Muslim world, save for a few contemporary scholars.

Ali's name is associated with almost every Islamic organization formed in Trinidad and Tobago. On leaving the TIA due to ideological differences, he was a founding member of the Trinidad Muslim League (TML). His movement from one organization to the other was the result of his unorthodox religious views, some of which were influenced by the Amadhiyya tradition as well as his progressive views on women. For example, he is credited with the introduction of what are called "stage marriages" in Trinidad: those Muslim marriages where both parties sit together for the ceremony. This contrasted with the proxy marriages that were the norm at that time, in which the bride is secluded from the groom and the communications take place through interlocutors or representatives. Ali played an important role in the movement for the recognition of Islamic marriages through the passing of the Muslim Marriage and Divorce Act of 1936 (see Reddock 2008). He also campaigned for the opening of non-Christian schools with the coeducational El Socorro Islamia School, the first of its kind, which opened in March 1942 and with which he was associated.

As a reformer, Ameer Ali encouraged reading the English version of the Quran so that more people could understand the faith. He encouraged women to participate in the TIA's religious activities and be involved in singing, reading, poetry, delivering lectures, and participating in debates.[19] He especially encouraged TIA members to allow their female relatives to join and participate in their activities, and he encouraged women to speak on public platforms. He publicly condemned Hindu and Muslim fathers who prevented their daughters from getting formal education (Kassim 2002: 22) and argued that the seclusion of women was not in conformity with the spirit of *purdah*, or female seclusion, as propounded in the Holy Quran. Women, he argued, should work side by side with men and be given equal opportunities in the social development of the community (Wahid 1974: 15). Ali's wife, Nurrn Nahar Ali, became the first Muslim woman to give a public lecture, and she was active in the movements to increase Muslim women's involvement in Islamic affairs in the 1930s (Zaffar Ali, interview). As reported in one source,

> The Moulvi set the example by allowing his wife to deliver a speech prepared by him on the topic "Muhammad, the Exalter of Women" on 6th July 1933. The occasion was the commemoration of the Prophet's birthday, organized by the San Juan Men's Muslim Association, and Mrs. Ameer Ali was greeted by thunderous applause when, in the course of her speech, she said: "The Arabs, in the days of ignorance, used to murder their daughters physically, but many a Muslim father here today murder their daughters spiritually." (AAIIL n.d.)

These positions brought him much criticism from TIA members, resulting eventually in a split in the association and the formation, in 1932, of the more conservative Anjuman Sunnat ul Jamaat (ASJA), which advocated stricter segregation of the sexes in all areas as one of its basic teachings.[20] The ASJA disagreed with the proposed Marriage and Divorce Ordinance (Jha 1985: 138) and denounced the "revolutionary ideas" about women voiced by Ali (Wahid 1974: 4, 16). The ASJA would eventually replace the TIA as the most influential Islamic body in the country.

The 1930s were an important period of organization and activism of women in Trinidad and Tobago (Reddock 1994), and from the titles of talks presented and news media articles it is obvious that Muslim women were also aware of changes taking place in other parts of the Muslim world (*Trinidad Guardian*, May 21, 1936: 4).[21] So it was in this context, as well, that the local newspapers recorded an increase in public activity by Muslim women. The *Comforter*, organ of the TIA, at that time edited by Ameer Ali, published the texts of the public debates and lectures and announced the intention of various *jamaats* (congregations) to host activities with female participation.

Kassim summarized these as follows:

Muslim women began holding meetings in the privacy of an individual's home, organizing fundraising activities or attempting to gain support for the development of a Muslim Ladies body. They also began to utilize the Muslim religious magazines to educate or appeal for the support of a cause, or to remonstrate against the inaction or apathy of females. It was therefore within the *masjid* Halls and through the printed word that Muslim women began to take a stance and raise their voices. (Kassim 2002: 23)

They eventually moved out of private space into the public religious space, and although *purdah* continued, they were now active participants in masjid life and worship. This was an important development in the history of Trinidad and Tobago. For example, in a public lecture at the Prince Albert Street Mosque Hall in San Fernando, Amina Rahamut responded to critics of these developments as follows:

You hurl ridicule upon those innocent girls, women who dare to stand upon a religious platform to sing praises in the name of Allah and His Holy Prophet. You screen them off with the purdah from the sight of your Ministers and Lecturers as though these poor ladies were some inferior objects, some base and mean animals untouchable whose every shadow pollute the holy atmosphere of the halls, whose sight is something hideous and whose presence alone carries some infectious disease. (*Trinidad Guardian*, March 12, 1936: 14)

As a result of this movement and the influence of Moulvi Ameer Ali, Trinidad and Tobago became one of the first few places in the Indo-Muslim diaspora to have women involved in public mosque worship.[22] Again according to Kassim,

Women delivered lectures on numerous topics that included: *Mohammed, the Exalter of Women, The Force of Muhammed's Character, The present Need for a Muslim Ladies Organization, Islam and Socialism, The Responsibility of a Young Woman, Spotlight on Truth, The Spirit of Islam, The Virtue of Namaz* [sic], *Rights and Duties of Women in Islam, Education and Islam, Meeraj, Our Needs Today, Mohammed Women's Greatest Benefactor.* ... Poets Nights were also held and females participated reading their own composed works. (Kassim 2002: 24)[23]

Women also participated in segregated and mixed debates on matters of local social and economic importance, but issues of gender equality and women's rights were included. One debate was titled "Be it resolved that Muslim women deserve an equal social status with men."[24]

The impact of this early period resulted in a much more inclusive Islam in Trinidad and Tobago. Women became members of elected mosque boards, and although segregation continued within the masjids, they attended prayers and were involved in a range of activities in the masjid halls and compounds. Even in the 1940s, with the increasing influence of the more conservative ASJA, a number of Muslim "ladies organizations" were formed, each associated with a particular *jamaat*. These included the Young Muslim Women's Organization, the Ladies Section of the Islamic Missionaries Guild, and the Islamic Ladies Social and Cultural Association (Wahid 1974: 15), which were involved mainly in social, cultural and fundraising activities such as concerts, excursions, tea parties, and dinners.

Speaking about his experience as a young Muslim growing up in Trinidad, Nasser Mustapha, university academic and member of the Trinidad Muslim League Mosque Board, noted:

> Women attended *maktab*, the *hijab* was not heard of. Nijhoff and Nijhoff, who carried out research here in the 1950s, reported that only older women wore the *ohrni*.[25] Up until the 1970s no woman under fifty would wear an ohrni. I remember that in the 1970s only about five people would wear the hijab. They were influenced by the Iranian revolution, and the growth of U.S. Islam, which is very influential; women saw women combining careers with a "Muslim" lifestyle such that the place of the women was no longer in the home. (Mustapha, interview)

In the 1970s, with the reemergence of the international women's movement, a National Muslim Women's Organization was formed, led by Feroza Rose Mohammed—interestingly, not referred to as a "ladies organization."

The question could be asked: what was it in Trinidad and Tobago that allowed for this autonomy for Indo-Muslim women in the practice of Islam? What accounted for the reduction in segregation and separation so early in the twentieth century? And does this account for the resistance to contemporary efforts to remove them from mosque worship?

A number of explanations could be given. These range from the leveling experience of immigration and indentured plantation labor, which for a time removed some of the direct patriarchal control that would have existed previously.[26] Gender segregation would have been virtually impossible in the plantation, and the experience of living among Africans and Europeans with contrasting social mores, less characterized by segregation, would have been a significant influence. In addition, due to the lower ratio of women to men, many men were unable to marry, and there is evidence of migrant Indian women in plantation contexts exercising some relative autonomy in the selection of partners and spouses (Jain and Reddock 1998).

Rose Mohammed recalled that her mother had read poetry in the mosque in El Socorro, San Juan, at the age of ten (Feroza Rose Mohammed, interview), which suggests that females' participation in mosque activities was evident even prior to the return of Moulvi Ameer Ali.[27] The experience of the Claremont Road Mosque suggests further that in the Indian diaspora, including the South African context, the potential for change may have been greater than on the Indian subcontinent.

Sarah Nabbie argues further that because of their early grounding in Islamic scripture, Arabic language, and reading of the Quran, women from long-established Islamic communities in Trinidad and Tobago have a strong understanding of their religion. They are therefore less easily swayed by the new thinking and practices being introduced. Nevertheless, there has been increased pressure brought on women to conform. Some have done so by changing their way of dress, adopting the hijab, niqab or other forms, while others had started staying away from the mosque, which is probably what is desired (Nabbie 2008; Kassim, interview).

The Global Revival of Islam and the Islamization Projects

The global Islamic revival, however, would significantly influence the local Islamic context. The more active role of Saudi Arabia and the Middle East in promoting Islam caused a shift in influence from South Asia (India and Pakistan). One imam describes this process in Trinidad in the 1980s:

> The literature that was being read by young Muslims came from Islamic activists in the Middle East, for example the Muslim Brotherhood in Egypt. Magazines were coming from England, for example the *Muslim*. Also, the writings of Maulana Abul Ala Maududi, leader of the Jamaati Islami of Pakistan, played an important role in the understanding and practice of Islam among the progressive young Muslims. The Iranian Revolution was a major inspiration during this period. Young people were being encouraged to go to Medina University to study in Saudi Arabia and no longer Pakistan/India. They were now seen as backward.

The literature in Arabic and Urdu was being translated into English and so available to Trinidadians. (Asim Abdullah, interview)

In addition to the Tabliqh influence from India, which had been a conservative influence in some *jamaats*, there is now the newer influence of Salafis: fundamentalists associated with the Wahabi tradition of Saudi Arabia, which follows the Hanbali school of law.[28] The young men who had studied there, according to one report, were idealistic and strongly influenced by their sheik or teacher in Saudi Arabia. They also tended to see things in sharp distinction, with no gray areas or room for flexibility. This group advocates a "return" to orthodox Islam based on Sharia principles, thus purifying Islam of other "non-Islamic" influences (Asim Abdullah, interview). Their influence has been greatest on other young people. Because of their newfound Islamic knowledge with which the local community is not familiar, they seek to assume leadership positions, which can result in power struggles within communities (Asim Abdullah, interview).

This wind of change affected local Islam especially in the north of the country from the 1980s. The north of the country, which includes the capital and the main university, has greater exposure to literature and people considered to be learned in Islam from the United States, Canada, and the Arab world.[29] In the south of Trinidad, the Asian subcontinent, especially India and Pakistan, continued to be the primary influence, resulting in differences in philosophy and approach to practice (Asim Abdullah, personal communication, June 16, 2012). These developments in Trinidad and Tobago have many of the characteristics of the Islamization project identified by Nageeb (2007) and mentioned earlier.

Women and Masjid Space in Trinidad and Tobago

In the rest of this essay I explore three cases: two in which women have had to fight to reclaim masjid space and reject efforts to curtail their use of it, and one where until recently, women for some time felt part of the mosque process, including the design of the new masjid, and participated actively. During the period of writing this essay, however, the situation changed drastically.

The Nur E Islam Masjid

The Nur E Islam (Light of Allah) masjid was the largest masjid in Trinidad and Tobago for many years. It began in the early 1900s as a simple wooden structure on two lots of land purchased from the El Socorro Plantation by private individuals (Nafeesa Mohammed 2008). Over the years the land would remain privately owned, but its use would function in a religious, social, and communal capacity. In 1924 a new masjid was built, and in 1936, although originally a TIA masjid, the deed for the building was transferred to the ASJA, which became incorporated in that year.[30] In 1947 Moulvi Ameer Ali and a group of his followers left this mosque to form the Trinidad Muslim League, which was incorporated in 1950 (Nafeesa Mohammed 2008: 25).

In October 1957 and January 1958 the Islamic Youth Movement (IYM), consisting of men, and the San Juan Muslim Ladies Organization (SJMLO) were established. Under the masjid's constitution the attendance of three representatives from the IYM and two from the SJMLO was expected at Mosque Board meetings. Because of the expansion in the membership and work of these two groups it was decided to build a larger two-storey masjid. This idea was put forth by the Ladies Organization, and in order to raise funds the Mosque Board, in collaboration with the Youth Movement and Ladies Organization, organized fundraising activities such as tea parties, bazaars, excursions, and dinners and accepted individual donations from all members of the *jamaat* to finance the new masjid. All members of the Mosque Board contributed toward the construction and design of the concrete renovation of the third masjid, which was completed in 1966 by Mohammed Haniff Hosein, a builder by profession and a member of the Mosque Board.

The inspiration for the design of the masjid, according to board member Kamaluddin Mohammed, was drawn from a masjid he had seen on a visit to Senegal.[31] He reported that the masjid that had impressed him had individual facilities—hall, library, and kitchen—for the "ladies," youth, and men within the masjid compound itself. Even the choice of name of the Nur E Islam Masjid was a product of consultation and deliberation of the then functioning Mosque Board. Prior to 1967 it was known simply as the San Juan or El Socorro Masjid.

In my interview with Nafeesa Mohammed (an active member of the SJMLO and a lifelong jamaat member of the masjid, whose ancestors were founding members of the jamaat), she reported that the new masjid was organized as follows (Nafeesa Mohammed, interview): "Upstairs was for worship with women and men in separate sections. Downstairs acted as a community center, a big hall with a stage for community activities. There was also a library with a partition to separate women and men and separate entrances. There was also a big kitchen for the ladies." Nafeesa reminisced further:

In 1966 when this new structure was built, there were new activities, there would be big bazaars every year—people coming from all over the country, it was a big hit. Through these activities we were able to purchase another parcel of land. It was seen as a space to attract youth with sport, football, etc. including girls' sport because it was felt that the ladies and girls should also use the space including for sport although an elder would be present.

There were excursions to the Hollis Dam, Tobago, Mayaro, Bird Sanctuary—the Mosque Board, the IYM and the MLO. Everyone went together, although there was [sex] separation. (Nafeesa Mohammed, interview)

For the women of the SJMLO, those were the good old days. Despite this history, since the 1970s, with the spread of Islamization projects, the SJMLO has been struggling, increasingly excluded and marginalized from the affairs of the Nur E Islam masjid and from their occupancy and use of the masjid as their headquarters and venue for events. Over the years the partition in the prayer area was pushed to decrease the amount of space available for the women, as Ms. Mohammed observed:

The partition was moved to the side and then placed in front of the women, a big wooden partition. They were told not to use shoes downstairs of the Masjid, but we refused because this floor had been designated a community center. The kitchen was also demolished without any consultation with the SJMLO and they tried to prevent us from hosting activities within the masjid. The women nevertheless continued with their activities—tea parties, Eid dinners and Moulood functions but have refused to use the kitchen which was constructed outside, preferring to use basins in the open yard.[32] They have also been completely ignored and left out of the decision-making processes since the collapse of the Nur E Islam Mosque Board in or around 1978 and the emergence of the Tabligh Movement in the Nur E Islam Mosque. This has been challenged on the grounds that according to the original deed no activities could be organized without the involvement of the Islamic Youth Movement and the San Juan Muslim Ladies Organization but so far with limited effect. (Nafeesa Mohammed, interview)

Mohammed recounted an incident when she was the sole female attendee at a consultation (*shura*) in the masjid, and in order to give her opinion on a particular subject, she defied the practice of total gender segregation. Ignoring the pen and paper sent over the partition to her in order to write out her concerns, she marched over to the other side, where the men were sitting, and voiced her opinion. She explained that this exclusion started in the 1970s with the arrival of a missionary originally from Gujurat, India, but now resident in Barbados, who was invited by the Nur E Islam Mosque Board to teach Islamic classes (in Urdu and Arabic) at the masjid. A follower of the Tabligh tradition, he objected to the participation of Muslim women in masjid activities in Trinidad. In particular, he felt that women ought not to attend and participate in the masjid. This eventually led to a major schism in the Mosque Board, which Mohammed recalled as negatively affecting the future of the organization:

> There were reports that he was encouraging women to stay away from the mosque and telling the women that they should have *Taleem* [educational] readings in someone's home instead of coming to the mosque. The board called on him to account and told him to make a declaration to carry out the policies of the board, which included having women attend the mosque. It was near to the end of Ramadan and a trustee (name withheld) sided with the *hafiz* and he did not turn up to sign the declaration, so Uncle Kamal [Mohammed] resigned as well as the other members of the Mosque Board. With the collapse of the Mosque Board, the power over the affairs of the jamaat reverted to the trustees, and since then, it has been dominated by the Tabligh Movement, which frowns upon women attending Masjids." (Nafeesa Mohammed, interview)

These developments at the Nur E Islam masjid were supported by other contemporary trends in the Islamic world—significantly, the growing popularity of the teachings of Abdul Wahab and the Wahabi school of thought dominant in Saudi Arabia. Its permeating influence in Trinidad and Tobago is undeniable, especially in the context of the boom in the oil industry at this time.

With the departure of the missionary, the predominant influence at the Nur E Islam masjid has shifted from the Tabligh school of thought to Salafi influence. A key indication of this shift is the issue of entry into and allocation of *salaah* (*salat*, prayer) space. The Nur E Islam masjid is situated at a busy intersection. The former *main* entrance facing the southern side of one of the streets has been assigned to the men, and the more recent side entrance located to the west of the building and facing the other street is used by the women. The masjid is now designed to facilitate the practice of purdah at almost every stage. Even after entry there are barriers that inhibit the men and women from seeing one another. The *salaah* area itself is completely sealed off. According to Sarah Nabbie, a practicing Muslim: "I can attest from personal experience that during the 1990s while visiting the masjid during the months of Ramadhan over some years, the barriers denoting the sisters' space would become more enclosed over time but through growing popularity had to once again be extended within the last decade" (Nabbie 2010b).

As a center for Salafi religious practice, this masjid has been growing in popularity. It rejects many of the traditional practices of the Hanafi school of thought and its influences, from India as well as local influences, as non-Islamic. The men wear the long gowns of the Middle East, and women wear the *niqab*—full face veils with long black gowns. Sarah Nabbie reports that the bakery that was situated next to the masjid has now been replaced by a *sunna* store selling all the paraphernalia needed for Salafi worship, including niqabs, gowns, gloves, etc.

The new leadership has also created an alternative women's organization to compete with the older existing one. While the scene at this masjid has been significantly transformed from the time of its origin, this has not been without a fight, a fight against the physical and symbolic exclusion and marginalization of women from the mosque they helped construct and that had provided them with a space of community. In the context of this new Islamic orthodoxy they are caught in a bind—negotiating between conformity to a new triumphalist and more visible Islam, of which they are an important symbolic representation, and their pious and democratic desire to have access to collective worship and to their masjid.

The Jinnah Memorial Masjid of the Trinidad Muslim League

The Jinnah Memorial Masjid is more popularly known as the St. Joseph Mosque because of its location in the town of St. Joseph, or as the TML Masjid, because that is the organization that runs it. As described earlier, the Trinidad Muslim League was founded in 1947 by Moulvi Ameer Ali (mufti), Mohammed Hakeem Khan, and Mohammed Rafeek, as a nonconformist or *ghair mulkalid* jamaat.[33] Members of this jamaat were free to adhere to any of the four schools of Islam, and this remains the character of the TML today. It was incorporated in 1950 by an act of the pre-independence colonial parliament. The compound at St. Joseph includes, in addition to the Masjid, administrative offices, kitchen facilities, a conference room, counseling room, science laboratory, the TML Primary School and Kindergarten, and the TML Archives (Trinidad Muslim League 2009).

The masjid was designed by the British architectural firm Mence and Moore (Zaffar Ali, interview). The land was granted by the government, and women were heavily involved in the fundraising activities. The foundation stone was laid by a visiting Pakistani missionary, Maulana Isfahani. This masjid is a single open chamber and for most of its existence has had no barriers. There was separation—women in the back and men in the front—but no barriers. Through the influence of Moulvi Ameer Ali the TML has developed a tradition of relative inclusiveness of women. From its inception women served on the council or board of the TML and in almost every position up to vice president. Current president Nasser Mustapha suggests that the TML has done for Muslim women what Presbyterianism has done for Indo-Presbyterian women (Mustapha, interview). The Canadian Presbyterian Mission was very important for education among the Indian population in Trinidad, and to a lesser extent Guyana, and provided key opportunities for girls' education.

It is in this context, therefore, that we have to see Feroza Rose Mohammed's shock when she turned up for Eid prayers in 2007:

> When I entered the mosque happy and smiling on that Eid day October 13th 2007, I froze when I saw the barriers separating the men from the women. I felt so strongly against this segregation that I could not contain myself. However I waited until after the sermon was completed. I rose and asked Dr. Nasser Mustapha, the scholar who delivered the *Khutbah*, for permission to say something. He agreed." (Mohammed 2009: 47)

In her speech she congratulated the scholar on his sermon, then "firmly expressed my objection to the sudden appearance of these barriers in *our* mosque" (emphasis added). She then pointed out that this was not the practice of Prophet Mohammed in his time and that it was wrong. She noted that the three most important mosques in the sixth and seventh centuries—the Haram mosque in Mecca, the Prophet's mosque in Medina, and the Aqsa mosque in Jerusalem—never had barriers. "Prophet Mohammed used to walk over and talk to the women on any matter when he wished" (Mohammed 2009: 47).

In response to this, she reported, "within two minutes of my complaint, while [I was] standing and still talking, a man suddenly crossed these very barriers and put his hand over my mouth to silence me. At the same time a woman grasped my hands to restrict me, another shouted, 'Shut up!' . . . In distress I shouted 'Remove the barriers!' In the process five males physically removed the barriers from the mosque. It became chaotic . . . shortly after the incident our TML president approached me in the mosque. The only thing he said was, 'Don't worry, Rose, the barriers will be back later today.' He did not say a single word to the man who touched me" (Mohammed 2009: 48).

Rose Mohammed, as she is popularly known, wrote and published a book, *Speak Out: Perspectives of a Muslim Woman from the Caribbean*, in 2009 to give her version of the events that occurred that Eid morning.[34] In my interview with Nasser Mustapha on these events, he justified the introduction of the barriers as a response to a request from women who complained that their space was continuously being encroached upon by men, hence the barriers, which he said were really short balusters installed to "stabilize the space available to women within the mosque" (Mustapha, interview).[35]

This explanation, however, was perceived quite differently by a contributor to the Web site trinimuslims.com, Youth of Islam, who accused Rose of rejecting the "parda" set up to prevent the women and the men from "bouncing [touching] during salaat." She was accused of being an excessive feminist and a wannabe liberal, and her behavior was seen as disgraceful. In the debate that followed, Rose Mohammed received much vilification from women and from men. Writer Yvonne Teelucksingh, in a newspaper article, accused her of "shrieking at the top of her voice" that "my father built this mosque" and embarrassing Muslim women of the country (*Sunday Guardian*, November 11, 2007). In the article it is suggested that the barriers were temporarily in place for Eid prayers, but today these barriers are still in place.

Some time later, in response to the publication of the book, another article was published on the Web site trinimuslims.com, titled "Rose Mohammed has done it again!" One responder noted that

> Allahu Musta'aan, No doubt this book is a trial for the Muslim sisters who live in Trinidad and throughout the world. It is one that seeks to misguide the masses and in specific our sisters who wear the Hijaab and try to live according to the Book and the Sunnah.
>
> Yes, without doubt the West keeps on taking their Islam from people who do not know about Islam. Moreover, they promote such Muslims in order that they become the ideal for other Muslims. But we refuse to accept this because we already have the best of examples.[36]

Speaking with Rose herself, it becomes clear that her personal history in many ways accounts for her public actions. She recalled that her parents were strongly involved with Moulvi Ameer Ali and were the first couple to be married using "stage marriage." She recounted, "My family was so much involved that my mother was one of the first persons to get married on a stage in 1936. They were angry with my grandfather for allowing his daughter to get married on a stage. This broke up our family" (Feroza Rose Mohammed, July 3 interview).

Rose noted also that there was a period of about ten years in the past during which barriers had been installed at the TML masjid, but they were removed on the advice of missionary Maulana Tufail, who advised that this was non-Muslim.[37]

Feroza Rose Mohammed's immediate response to the reinstallation of barriers in many ways reflected her realization that the global Islamization process had reached her jamaat, her community, and the masjid that her father along with Moulvi Ameer Ali and others had built. It was an immediate response to what she saw as a real threat, an omen, perhaps, for the future.

The Bamboo Masjid

Bamboo Settlement is located in the area south of the main east-west Churchill-Roosevelt highway in North Trinidad.[38] It was established during the 1960s and was a result of the state's relocation of residents from the Bejucal area of central Trinidad (Asim Abdullah, interview). The majority of residents were farmers, and over time the Bamboo Settlement expanded from one area to the west of the Uriah Butler Highway, which is now Bamboo Settlement No. 1, to an additional settlement situated to the east of the same highway and west of the South Valsayn area (Bamboo No. 2). The area's growth and development were augmented by the addition of some squatters who settled and sandwiched themselves between Bamboo Settlement No. 2 and the Uriah Butler Highway. This area is now known as Bamboo Settlement No. 3.

In order to meet the religious requirements of Muslim community members to offer daily congregational prayer or *salaah*, the Muslim residents used to congregate at the house of the late Brother Khan (Nabbie 2008). However, due to the rapid growth in attendance it was decided to erect a masjid at Bamboo Settlement No. 2. The land where the masjid is currently located was leased by the TIA on behalf of the Bamboo Settlement *jamaat*. This grant allowed the villagers to construct a wooden building with a galvanized roof generally used for *salaah* purposes.

Over time, through the efforts and sacrifices of the local residents, the wooden structure was replaced by a concrete structure that provided prayer areas for both men and women, separated by a wooden partition. This space also included a general hall, kitchen, parking lot, bathrooms, store room, and library. The new building permitted the masjid to function as more than a place of worship. At the time of this study in 2010, Islamic classes (*maktab*) for both boys and girls were taught in the hall. The kitchen was used by both men and women at the weekly Friday Night Family Sessions; the building was the location for Sisters' Hour, a monthly program for women; and in 2010 the Bamboo Settlement masjid was the facility for a Community Education Seminar hosted by the Ministry of Social Development. The facility was also used to host annual dinners and fundraising events and bazaars.[39] All these activities were coordinated by both male and female members of the Bamboo Settlement masjid. In 2005 it was registered under the Companies Act under the name Bamboo Jamaah and was in the process of being registered as a not-for-profit organization. In 2012 it was managed by a board of directors comprising both men and women and was drafting by-laws. Former imam Asim Abdullah described this masjid as follows:

> Although predominantly Sunni, people attend from every kind of tradition. People from east, west, and south Trinidad are able to attend because it is convenient and close to the highway. Men and women, boys and girls are encouraged to participate in the same way. In sermons on International Women's Day for example, I would give time and effort to speak on these issues giving women their due rights and encourage them to participate. Even prior to us being married my wife was a member of the committee that runs the mosque. Women give lectures, head committees, run their own women's groups with monthly lectures and meetings, there is a family night where women are encouraged to participate and talk, etc. I have made a special effort." (Asim Abdullah, interview)

In 2010, at the time of these interviews, this was perceived as an independent and nonconformist jamaat, and the masjid was seen as liberal and friendly to women. According to the then imam of the masjid, strict purdah was not practiced or encouraged at this masjid (although a partition of approximately three feet did exist).[40] The complete separation of males and females he perceives as a misunderstanding of Islamic ideology, although it "came to Trinidad with the Indian Muslims and was accepted as a norm." Physical partition in the masjids, he suggests, is extreme and counter to the traditions of the early Muslims (Asim Abdullah, interview). This view is supported by Sharifa Ali Abdullah, wife of the then imam, who organized the Sisters' Hour and was a member of the mosque board. She was also previously a member of the TML council and expressed surprise that barriers had been installed at the Jinnah Masjid.

Sarah Nabbie was then secretary of the Bamboo Settlement masjid board.[41] She reflected on her involvement as follows:

As a young Muslim female citizen and resident of Trinidad, I have always been curious about the different policies and rules adopted by Muslims regarding mosque space (the term "mosque" will be used in reference to the masjid buildings themselves). Not just the policies between various masjids but rather the policy changes within one single masjid. I remember at the age of nine accompanying my father to our neighborhood masjid in San Juan and we would use the same main entrance together then head towards our specified prayer area but two years later, a fellow male Muslim stopped my father and told him that I had to go around to the other side of the masjid and enter through the ladies section.[42] Furthermore, upon entering I was faced with blackboards placed in such a way to create a visible barrier among the main hall to restrict any visibility between males and females. This seemed even more perplexing when considering that the masjid at my then school was completely barrier-free.

This highlighted to me that the rules in the masjid were apparently negotiable and subject to change. The question I then always wondered was "who was negotiating with whom and who had the final say?" (Nabbie 2010a)

As secretary of the Bamboo Masjid board, Sarah Nabbie had been actively involved in the consultations and plans for the construction of the new women-friendly Bamboo Settlement masjid. Similar to the Nur E Islam masjid, there were plans to have two floors, one with a sisters' prayer room as well as a room for mothers with babies and small children. Sharifa Ali Abdullah described the plans for this masjid:

In this (current) mosque the women's entrance is at the back, so although we have security during the month of Ramadan it could be dark and insecure. We wanted to ensure that males and females would have a safe and secure space, we wanted a room for young mothers so that women with young children would have their own room—a comfort room; a space where they could participate, see what is taking place (I saw this in the mosque in Geneva). We also plan to have facilities for classes, for exercise.

Asim has suggested that there should be no purdah. We now have a very short barrier; he wants it totally removed. There may be some negative reaction but he thinks it should be an open space with men in front and children in the middle, like the TML used to be. I have advocated for one main entrance for everyone. Already (in the current mosque) we put an entrance at the left side to facilitate women but we still have women using the back entrance. The Jamaat al Muslimeen is a local example of a mosque with no barriers with one circular space for all."[43] (Ali Abdullah, interview)

Not long after this interview, Asim Abdullah resigned his position as imam of this masjid, and some time later Sarah Nabbie was no longer serving as secretary due to objections to a woman holding that position. There is new management and there has been no further progress in the construction of the new masjid at the time of writing.

Conclusion

In Trinidad and Tobago, as in other parts of the world, Muslim women are involved in continuous struggles to negotiate and renegotiate their relationship to Islam and their right to congregational worship. Many feel called upon to respond to the growing strength of global Islamization projects with their main center in Saudi Arabia and the Middle East, which have become more evident since the 1980s. Even where they have accepted the inevitability of their changing location within Islam, they have sought to create their own spaces through their own forms of agency. This agentive potential, however, varies and is shaped by different histories and sociocultural contexts.

In Trinidad and Tobago, this struggle is also a generational one for women who grew up in a period of a more inclusive Islam because of the progressive Islamic and women's movements of the early and late twentieth century. Their experience of growing up Muslim, attending *maktab*, reciting the Quran at early ages, attending mosque, and learning about their religion contrasts greatly with what is now being presented as Islamic practice. These women, interestingly, may not find common purpose with new converts, less steeped in the more egalitarian local religious culture. Central to all these negotiations is the issue of spatial boundaries and how they should be understood and expressed.

This spatial segregation, or "purdah," represented both physically as in masjid space use and corporeally in the public presentations of Muslim women's bodies, becomes an important marker or distinction for Muslim activists as they seek a new recognition and power on the global stage. Conformist and Islamist-influenced women are content with sex-segregated masjid space. They, and other women who may not necessarily be conservative, often wear the hijab or niqab as markers of belonging to the Muslim *ummah* (global community or "nation"). These women remain within a patriarchal understanding of Islam and operate within the larger sphere of political Islam, or what I have referred to as the global Islamization projects.

Other activist Muslim women push for a gender egalitarian model of Islam in local and global arenas, and these women—like some who appear in this essay—challenge more conformist women, Islamists, and even "mainstream" Muslim men comfortable with patriarchal practices that they perceive as authentically or traditionally Islamic.

This has clearly been the case in Trinidad and Tobago, where women and progressive men have demonstrated agency and presented resistance to these developments, although independently in their particular mosques and jamaats and not through more public collective action. This takes us back to the earlier debates on agency and resistance in relation to similar movements in other parts of the world and how we should interpret these actions by religious women in patriarchal contexts.

I have argued that the liminal space where women's representation of Islamic identity clashes with their desire for congregational worship provides the possibilities for the challenges to patriarchal power that these women's mosque struggles and movements have come to represent.

Recent developments in Trinidad and Tobago, however, suggest that even for these women and their progressive male supporters, this struggle is becoming increasingly difficult as new orthodoxies emerge and become accepted as normative. These orthodoxies, combining versions of "tradition" with versions of "modernity," emerge as a powerful, visible counterpoint to western hegemony and globalizing cultural practices and influence. In this situation, control over women becomes an important symbol of difference in contests among men for power and prestige.

Notes

1. It is difficult to be consistent in the use of the terms *mosque* and *masjid* for a Muslim place of worship. Although I prefer the term *masjid*, the term *mosque* is more popularly used in Trinidad and Tobago and was mentioned in interviews, books, and other sources. As a result the two terms tend to be used interchangeably in this essay. I have tended to use *masjid* in relation to the actual building and *mosque* in relation to the building and the community.

2. I would like to acknowledge the assistance of Sarah Nabbie in the production of this essay as well as the advice of Margot Badran and Val Moghadam.

3. Malak Hifni Nasif is known under the pen name Bahithat Al-Badiya, http://www.progresiveislam.org/badran_womens-mosque_movement.

4. These prayers were originally planned for the Sundaram Tagore Gallery, but after refusals by three mosques and a bomb threat to the art gallery, the event was transferred to the Anglican Church of St. John the Divine. More than a hundred men and women attended the prayers, which took place among strict security measures. Among those objecting were Sheik Sayed Tantawi, the imam of the mosque of the University of al-Azhar in Egypt; the great mufti of Saudi Arabia; the imams of Makkah and Medina; and other "religious authorities" of Morocco, Pakistan, and Jordania. See http://abdennurprado.wordpress.com/2005/03/10/about-the-friday-prayer-led-by-amina-wadud and http://news.bbc.co.uk/go/pr/fr/-/2/hi/americas/4361931.stm.

5. See also http://caledoniyya.com/2008/04/21/amina-wadud/.

6. The aside stands for "Sallalahu 'alayhi wa sallam," usually translated as "peace be upon him." It is compulsory for every Muslim to add this salutation in wording and speech whenever the Prophet (s.a.w.) is mentioned.

7. Rawoot (2010) uses the words: "Do not prevent the female servants of Allah from going to the mosque of Allah" (Dawood, vol. 1, ch. 204, hadith no. 570); Al Bukari, Sahih *Hadith, Bukhari 1:832, narrated Salim bin 'Abdullah*, also in 7:165; see also Islam Online. Net, http://www.islamonline.net/servlet/Satellite?pagename=Islamonline-English-Ask_Scholar/FatwaE/FatwaE&cid=1119503544352; and Sahih Muslim, 4/161, 162, Kitab al-salah, bab khuruj al-nisa' ila'l-masajid.

8. Thanks to Laurence Waldron for this insight; http://www.islamonline.net/servlet/Satellite?pagename=Islamonline-English and http://www.allaboutturkey.com/mosque.htm.

9. For the hadith see Bukhari 1:832, narrated by Salim bin 'Abdullah, also in 7:165. In preparing this essay what became very interesting to me was the spatial organization or geography of masjid space, which I hope will be the subject of another paper.

10. By *movement* I mean the effort to desegregate main hall space and to involve women in conducting religious ritual.

11. After the British abolition of the slave trade in 1807, slave ships were captured by the British and the slaves were "liberated"; many ended up in the Americas with indentureship contracts.

12. The West India Regiment was an infantry unit of the British Army recruited from and normally stationed in the British colonies of the Caribbean between 1795 and 1927. Many recruits were Africa-born. Brereton (1981) reports that in the isolated East Coast settlements not reached by Christian missionaries, some of the settlers were converted to Islam by Mandingo ex–West India Regiment soldiers (Brereton 1981: 69).

13. Mainly from the United Provinces and Bihar in the north and Madras in the south of India.

14. J. C. Jha was visiting Indian professor to the University of the West Indies, St. Augustine Campus, in the early 1970s.

15. *Hafiz* is an Arabic term of respect for someone who has memorized the Quran; its literal meaning is "guardian."

16. The name means "Society for the Strengthening of Islam," and it was nonsectarian in being open to adherents of any of the four schools of thought: Hanafi, Shafi'i, Maliki, and Hanbali.

17. Badran (1995) speaks of the cluster of Islamic modernist, secular nationalist, and

humanitarian threads in this pioneering feminism, often called secular feminism but with a religious thread.

18. Zaffar Ali is the son of Moulvi Ameer Ali.

19. During the mid-twentieth century there was a strong tradition of literary and debating societies that organized public debates and poetry recitation.

20. By *conservative*, I mean accepting of patriarchal notions and practices that are perceived as authentically or traditionally Islamic and as returning to the fundamentals of the tradition.

21. The *Sunday Guardian* reproduced the text of a paper by Nawabzadu Nushat Ara Begum that dealt with the "freedom and equality" then being experienced by women in Iraq, Turkey, Arabia, and Egypt, who reportedly were able to move about the streets freely and to attend university locally and abroad (cited in Reddock 1994: 119).

22. Moulvi Ameer Ali was invited to visit British Guiana, so his influence may also have been felt there.

23. The lectures were often published in the "Indian News and Views" section of the *Trinidad Guardian*.

24. Topics included cocoa and oil, the arming of nations, marriage, home lessons, male-female social equality, and women accessing seats on the municipal council. Women-only debates included topics like education, social equality, political representation, and cinema (*Trinidad Guardian*, 1936–1939, various issues, cited in Kassim 2002: 24).

25. The *ohrni* is a head covering worn by women from the Indian subcontinent, usually made from a fine or thin material.

26. For more on this, see Jain and Reddock (1998).

27. She stated that this information was recorded in a book that is still available.

28. Tabliqh was a reforming tradition originating in the early twentieth century in New Delhi, India, seeking to reform the existing grassroots practices of Islam in Muslim communities in India that had been strongly influenced by Hinduism.

29. One example was the magazine published by the Islamic Trust in the late 1970s and early 1980s, which created a stir, especially in the north of Trinidad (Asim Abdullah, personal communication, June 16, 2012).

30. Many mosques become affiliated with a Muslim organization in order to get state recognition, which is necessary to get financial support, access to state lands, and recognition of marriage officers.

31. Much of the information in this section is drawn from a three-part video produced by the San Juan Muslim Ladies Organization to show, document, and publicize their role in the construction and development of the masjid. This video is available for viewing on You Tube, http://www.youtube.com/watch?v=n8Blo3UFGyM. Note that head coverings were seldom worn in the older video footage.

32. Moulood functions include coming together to read Tazeem or sing *qaseedas*, a form of Persian-Arabic lyrical poetry sometimes disapproved of by some traditions.

33. *Nonconformist* means open to all four accepted traditions, not linked to any specific one.

34. Feroza 'Rose' Mohammed is founder of the National Muslim Women's Association of Trinidad and Tobago.

35. Nasser Mustapha was not president at the time of the incident.

36. The controversy and threads of response were aired online at http://aa.trinimuslims.com, but these posts were later removed.

37. Sheik Maulana Tufail was the Ahmadiyya missionary who strongly influenced Moulvi Ameer Ali. He first came to Trinidad in 1964 and spent three months. He returned in 1966 with his elder son, Basharat. The rest of his family joined him later and stayed for two years. The maulana and his family returned to England in 1969 but came back to Trinidad regularly; see http://aaiil.org/text/biog/biog/smtufail.shtml.

38. Much of this section is drawn from an Eid program presentation prepared by Sarah Nabbie, secretary of the Board of Directors (Nabbie 2008).

39. This information is based on interviews carried out in 2010; the situation may now have changed as the masjid leadership has changed.

40. I have come to realize that this is in comparison with some other masjids, which have an entire wall as a partition, so this statement is relative.

41. Since the period of these interviews Sarah Nabbie has resigned as secretary of the masjid board due to objections by a newly dominant faction to having a female on the board.

42. This would have been around the 1980s.

43. Jamaat al Muslimeen is a controversial group of predominantly African Muslims, associated with an attempted coup in 1990. With the change in leadership of the masjid, the proposed renovations had not started at the time of writing.

References Cited

Ahmadiyya Anjuman Ishaat-e-Islam Lahore (AAIIL)
N.d. The Life and Works of the Late Al-Hajj Moulvi Ameer Ali. http://aaiil.org/text/biog/biog/ameeralimoulvi.pdf.

Ali, Zaffar
2010 Interview by author, April 24.

Ali Abdullah, Sharifa
2010 Interview by author, May 8.

Appadurai, Arjun
1991 "Global Ethnoscapes: Notes and Queries for a Transnational Anthropology." In *Interventions: Anthropologies of the Present.*, ed. R. G. Fox, 191–210. Santa Fe: School of American Research.

Asim Abdullah, Imam of Bamboo Masjid
2010 Interview by author, April 8.

Asim Abdullah
2012 Personal communication, June 16.

Badran, Margot
1995 *Feminists, Islam, and Nation: Gender and the Making of Modern Egypt.* Princeton, N.J.: Princeton University Press
2006 Rites and Rights: Margot Badran Traces the Mosque Movement from Mecca to Main Street. Al-Ahram Weekly Online, no. 816, October 12–18.

Brereton, Bridget
1981 *A History of Modern Trinidad, 1783–1962*. Kingston, Ontario: Heinemann.

Gamieldien, Fahmi
2004 *The History of the Claremont Main Road Mosque*. Cape Town: Claremont Main Road Mosque.

Islamic Research Foundation International
2010 "Women in the Mosque." http://www.irfi.org/articles/articles_301_350/women_in_the_mosque.htm.

Jain, Shobhita, and Rhoda Reddock (eds.)
1998 *Plantation Women: International Experiences*. Oxford, UK: Berg.

Jaschok, Maria, and Shui Jingjun
2000 *The History of Women's Mosques in Chinese Islam: A Mosque of Their Own*. Richmond, UK: Curzon Press.

Jha, J. C.
1985 "The Indian Heritage in Trinidad." In *From Calcutta to Caroni: The East Indians of Trinidad*, 2nd rev. ed., ed. John La Guerre, 1–18. St. Augustine: University of the West Indies, Extra Mural Studies Unit.

Kassim, Halima-Sa'adia
1999 "Education, Community Organisations and Gender among Indo-Muslims of Trinidad, 1917–1962." M.Phil. thesis, University of the West Indies, St. Augustine, Trinidad.
2002. Transformation of Trinidad Islam: The Works of Moulvi Ameer Ali and Moulvi Nasir Ahmad, 1935–1942. Typescript.

Kassim, Halima S'aadia
2013 Interview by author, St. Augustine, February 15.

Khanam, Daud Sharifa
2010 Interview by Vanessa Baird. http://www.newint.org/columns/makingwaves/2004/05/01/daud-sharifa-khanam/.

Jayawardena, Kumari
1986 *Feminism and Nationalism in the Third World*. London: Zed; New Delhi: Kali for Women.

Korom, Frank J.
2003 *Hosay Trinidad: Muharram Performances in an Indo-Caribbean Diaspora*. Philadelphia: University of Pennsylvania Press.

Mahmood, Saba
2005 *The Politics of Piety: The Islamic Revival and the Feminist Subject*. Princeton, N.J.: Princeton University Press.

Mernissi, Fatima
1987 *Beyond the Veil: Male-Female Dynamics in Modern Muslim Society*. Rev. ed. Bloomington: Indiana University Press.

Mohammed, Feroza Rose
2009 *Speak Out: Perspectives of a Muslim Woman from the Caribbean*. Caroni: Lexicon Trinidad.
2010 Interviews by author, July 3, 4.

Mohammed, Nafeesa
2008 "Facts about the Nur-E-Islam Masjid." In *San Juan Ladies Muslim Association 50th Anniversary Souvenir Brochure*. San Juan: SJMLO.
2010 Interview by author, April 29.
Mustapha, Nasser
2010 Interview by author, May 12.
Nabbie, Sarah
2008 Eid Programme Presentation, Bamboo Masjid.
2010a Reflections (written statement), April 20.
2010b History of the Nur E Islam Masjid. Written statement.
Nageeb, Salma
2007 "Appropriating the Mosque: Women's Religious Groups in Khartoum." *Africa Spectrum* 42(1): 5–27.
Rawoot, Ilham
2010 "Opening up the Mosque." *Mail and Guardian* (Johannesburg). http://mg.co.za/article/2010-04-01-opening-up-the-mosque.
Reddock, Rhoda
1994 *Women, Labour and Politics in Trinidad and Tobago: A History*. London: Zed.
2008 "Gender, Nation and the Dilemmas of Citizenship: The Case of the Marriage Acts of Trinidad and Tobago." In *The Global Empowerment of Women, Responses of Globalization and Politicised Religion*, ed. Carolyn Elliot, l43–60. New York: Routledge.
Samaroo, Brinsley
1988 "Early African and Indian Muslims in Trinidad and Tobago." Paper presented at Conference on Indo-Caribbean History and Culture, May 9–11, Centre for Caribbean Studies, University of Warwick, Coventry, England.
Taakveyatul Islamic Association
1974 Silver Anniversary Souvenir Brochure.
Trinidad Muslim League
2009 A Historical Review of the TML. http://www.caribbeanmuslims.com/articles/1107/1/A-HISTORICAL-REVIEW-OF-THE-TML-/Page1.html.
Trotman, David V., and Paul E. Lovejoy
2004 "Community of Believers: Trinidad Muslims and the Return to Africa." In *Slavery on the Frontiers of Islam*, ed. Paul E. Lovejoy. Princeton, N.J.: Markus Weiner.
Wahid, Jennifer
1974 The Role and Influence of Muslim Women and Women's Organizations in the Islamic Community in Trinidad. Caribbean Studies Project, University of the West Indies, St. Augustine, Trinidad.
Wieringa, Saskia
1995 "Introduction: Sub-Versive Women and Their Movements." In *Subversive Women: Women's Movements in Africa, Asia, Latin America and the Caribbean*, ed. Saskia Wieringa, 1–22. London: Zed; New Delhi: Kali for Women.

11

Democracy, Gender, and Indian Muslim Modernity in Trinidad

GABRIELLE JAMELA HOSEIN

In this essay I explore how Indian Muslim modernity is both accomplished through and ruptured by gendered democratic processes and community and citizen belonging. This dynamic appears in deliberations regarding the spiritually "correct" practice of racial, class, and religious distinctions as well as participation in bureaucratic, democratic, and constitutional sources of power. These sacralize forms of associational governance and mark gendered contestations as potentially corrupting. It is in this context that the lived meanings of Indian Muslim modernity become significant. Conceptions of modernity service idealizations of Indian Muslim "purity," intersect religious sentiments with secular-rational forms of authority, and establish the terms on which scales of associational, ethnic, national, transnational, and diasporic belonging are managed. Such conceptions powerfully define Indo-Muslim negotiations with gender, democracy, and citizenship in Trinidad.

In the following pages, Indo-Trinidadian Muslims' approaches to modernity are explored in relation to a 2004 election in the Anjuman Sunnat ul Jaamat Association (ASJA), a Muslim organization that represents the majority of Muslims in Trinidad and Tobago.[1]

Drawing primarily on ethnographic data collected among members of the San Fernando Jama Masjid, a mosque affiliated with the ASJA and located in urban, southern Trinidad, I explore the exclusion of Indo-Trinidadian Muslim women from the election of the ASJA's executive and leadership.[2] Muslim women's and men's experiences of and perspectives on the ASJA election highlight the extent to which democratic participation provokes anxieties regarding "spiritual correctness" in Islamic knowledge and practice and the differential implications of these anxieties for women and men. Gender differential experiences of democracy for those in the ASJA are therefore discussed in the following pages with regard to the following questions: What are the anxieties that give the associational election its gendered meanings? How does the ideal of spiritual correctness respond to these anxieties? How does attention to gender explain when and how democracy becomes meaningful to the women and men in this association? What do women's and men's negotiations over democracy, correct Muslim practice, and gendered power relations suggest about conceptions of an acceptable Muslim modernity in Trinidad?

Gender Differential Modernity and Creolization among Indo-Trinidadian Muslims

The Indo-Muslims discussed here are "Indo-creoles" deeply identified with the post-colonial nation-state. Yet their own experience highlights that the meanings of "creole" cannot simply be reduced to intermixture or localization in the New World. As Keith McNeal, among others (e.g., Khan 1993; Munasinghe 2001; Segal 1993), points out, "In the case of Trinidad and Tobago, for example, 'Creole' refers primarily to people of African and mixed Afro-Euro descent, a regulating discourse positing Indo-Caribbeans as foreign, hence 'East' and not ultimately 'West' Indian, thus also not 'Creole'" (McNeal 2011: 326). There are thus competing and unstable conceptions of creolization, and its intersections with modernity, in the scholarship on ethnicity, class, gender, and religion, and on notions of respectability, in Trinidad.[3] For the purposes of this chapter, I draw primarily on the literature that has theorized modernity and creolization as gendered experiences in the lives of Indo-Trinidadians.

Patricia Mohammed (1988) first theorized Indo-Trinidadian women's creolization, arguing that it was "interlocked" with modernity. For her, creolization referred to processes of acculturation or assimilation to dominant European and African cultural norms that had come to define national culture in Trinidad as well as processes of interculturation or cultural mixing (Mohammed 1988: 382). Modernization was associated with the intrusion of external and metropolitan Euro-American influences and the readiness to accept them. For Mohammed, creolization and modernization were interlocked "as new values are formed and shared between and among the various groups" (1988: 393) through their participation in and commitment to their country of birth. Aisha Khan (2004: 12) has also pointed out that for the Trinidadian nation-state, mixing and being mixed "connotes modernity—democratic political representation, racial and ethnic tolerance, and a cosmopolitan world view." While Mohammed (1988: 395) considered modern Indian Trinidadian women to be "selective" in their acculturation, in her view to speak of the creolized Indian woman was to employ both the concepts of creolization and modernization simultaneously.

In essence, modernity for Indo-Trinidadian women is a creole modernity, forged in the colonial encounter of heterogeneous and unstable racial, religious, and class relations, European domination, and Afro-Caribbean histories.[4] Rather than simply being a "Western" modernity, Indian encounters with the West were refracted through the creole, creating conditions where "Indian tradition (and Indian women) in Trinidad [came] to be defined as that which is not, cannot be allowed to become, African" (Niranjana 2006: 123). Indian womanhood also became symbolically significant in relation to nationalist conceptions of womanhood in India, as debates over and attempts to recruit, create, and control the right kind of indentured Indian woman defined both Indians' indentureship experience (Reddock 1986) and the reconstitution of patriarchy in village life after the end of indentureship in 1917 (Mohammed 2002). Historically then, Indian women's creolization and modernity—that is, the reshaping of Indian femininities in the context of Trinidad—have posed difficulties for the establishment of racial and cultural boundaries and Indian men's place in the "competition among patriarchies."[5] As I show in relation to the 2004 ASJA election, gender differential approaches to creolization are still significant to Indian Muslim men's struggle for status in relation to whites, Africans, and Christians as well as Indian Hindus in post-colonial Trinidad.

Niels Sampath (1993) was the first to flesh out further what Mohammed's conceptualization meant for masculine privilege and gendered power relations among Indo-Trinidadian women and men. Examining the lives of young men, Sampath concluded that creolization was an instrument of masculine power. This was because young Indian men could—and were compelled to—seek status on terms set both by Indian notions of honor and shame and by creole notions of reputation and bad-boy machismo. Across different life stages, and as defined differently by a new generation, Indian men could be both successfully Indian and creole, but this could only take place if Indian women's creolization remained reduced or unenhanced and Indian domestic patriarchal power was unchallenged. Indian men could become creolized without challenging "tradition" because their creolization did not challenge patriarchy as expanded options for Indian women's cultural, racial, and religious mixing would do.

Other scholars have pointed to the interplay of racially, culturally, and religiously defined multiple modernities. Tejaswini Niranjana argues that historically in Trinidad, "there seem to be competing modernities—'Indian' and

'Creole,'" and "cultural anxieties produced by different vocabularies of modernity that were not always in alignment" (Niranjana 2006: 173, 174). For Niranjana, "Indian modernity" in Trinidad reflects continuities and discontinuities with the national creole-modern conceptualization of Trinidad and nationalist conceptualizations of modernity in India (Niranjana 2006: 54), which together make issues of racial and cultural difference, caste-class, and Indian women's sexual respectability salient. I would add that continuities and discontinuities are not only with India, conceptualized as the motherland, but also with Mecca and the Middle East, conceptualized as the homeland (Khan 1995).

Yet creolization compels the Indo-Trinidadian Muslims discussed in this chapter to define their community boundaries and structures of authority within them against *too much* mixing of racial identities associated with cultural inheritances from India (and therefore, potentially, Hindus) and religious identities defined by Islamic orthodox teachings. Anxieties regarding how to be Muslim, middle class, and Indian are also articulated in relation to the working class, the unlettered, and other sects of Muslims such as Shi'a (Khan 2004: 15). This group also wrestles with the potential for social mobility to lead to forms of assimilation that result in cultural subordination to Afro-Trinidadians, Western Christianity, and the nation-state, or alternatively for social mobility to fortify "identities as distinct, nationally recognized, racial-cultural constituencies" (Khan 2004: 63). The 2004 ASJA election exemplifies Muslims' attempts to resolve such anxieties regarding group cohesion—anxieties that creolization and modernity have brought on—by setting and maintaining gendered boundaries.

These efforts to consolidate the meanings of women's and men's religious and racial identities come at a time when Indo-Trinidadians' expanded political visibility has broadened "spaces of assertion" for women as well as men (Niranjana 2006: 123). If acceptable Indo-Trinidadian Muslim modernity can be broadly understood as the "concurrence of cosmopolitanism with morality, dignity, and an unbroken connection with religious heritage—a modernity with limits" (Khan 2004: 95), the construction of creole, hybridized space as secular, Western, immoral, Afro-Trinidadian, and masculine establishes Indo-Trinidadian religious space as a site for retention of honor, identity, and "tradition" (Hosein 2004a). Within this religious context, the purity and protection of women and community become "the specific mode in which the entry into modernity is 'managed'" (Khan 2004: 53). I therefore focus particularly on the role of Islamic discourses of spiritually correct gender identities in this process of managing creole modernity and as seen through democratic participation in the ASJA election.

The associational election can be seen as a technique for articulating, institutionalizing, and habituating an "acceptable" Muslim modernity that can help resolve anxieties about religiously defined community boundaries, secular democratic ideals, and gender relations as well as points of convergence and difference among "Indo-Trinidadian," "Trinidadian," and "Islamic" identities (Khan 2004: 189, 207).[6] Women's exclusion from the election was not simply about Sharia law (the code of law based on the Quran) but about a community working through how to participate in modernity and creolization while idealizing racial purity and religious piety (Khan 2004: 222).

Discourses of Indian Muslim purity speak to a mix of at times contradictory meanings, including being Indian culturally, avoiding miscegenation (even with Afro-Trinidadian Muslims), and cleansing Islamic practice of the cultural innovations and traditions associated with Hinduism and India. Piety refers to a commitment to sincerity, worship, "right" (correct) knowledge, and community, in attempts to live up to ideals of purity (Khan 2004: 189). Purity and piety became salient discourses because of the historical experiences of Indian Muslims in Trinidad.

In the Anglophone Caribbean, Islam first came to Trinidad with enslaved Africans (Campbell 1974). A later resurgence came with indentured Indians' arrival (Samaroo 1988). Of the 145,000 Indians brought to Trinidad between 1845 and 1917, approximately 23,600 were Muslim (Ali and Mansoor 1995: 7). Throughout the twentieth century, efforts to "preserve a Muslim identity in a predominantly non-Muslim state" (Samaroo 1988: 11) included regular contact with missionaries who traveled to Trinidad from Egypt, Pakistan, India, and Guyana, performance of *hajj*, and the establishment of masjids (mosques), *maktabs*, primary and secondary schools, and social organizations (Samaroo 1987) such as the ASJA.[7]

Conceived in 1931 and incorporated by an act of Parliament in 1935, the ASJA has prioritized the propagation and practice of orthodox Islam, leadership of imams, and synchronization and strengthening of customary practices (Rahaman, interview). There has been an elected president general of the ASJA since its establishment. Only men have held Executive Council positions. While ASJA men ritually hold associational elections, politics is considered potentially and powerfully corrupting, a source of confusion, and is associated with other kinds of men such as non-Muslims and state politicians. Women cannot fill Executive Council positions such as president or vice president, which involve meeting with non-Muslims, non-Indians, and especially men. It is also seen as potentially dishonorable for women to sit at ASJA meetings with men and for men and women to mix too freely socially.

An "ASJA Ladies Incorporated" is recognized in the constitution of the ASJA. It was established in 1938 and has its own constitution (Ali 1995: 32).[8] Its constituency comprises all women in the ASJA who pay membership dues at an annual general meeting. Executive positions are elected. It is positioned parallel to the Executive Council while at the same time being under the oversight of the president general. This association has no formal right to representation on the ASJA Executive Council. The group's function is to have regional events and classes, and to help people, for example through charitable and fundraising activities.

The San Fernando Jama Masjid is affiliated with the ASJA. It was founded in 1913 but was not officially established as part of the ASJA until 1931. There is a functioning mosque board with elected positions such as president, vice president, treasurer, and secretary. The imam of the masjid also sits on the board. Voting is by consensus.

The Young Women's Muslim Association (YWMA) is based at the San Fernando Jama Masjid and was established in 1950. The group has no mission statement other than that contained in its letterhead: "God hath granted higher to those who strive and fight with their wealth and persons than those who sit (at home)" (Quran ch. 4, verse 95). The YWMA is independent from the ASJA Ladies Incorporated and is not directly affiliated with the ASJA. It has no formal right to representation on the mosque board. The group has its own executive, with a female president, vice president, secretary, treasurer, and members. Usually decisions are made by open voting by a show of hands, but elections go through a process of nomination and secret ballot. Traditionally the YWMA has held events such as lectures, fundraising teas and dinners, and *iftar* and Eid ul Fitr dinners.[9] This "caretaker and caregiver" role, as one member described it, is quite typical. Women's groups at other ASJA-affiliated mosques also focus on what she described as "women's things."

The role of president of the ASJA and of individual mosque boards requires interaction with non-Muslims, Muslim men in the community, and imams who head affiliated mosques. It involves leading the *jamaat* (congregation) in prayer. These are all considered male roles. At different times over the mosque board's history, representatives of the YWMA have been invited to attend meetings. These are short-lived and sporadic instances, usually related to Ramadan or special dinners.[10] Women have also asked to be invited without consistent success. When women attend meetings, they are usually the family of board members or older and married. As the president of the San Fernando masjid outlined, the ideal of women's nonparticipation in religiously and culturally heterogeneous public spaces aims to protect them "from the influences of non-Muslims who might degrade them." By contrast, religious, family, and associational male leaders consider Islamic social space to be protected and private.

Yet the 2004 ASJA election highlighted precisely how masculine spheres within Muslim social space mark a potentially dishonoring inner public. In attempting to fulfill theological expectations, women and men therefore make politics another place where appropriate gendered roles and spaces can be established as God intended. Such an approach, grounded in ideals of balanced and complementary gender roles, informs the way that power is ordered in the ASJA. For example, many women declined to attend the election without permission of the president general, their imam, and to some extent their male family because they were afraid of censure for seeming to defy Islamic gender ideals regarding sex segregation and women's appropriate roles in Islamic political life.

Such issues as women's organizational enfranchisement and participation and leadership in Indo-Trinidadian Muslim organizations have been contentious for decades. Women were remarkably absent from mosques until the 1930s and from Muslim organizations until the 1950s (Kassim 1999). When they began to access greater secular and Islamic education, they were seen by imams, Islamic scholars, and associational leaders to be (silent) receptacles but not deliverers of knowledge (except to children). Over the last several decades, women's admittance to mosques, meetings, and lecture podiums has been and remains a source of intense inter-organizational and ideological conflict (Kassim 1999: 141). Yet Indo-Trinidadian Muslim women's expanding visibility highlights their success in slowly undermining patriarchal strongholds throughout the early decades of the twentieth century (Kassim 1999: 128).

Building on Kassim, I examine how questions about Muslim women's visibility were enmeshed in the ASJA election. The following section is an exploration of how an ideal of and debate about spiritual correctness responded to contemporary anxieties regarding creolization and modernity. Additionally, it is focused on when and how gender and democracy become significant in attempts to establish acceptable forms of Muslim modernity in twenty-first-century Trinidad.

When Choosing a Leader . . . Choose a Return to Spirituality!

While the election was held to elect an incoming president general and executive, at its heart was a struggle against corruption and creolization. The election campaign embarked upon by the San Fernando Jama Masjid sought to establish an Islamic public sphere committed to keeping politics in the realm of the sacred. This was reflected in the mosque-led campaign's slogan—'Return to Spirituality!'[11]—which articulated the campaign's critique of the association's incumbent president general and the claims that his bureaucratic and financial administration was corrupt in terms of decision-making processes and disbursement of patronage. As the San Fernando masjid president described, the men imagined themselves "fighting a battle of spirituality," while "the other side was trying to gain power through deception, money and fear." Their campaign aimed at restoring respectability and reawakening the idea of personal leadership based on spirituality rather than patronage, constitutional power, and votes. The election was therefore a technique for articulating an Islamic aesthetic or ideal out of a mixed liberal-democratic and Islamic habitus.

One difficulty faced was that some religious scholars involved in the campaign team considered elections, as secular liberal-democratic rituals, to be inauthentic to Islam. As the masjid president explained, "You could use a secular method to set up structures for governing a religious organization, but this is the wrong approach because the Surah should determine everything."[12] Yet in a post-colony that is politically organized according to the British parliamentary system, the men of the San Fernando jamaat were themselves already habituated to Western democratic politics and forms of legitimization. Politics, as potentially and powerfully corrupting, had to be kept interlocked with the sacred.

In meetings the men would therefore assert that "Islam is political" or "Islam is about democracy" as they grappled with the contradiction of both defining Islam against Western democratic ideals of universal suffrage and using democracy to define authenticity in Islamic leadership and to challenge the association's president general. What made the election creolized was not only its association with secular democracy but also the ways that the San Fernando Jama Masjid–led campaign drew in politicians, activists, and campaigning strategies from national politics; the ways that the incumbent leadership drew resources for campaigning and patronage from state support for denominational primary and secondary schools; and the "comess," or bacchanal, of election day itself.[13]

On election day, open-mic public deliberation among ASJA men about the leadership and accountability of the reigning executive preceded voting, and there was protracted tussling for the microphone by speakers for and against the incumbent president general, not to mention shouting, interruption, accusation, heckling, disagreement, condemnation, and rebuttal. During the voting process there were no controls over delegates, no voters' lists, no numbered ballots, and no idea how many men voted in relation to how many were eligible to vote. No one knew if any men had voted more than once. Several of the men attending complained that the ASJA election was conducted like a "carnival" and appeared less like an exercise guided by piety and decorum than one guided by irreverent chaos and confusion. This failure at piety illustrates the potential for impurity presented by democracy and helps to explain women's exclusion from associational enfranchisement and participation.

ASJA men locate women's "natural" roles in the home, and they place the risks posed by mixed-sex gatherings to women's respectability and honor at the heart of considerations about their electoral participation. Yet the only ASJA woman who rebelliously attended the election (Hosein 2009), Rashida, felt that rather than seeing "what is right" or "genuine leadership," she instead saw "desire for power, control, prestige, fame, and personal gain."[14] In an ironic speaking back to that power, Rashida's witnessing of the election enabled her to put men's respectability, religiosity, and gender-appropriate behavior at the heart of their own participation. Responding to men's argument that the election was not "a suitable domain for ladies" because of the "rough and tumble nature of politics," "hooliganism," and "men's behaviour at elections," Rashida asserted: "They are not behaving according to the Sunnah, their practice is unIslamic, and maybe women should discipline them. Meetings should not be rough, and if they are, the entire format of the meeting is corrupted."

Men in the mosque-led campaign somewhat weakly countered that elections should become more "dignified" before women participate, but it is also clear that keeping women away from the election prevents them from potentially exercising greater moral authority in political affairs and shaming men for failing to live up to their own ideal of Indian Muslim middle-class masculinity as a guardian against incorrect Islamic practice. In other words, while revitalizing or defending correct ways to be Muslim may legitimately involve secular democratic processes, these processes pose the risk of pollution of pious gender identities, including masculine ones. Election campaigning and voting were precisely about contestation over the respectability and piety of Muslim leadership. For women and men, such notions of respectability and correct Islamic practice created gender differential relations to democracy. For men, ideals about "what is right" became intermixed with a corrupted meeting. For women, these ideals enabled them to challenge masculinist-defined gendered boundaries and power.

As the election showed, ideals of Indo-Muslim masculinity enable men to be both modern, by advocating equal rights and enfranchisement within their association and society, and creole, by participating in spheres and activities that they associate with spiritual corruption and impurity. They participate in both modernity and creolization without losing masculine authority or prestige as Indo-Muslims, certainly in the eyes of other Muslim men. This was one of the reasons why the campaign failed to secure more than one-third of the votes despite its valid critiques of association leadership and its calls for a revitalized spirituality. Indo-Muslim men, like the ASJA leadership they were contesting, can engage different sources of status while benefiting from a privileged freedom from shame. Their engagement with democracy therefore reflects both modern, orthodox articulations of religion and practices that appeared more like those typical of the heterogeneous, non-Islamic, creole "national-modern formation" (Niranjana 2006: 173). Yet simultaneously, men's role in protecting Islam, women, and community from too much mixing with the secular nation-state and non-Indian, non-Muslim cultural influences also strengthens their gendered privilege and authority in the national "competition among patriarchies" (Mohammed 2002).

By contrast, and as contested by Rashida, Indo-Muslim women cannot engage in such creolization without conveying irreverence, misinterpretation, and failure to fulfill appropriate forms of womanhood associated with Islamic authenticity and piety. For these women, to be creole is to be like non-Muslim women, and men, and to risk a damaging reputation, which is associated with a lack of respectability. This is why women's challenge to their exclusion from the election was associated with censure, dishonor, gossip, and fear.

Yet modernity intervenes here, enabling a vocabulary of "right" or correct knowledge to create greater potential for women's respectability as Indo-Trinidadians, Muslims, and citizens. For this group of women, it is the potential association of modernity with middle-class propriety, edification, and text-based knowledge, tutoring, self-discipline, and respectable femininity in both private and public spheres that prevents modernity from being equivalently interlocked with shame. Modernity offers an alternative to tradition as a source of honor, and unlike creolization, it potentially expands women's access to status through respectable enactments of democracy, enfranchisement, and citizenship. Given this, modernity becomes the ground for the retention, reproduction, and resignification of "correct practice," and it explains the gender negotiations sparked by the AJSA election. It makes sense, then, that debate about gender differential creolization and modernity would take place through discourses regarding correct Islamic knowledge, who can lay claim to it, and how it is enacted in those moments, such as elections, when the piety of practice is both most emphasized and potentially threatened.

Rashida entered this debate by circulating a petition declaring that women's exclusion had no basis in Islamic law or custom or in the ASJA constitution. Other women also completely disagreed with their disenfranchisement, viewing voting both nationally and in the ASJA election as their "right." As Lateefa, a YWMA member for more than fifty years and a signer of Rashida's petition, protested, "Women can't vote because they [male leadership] misunderstand the Quran. We are equal in the Quran. We are part of the jamaat, men alone shouldn't have that right [to vote]." Thus rather than reaffirming the appropriateness of gender differential democratic practice, the election opened the question of what sources of knowledge should determine it. Rashida acknowledged that the guardianship of men is considered to be part of nature (*fitra*; see Esposito 1998: xvii). However, she challenged, "Yes, leadership means headmanship, but I do what Allah, not my husband, tells me. Women are certain to speak to issues men won't speak to. They have an opinion and a role to play." Her insistence on women's unmediated relationship with God, and therefore their capacity for correct understanding, strikes directly at patriarchal definition of an Islamic ideal of order and women's obedience (Mahmood 2005).

Women's fear ultimately kept them from attending the election. So too did ideals of respectability, femininity, and complementary gender roles. Yet women's arguments about their knowledge of economics, gained "from running the house," and their moral authority in relation to men's corruptibility as well as their equality in Islam show ways of resisting gender differential and unequal experiences of creolization and modernity, and their arguments also open room for women to assert moral authority and critique male privilege and practice, from which they were excluded for their own "protection," as insufficiently honorable. For Taimoon, one of only two women involved in the mosque-led campaign, such exclusion was undemocratic, un-Islamic, and beyond what is "right." As Shazeeda, the other ASJA woman on the campaign team, described, accepting their disenfranchisement meant "accepting a role as housemaker, responsible for children only and not being able to move around on our own or not voting because your husband told you not to." Her life choices to work, to participate in feminist, union, and political organizing, and to move around on her own are forms of power that create different articulations of Indo-Muslim female subjectivity from those foregrounding women's "natural" familial roles, greater morality, and strength in piety.

Some men also saw women's exclusion as unsuited to Indo-Trinidadian Muslim modernity. As a community elder in his seventies, Haji Raffi felt that "there are women with good Islamic training who do a lot of work for the organization and have good qualities. It is up to the women to fight for that right [to vote]. Because if you follow custom and tradition, where are you going?" His view may have reflected a more Indian rather than Middle Eastern Islam, which overlaps with Indo-Trinidadians' challenge to their marginalization as an ethnic group and their pride in women's empowerment and entry to the public sphere as a sign of community success. Similarly, Saleem, a politician involved in the mosque-led campaign, asserted, "I don't think people in community feel that women shouldn't be at the head of executive positions. I think they can participate across the board whether in religion or industry. If we deprive women of executive leadership roles, we exclude 50 percent of our human resources. I don't see their disenfranchisement as natural or right whether in the context of a general election or the ASJA."

Ultimately, however, as a technique, the election failed to establish authoritatively what women's or men's relationship to Islam and democracy should be, and it left debate about the relationship between religion and politics unresolved. One day Saleem unexpectedly approached the mosque-based Young Women's Muslim Association (YWMA) during their meeting to explain the campaign and its challenges. He asked them to speak to their male family members and to write to newspapers. The women were a surprising combination of skeptical and disinterested. One exclaimed, "Why should I help? I pay my membership and I cannot even vote." Others threw in, "Too long ASJA has been a boys club!" and "Why are women thrown out of meetings?!" The women also disliked the ad hoc way they were approached and were a tougher crowd than the politician anticipated. Saleem retreated, suggesting that they should put forward a policy for women in the ASJA. Yet he did not consider the election an appropriate time to challenge the status quo. Nor has he advocated generally for change in ASJA practice. Also showing underlying ambivalence, Waliyudeen, the San Fernando Jama Masjid president (2002–present), felt women should be able to vote but idealized how "wives let men feel they are the bosses" while in reality women ran the jamaat "using *hikmat*" (wisdom).

As articulated in the mosque's campaign, ideals of spiritually correct, democratic practice therefore put Islamic Sharia law, ASJA constitutional law, non-Islamic masculinist Trinidadian political culture, and both Islamic and secular-democratic notions of gender equality in negotiation with each other. Ultimately then, what occurred was not an exercise in purity but managing creole modernity and the potential for failed enactments of orthodox knowledge, moral practice, and pious subjectivities. The election showed how democracy both helps to create Islam and is defined against it as a governance model that competes with Sharia law. Its practice leaves the ASJA community open to creolization (Mohammed 1988), which poses problems of corruption, mixing, carnivalization, and confusion for a Muslim modernity premised on clear community boundaries marked by gendered ideals of piety and purity. Thus democracy becomes a technique for reproducing patriarchal interpretation of spiritual ideals and revitalizing action against masculinities considered un-Islamic. At the same time, it undermines those ideals, by provoking debate about theologically "correct" knowledge and practice of women's and men's equality and leadership.

Navigating Knowledge: Gender Negotiations with Modernity

Orthodox knowledge therefore opens a respectable space for gender negotiation and women's agency (Mahmood 2005). Such knowledge is important because it explains women's presence in the democratic processes of women's groups and the nation-state but not in their mosque or association. At the same time, it explains how they challenge this stratified participation. "Right," or correct, knowledge enables women to articulate a sense of citizenship or a "right to rights" (Isin 2008) that ruptures boundaries between tiers of enfranchisement defined by tropes of purity and piety. It enables Indo-Muslim women to be creole, or mixed in their political ways of knowing (Khan 2004: 153) and authority, while presenting themselves as acceptably Muslim and modern. Thus, Rashida argued, "the traditional Muslim woman has been timid and she has not paid attention to the role she is supposed to play in the community. Also, there are forces pushing them not to participate. Education in Islam makes a difference, gives them a different sense of their role. Unless women feel they can make a statement about scriptures, they are likely to challenge less."

Rashida felt grounded in knowledge of Islam and that she knew the laws and "when men are talking stupidness." "Plus," she added, "I fear Allah more than I fear men." Certainly women in the ASJA have not claimed (and may not all want to claim) this kind of power. As Muneera, the 2004 YWMA president, described, "There is something about women—they don't always stand up for their rights. Their husband's view is important, and even in [general] elections, if they tell them not to vote, some women wouldn't." Naila wondered, "Is it that we are afraid of religion or the men in our religion or just from time immemorial do you have it in your head that you are supposed to be like that? Is it the influence of history? Maybe no one cares. Maybe we are intimidated by men and religious politics, you know, the male aspects of the organization."

Yet drawing on the importance of "right" knowledge, creole nationalism, and women's independent reasoning, she continued, "They preach in Islam that men and women are equal. But *maulanas* [religious leaders] might tell you things women can't do and sometimes you disagree. Plus we are not living in an Islamic state and you have to live with others and your neighbors. I listen and decide for myself. You have to have it up here [pointing to her head] to know what to do and not be brainwashed." However, Naila also observed the risk involved in advocating reforms because "maybe nobody would go for it and you would get pelt out [forcibly removed]."

It is clear that women who are involved in political parties, state governance structures, full-time independent employment, and non-Muslim organizations are more likely to contest disenfranchisement and marginalization. It is this small group that most often raised themes of equality and rights. However, more than this language, what seem to shape women's perspectives most are ideas about living in a non-Muslim state, conceptualizing the self as a human being, accessing the power that comes from a personal relationship with God, and asserting an authority that comes from women's right to *ijtehad* (independent reasoning). In this way they reflect forms of "Islamic-modernist" (Esposito 1998: xxi) feminisms that advocate reinterpreting Islamic codes to emphasize the Quran's egalitarian and emancipatory message. Such claims to knowledge and acceptable modernity can both reproduce and rupture stratified democratic participation as ASJA women currently experience it.

Governance and democracy remain key to establishing correct and authentic gendered power relations and politics. Thus men cast the YWMA as a space where "women can do what they want." Men claim that the organization has "influence and power in decision-making because they can make suggestions to the president general if they want, and he will listen." However, women's responses suggest that this is easier said than done, and women can be left feeling "there is no cooperation, no love, no thanks." Rashida acknowledged, however, that women press their concerns less than they should because "when women meet they are afraid to deal with contentious issues because of cultural and social patriarchy."

While women may argue that they have no direct influence, they frequently claim that they influence their husbands. Lily, the 2004–10 YWMA president, maintained, "Our husbands take into account what we feel when they vote. Unofficially we have great say. We let people know if there is somebody we don't like." Successful tactics may not directly challenge, but some feminists have suggested that the political significance of women in the private and informal sphere cannot be overlooked (Riphenburg 1998: 147). Through their husbands and sons they may play an invisible political role influencing decisions taken in the public sphere.

Yet without formal right to representation, women must rely on letters to the mosque board or informal means of access to spheres of male power. In particular, family networks enable this. Family is itself associated with protection of women, morality, and male headship. Therefore it facilitates a great deal for women by being a "safe" space legitimizing their participation in public and male domains. In the past, when female family members of the masjid president have held the leadership of the women's group, informal communication was more effective, and they could listen in when informal discussions were held at their own or a family member's home.

"Right" knowledge ideally represents "progress away from ignorance and, importantly from vulnerability" (Khan 2004: 165). Yet it is not a source of power to which all women are willing to turn. For Indo-Trinidadian Muslim women, itjehad and refusing to be "brainwashed" are "Islamic-modernist" ideals of women's rights, but they inevitably mix modern and Islamic sources of authority with creole-national ones. Separately and together, these can legitimize women's challenge to rules established by men. However, they can present the risk of reputation, impurity, and incorrect knowledge if women's claim to "respectable citizenship" (Thomas 2006), as a basis for blurring democratic boundaries, is rejected by men. As Waliyudeen, the masjid president, cautioned, women should influence decisions by "not directly challenging or rocking the boat because they will be sidelined or thrown off." This is because "they are women first, before they are someone who holds office."[15] These are the negotiations among democracy, gender, modernity, and Islam highlighted by the ASJA election.

Conclusion

This essay has explored the ways in which governance establishes religious and gender ideals and explains the "controlled emancipation" (Hansen 1995: 82) of Muslim women. Ideals of patriarchal leadership among ASJA members are based on interpretations of respectable gender roles in Islam but also on larger non-Islamic and national gender ideologies (Barriteau 2003; Reddock 2004). This is key to understanding how dualistic definitions of secular and spiritual space can provide only porous community boundaries.

Women's greater participation in leadership and democracy would feminize an Islamic public sphere overtly defined by and for masculinity and masculine domination. This would expand women's options for both respectability and reputation, an experience central to male privilege, and it would make men more accountable to women both formally and informally. Putting the register of authority in the ASJA in such flux would shake up the formations of power and meaning associated with gender as well as those associated with community and religion. Situated in the larger non-Islamic public sphere, this could lead to increased feelings of community vulnerability and, for men, lesser status in the national (and international) competition among patriarchies. It would also render politics even more capable of producing failures of piety and "correct practice."

Women's contestations seek both to embody the divine, or what is beyond politics and to participate in forms of associational governance associated with corruption, reputation, and worldly authority. Interestingly, their attempts to maintain gendered notions of purity and authenticity expand their power to insist that authority, and even patriarchal authority, must not be power by any means. This illustrates how Indo-Muslim investments in patriarchal status, religious authenticity, and middle-class respectability produce nuanced configurations of and anxieties regarding gender and democracy in Trinidad. Rituals like the ASJA election are therefore not just gendered contexts of negotiation but are "practical engagements" (Mahmood 2005: 188) through which particular modes of subjectivity, religion, and modernity gain lived meaning.

Notes

1. According to the 2000 census, ASJA membership is approximately 25,297 persons (12,196 females and 13,101 males). The 2011 census counted 13,992 persons (6,657 females and 7,335 males), but comparability of the data is an issue as the "Sect" of more than 41,000 Muslims is listed as either "not stated" or "not known." The 2011 census enumerates a total of 65,705 Muslims (30,813 females and 34,892 males) in Trinidad and Tobago. Within this, the ASJA membership is primarily Indian, as is the Islamic population, which comprises 54 543 Indians. Government of Trinidad and Tobago 2000, 2011.

2. I use the terms Indian Muslim, Indo-Trinidadian Muslim, and Indo-Muslim interchangeably. I gained access to the masjid primarily as "Maulana's niece" and because

of my great, great grandfather Syed Abdul Aziz (Seesaran 1994: 345; Niehoff and Niehoff 1960: 182); my father's brother, the Pakistan-trained Islamic scholar Maulana Imran Hosein; and my mother's male cousin, who regularly had coffee with the masjid president.

3. See Munasinghe (2001), Khan (1995, 2001, 2004), and McNeal (2011) for more engagement with this literature.

4. After the first encounter with Europeans in 1498, Spanish colonial control of Trinidad stretched from the sixteenth century until British takeover in 1797 (Brereton 1979: 8). By the end of the nineteenth century, and following the abolition of slavery in 1834, Indians, Chinese, Syrians, Portuguese, and others had been brought to the colony as laborers or had migrated as traders. Indians were the largest group of these migrants. Today Indians and Africans each make up 40 percent of the population. Almost 50 percent of Indians are Hindus, 11 percent are Muslims, and 25 percent are Christian.

5. Mohammed (2002: 32) described a post-indentureship system of three "competing patriarchies" jostling for economic, political, and social status and power in the early twentieth century. In this hierarchical system, "Indian men found themselves at the lowest end of the ladder," beneath the dominant white patriarchy and the "creole" patriarchy of the time. While Indo-Trinidadians' significant social mobility over the last decades has reconfigured this hierarchy, setting and maintaining one's own position and challenging other groups' boundaries remains a significant part of "contestations" over political power and national culture (Reddock 1995).

6. Gender refers to "complex systems of personal and social relations of power through which women and men are socially created and maintained and through which they gain access to, or are allocated status, power and material resources within society" (Barriteau 2003: 30).

7. The *hajj* is the holy pilgrimage to Mecca; *maktabs* are Islamic classes.

8. Reddock (1994) has suggested that the label *ladies* "reflects the adoption from the British tradition of class-based and moralistic separation between 'good ladies' and 'bad women.'" Kassim (1999) has commented on the contrast between this "ladies'" group, which was founded as an appendage to the ASJA male executive, and the Young *Women's Muslim Association*, which was formed independently.

9. *Iftar* is the evening meal for breaking the daily fast during the month of Ramadan; Eid ul Fitr is the Islamic holiday marking the end of Ramadan.

10. Ramadan is the ninth month of the Islamic lunar calendar and the Muslim month of abstaining from eating, drinking, and sex from dawn to sunset.

11. At one point a campaign team member suggested printing T-shirts saying, "When choosing a leader . . ." on the front and "choose a return to spirituality" on the back.

12. Quotations from the masjid president were personal communications to the author. A *surah* is a chapter of the Quran.

13. According to Tiab Rahman, one of the masjid's oldest members, ballot fixing, miscounting, and patronage began with development of schools in the 1940s. A past secretary for the Education Board defined patronage as the ability to "get people's children in school, give contracts to do work and make promises to help mosques." He explained that these promises are "fulfilled by [excess] money from the Education Board" and felt it impacted the 2004 election.

14. Rashida is a pseudonym, as are other names used in the following discussion.

15. Signaling heterogeneity in ASJA men's politics, a past ASJA president reported that during his tenure, he invited women to participate and present papers at biannual meetings and vote and participate in decision making. Sometimes women sat in on his jamaat's mosque board meetings. He added, "Not only when dinners are being planned."

References Cited

Ali, Amina Ibrahim, and Ibrahim Mansoor
1995 *Islam in Trinidad and Tobago.* Port of Spain, Trinidad: ASJA.

Barriteau, Eudine
2003 "Theorizing the Shift from 'Woman' to 'Gender' in the Caribbean Feminist Discourse." In *Confronting Power, Theorizing Gender*, ed. Eudine Barriteau, 27–45. Kingston, Jamaica: University of the West Indies Press.

Brereton, Bridget
1979 *Race Relations in Early Colonial Trinidad, 1870–1900.* Cambridge, UK: Cambridge University Press.

Campbell, Carl
1974 "Jonas Mohammed Bath and the Free Mandingo in Trinidad: The Question of Their Repatriation to Africa, 1831–1838. *Pan African Journal* 7(2): 129–52.

Esposito, John L.
1998 "Introduction: Women in Islam and Muslim Societies." In *Islam, Gender and Social Change*, ed. Yvonne Yazbeck Haddad and John L. Esposito, ix–xxvii. Oxford, UK: Oxford University Press.

Government of Trinidad and Tobago, Central Statistical Office
2000 *Population Social and Vital Statistics.* Port of Spain, Trinidad: CSO.
2011 *Population Social and Vital Statistics.* Port of Spain, Trinidad: CSO.

Hansen, Thomas Blom
1995 "Controlled Emancipation: Women and Hindu Nationalism." In *Ethnicity, Gender and the Subversion of Nationalism*, ed. Fiona Wilson and Bodil Folke Frederiksen, 92–94. London: Frank Cass.

Hosein, Gabrielle
2004a "Gender, Generation and Negotiation: Adolescence and Young Indo-Trinidadian Women's Identities in the Late 20th Century." M.Phil. thesis, University of the West Indies, St. Augustine, Trinidad.
2004b "Ambivalent Aspirations: Assertion and Accommodation in Indo-Trinidadian Girls' Lives." In *Gender in the Twentieth Century: Caribbean Perspectives, Visions and Possibilities*, ed. Barbara Bailey and Else Leo-Rhynie, 529–63. Kingston, Jamaica: Ian Randle Press.
2009 "Food, Family, Art and God: Aesthetic Authority in Public Life," In *Anthropology and Individuals*, ed. Daniel Miller, 159–78. London: Berg.

Isin, Engin
2008 "Theorizing Acts of Citizenship." In *Acts of Citizenship*, ed. Engin Isin and Greg Nielsen, 15–43. New York: Zed Press.

Kassim, Halima Sa'adia
1999 "Education, Community Organisations and Gender among Indo-Muslims of Trinidad, 1917–1962." PhD thesis, University of the West Indies, St. Augustine, Trinidad.
Khan, Aisha
1993 "What Is 'a Spanish'? Ambiguity and 'Mixed' Ethnicity in Trinidad." In *Trinidad Ethnicity*, ed. Kevin Yelvington, 180–207. Knoxville: University of Tennessee Press.
1995 "Homeland, Motherland: Authenticity, Legitimacy, and Ideologies of Place among Muslims in Trinidad." In *Nation and Migration: The Politics of Space in the South Asian Diaspora*, ed. Peter van der Veer. Philadelphia: University of Pennsylvania Press.
2001 "Journey to the Centre of the Earth: The Caribbean as Master Symbol." *Cultural Anthropology* 16(3): 271–302.
2004 *Callaloo Nation: Metaphors of Race and Religious Identity among South Asians in Trinidad*. Durham, N.C.: Duke University Press.
Mahmood, Saba
2005 *The Politics of Piety: The Islamic Revival and the Feminist Scholarship*. Princeton, N.J.: Princeton University Press.
Maingot, Anthony
1998 "The Caribbean: The Structure of Modern-Conservative Societies." In *Latin America: Its Problems and Its Promises*, ed. J. Knippers Black, 375–91. Boulder, Colo.: Westview Press.
McNeal, Keith
2011 *Trance and Modernity in the Southern Caribbean: African and Popular Religions in Trinidad and Tobago*. Gainesville: University Press of Florida.
Mohammed, Patricia
1988 The Creolisation of Indian Women In Trinidad." In *Trinidad and Tobago: The Independence Experience, 1962–1987*, ed. Selwyn Ryan, 381–98. St. Augustine: University of the West Indies Institute of Social and Economic Research.
2002 *Gender Negotiations among Indians in Trinidad, 1917–1947*. Basingstoke, UK: Palgrave Macmillan.
Munasinghe, Virangini
2001 *Callaloo or Tossed Salad? East Indians and the Cultural Politics of identity in Trinidad*. Ithaca: Cornell University Press.
Niehoff, Arthur, and Juanita Niehoff
1960 *East Indian in the West Indies*. Publications in Anthropology, vol. 6. Milwaukee: Milwaukee Public Museum.
Niranjana, Tejaswini
2006 *Mobilizing India: Women, Music, and Migration between Indian and Trinidad*. Durham, N.C.: Duke University Press.
Rahaman, Tiab
2004 Interview with author, August 23.
Reddock, Rhoda
1986 "Freedom Denied: Indian Women and Indentureship in Trinidad and Tobago, 1845–1917." *Caribbean Quarterly* 32(3–4): 27–49.
1994 *Women, Labour and Politics in Trinidad and Tobago: A History*. London and Kingston: Zed Books and Ian Randle Publishers.

1995 Contestations over National Culture in Trinidad and Tobago: Considerations of Ethnicity, Class and Gender. Mimeograph.

2004 *Reflections on Gender and Democracy in the Anglophone Caribbean: Historical and Contemporary Considerations*. The Hague, Netherlands: SEPHIS, and Dakar, Senegal: CODESRIA.

Riphenburg, Carol J.

1998 "Changing Gender Relations and the Development Process in Oman." In *Islam, Gender and Social Change*, ed. Yvonne Yazbeck Haddad and John L. Esposito. Oxford, UK: Oxford University Press.

Samaroo, Brinsley

1987 "The Indian Connection: The Influence of Indian Thought and Ideas on East Indians in the Caribbean." In *Indians in the Caribbean*, ed. I. J. Bahadur Singh, 103–21. New Delhi: Sterling Publications.

1988 "Early African and East Indian Muslims in Trinidad and Tobago." Paper presented at Conference on Indo-Caribbean History and Culture, May 9–11, Centre for Caribbean Studies, University of Warwick, Coventry, England.

Sampath, Niels

1993 "An Evaluation of the 'Creolisation' of Trinidad East Indian Adolescent Masculinity." In *Trinidad Ethnicity*, ed. Kelvin Yelvington, 235–53. Knoxville: University of Tennessee Press.

Seesaran, Rosabell

1994 "Social Mobility in the Indo-Trinidadian Community, 1870–1917." PhD thesis, University of the West Indies, St. Augustine.

Segal, Daniel

1993 "'Race' and 'Colour' in Pre-Independence Trinidad and Tobago." In *Trinidad Ethnicity*, ed. Kelvin Yelvington, 81–115. Knoxville: University of Tennessee Press.

Thomas, Deborah

2006 "Modern Blackness: Progress, 'America,' and the Politics of Popular Culture in Jamaica." In *Globalization and Race: Transformations in the Cultural Production of Blackness*, ed. Kamari Clarke and Deborah Thomas, 335–54. Durham, N.C.: Duke University Press.

12

More Than Dawud and Jalut

Decriminalizing the Jamaat al Muslimeen and Madressa in Trinidad

JEANNE P. BAPTISTE

Peter E. Hopkins, Mei-Po Kwan, and Cara Carmichael Aitchison contend that "just as global migration and mobility are important to the geographies of Muslim identities, so too are local and regional experiences.[1] Local experiences of negotiating Muslim identities, creating Muslim space, and managing other identities alongside this, are significant in helping to understand the experience of being Muslim in various places" (Hopkins et al. 2007: 3). In this essay I explore the construction of a postcolonial Muslim identity called Muslimeenism, in a particular local space; examine the ambiguous relationship that may arise between Muslim communities and a non-Muslim nation-state as a result of the racializing, gendering, and criminalizing of Muslim identity; and seek to illuminate how Muslim communities may provide alternative forms of social justice and social relationships.[2] The material I discuss surveys contemporary feminist, race, and Islamic discourses and draws upon five years of ethnographic research—specifically participant observation, structured and semi-structured interviews, and informal discussions with about sixty members of the Jamaat al Muslimeen, a mosque in northwest Trinidad.

Despite the attention of international and national media to the Muslims in the Muslim world, the "life-worlds of Muslim women [and men] residing in predominantly non-Muslim countries ... are one of the most striking unknown facets of the contemporary phenomenology of globalized modernity" (Dietz and El-Shohoumi 2005: 1). This exploration is an effort to bring into view critically—as actors rather than as spectacle—Muslim men and Muslim women in non-Muslim countries and to examine their constitutive individual as well as collective religious and social identities (that is, their contextual realities as opposed to just the ideal of Islam).

Being a Trinbagonian (a citizen of Trinidad and Tobago) but not having been *in* Trinidad at the time of the 1990 Muslimeen coup attempt, I have no firsthand experience of the trauma of the insurrection, nor do I harbor a subjective memory of it. Yet this lack of primary sensibility, not synonymous with absence of sensitivity, gives me the critical, emotional, and psychological distance and detachment of an outsider, which I combine with the cultural, social, political, and personal consciousness of an insider. The simultaneous outsider/insider location allows me to see the Muslimeen through a lens of Derridean multitextuality.

Similarly, from the Muslimeen's perspective, visitors can be either antithetical to their ideological and political positioning or be potential allies. I was at different times viewed both with suspicion and with camaraderie, perspectives congealing after a year or so into one of possible convert, especially as I continued to attend Sister classes after my field research officially ended.

Setting and (Unsettling) Actors: A Collage of the Jamaat al Muslimeen

Contested land. No deed of ownership by the occupants. A people simultaneously set apart from and a part of a greater whole, a nation. On the outside of the contested territory, west of the main structure: a large grassy field, a manual car wash. Framing the front, white walls with green trim and an open gate until darkness descends.

On the inside and just beyond: a crescent moon, geometric shapes, and Arabic symbols. Remember: allegations of no deed of ownership so no permits to build on the land; therein, according to the nation-state, stand illegal structures. First, a relatively new guard booth, usually unoccupied, except for special occasions; a large paved area for parking, and for erecting tents when observing Islam's most religious observances: Eid ul Fitr and Eid al Adha. Brother Tambu, African Trinidadian, usually the first face one meets on the compound.[3] A special cemented area with an outdoor pipe, used for animal sacrifice during Eid al Adha. One is certain to see Sheikh Tariq, African, eight score plus, perform the sacrificial rituals annually.

A print shop, operated by a couple—the husband Indo-Trinidadian; the wife, African Trinidadian. Schools: infant/kindergarten through secondary/high school located toward the back of the compound. Offices upstairs for the principal; vice principal; and one of the imam's wives, African, very well educated, who oversees the academic operations. A tiny shop, selling snacks and sandwiches, tucked away at the back of the compound but allowing easy access from the school. Operated by an African couple.

A large kitchen: the cook, Sister Saida, African. It took four years for Sister Saida to inform me that like Sister Sara, she liked to watch the popular American television show *Dancing with the Stars*.[4] A large covered area for eating and communing; and at this entrance usually stands Brother Abdul, African, always dressed in elaborate Arabic-style clothing and wearing a smile, with a ready greeting of *asalaam alaikum* (peace).

A green internal wall on which are painted in italics various affirmations of the power of Islam: "Islam/Working for me and/it could work for you"; "Over 1 billion and growing"; "Islam/Let's all try to understand it/You cannot imprison it/You cannot shoot it/You cannot extradite it/It will not go away; and the Five Pillars of Islam: *shahada* (declaration of faith); *salat* (prayer); *sawn* (fasting); *zakat* (charity; a percentage of one's annual income); and *hajj* (pilgrimage).

Two offices toward the southeastern side: one, the imam's, African. Surname: Abu Bakr. Yasin Abu Bakr—insurrectionist, put his country in the international news in 1990 and subsequently on the North American no-fly list. On the walls of the second office, maps of the Prophet Muhammad's *hijra* (flight) from Madinah to Mecca. Fuad Abu Bakr, *dougla*, used this space as headquarters for his New National Vision (NNV) political party to contest the nation's 2010 general election.[5]

To the north, separate wash areas for men and women to perform *wudu* (the cleansing ritual) before *salat* (prayer). A mosque, reconstructed as two levels after the state demolished it in 1990 as a result of the insurrection. The upper level for women and girls—to be protected in case of another incursion by the state. One of the imam's wives, Indo, holds Sister classes here on Saturdays from four or five o'clock in the afternoon and at times until after dark. The men are relegated to the lower level. *Nikhas* (marriage ceremonies) are performed on the lower level, so women occupy this space too on special occasions. Also on the lower level, during *juma* (Friday prayers) especially are members of the imam's security detail dressed in black, military-style clothes and boots; the small, round, and on this occasion red head covering called *taqiyah* or simply *topee*; and dark sun glasses. Hypervisible. Hypermasculinized. Hypermilitarized.

At the entrance to the compound, a sign: Masjid al Muslimeen and Madressa. Translation: a complex Dawud and Jalut (David and Goliath) enactment woven together with historical, geographical, economic, and sociopolitical subtexts and counter-narratives. But not only.

More Than a Tale of Dawud and Jalut

From its inception, the Jamaat has been disruptive to a cohesive Trinidad and Tobago national identity, literally and symbolically embodying the contradictions of race, ethnicity, sexuality, religion, and nation. Founded on land given by the government to the Islamic Missionaries Guild to build a cultural center, but later rescinded when the guild sought a different location, the masjid was formed in the late 1970s on the abandoned land "through the merging of Dar Al Islam Al Muwahiddin (a splinter group from the Islamic Party of North America), followers of Ansar Laah" (Ibrahim 1995: 65), and black militants from Laventille, reputedly one of the most depressed and dangerous areas in Trinidad. Ansar Laah is a black Muslim group that emerged out of New York in the 1970s.[6]

After receiving his college education in Canada, where he converted to Islam, Lennox Philip, a former Trinidad and Tobago police officer attached to the Mounted Branch Division, returned to Trinidad as Yasin Abu-Bakr and was selected as imam of the Jamaat al Muslimeen in the early 1980s. This African Trinidadian Muslim triangulation among Canada, the United States, and Trinidad congealed into a Muslim identity that bears resemblance to but is still different from even its closest ally, the Nation of Islam, and manifests itself in a postcolonial ideology and politics of Muslimeenism specific to the Jamaat.

Given the Jamaat's reputation of being a criminalized space, going to the compound whether as a Muslim or non-Muslim is immediately construed by the larger society as an act of transgression. On my initial visit in 2007 to obtain the imam's consent to do my dissertational research, my brother accompanied me and waited the nearly two hours it took for me to meet with the imam. It was the month of Ramadan at the time, and the imam was swamped with petitioners. The pillar of zakat is itself an alternative form of social security, a social safety net for the poor, including poor non-Muslims. Thereafter I had to use public transportation to get to the compound since I did not own a car until nine months later.

In order to stop at the Jamaat, I would say to the driver as I entered or was about to alight from a maxi-taxi, "Jamaat please?"[7] Invariably, that phrase would elicit some kind of reaction from the other passengers, either tacit or vocal—"You belong to the Muslimeen?" Not Muslim but Muslimeen, and not "are" but "belong to." Somehow I knew it would be merely for confirmation, for in Trinidad most African Trinidadian Muslims are marked Muslimeen, and negative emotions attach almost automatically both to black Muslim bodies generally and the Muslimeen specifically. "No," I would respond. In the early phases of my ethnography, to distance myself even further from any alliance with this stigmatized community, I would offer, "I'm just doing research there."

"You brave." "Be careful." "Next thing you one of them," were the standard responses of caution, infused simultaneously with fear and intrigue.

The collage opening the essay accounts for public perception and affect as articulated in the taxi anecdotes, and the rhetoric is not without basis. On July 27, 1990, the Jamaat marshaled its defiant stance against the state, and like a symbolic Dawud, with a negligible number of insurgents, they sought to bring down Jalut, emblematic of religious persecution, sociopolitical injustice, and economic inequities.[8] One group of insurrectionists blew up police headquarters in the capital city, stormed Parliament as it was in session, and held hostage the prime minister, other government ministers, and employees in the building. Another faction took over the sole television station at the time and a radio station, holding media employees captive. There were more than thirty fatalities as a result of the coup attempt. The insurgents surrendered on August 1, 1990, after sealing an amnesty agreement that was later contested by the state but was upheld by the highest court of appeal, the Privy Council in London.

Another blow to Jalut.

Traditionally then—given the colonial shaping of race, ethnic, and gender relations in Trinidad; vestiges of racial and ethnic tensions; and Muslimeen hypervisibility—discourses on the Muslimeen are mired not only in the production and consumption of male Muslimeen bodies but in the production of them as already criminalized and thus antithetical to the commercialized, homogenized Trinidadian identity. Among the Muslimeen, Islamic doctrine and religious affiliation transcend allegiance to local and national centers of government and destabilize the national social imaginary of "all ah we is one family."[9]

Yet the very presence of the Muslimeen designates the nation-state a unique Muslim space, both a part of and apart from the global *ummah*. In Trinidad itself, too, more than thirty years after their formation and twenty-two years after the coup d'état attempt, the Muslimeen continue to shape actively the history of Trinidad and Tobago as they persist in the preservation and hypervisibility of their Muslimeenism.

On August 1, 1985, Trinidad and Tobago ceased observing Christopher Columbus's "discovery" of Trinidad and replaced Discovery Day with Emancipation Day, marking the historical freeing of African slaves in the British colonies. In 2012 both July 27 and August 1 fell during one of the holiest periods for Muslims, Ramadan. The year 2012 also marked the fiftieth anniversary of Trinidad and Tobago's independence. Interestingly, the Jamaat was probably the only site in the nation that marked simultaneously this complex national story, coalescing in an alternative religious, social, and cultural history.

The eastern interior wall displayed traditional African outfits, primarily from Nigeria and Ghana, Trinidad's closest allies from the continent. On the western and southern walls, below the affirmations of Islam inscribed on them, Brother Jomo coordinated the hanging of laminated newspaper clippings of every article written on the 1990 attempted coup and its aftermath. On the outside wall framing the compound, a large banner remaining from the July 27, 2012, commemoration of the insurrection affirmed: "To the Men and Women Who Struggled Inside and Outside the Prison Walls."

The tension between the Jamaat and the state is easily a metonym for the Dawud and Jalut narrative. To continue, however, to mire the Jamaat al Muslimeen, now estimated arguably at a mere five hundred members, between positive symbols of resistance—and thus as a place of possibilities for the disempowered and dispossessed—and negative signifiers of criminality and terror is to elide completely an alternative social reality.

Trajectories of African Trinidadian Muslim Presence in the Americas: Black Muslims, Nation of Islam, Orthodox Islam, and the Muslimeen

Transnationalism has shaped the development of Islam in the Americas, for "experiences of migration and mobility are important to the construction, negotiation and contestation of various identities, including religious identities" (Hopkins et al. 2007: 2). The majority of African slaves brought to the Americas during the Atlantic slave trade were Muslims from West Africa (Diouf 1998; Gomez 2005).

Yet like in many countries comprising the Americas, this Muslim presence has been ignored or eradicated from these regions' annals. Tenets of Islam, such as defending the faith, solidarity, and self-affirmation, arguably made African slaves appear rebellious and difficult to control. Slave owners made every attempt to suppress not just the practices of Islam but also what they saw as the essence of rebellion in these recalcitrant slaves.

Scholars, however, still maintain that despite rigorous imperial efforts to militate against the Islamic practices of slaves, Muslim slaves refused to divorce Islam from their heads and hearts, using it instead to rally against the dehumanizing effects of human bondage (Diouf 1998: 1–3; Reis 2001: 306–9; Samaroo 1988: 1; Warner-Lewis 2000: 118, 119, 125).

West African Islam itself was a syncretism of indigenous West African law and governance and Islam brought by the invading Almoravids, orthodox "Muslim militants" led by Abu Bakr who organized the Sanhaja Berbers in a holy war against non-Muslims in the western Sudan (Turner 1997: 17). In Ghana and Mali, as in the Sudan (where some posit that Islam first emerged on the African continent), Islam contained aspects of universalism, particularism, and separatism as "rich and powerful black rulers ... attempted to reconcile their new religion with African traditional religious and cultural praxis" (Turner 1997: 17). West African Islam gave birth to a new signification, *black Muslim*. This signification, which itself signaled syncretism and separatism, carried over and played out in telling ways in the United States and other parts of the African Muslim diaspora, including in the Caribbean.

In keeping with the concepts of naming and signification in West African Islam that Richard Brent Turner analyzes, Noble Drew Ali was uncompromising in teaching African Americans to repudiate the terms *black, colored,* and *Negro* and to adopt the identity of *Asiatic,* since, he said, African Americans were originally Moors, whose initial religion was Islam (Curtis 2009: 34–35; Marsh 1996).

From the 1800s African Americans and African Caribbean figures made interventions into returning people of African descent to the continent. Paul Cuffee, Edward W. Blyden, Henry Highland, and Marcus Garvey led some of the most notable movements to reconstitute an African identity. These themes of deracination and resignification continue to permeate and shape African Islam in the diaspora to the present day, especially in the United States as well as Latin America and the Caribbean, where there are a Nation of Islam revival and other forms of African Islamic communities, such as the Muslimeen in Trinidad.

In the late 1920s and early 1930s W. D. Fard Muhammad, an itinerant, self-identified Arab immigrant from Mecca, realized a social, economic, and political void felt by black Americans and introduced a new religious ideology, a black Islamic concept (White 2001: 3).[10] This new Islam took root easily in a milieu of unbridled racist, discriminatory, demoralizing, and exclusionary policies and practices by white racism against blacks (White 2001: 21) and an already existing African Islam in America. As a young boy in Georgia, Elijah Poole had witnessed the lynching of a deacon of his father's church. Fleeing racism as an adult, Elijah Poole left Georgia for Michigan; and it was there that he met Fard Muhammad. Poole would rename himself Elijah Muhammad.

Elijah believed that W. D. Fard Muhammad was God. This belief led to persistent and even vitriolic critiques from orthodox Muslims globally and created tensions within the Nation of Islam. Islam is a monotheistic religion, and its first pillar is the declaration of faith: "La ilaha illAllah, Muhammad-ur-Rasul-Allah" (There is no other God but Allah, and Muhammad is his prophet). To declare otherwise is *shirk,* the most egregious sin a Muslim can commit.

Furthermore, owing to Elijah's steadfast separatist and particularist politics and ideologies and his unwillingness to bring the Nation of Islam in line with orthodox Islam, he would come to be at odds with one of his most revered students and leaders, Malcolm X, as well as with one of his own sons and successor, Warith Deen Muhammad. Later in his religious and political life, Malcolm X supported the Nation of Islam's realignment. After his father's death W. D. Muhammad, whom his father excommunicated several times from the Nation, shifted Elijah Muhammad's anti-orthodox ideologies from particularist, separatist forms of Islam to a more universal, orthodox Islam, in the form of Sunni Islam. This paradigmatic shift, however, was not incommensurable with a progressive black consciousness and politics.

The postcolonial commitment to reifying African antecedents remains indelible and even necessary, especially when the legitimacy of African Muslim identity in the African-Indian diaspora is called into question repeatedly. In Trinidad, Islam seems indelibly marked as an Indo religion.

Islam in Trinidad: The 150-Year Gap between Yunus Mohammed Bath and Yusuf Mitchell

The mapping of the history of Islam in Trinidad facilitates the amputation of "African" from "Islam." Yunus Mohammad Bath, also recorded as Jonas Mohammed Bath and John Mohammad Bath, is one of the most notable and revered names to African Muslims in Trinidad; but to this day his name and the African Muslim presence in the Caribbean remain absent from most Caribbean history books written even by Caribbean historians.[11] In the 1800s, Bath, who claimed to be a sultan in Gambia, became the imam of a Port of Spain commune of Mandingo Muslims captured from Senegal and concentrated on purchasing the freedom of Muslim slaves and returning them to Africa. This group of Muslims seemed "uncrushed psychologically and bore no traces of dehumanization" (quoted in Ibrahim 1995: 3).

The history of African Muslims in Trinidad is not picked up again for 150 years. Ibrahim also documents one of the first African Trinidadian reverts to

Islam. A disenchanted twenty-three-year-old Yusuf Mitchell reverted to Islam in 1950. "By chance" he was passing the Jama Masjid in Port of Spain, Trinidad, when he heard the words of a Pakistani missionary Maulana Abdul Aleem Siddiqui. After following the missionary, around for months, Yusuf took shahada (declared faith), describing his reversion as "the most beautiful turning point in his life" (Ibrahim 1995: 63). Yusuf's conversion story mirrors Elijah Muhammad's and, as we shall see, that of several of the Muslimeen. The fact that his conversion was "by chance," however, perpetuates the portrayal of African Trinidadians' reversion to Islam as happenstance and thus inauthentic.

The disappearing or at least significant diminution of an African Muslim presence from Trinidad for a century and a half lays bare a systemic and epistemic erasure that opened the discursive space for a counter-narrative of Islam, not even a chronological or parallel one, to be reinscribed upon the spatial and psychic landscape of the nation. Thus, given the colonial attempt to stamp out African slaves' own religion and the colonialists' relative permissiveness with the religious practices of Indian indentured laborers, although Islam in the Caribbean was given a *re*-birth by Indo-Trinidadian Muslims, a common re-creation story attributes the origin of Islam in Trinidad to Mother India.

It is almost logical, then, that an African Muslim revolutionary spirit born out of a need for self-actualization would remain discursively disconnected from a Trinidad national history and consciousness, from liberation struggles, and from black power movements in the region. Though the prevailing signifiers of revolution in the region intersect at the site of race and gender, race equals black and gender equals masculinity; so black men are seen as the primary agitators. Religion, women, and South Asians are excised for the most part. In an inversion of the resistance narrative, though, black men are not portrayed as emancipators. Disembodying the legacies of slavery and its production of black men as nefarious perpetuates the symbol of the black/African body as inherently, and only, criminal.

Politics of Muslimeenism: Negotiating Racialization of Islam in Trinidad

In Trinidad and Tobago Muslims constitute about 6 to 8 percent of the entire population. According to one of the imam's wives, the Muslimeen numbered no more than five hundred in 2012, although some scholars estimate that after the 1960s and 1970s uprisings, their numbers reached as high as two thousand. Owing to the strained and ambivalent relationship between the Jamaat and the state as well as the insurrection, the Muslimeen occupy a very contentious position on the social, political, and cultural landscape. But they traverse this space strategically. Young women and men, escaping the challenges of the *dunya* (world, worldliness), come to the Jamaat seeking refuge, protection, self-renewal, and restoration of their respectability. Those born into the Muslimeen community retain their connections whether abroad or at home. A group of young Muslimeen who were toddlers during the 1990 attempted coup is currently engaged in a book project called *Children of the Islamic Renaissance.*

During my research Muslimeen women numbered arguably no more than 150 members. Muslimeen women are among very few women in Trinidad who live in openly polygamous marriages. They are also among the minority of Muslim women who on a daily basis cover completely in public, including wearing *hijab*, an indicator Saba Mahmood sees positively as part of the "religious ethos and sensibility" of the Islamic revival and piety movement in Cairo, Egypt (Mahmood 2005: 3). The intersection of these three identifiers—polygyny, place, and ethnicity—results in a visibility for Muslimeen women unlike other Muslim women, militated through the hypervisibility of Muslimeen men. Their covered visibility is made even more apparent up against "indecent dress of young women" in Trinidad society (Jamaat exchange 2009a).

Muslimeen women and men use this mediated visibility to perform their politics of Muslimeenism.

The imam preaches frequently about Muslims being pillars of the ideal Islamic life in their communities. He demonstrates no patience for idleness, admonishing in one *khutbah*, "Does a bee wake up and say, 'I don't feel like working this morning'? Does a bee say, 'I can't find work'? Does a bee say, 'I have nothing to do'?" (Jamaat exchange 2008a).

Paradigmatic shifts do not occur in a vacuum. Global, local, and personal politics create reverberations across space, time, and culture. Muslimeen politics emanated out of postcolonial, decolonizing, and nationalist currents. Many older members of the Jamaat al Muslimeen rode the waves of Pan-Africanism and its mantra of black consciousness and reaffirmation of black identity. Sister Naima was a supporter of the 1970 Black Power Revolution in Trinidad and changed her Christian name to an African Muslim name. Like her name change, her conversion to Islam was yet another self-affirming signification of her pride in her African roots and her resistance to lingering but persistent effacing imperial narratives of black bodies.

Although, on one hand, the Muslimeen admit that Islam does not subscribe to ethnic and racial differentiation, on the other hand, in the context of Trinidad during the 2011–13 Commission of Enquiry into the events of the 1990 coup attempt, Kala Akii Bua, Jamal Shabazz, Muhammad Shabazz, and Lorris Ballack attested to black consciousness as an irreducible component of Muslimeen identity and a predominant reason for the state's antagonistic position toward the Muslimeen (see Commission of Enquiry 2014). Muhammad Shabazz iterated that the coup was necessary to address inequities in race and class. African Trinidadians are stereotyped negatively, and Muslimeen are stigmatized even more.

Muhammad Shabazz claimed further that African men must fight for everything because of what they have to endure through their racial categorization and class position. "My race in the social order is the lowest class. Africans killing each other because of what society teaches them . . . African people are misrepresented in society and these issues of misrepresentation need to be addressed" (Commission of Enquiry 2014). Muhammad Shabazz bemoaned that when issues are raised of African Trinidadians suffering race and class discrimination, the response is, "Look, the Indians suffer like us." He contended further, "But I can't solve the Indian suffering. I have to solve mine." He testified that prior to 1990, as prior to 1970, signs of a coup were imminent, but no one paid attention. He warned that under the present conditions the signs tell the same story of the need for a coup.[12] During Trinidad and Tobago's TV6 seven o'clock news on April 25, 2012, the announcer retracted a statement she had made earlier in the broadcast when reporting on Muhammad Shabazz's testimony to the commission, saying instead that Muhammad Shabazz, "was not a former insurrectionist but a former People's National Movement senator."[13]

The collapsing of Muslimeen and terror, however, operates in a unique and paradoxical way in Trinidad. The conflation of Muslim and terrorist is ubiquitously mapped onto African Muslim (black) bodies but not necessarily onto Indo-Muslim (brown) bodies. Their histories are different, but there are exceptions of course. Despite the Jamaat's strong connection to an African origin, some Indo-Muslims are Muslimeen; and once this declaration is made, their Indian bodies are also racialized. One Indo-Muslimeen brother recounted a job interview: "The boss asked me if I was a Muslim. I said yes. He asked me where. I said the Jamaat. Then he asked me if Abu Bakr puts a gun in your hand and asks you to kill a family would you? I said I can't answer that. Abu Bakr would not ask that. Plus Abu Bakr is the imam, my leader, not my Lord. I have a mind of my own" (Jamaat exchange 2009b).

Since it is difficult to dislodge the origin of Islam from an Indian Muslim default, so mired is the Caribbean region in this belief, African Muslims are constructed putatively as "other" and as problematic. Sheikh Tariq—at eighty-three years old (or, as he put it, four score and three) probably the oldest living member of the Jamaat al Muslimeen—bewailed that even the most current social studies books used in Trinidad contain erroneous information about Islam and Muslims, negating the presence of African Muslims.

Paget Henry offers reasons for this delegitimizing of African cultural formations. One is peripheral cultural systems, where external imperial forces influence indigenous, internal configurations, namely "ego-genetic processes" like identity formation (Henry 2000:10). Another is the polarized internal competition between imperial and indigenous reproductive sites to determine whose narrative of the colonized is privileged, that of the colonizer (Prospero) or the colonized (Caliban; Henry 2000: 11). Finally there is the racializing of group cultural identities, which produces categories of people along a hierarchical color spectrum, a perpetuating colonial instrument that continues to facilitate the color coding of criminal acts generally with white as the most innocuous and black as the most insidious (Henry 2000: 11).

Polygyny among the Muslimeen is a site for this discursive reclaiming. Gender relations and practices between men and women on a quotidian basis, including sexual intercourse, procreation, childbearing, and polygamy are all performed and negotiated by both Muslim men and women within a domain bounded by what they understand as pious sexuality. Brother Kala also spoke of how demanding it is to pay equal emotional commitment to wives and children in different households; so polygamy, if practiced within the guidelines of Islam, is not an intoxicating experience but an intense metaphysical responsibility. That is not to say polygyny is devoid of pleasure and sensuality for either husband or co-wife.

Politics of Pious Sexuality

In surveying contemporary feminist scholarship on Islam, and even within Islamic feminism, it emerges that Western-based feminists too often gloss over Muslims' diasporic mundane and specific contexts, reproducing the perception that generically interprets Muslim men and women according to what is referred to as the Muslim or Arab world. Additionally, Muslim men are portrayed as fundamentalist and oppressive, regressive patriarchs and Muslim women as inherently subordinated (Falah and Nagel 2005; Mernissi 1991). Two major feminist critiques of Islam are veiling and polygyny.

Polygyny is spurned by non-Muslims for its alleged privileging of male sexual prowess over female sexual desires. Such a perception of Islamic sexual arrangements catering to male sexual appetite, while not only regulating but also stymieing female sexuality, is not, on the surface, without validity in a predominantly Christian state. Muslim men can marry non-Muslim women and have up to four wives (if they can treat them equally), once the wives are people of the Book: Muslims, Jews, or Christians. Muslim women, however, can marry only a Muslim man and are allowed only one husband at a time.

During my ethnography I did not encounter any men who admitted to converting to Islam just to marry a Muslim woman. But if certain versions of feminism continue to highlight polygyny and veiling over all other Muslim gender relations and practices, then female Muslims can only be sexually repressed and socially oppressed women. Such a reading, however, is incompatible with the gender performances of the Muslimeen.

Muslimeen women and men navigate mindfully and strategically the space and time between the dunya and shahada through a politics of Muslimeen-ism including pious sexuality, where piety and sexuality are not diametrically opposed but coterminous and extend beyond the borders of the bedroom. Not wishing to reproduce tired rhetoric, I must clarify that my idea of pious sexuality complicates the public/private dyad. While the validating gaze for heterosexual women is generally that of a male observer, the degree of validation is heightened by an external, more public and collective gaze.

Muslimeen women, however, opt to reserve the physical expression of their sexuality and sensuality for their husbands; and for Muslimeen women this limitation of the male gaze spawns from and is shaped by the empowering Islamic doctrines of sanctioned sexuality and pious commitment. Submission to the will of Allah includes obedience to husband—gender practices and formations antithetical to liberal and radical feminist notions of agency and subjectivity. Shahnaz Khan argues that "at intersection[s], women find themselves thrust into predetermined discourses and practices that help shape their agency and determine their strategies of resistance, often to the extent that progressive politics do not appear possible within the category Muslim" (Shahnaz Khan 2002: xix). Yet when Muslimeen women veil, they claim a no-tolerance zone around their bodies, a privilege less readily available to uncovered women in a sexist and patriarchal society with rising incidences of violence against women.

For Muslimeen women and men, polygamy transcends physicality and sex. In the context of the Muslimeen, polygyny is least about sexuality and mostly about piety, family, community, and the care of women and children, with special attention being given to the well-being of widows and orphans. During one *juma khutbah* (Friday sermon) before a *janazah* (funeral), the imam reminded the men of their responsibility to marry widows in order to ensure that widows and children are cared for and not left to fend for themselves. "Give women their respect and honour. Marry the women you are having children with.... If you are financially able, marry the widows" (Jamaat exchange 2008a).

After juma, the mourners moved to the compound's common meeting area, just outside the mosque, to pay final respects to the dead. The body is never brought into the mosque. Cleansing rituals are endemic to an Islamic way of life; so in preparation for janazah, the body is washed according to the same criteria observed for *salat*, wrapped in a simple white fabric called a *kafan*, and placed in a simple wooden coffin.[14] The *salat-l-janazah* delivered by the imam is simple and dignified, symbolic of the ideal Islamic lifestyle. The deceased's biological brother and other men eulogize him, but the widow and women remain silent. While women can go to the cemetery for the *al-dafin* (burial), they are not allowed at the graveside.

Ideally, Muslims are to be buried before sundown of their passing; and while they recognize that there will be the need to mourn, there is no excessive emotive performance like wailing and gnashing of teeth or prolonged grieving periods. As during a divorce, the widow is to observe a waiting period, or *idaat*, during which she has no sexual intercourse. The idaat is three months for a divorce and almost four months for the death of a husband, to ensure that the wife is not pregnant. Establishing paternity is critical since it is the father's responsibility to care for his child for the first seven years at least.

With polygyny there is a responsibility on the husband's part to ensure fairness, justice, and equality among his wives and children; for the Quran "not only restricted polygyny, but it made the practice contingent on ensuring justice for *women*" (Barlas 2002: 157, emphasis in original). Although not attributing the origins of androcentrism, misogyny, and sexism to Arab culture, Barlas theorizes that these characteristics of Arab culture perverted polygyny through acquisition of harems and other sexual unions (Barlas 2002: 157, 169).

For the Muslimeen, conversion is more for self-fulfillment, as a twenty-three-year-old who reverted at age fifteen iterated. In 2008 Fawaz had already been a convert for eleven years. He married soon after his conversion and started a family immediately. He is a strict adherent to the Islamic nondating principle. He abstains from all alcohol and tobacco, which he claims are toxins in the body. He is also vegan, practicing a disciplined body ethic similar to that of members of the Nation of Islam under Elijah Muhammad. He is an extremely disciplined observer of Ramadan, not even drinking water when fasting. With little formal education, unlike his wife, he is nevertheless a deep thinker and philosopher working through and interpreting hadiths and Quranic texts. Fawaz never pressured his Christian wife to convert to Islam, confident that she would do so when Allah decreed.

His Islamic way of life and his submission to the will of Allah sufficed for both of them. His immediate consummation of his marriage, his procreation with his wife, and his unequivocal devotion to his wife and children are as much practices of pious sexuality as is Muslimęen women's monogamy. Fawaz is not a Muslimeen anomaly (Jamaat exchange 2009d).

Contrary to the putative image of Muslimeen men as oversexualized and criminal, Muslimeen men are as a rule protective and respectful of their women—in fact, all women. Having been on hajj, Brother Kala classified Saudi Arabia as "the most oppressive place [he] had ever been," in terms of how inhumanely women were treated and the lack of women's rights, including not being allowed to drive. "We [Muslimeen] would never mistreat our women. They [Saudi Arabian women] get knocked down [run over] crossing the street because they cannot see through their veils. Women are to be valued and respected. That [repression] is not Islam; that is culture." He added immediately to the assent of all within earshot, "Neither would our women tolerate such treatment" (Jamaat exchange 2007a).

The Muslimeen picture is not as completely romanticized as it appears, though. Despite the hermeneutics of the Muslimeen women we will encounter later in the chapter, in a conversation that predated this exchange among them, a divorced, forty-four-year-old Muslimeen brother with a master's degree contemplated the "pull factor that encourages women, particularly young women to marry into Islam" (Jamaat exchange 2008b). This pull factor consisted of "poor socioeconomic conditions" in the dunya coupled with the fact that Muslims are discouraged from dating (Jamaat exchange 2008b). Before marriage, a couple can only be in each other's company when there is a third party "to help prevent indiscretions of the flesh, since even Muslims are human" (Jamaat exchange 2009e). The divorced brother further critiqued, "It's usually younger women and older men, older men who have discarded older wives." He continued, "All for material objectives . . . no spirituality." After a few moments of silence he concluded, "Western culture does that" (Jamaat exchange 2008b).

Muslimeen Women: Voice, Sexuality, Obedience

One of my first revelations at the Jamaat al Muslimeen, however, was that Islam as lived by the Muslimeen women was neither the concept of Islam nor the idea of Muslim women I had come to imagine from Western scholarship, course textbooks, and online publications on Muslim women—from the United States media, from the Trinidad and Tobago media, and from the Muslim world. Many long-standing women members of the Jamaat al Muslimeen are well versed in the Quran, are formally educated, own property and businesses, and negotiate tenets of Islam like polygamy and obedience differently and strategically, especially across generations and educational levels.[15]

Most Muslimeen, nevertheless, are in monogamous marriages, with the majority of polygamous marriages among the upper echelons of the Muslimeen social structure; that is, the older heads like the imam and his closest advisers. Conditions and the state of Muslim women globally—stereotyped or actual—do not map epistemologically or ontologically onto the lives of these local Muslim women, some of whom reverted to Islam and some of whom were born into Islam, including into wealthy Indo-Trinidadian Muslim families.

Given the multidimensionality of Trinidad's cultures, religions, and ethnicities, immediately realizable is that choice is part of Trinidadian Muslim women's lives in ways that perhaps are not available to or feasible for women in Islamic countries. Yet the fact that Trinidadian women are not subjected to the patriarchal violence to which women in the Muslim world are subjected does not mean that Muslimeen women's negotiations or choices—as Trinidadians and especially as Muslimeen women in a predominantly (and oxymoronically) Christian-bacchanalia state—are irrelevant or meaningless.[16] *That* configuration would be romanticizing the alleged "freedoms" of the West and infantilizing Muslimeen women.

In fact, rather than opting to be *other than* Muslim women, Muslimeen women elect to remain or become Muslim, to negotiate daily the metaphysical and mundane realities of being members of the Jamaat in spite of national and international surveillance and in spite of local expressions of Islamophobia that I term *Muslimeenphobia*. These choices also speak to a tacit but profound rejection of the local dunya.

When a Muslimeen woman marries, polygamy is only one of her considerations. Maintaining good relations with her extended family, bearing children, parenting, being able to pursue her education if she so desires, and being a good (observant) Muslim are other important deciding factors in a Muslimeen woman's opting to become part of the Jamaat. By the same token, however, polygamy is a central concern. Wives sharing the same husband are very deliberate in how they use their time in the absence or presence of their husband. Some wives are able to appreciate polygyny. One older sister confessed, "I am so at peace when [my husband] is not with me. I can stay in bed much later and do not have to get up for husband care. For you know that sometimes these men are like babies, and you have to take care of them like children. I like to read so I read. Well, I can laze around and get up only when I have to" (Jamaat exchange 2007c).

Mostly the younger ones simply cope, but polygyny is even rarer among young couples than it is among older men. None of the couples below their thirties with whom I interacted directly were in polygamous marriages. In fact, after multiple years of marriage, a husband generally marries a younger woman, with whom he might have more children.

Sister Rianne confessed, "Of course after so many years of marriage I was hurt when my husband told me he wanted to marry another wife. But I accepted it as the will of Allah, *al-hamduallah*; and now as I get older and older I appreciate the help of the other women and children" (Jamaat exchange 2007d). As another sister explained, "By the fortieth day in the womb your destiny is sealed. So if the imam is to have four wives, it is no more his choice than hers; for it is Allah's" (Jamaat exchange 2009c).

Early in my research the issue of sexuality and sensuality arose without my posing the question directly. After admitting that she had no idea why wearing Islamic clothing was considered oppressive, an older wife explained that Muslim women were actually quite liberated. "Liberated" in this context did not signify a feminist consciousness but rather a comfort with adhering to Islamic doctrine, as her subsequent explanation revealed. "When my husband comes back [from either business trips or other wives], I wear negligees and seduce him. There is nothing in the Quran that says a wife is not supposed to be sexy." Ironically, one can argue that by invoking the Quran in validating her right to be a sexual and sensual being, Sister Amina is engaging Islamic feminism, Quranic exegesis promoting gender equality and justice for Muslim women; that is, relying upon theology to validate her point (Jamaat exchange 2007c).

If we were to draw upon Mahmood's "politics of piety" and push the boundaries of the meanings of piety, Sister Amina embodies pious sexuality. Amina was not only admitting her enjoyment of her desirability but claiming her right to her sexuality, even into her seventies, and grounding it in Quranic exegesis.

Amina's sexuality is not divorced from her piety; there is no dichotomy. Feminists are apt to take a position between the binaries of complicity or empowerment, virgin or whore. But Muslimeen women do not see their behavior and practices according to gender binaries or hierarchies. They do not conceptualize piety as oppressive and understand that ordering their lives along contingencies is not akin to compromising self. Barlas underscores this point on Muslim sensuality, stating, "While the Qu'ran . . . closes off the body to scopic activity, it does not mean it de-eroticizes or de-sexualizes the body" (Barlas 2002: 159). Sister Amina testifies to the Muslimeen quotidian and in their view ordinary practice of pious sexuality.

Similarly, in an Eid ul Fitr sermon, the imam revealed that Muslim women are not required "to look dowdy" and can "put on a li'l eye thing [mascara, eye liner, eye shadow] to look pretty." He suggested they put on a "nice *dan dan* [outfit] and instead of coming to mosque "with their aprons as part of their dress" to "walk with the apron in a bag" (Jamaat exchange 2007b). The imam also encouraged men to pay similar attention to their deportment.

A holder of two master's degrees, a retired teacher, and now a school administrator, Sister Amina responded to my question about public perception of Muslimeen women's quotidian practice of covering their bodies according to Islamic dress codes:

> I have no idea why they [non-Muslims] feel wearing a hijab and covering yourself [head, face, breasts, arms, and legs] is oppressive. This is very liberating to me. I am happy to cover. I do not have to think about my body, and if I look sexy or I am too fat. My mind is free to think about important things like reading the Quran and teaching my students, not foolishness like if I am looking good. (Jamaat exchange 2009c)

On the surface, Sister Amina's sentiments may seem paradoxical relative to those of other sisters since sometimes posted on the notice board in the common area are advertisements for weight loss agents, and several Muslimeen women go to gyms. But the declaration really speaks to sexual and asexual as well as to eroticized and de-eroticized bodies and to whether sexual and erotic are synonymous on the female Muslimeen body.

Nadra recounts her conversion story. "I didn't become a good Muslim all in one shot. I did it in degrees. Even after I had taken shahada I used to lime [hang out] on the corner with my brothers and friends. I also used to hide the fact I was a Muslim from my family. I would leave the house in regular clothes and put on my hijab in the taxi" (Jamaat exchange 2009c).

The point is that Nadra would not be covered until she boarded a taxi, so she would be exposed to non-*maharym* men.[17] Yet this was her way of negotiating the ambivalences between her way of life and her family's. What made Nadra's conversion even more problematic was that she was a Muslimeen. For months Nadra kept up her charade until one day she forgot to unveil before she entered the house, and her brother saw her and confronted her. Once her veiling secret was revealed, she was able to complete her conversion and no longer needed to straddle the dunya and the jamaat.

When attending the mosque, Muslimeen women are required to cover the head, including ears, neck, breasts, arms to their wrists, and legs at least to their ankles. While preference is for all women attendees, even non-Muslims, to cover at least the head and breasts when entering the mosque, it is not a requirement. During a Sister class, however, Sister Fatima reminded a teenage convert that the hijab must also cover her breasts; and she is not to leave the veil just to drape, cowl style, from her neck. A few weeks later Sister Fatima brought several white veils to class and gave one to each of the new converts. She also gave me an intricately embroidered one.

Still, Muslimeen women dress in differing degrees of modesty and conspicuity, showing postcolonial cultural, ethnic, and generational conformity as well as fissures. Barlas states: "Veiling ... inscribes the body literally, by covering it and figuratively, by serving as a marker of identity. That is not to say that veiling has only one form or that veiling means the same thing to all women" (Barlas 2009: 2). While all Muslimeen women wear headscarves, some of the younger Muslim girls and women allow some "baby hair" (hair around the temple and neck) to show. Some mothers cover the heads of their young girls when the children are as young as two years old; others leave it up to their daughters to choose before puberty. But most girls with whom I chatted chose to wear a hijab well before puberty. In fact, many school girls wear their school skirts ankle-length and their school blouse sleeves to their wrists.

The middle-aged to older women are primarily of African-Trinidadian descent and, in public, less ostentatious in their colors and fabric than the younger Muslimeen women or girls, who are more visually expressive of their individuality via their clothing. The women who embody a black consciousness, though displaying a strong sense of black female identity and pride, tend to be relatively conservative in dress, their Islamic clothing made from monotone, plain, heavy cotton fabric. Some wear a *burkha* or *chador* as one would see in pictures of Saudi Arabian and Afghani women, for example. Some of the older women wear a *niqab* and cover from head to toe, including black gloves and black stockings, with only their eyes visible. These women seem to recall the historic hypersexualization and exploitation of African female bodies especially during colonialism and may use Islamic attire as a counter-narrative and restoration of respectability to black female sexuality.

On the other hand, the younger Muslimeen women, not shackled psychologically by the chains of colonialism, slavery, and indentureship, dress in what was traditionally considered Indian fashions: elaborate and lightly textured sari material with brightly colored, beaded, sequined *shalwar* chemises and ostentatious yet color-coordinated headscarves. While many Muslim women reserve their most elaborate and conspicuous wear for Eid ul Fitr, many young women dress elaborately every Friday for juma. A group of young women ranging from late teens to early twenties, two already married and one of them a mother, attend juma very ornately adorned, including wearing a noticeable amount of gold jewelry, sporting several piercings in each ear and multiple rings on each finger, so many that some fingers are invisible for all the jewelry adorning them.

Conversion Narratives

At the first shahada I witnessed on August 8, 2008, Sister Fatima said to me slyly, "It should be you taking shahada, Jeanne [she had not yet changed my name to Jihanne]. After all, you have been here a year already. But *inshallah*." Sister Fatima explained to this shahada's seventeen-year-old convert-to-be that cleanliness was paramount to being a good Muslim. Muslims therefore should at least perform *wudu* before each of the five daily salats, immediately after sexual intercourse, and after using the bathroom. Ideally, *ghusl* (the full cleansing ritual, in essence, a shower), should be performed; but wudu is a more practical daily form of cleansing, particularly before prayer.

Fatima explained practically: Muslim women fold toilet paper into a wad, wet it, and leave it on the tank of a toilet. After urinating or defecating, the wet toilet paper is used to clean the vagina, the anus, or both as necessary, each area being cleaned separately. The woman must be careful to use the side of the paper that did not touch the surface of the tank. A woman can also use disposable wipes to cleanse, provided the solution does not contain oil, for oil traps dirt. One day during instructions for a shahada, one older sister joked that one would have to be "a really good Muslim to perform ghusl after sex at 2:00 a.m.," since ghusl involves washing one's hair also.

Sister Zara and her husband have three children. After more than three decades of marriage Brother Hassan has never taken another wife, and according to Brother Hassan (but mostly Sister Zara), he does not intend to do so. Sister Zara, significantly younger than Sister Amina and also of African descent, co-owns a business with her husband. She expressed a similar sentiment to Amina's about covering, choosing to invest her mental energy in running her own food business rather than in worrying about her physical appearance. Sister Zara took shahada when she was seventeen years old (Jamaat exchange 2008c).

Sister Rita, also of African descent, co-owns a printing business with her Indo-Trinidadian husband. They are a young couple in their early thirties. Rita expressed the liberating feeling of "covering the body." She was married for four years before she decided to take shahada. The couple has four children, two boys and two girls, ranging in age in 2009 from ten months to ten years. Rita told me that although girls are not required to wear the hijab until puberty, her daughter decided at eight years old that she wanted to cover all the time. Sister Rita explained:

> We would take them to the Savannah to play, and although I tell Risah she does not need to wear long-sleeved tops and long skirts or pants, she does not want to go out in shorts or T-shirts.[18] She also insists on wearing hijab all the time. She does not feel comfortable wearing armholes (sleeveless vests) with her hijab, so she just covers completely. (Jamaat exchange 2008d)

Her husband, Fawaz, interjected that because they live in a communal compound with his family, his wife chooses to cover at home too. "So, from a very young age, Risah chose to cover. Although she is allowed to, Risah does not wear short skirts, lip gloss, earrings, chains, or armbands. I have no say. I leave it up to her mother."

After a brief reflective pause Rita continued, "She also covers the eyes in all her dolls or animals people give her, for you know, you are not supposed to have pictures with eyes or portraits in your house because evil comes through the eyes."

Whatever the personal clothing, these choices—Islam in general and covering the body from public view, particularly the male gaze—are conscious and empowering decisions by Muslimeen women in a country given to high incidences of violence against women as well as to what many deem as overexposure and hypersexualization of women's bodies at particular cultural moments and events. Mernissi (1987: 167) argues, "While Muslim exploitation of the female is cloaked under veils and hidden behind walls, Western exploitation has the bad taste of being bare and over-exposed."

Although it seems antithetical to the ways non-Muslims are accustomed to constructing their own existence, by persisting in the ordinariness of their lives the Muslimeen tell extraordinary stories of "engaged submission" as Muslimeen women and men are "enlisted . . . in the creation of [an alternative] social and moral space" (Moxley Rouse 2004: 6), including harmonious gender relations and practices in a nation with staggering crime rates, increasing statistics of violence against women, and hypervisible sexuality around Carnival time.

This small community's mundane yet resilient existence amid national, global, historical, geographical, physical, and sociopolitical ambivalences and contradictions begs revisiting how we read, interpret, represent, and deploy existing categories, theories, and methodologies that articulate gender, sexuality, race, religion, and nation.

Notes

1. Thanks go to a friend, Ronald Chandleur, who often listened and advised as I talked my way through this essay. He suggested the David and Goliath hook. Trinidad and Tobago is a twin-island state, but I refer to Trinidad only because Tobago has its own political and cultural aesthetics, and I did no research in Tobago.

2. Muslimeen refers specifically to both men and women members of the Masjid al Muslimeen and Madressa, called locally the Jamaat al Muslimeen or just Jamaat, although in popular culture the term seems to attach to male Muslimeen only. As Ethel Brooks clarified during my dissertation proposal defense in October 2006, *jamaat* refers ideally to a body of people, whereas *masjid* or mosque refers to the physical structure. With this distinction in mind, when I refer to the physical structure I capitalize Jamaat; and when I refer to the people, I use the lower case form jamaat. Note, however, that Muslims can pray anywhere and do not need a physical structure to perform *salat* (prayer).

3. African Trinidadian refers to a person of predominantly African descent, as opposed to someone of South Asian descent, called East Indian or Indo-Trinidadian. Although arguably the majority of people in Trinidad are actually mixed with African and South Asian, individuals often choose or are ascribed to one or the other ethnic group. I qualify African and East Indian with "predominantly," as ethnicity is often ascribed through the visual realm. At times too, I use African and Indo meaning African Trinidadian and Indo-Trinidadian.

4. Saida and Sara are pseudonyms.

5. A *dougla* is a person of mixed African and Indian descent.

6. In this essay black is synonymous with African descent.

7. Regular taxis in Trinidad do not operate like cabs in the United States. Particular cars and minibuses, called taxis and maxi-taxis (or maxis) respectively, ply routes in designated zones: east, west, central, and south Trinidad. Passengers wait anywhere along the routes for transportation. These vehicles seat from four to more than twenty-five

passengers. Since there are no designated stops, passengers board and alight wherever they choose.

8. Although all media and academic reports number the insurgents at 114, during one session of the Commission of Enquiry one of the insurrectionists, Jamal Shabazz, called this total into question, saying the number was fabricated by the state and there were more; but according to Shabazz, this reconstructed figure "proves the will of Allah as there are 114 suras in the Holy Quran."

9. "All ah we is one family" is the chorus of one of Lord Nelson's most famous calypsos, "One Family." Although the song refers specifically to social relations in Trinidad's twin isle of Tobago, the calypso has become almost a national anthem and a rallying cry in times of racial and ethnic fractures in Trinidad.

10. W. D. Fard Muhammad has a very controversial history, starting from his point of origin in Mecca to having multiple identities, including being the reincarnation of Noble Drew Ali. Nation of Islam followers claim such a history is a white conspiracy to discredit Professor Muhammad. I defer from such a discussion, as irrelevant to believers as to my analysis.

11. Brinsley Samaroo and Ibrahim Ali's texts are housed under Religion, according to the Library of Congress classification system.

12. Testimony at the Commission of Enquiry into the Events of 1990, session televised April 25, 2012. My source was the broadcasts; the 2014 commission report was completed two years after my research. The commission consisted of Barbadian Sir David Simmons, chair; Barbadian jurist Sir Richard Cheltenham, QC; retired teacher and former independent senator Dr. Eastlyn McKenzie from Tobago; Diana Mahabir-Wyatt from the Coalition against Violence and also a former independent senator; and Dr. Haffizool Ali-Mohammed, a U.S. military expert (Commission of Enquiry 2014).

13. PNM is the acronym for People's National Movement, the current opposition party.

14. The cleansing rituals of *ghusl* and *wudu* are explained in detail in the section on conversion or shahada, the first pillar of Islam, the declaration of one's monotheist belief in Allah.

15. By regular member I mean any female who has been involved with the Jamaat al Muslimeen for at least a year consistently despite the date of shahada. While I can provide no logic for my numeric choice, it seems one year is a sufficient time period to determine one's commitment to and knowledge of Islam. That is not to say that newer members' testimonies are discounted.

16. I am not denying that social and cultural performances at Carnival time can be read as embodied acts of subversion, whether against heteronormativity or against class and color hierarchies, race and ethnicity, or colonial formations. In arguing a politics of pious sexuality, however, I am turning to an alternative site, the bodies of Muslimeen women, upon which even feminism has already inscribed and fixed a subordinated identity owing to feminism's privileging of specific sexualities and a particular kind of sexual agency.

17. Muslim women are only allowed to be unveiled in the company of certain men and specific male relatives. In Muslim countries, Muslim women can only go out in public if

they are accompanied by these sanctioned men. Muslim women in Trinidad go out in public unaccompanied or in company of other women if they so choose.

18. The Savannah is a large circular grassy area in Port of Spain. An important cultural and social space, it is a popular spot for "liming" (hanging out), playing sports, drinking coconut water, walking, and jogging.

References Cited

Aitchison, Cara, Peter Hopkins, and Mei-Po Kwan (eds.)
2007 *Geographies of Muslim Identities: Diaspora, Gender and Belonging*. Burlington, Vt.: Ashgate.
Barlas, Asma
2002 *"Believing" Women in Islam: Unreading Patriarchal Interpretations of the Qur'an*. Austin: University of Texas Press.
2009 "Islam and Body Politics: Inscribing (Im)morality." Conference on Religion and Politics of the Body, June 26–28, Nordic Society for Philosophy of Religion, University of Iceland, Reykjavik. http://www.asmabarlas.com/PAPERS/Iceland.pdf.
Butler, Judith
2009 *Frames of War*. London: Verso.
Commission of Enquiry
2014 *Report of the Commission of Enquiry Appointed to Enquire into the Events Surrounding the Attempted Coup d'État of 27th July 1990*. Report to the president of Trinidad and Tobago. http://www.ttparliament.org/documents/rptcoe1990.pdf.
Curtis, Edward E.
2009 *Muslims in America: A Short History*. Oxford: Oxford University.
Dietz, Gunther, and Nadia El-Shohoumi
2005 *Muslim Women in Southern Spain: Stepdaughters of el-Andalus*. San Diego: Centre for Comparative Immigration.
Diouf, Sylviane A.
1998 *Servants of Allah: African Muslims Enslaved in the Americas*. New York: New York University.
Falah, Ghazali-Walid, and Caroline Nagel
2005 *Geographies of Muslim Women: Gender, Religion, and Space*. New York: Guilford.
Gomez, Michael A.
2005 *Black Crescent: The Experience and Legacy of African Muslims in the Americas*. Cambridge, UK: Cambridge University Press.
Henry, Paget
2000 *Caliban's Reason: Introducing Afro-Caribbean Philosophy*. New York: Routledge.
Hopkins, Peter E., Mei-Po Kwan, and Cara Carmichael Aitchison
2007 "Introduction." In *Geographies of Muslim Identities*, ed. Cara. Aitchison, Peter Hopkins, and Mei-Po Kwan, 1–9. Burlington, Vt.: Ashgate.
Ibrahim, Mansoor
1995 *Islam in Trinidad and Tobago*. Researched and coordinated by Amina Ibrahim Ali. Port of Spain, Trinidad: Anjuman Sunnat ul Jamaat Association.

Jamaat exchanges
2007a Brother Kala Akii Bua, interview, October 13, 2007.
2007b Eid ul Fitr khutbah, October 13, 2007.
2007c Sister Amina (not her real name), interview, September 2007.
2007d Sister Rianne, interview, September 2007.
2008a Imam Abu Bakr, sermon during juma, April 18, 2008.
2008b Usmaan Dan Fodio, conversation, November 14, 2008.
2008c Sister Zara, conversation, May 12, 2008.
2008d Sister Rita, conversation, May 12, 2008.
2009a Muslimeen brother 1, conversation, June 3, 2009.
2009b Muslimeen brother 2, conversation recounting recent job interview, June 3, 2009.
2009c Sisters at the Jamaat, informal discussion, June 3, 2009.
2009d Fawaz, conversation, June 3, 2009.
2009e Instructions given at shahada, August 22, 2009.

Khan, Aisha
1995 "Homeland, Motherland: Authenticity, Legitimacy, and Ideologies of Place among Muslims in Trinidad." In *Nation and Migration: The Politics of Space in the South Asian Diaspora*, ed. Peter van de Veer, 93–131. Philadelphia: University of Pennsylvania Press.

Khan, Shahnaz
2002 *Aversion and Desire: Negotiating Muslim Female Identity in the Diaspora*. Toronto: Women's Press.

Mahmood, Saba
2005 *Politics of Piety: The Islamic Revival and the Feminist Subject*. Princeton, N.J.: Princeton University Press.

Marsh, Clifton
1984 *From Black Muslims to Muslims: The Transition from Separatism to Islam, 1930–1980*. Lanham, Md.: Scarecrow Press.

Mernissi, Fatima
1987 *Women and Islam: An Historical and Theological Enquiry*. Trans. Mary Jo Lakeland. New Delhi: Kali for Women.
1991 *The Veil and the Male Elite: A Feminist Interpretation of Women's Rights in Islam*. Trans. Mary Jo Lakeland. Reading, Mass.: Addison-Wesley.

Moxley Rouse, Carolyn
2004 *Engaged Surrender: African-American Women and Islam*. Berkeley: University of California.

Reis, Joao Jose
2001 "*Quilombos* and Rebellions in Brazil." In *African Roots/American Cultures: Africa in the Creation of the Americas*, ed. Sheila S. Walker, 301–13. Lanham, Md.: Rowan and Littlefield.

Samaroo, Brinsley
1988 "Early African and East Indian Muslims in Trinidad and Tobago." Paper presented at Conference on Indo-Caribbean History and Culture, May 9–11, Centre for Caribbean Studies, University of Warwick, Coventry, England.

Turner, Richard Brent
1997 *Islam in the African-American Experience.* Bloomington: Indiana University Press.
Warner-Lewis, Maureen
2000 "Ethnic and Religious Pluralism among Immigrants in Trinidad in the Nineteenth Century." In *Identity in the Shadow of Slavery*, ed. Paul Lovejoy, 113–25. London: Continuum.
White, Vibert L.
2001 *Inside the Nation of Islam: A Historical and Personal Testimony by a Black Muslim.* Gainesville: University Press of Florida.

13

Island Currents, Global Aesthetics

Islamic Iconography in Trinidad

PATRICIA MOHAMMED

The history of Islam in the Caribbean has not been rigorously traced (Khan 2004: 190).[1] No pure story of traditions that arrive and are transformed over time by individuals or groups emerges. As with all cultural phenomena, growth and expansion are influenced by factors of migration, global currents in religious thinking, and material culture. In this essay I focus on what surfaces as a recognizable Islamic iconography in Trinidad over the history of its British colonial settlement from the nineteenth century to the present.[2]

In order to locate elements of an iconography, I have drawn on several sources of data, including vignettes by historians who have commented on the Islamic presence; observations from anthropologists, especially in relation to practices and material culture in the twentieth century; online sources that recount histories of *jamaats* (Islamic assemblies); and architecture, festivals, and clothing, and my own experience. I interpret the practices of Islam not as a distant observer but as an eyewitness exposed to aspects of this religion for more than half a century. Some references to other religious practices in Trinidad and to the past development of Islam in Africa and India and in other Caribbean territories are also useful in establishing those Islamic elements that have become iconic of this society.

In its beginnings in Trinidad as a religion, Islam had a more indiscernible and muted presence. From the early twentieth century onward, the construction of mosques and Muslim schools predominantly by the Indo-Islamic community, along with the annual festival of Hosay, made for greater visibility of this religion. Islamic aesthetics have conventionally developed along geometric rather than figurative lines, characterized by minimalism rather than the more sensual ritualism found in the religious practices of Hinduism or

Catholicism. This is paralleled in the emergence and growth of the Islamic presence on this landscape, which is most evident in the architecture and architectural symbols of its places of worship and in the style of dress expected of its adherents, rather than in objects, utensils, or elaborate rituals of its altars or festivals, again with the exception of Hosay, a funerary rite presented as the public "passion play" (Thaiss 199: 38) of this religion. While there are differences in the development of the Afro-Islamic and Indo-Islamic traditions in Trinidad, common to both is the importance of the Quran as the single holy text to which all believers subscribe. Religious leaders are largely men, who in general must have the capacity to read or recite the Quran in Arabic. Women, though important as followers, are to be controlled in dress and public behavior to preserve the honor and authority of men.

The essay is divided into three sections, the first examining evidence from the work of early historians and writers for their insight into the iconic. It establishes the symbols that differentiate Islam from the other religions. The second section looks at the most recognizable visual elements in the society that have come to be associated with Islamic iconography and Islamic art, drawing on the Hosay celebrations as its public performance of art, music, and strong ties to Arabic origins. Section three explores the dress and covering of the male and female body in Islam, especially in the public sphere, and the significance of this for meanings of piety and control over women in the religion in this society. I conclude with a summary of the main iconic elements that have surfaced in this review of available evidence.

Tracing Early Iconic Elements in the Growth of Islam in Trinidad

Islamic culture and practice in the Caribbean cross ethnic divides, drawing their congregation from a wide mix of peoples. African Islamic populations introduced during and after slavery predate the arrival of the Islamic adherents who were brought from India as indentured workers. Although the Islamic presence was always recognized in Trinidad, demographically its followers make up a relatively small percentage of the population. The 2011 population census of Trinidad and Tobago indicates that 5 percent of a population of more that 1.3 million now belong to the Islamic faith, indicating a decline in adherents from 2000.

The first known Muslims were from West Africa. It is thought that up to the early nineteenth century, there was a Muslim community in Port of Spain led by Yunus (Jonas) Muhammad Bath. Historians Carl Campbell (1974) and Brinsley Samaroo (1996) both confirm that the earliest introduction of

Muslims to the Caribbean region was by the Spaniards, who brought African Muslim slaves with them. This continued in the international slave trade, which flourished from the seventeenth century onward. "By the eighteenth century," writes Samaroo, "there were black Muslims throughout the region holding their rites, teachings and ceremonies openly under the eyes of the Christians, undergoing intense persecution but steadfastly persisting in their faith" (Samaroo 1996: 203). Campbell notes that "Jonas Mohammed Bath, who claimed that he was a Sultan in the Gambia, was well-versed in the Qur'an, dressed as an Imam and was well regarded as chief priest and patriarch of the Mandingos who set up their society in Port of Spain" (Campbell 1974: 145). Bath Street, located between Observatory and Picadilly streets in Port of Spain, still carries the memory of his Islamic leadership today (Brereton 2013).

Maureen Warner-Lewis confirms that "the African presence in Trinidad begins by naming the Mandingo. This might have to do with force of numbers, but it might just as well have had to do with the cohesion wrought by their Moslem faith, the favourable rating of their monotheism, the Arabic literacy of their spokesmen, and their repeated petitions to the colonial authorities"(Warner-Lewis 1996: 35). Fitzroy Baptiste also corroborates that a Black Muslim community or the "Mandingoes" could be found in the district of Belmont in Port of Spain up to and including the 1850s. He points out, however, that this was a generic term to describe African Muslims, among them the Hausa, Fulani, and some Yoruba, who were not of Mande linguistic and ethnic stock (see Baptiste n.d.). Agreeing with this metanarrative of African Islamic settlement, Aisha Khan recounts archival evidence of a meeting between 1840 and 1841 in Trinidad, where "a Mahometan priest named Emir Samba Makumba" greeted three Society of Friends representatives in Arabic. Makumba said he was brought to Trinidad in 1795, purchased by a French planter from a slave ship, and given the name Simon Boissiere. Having bought his freedom and with others sustained the Islamic faith, he in turn would greet other Mandingoes arriving on the island and enjoin them to subscribe to this group (Khan 2004: 191).

Warner-Lewis notes "that the kaftans worn by the Moslem men were thought of as 'night gowns'" (Warner-Lewis 1996: 38). Ethnic differences and distances among the African populations were fueled, as Warner-Lewis notes, by religious beliefs of the groups in Trinidad: "Moslems were offended by the physical and spiritual pollution of non-Moslems and it appears that the Moslem faith formed a bond across ethnic divisions. The Hausa considered the Yoruba polytheistic infidels, and the Yoruba in turn applied to the

Hausa their own Hausa term for foreigners, *gambari*." After 1841 the African-born slave population was increased by another group. These were African soldiers who served in the British West India Regiment during the Napoleonic wars (Hamid 2010). Brereton writes that soldiers of the disbanded group were given lands on the east coast of Trinidad in Manzanilla, and "smaller settlements were established along the bridge path from Arima to the coast" (Brereton 2013). They swelled the ranks of the Islamic Africans but remained relatively low in numbers; more isolated on the island, many accumulated elements of African Christianity. This surviving information establishes the earliest signs of an Islamic presence of "black Muslims" or Muslims of African descent, as they were and continue to be called in Trinidad.[3] Designation as black Muslims differentiates this group from the Indian-descended followers of Islam. Images of the African population in the early settlement period are not available in sketches, paintings, or photographs; sadly, we have no visual archaeological evidence of their dress styles, household items, implements, or the markings in their place of worship.

The introduction of Muslims from India began to increase the visibility of Islam in Trinidad dramatically from the nineteenth century onward. Although the majority of Indian migrants who were brought between 1845 and 1917 under the indenture system were of the Hindu faith, it was soon clear that Islamic practice presented some differences among them. It is estimated that Muslims accounted for 13 percent of the Indian immigrant population who came to Trinidad during the entire period from 1845 to 1917 (Comins 1893).

While there were marked tribal differences in dress and language that may have differentiated the African groups, among Indians in the early stages of migration there were few obvious markers in dress between Hindus and Muslims, at least to our untrained eyes—although no doubt these were well known among the migrants themselves. If we examine one of the iconic images of an early group of new arrivals into Trinidad quarantined at the Depot in Nelson Island (figure 13.1; Stark 1897), how does one differentiate the Islamic from non-Islamic?[4] The women and girls all have their heads covered rather similarly by the *ohrni* or headscarf, regardless of age. There are wide variations in the headdress and styles worn by men, however, with different patterns of tying the *pagree* head covering.

The Muslim migrants who came from India to the Caribbean practiced Islam that was syncretized with aspects of Hindu culture. These practices continued well into the early twentieth century. Patriarchy was reasserted in the establishment of the village *panchayats* (council of five elders), where imams or Islamic community leaders acted as the makers and enforcers of law, along

Island Currents, Global Aesthetics: Islamic Iconography in Trinidad · 299

Fig. 13.1. "Newly Arrived Coolies," from *Stark's Guide and History of Trinidad*, ca. 1897, p. 73. Indian migrants were quarantined on Nelson Island before they were selected by estates.

with *pundits/pandits* or Hindu community leaders. Imams and pundits were, and continue to be, primarily male. Although early missionary influences from the Middle East helped to shape the development of a separate Muslim identity by the 1930s, ethnic and cultural similarities among all Indians in the Caribbean provided a common base for their cuisine, musics, agriculture, and domestic life and expectations of gender roles. We should recall that the Indian migrants to Trinidad came from pre-partitioned India, decades before the independence and separation of Pakistan from India.

In *White Mughals*, William Dalrymple notes that "Islam has never been monolithic and has always adapted itself to its social and geographical circumstances ... over the centuries of Hindu-Muslim co-existence in India, much mutual exchange of ideas and customs took place between the two cohabiting cultures"(Dalrymple 2002: 168). Examples of syncretic rituals were evident in the earliest periods of indentureship from 1845. In the traditional Islamic wedding, women are not allowed to follow the procession from the groom's residence to the bride's house where the main ceremony takes place. However, Muslim women in the Caribbean not only followed the procession but actively participated in the dance celebrations and the anointing of the bride and groom before the marriage. In a village in south Trinidad containing both Hindu and Muslim families, Yakoob reported that when he was married in 1951 according to Muslim rites, his wife Zalayhar being also of this faith, the ritual he underwent the night before his wedding was similar to the Hindu practice. Yakoob was anointed by the village women with a mixture of *dahi* (yoghurt) and turmeric, a traditional preparation for both the bride and the groom to beautify their skin and prepare them for the first night marriage bed, all carried out with much ribaldry while he was being anointed (Mohammed 2002: 30).

Halima Kassim (1999, 2008) has noted other similarities between the early practices of Hindus and Muslims in the Caribbean. She argues that the model of womanhood that informed both Hinduism and Islam did not seek to empower women but rather to control their sexuality. Paralleling the Hindu view of women's *prakti* or untamed nature, which must be kept in check by men, was the Islamic notion of *fitna*—the chaos provoked by sexual disorder that is initiated by women. Islam presents women's sexuality as a threat to men and to the social order if left unchecked (Mernissi 1987: 31). While control of Islamic or Hindu women endures to this day, the growth of organized religion led to further differentiation between the two religions. In the second decade of the twentieth century the earliest Islamic missionaries came from India, among them Peer Hassan, who arrived in 1914. By 1923 with the arrival of the Middle Eastern Islamic missionary Karim Khan Durrani, there was growing conflict between India-derived beliefs and practices and the new fundamentals introduced by Middle Eastern missionaries. Sheik Hassim Muzaffar recounts in the history of the El Socorro Jamaat: "The Jamaat continued working harmoniously until the year 1920 when a Moulvi by the name of Fazal Karim Khan Durrani, B.A., came to Trinidad from London to do missionary work for and on behalf of the Ahmadiya Movement of Lahore, India. There was a heated debate with the Moulvi on one side and Hafiz Yacoob Ali and Haji Rooknudin Meah on the other side. A few months after the debate, Moulvi Durrani went back to London" (Muzaffar 2009).

With the introduction of self-appointed custodians, including the Tackveeyatul Islamic Association (TIA) in 1925, the Anjuman Sunnat ul Jamaat Association (ASJA) between 1931 and 1935, and the Trinidad Muslim League (TML) in 1947, each would establish identity markers that differentiated one group from the others, while still holding fast to some essential aesthetic lines and practices that were recognizably "Islamic," central among them the importance attributed to the reading of the Quran in any religious event (Khan 2004: 150).

The African tradition equally had privileged literacy and knowledge. In Muslim West Africa the written word was synonymous with the word and power of God. The Muslim traveler known as Leo Africanus observed about the town of Timbuktu on the Niger River in 1510 that "here are great stores of doctors, judges, priests, and other learned men, that are bountifully maintained at the king's costs and charges" (Goucher et al. 1998). This is consistent with the first glimpses of erudition we glean of the Fulani and other Islamic African ethnic groups in Trinidad.

Among those who came from India the mastery of the Quran was central to the survival of Islam as a religion (Jha 2005: 6). The Mughals or Moguls who consolidated Islam in South Asia spread Muslim and particularly Persian arts and culture as well as the Islamic faith throughout the sixteenth and seventeenth centuries. Wisely recognizing that full conversion was not possible, as the majority of the population were of Hindu or related faiths, the Mughals fostered a sophisticated civilization based on religious toleration, a mixture of Persian, Mongol, and Indian culture (BBC 2009). The Quran and fundamental adherence to its teachings remain the central difference in a very divergent yet tolerant Hindu and Islamic aesthetic that obtains in Trinidad to this day.

The migrant streams of Islamic Africans and Indians were not elites who had the luxury of travel and material goods. Both sets of migrants brought learning where possible and, as migrants do, drew heavily on memory of village and regional practices. Schematically in West Africa, from which the Africans were drawn, and in pre-partition, pre-Independence India, from which the Indians were drawn, indigenous belief systems had fused with the introduced Islamic traditions. In anthropological terms these traditions were commonly referred to as "little traditions," describing folkways and lived practices of peoples who interpret culture and religion in their varied contexts, and "great traditions," speaking to broader civilization and formalized origins. The sheer complexity of the past developments in art practices that influence religious iconography makes this systematic tracing of "big" and "little" traditions virtually impossible. For instance, there are both Mughal and Iranian influences on Islam in India at different historical periods, just as there are numerous other influences on Islam in African states. Such complexity must be acknowledged nonetheless as a precursor to the history of the migration of Muslims to the West Indies, a fertile history (Grey 1967: 97; Wiet 1967: 93) on which all Islamic cultures that continue to flourish have referenced.

Despite the study of migrant communities through the framework of "cultural persistence," as was the practice of early anthropology in the Caribbean (Herskovits and Herskovits 1947; Klass 1961), religious practices are embellished or amplified by new trends and traditions. For instance, "Around the late 1960s, missionaries from the Middle East began visiting Trinidad, along with returning nationals educated at Al-Azhar University in Cairo and universities in Saudi Arabia," and they continually altered the practices of Islam (Kassim n.d.) Thus tracing Islamic iconography is like piecing together a jigsaw puzzle where only segments of a picture will emerge.

Minimalism of an Islamic Aesthetic and the Suppression of the Senses

Compared to the major religious persuasions in Trinidad—Christianity and Hinduism—Islam in Trinidad has a muted aesthetic presence. In this island the presence of Islam is an interruption in an otherwise richly variegated landscape dotted with Catholic and Protestant churches, iconic statues of the Virgin Mary and Jesus, stained glass windows and bell towers, elaborate Hindu *mandirs* (temples), and brightly colored prayer flags or *jhandis* that identify gardens of Hindus. If architecture is a primary signifier of visibility, at present there are more than 200 Hindu temples in Trinidad and possibly twice as many Christian places of worship, with fewer markers of an Islamic presence.

There are fewer religious icons to be found in Muslim households than in Hindu households. In general (although these rules are not followed as stringently today), followers of Islam are not allowed to have any graven images or likenesses of the human body, either as sculpture or photographs or as decorative elements of their furnishings. Where the Hindu presence announces itself in a profusion of color and objects, Islamic prayer events are somber, austere, and focused primarily around the centrality of the word and the obeisance to Allah and the Prophet Muhammed. Aisha Khan captures perfectly the few ritual objects and highly sanitized minimal aesthetic that are typically found at a Muslim *niaj* (prayer meeting). "Around a table at the front of the area sat six men, including the imam and Jasmine's husband (being one of the hosts). On the table were the standard accoutrements—flowers, a pitcher of water and glasses, some incense sticks burning in a small vase" (Khan 2004: 200). Figure 13.2, showing a *niaj* I attended in 2011, mirrors her description. Only men sit at this head table, including the presiding imam and host, and the incense and flowers are obscured by water glasses. The open book is recurrent.

The aesthetic dissimilarity of the religions of Islam and Hinduism are clearly depicted in figures 13.3 and 13.4. The former shows the front of a mosque in Valencia, east Trinidad. The latter shows the interior of a modest temple in Chaguanas, central Trinidad. In the interior of the mosque in figure 13.3, as on the exterior, there is little to distract the senses of the devotee away from the primary purpose—to focus on the word of Allah and the teachings

Fig. 13.2. Arabic reading of texts as a prayer meeting component for the occasion of the sixtieth wedding anniversary of a Muslim couple in Trinidad. Photo by Patricia Mohammed, 2011.

Fig. 13.3. Mosque at Valencia. Photo by Patricia Mohammed, 2001.

Fig. 13.4. Interior of Hindu temple at Chaguanas. Photo by Patricia Mohammed, 2003.

of the Prophet Muhammed.[5] Yet as figure 13.4 indicates, Hinduism allows the photographic representation of *deotas*, marble or stone effigies of sacred characters, shrines, flowers, incense, and bright sparkling colors that immediately embrace the senses. During the Hindu prayer ritual the smell of ghee on burning sandalwood and smoke rising from the *bedi* presided over by the pundit draws one into an almost trancelike participation in the unfolding ritual of the prayer. John Bowen observes: "Viewed through a Western lens, Muslim rituals often do not appear to have . . . the intricate and apparently arcane procedures . . . that tend to characterize Hindu devotional rites" (Bowen 1989: 615, quoted in Khan 2004: 194–95)

Fundamental to the aesthetic of the religion of Islam is the belief that "there is no more perfect symbol of the Divine Unity than light. For this reason, the Muslim artist seeks to transform the very stuff he is fashioning into a vibration of light" (Burckhardt 1976). The interplay of light and dark in the elegant Arabic script calligraphed by an Islamic adherent in Trinidad (figure 13.5) and in the decorated front surface of the mosque in Valencia (figure 13.6) is itself the perfection of art that Islamic culture seeks to represent: repeated arabesque geometric patterns and carved designs that allow the shape and texture of light to emerge. In this recognition of form coalescing out of light, there is no dif-

Fig. 13.5. Drawing of first surah by Islamic adherent Ayoob Mohammed, Trinidad, 2012.

Fig. 13.6. Detail of Valencia Mosque surface decoration. Photo by Patricia Mohammed, 2001.

ference between Islamic art and the fundamental rules governing all painting and photography. This is the same effect that was aimed at in stained glass windows in Christian churches. Viewed from the ground, they appear not as a picture but as a network of geometric black lines and colored light.

Islamic calligraphy configures a repetitive geometry of patterns that facilitates a mental reckoning through the maze of a mind, thus forcing the believer to focus on the word and teachings of the monotheistic God of this religion. Similar to the Jewish relationship to the Talmud, the gaining of knowledge through the act of reading and writing itself embodies the sacred in this religion. Only those who knew and could read from the Holy Quran could become its leaders. This is very resonant with the way in which writing was originally conceived of as a religious experience: "The hieroglyph, referring to the characters used in the writing of ancient Egypt, means 'writing of the gods' from Greek *hieros*, meaning holy, and *gluphein*, to engrave. The act of writing and inscribing was therefore already beginning to be associated with wisdom and knowledge" (Mohammed 2010: 28).

In summary, the first iconic markers of an Islamic presence in the earlier years of settlement could be found in the different dress style of Islamic followers, in their literacy in the language of Arabic, and in the earliest architectural constructions of congregational places of worship, represented in their *masjids* and, as we shall see, in the festival of Hosay—the Caribbean's Muharram, commemoration of the martyrdom of the Prophet Mohammed's grandsons Hassan and Hussein at the Battle of Kerbala.[6] In the next section we look at how a more defined Islamic presence and iconography would emerge in the late twentieth and early twenty-first century.

Contemporary Defining Markers of Islam on the Landscape

In this section I select the most recognizable visual elements in the society that have come to be associated with Islamic iconography and Islamic art. Islamic art remains a footnote in the artistic sensibility of this island, which does not itself have a highly sophisticated visual grammar. It has no self-avowed Islamic artists or locally produced public Islamic art other than that constituted in the architecture of masjids and the festival of Hosay. The majority of Muslims retain the injunctions of the Quran that domestic spaces may contain no photographs, paintings, or reproductions of the human body. The latter rule, in my view, has not encouraged experimentation with form that might lead to robust iconic markers specific to the abstract geometry between light and dark, as is required of Islamic art. Islam emerges as a more private and austere religion.

An Architectural Presence

Several iconic mosques and dominant symbols and colors have come to be associated with Islamic architecture in Trinidad. I concentrate on the earlier structures, although renovations in older mosques or newly built ones began to take on more eloquent architectural statements. As communities and patronage by the wealthy grew, elaborate domes and architectural surfaces were introduced on masjid buildings. Jamaats and sects quietly competed with one another to present the magnificence of their place of worship.[7]

One of the earliest Muslims arriving in Trinidad for whom we have some biographical data is Haji Ruknuddeen Sahib, who came in 1897. It is said that he "started to preach Islam at secret locations, since the indentured servants were not allowed to use light or have public gatherings. He used to read the Koran by moonlight" (*Newsday* 2008). Muslims with resources were eager to establish institutions to cater for the educational needs of the community. Literacy was a prime objective for keeping those of Islamic faith in schools where the religion was taught, rather than attending the competing schools where Christianity was observed in daily practices. Mohammed Ibrahim, a prominent entrepreneur, built a school and a mosque in 1924 in El Socorro. The Islamic Guardian Association also started an Arabic and Urdu school in Princes Town in 1925. Hajji Gokool Meah, another wealthy entrepreneur, built a mosque (figure 13.7) and a school in St. James in 1929. Haji Ruknud-

Fig. 13.7. Haji Gookool Meah Mosque in St James. Photograph courtesy Nyla Singh.

deen also built a few small schools in other districts. This probably included the Lengua Islamic school, which started in 1929 in Princes Town (Mustapha 2009). All these buildings would begin to take on some architectural resemblance by the mid-1930s, consolidating a twentieth-century presence of Indo-Trinidadian Muslims in the society. The orchestrated building of mosques and schools was aided and abetted by overseas visitors like the learned missionary Karim Khan Durrani and facilitated Islamic religio-cultural organizations and thus the "codifying of Islamic doctrine of somewhat divergent traditions and pedagogies, explicitly in the spirit of learning, teaching and knowing" (Khan 2004: 204).

Examining the earliest examples of Islamic places of worship, Gaston Wiet describes the mosque of Sultan Hasan of Cairo during the Mamluk period 1356–62 as representing the high point of Mamluk art. "This impregnable edifice, a solidly built fortress-like structure of simple geometric plan, its minaret soaring heavenwards, represents the apotheosis of Islam" (Wiet 1967: 93). Domes, arches, spires, minarets, geometric balance, and clever illumination ushering in light were the typical vocabulary of Islamic architecture. The shape of the dome, its symmetric half circle as a powerful inverted capturing of space and light internally while soaring to heaven, represented balance. The minaret, from the Arabic for "the object that gives light," is said to be "light held by the Muezzin as he recites the call to prayer at night which gives the onlooker below the idea of a light-tower" (Gottheil 1910: 132). In Trinidad the domes of some mosques, topped by the sculptural form of the joined crescent moon and five-pointed star (see figures 13.8 and 13.9), and the dominant color of the building being white accented in green, would quickly become a signature of Islamic faith in Trinidad. The Jinnah Memorial Mosque was completed in 1954 and named after the founder of Pakistan, Quaid-I-Azam Mohammed Ali Jinnah. The mosque is owned by the Trinidad Muslim League, an organization that was founded by Moulvi Ameer Ali, Mohammed Hakeem Khan, and Mohammed Rafeeq on August 15, 1947, the same day that Pakistan was created.[8] The Jinnah Memorial Mosque is popularly referred to as the St. Joseph mosque due to its location at the intersection of the road that leads into St. Joseph, the first capital of Trinidad.

The crescent moon and star have been adopted as symbols of Islam and are readily apparent on many but not all the mosques in Trinidad, since not all sects subscribe to what can be viewed as pagan symbols that predate Islam by thousands of years. It is thought that during the time of the Prophet Muhammed the early Muslim community did not have a symbol, but Islamic armies and caravans flew simple solid-colored flags of black, green, or white

Fig. 13.8. TML Islamic Mosque in St. Joseph, Trinidad, with minaret and moon and star. Photo by Patricia Mohammed, 2013.

Fig. 13.9. A crescent moon and star top the dome of the Nur-e-Islam Mosque in San Juan. Photo by Patricia Mohammed, 2013.

for identification purposes. Not until the Ottoman Empire did the crescent moon and star become affiliated with the Muslim world. When the Turks conquered Constantinople (Istanbul) in 1453, they adopted the city's existing flag and symbol. It is also thought that the colors green and white are appropriated because these were the colors used by the Prophet Muhammad's tribe. Green represented paradise, the latter also being the Persian word for garden, the color green signifying survival to Bedouin tribes who depended on the green oasis for water and food in the desert. Green also became the dominant color in the binding of the Quran. Green was the accepted color for the large cloth screens in early mosques in Trinidad that divided the male and female populations from sight of each other during prayers.

The colors of green and white, the crescent moon, and the five-pointed star in Trinidad as iconic representations of Islam are directly linked to the founding of Pakistan, the flag of which bears the same icons and colors. Designed by Mohammad Ali Jinnah, the founder of Pakistan, as the national flag for its recognition as a separate nation in August 1947, the flag is dark green in color with a white vertical bar, a white crescent in the center, and a five-pointed star. The alliance with Pakistan at this time is not incidental. While Indian migrants had come from pre-partitioned India, the creation of two nations built on religious differences on the Indian subcontinent at independence in 1947 would create further distinctions between the Islamic and Hindu populations in Trinidad. By 1947 different places of worship, schools, and even separate laws pertaining to marriage and divorce had already created internal differentiations within this ethnic population—without the acrimony and bloodshed that had taken place in India.

There is no similar trajectory of Islamic architectural visibility among the African-descended Islamic population, with the exception of the Jamaat al Muslimeen led by Yasin Abu Bakr. From the early 1980s this movement combined a black liberation thrust founded around a religious base, unlike other mosques being constructed in Trinidad. The Port of Spain City Corporation had filed an injunction against the Jamaat al Muslimeen to stop them from erecting a mosque on lands belonging to the corporation in west Port of Spain, for which Abu Bakr was jailed. By 1985, nonetheless, the mosque was opened in the prohibited compound. The Jamaat al Muslimeen was later associated with political unrest and Abu Bakr's 1990 attempt to capture state power in a political coup.

In more recent years the architecture of primarily Indo-Trinidadian mosques has become increasingly ornate, with larger domes that stand out in the landscape, and with changing color schemes, but the architectural styles

Fig. 13.10. Charlieville Mosque. Photo by Patricia Mohammed, 2013.

have nonetheless retained a family resemblance to the earliest mosques (figure 13.10).

Architecture and Performance Art—The Commemorative Ritual of Hosay

Eid ul Fitr or the end of Ramadan—the month of fasting—has been recognized for the last decade as a national holiday in Trinidad. This public recognition of Islam is piously commemorated with an early morning prayer at the mosque, where donations are given to the poor, and later with private meals at homes for family and friends. Hosay or Hosea in Trinidad is the only celebration in this religion that has wide Islamic and non-Islamic public participation and is vibrant with color, sound, and movement. The symbolic markers identified—the architecture of Islamic places of worship and the crescent moon—recur in the ritual objects produced for this festival. The earliest observance of Hosay in Trinidad has been traced to 1854, eleven years after the first set of indentured laborers arrived from India. In the undated, circa 1910, image (figure 13.11) men, women, and children are gathered in a large crowd, many clearly dressed in their "Sunday best." At least five *tadjahs* or temples are vis-

Fig. 13.11. Earliest photograph located of Hosay festival in Trinidad, ca. 1910. Photo courtesy of Patricia Mohammed.

Fig. 13.12. Postcard of Hosay festival, Trinidad, 1930s. Courtesy of Patricia Mohammed.

ible, and even through the fuzziness of this photograph we can see that they are ornate creations. In the second postcard image, circa 1930s (figure 13.12), again set against the estate fields where permission would have been granted to hold this festival, the greater detail on the tadjahs confirms the artistry and skill of tadjah makers and the knowledge of this ritual that would have traveled with the migrants.

The largest celebration of the festival of Hosay is now held in St. James, an urban district of the main city of Port of Spain, although there continued to be performances in other areas such as Curepe for many decades, and Hosay is still observed in other areas, such as Cedros in the far south. It draws thousands of spectators from all ethnic groups and religions. Hosay is a remembrance and funerary rite, but its religious significance is lost to many, other than those who continue to make the tadjahs and perform its religious rituals.[9] The tadjahs (tombs or mausoleums) are labor- and time-intensive works of art. The actual festival lasts for five nights, with the procession of the tadjahs taking place on the third night (figures 13.13 and 13.14). They are built to be destroyed on the final day, when they are submerged into the sea, symbolizing both the violence of this moment in Islamic history and the transience of life.

Fig. 13.13. Current photograph of tadjah from Hosay festival in St. James, Port of Spain. Photo courtesy Noor Kumar Mahabir.

Fig. 13.14. Participatory event of mixed populations at Hosay in St. James. Photo courtesy Noor Kumar Mahabir.

The tadjah makers spend considerable time and money and are skillful artisans in their use of bamboo, wood, paper, and tinsel to produce tombs of Hussain, the grandson of the Prophet Muhammed who was killed in the Battle of Kerbala. The five tadjahs built for each Hosay range in height from 10 to 30 feet. They are hauled through the streets on parade days to the beat of *tassa* drums along with two standards in the shape of half-moons, each carried separately on the shoulder of one man at a time. The half-moons, one red and one green (figure 13.15), symbolize the deaths of Hussain and his brother Hassan; red for the blood of Hussain that was shed at Kerbala and green for the poisoning of Hassan, eleven years earlier.

The architectural elements in the tadjahs of domes, minarets, and the geometric decorative elements are all consistent with the style of the mosques described earlier, differing only in their vivid application of colour. The decorated crescent moon wreaths used for the moon dance during Hosay confirm the strong association of this symbol with the iconography of Islam (figure 13.15). The sight of the new moon, in the form of a crescent, is the signal for the start of the lunar month of Ramadan, which begins the discipline of fasting and the special prayers of *taraweeh* or reading of the Quran that is carried out every night until the cycle of the moon wanes again.

Elements of an Islamic aesthetic in Trinidad were recognized by Trinidadian artists in the 1940s and 1950s. Sybil Atteck depicted the whirling gestures of the moon dance in a painting that is now owned by the National Art Gallery and Museum of Trinidad and Tobago.[10] She was trained in art schools in Europe and South and North America and exposed to German expressionism. At a time when the newly formed Trinidad Art Society was attempting to define a national aesthetic, her nonphotographic representational style was viewed as "foreign," but the geometric lines that depict the movement of the moon dance are somewhat consistent with the aesthetic of Islamic art. M. P. Alladin (1919–80), a fellow painter of the Trinidad Art Society, also depicted the Hosay drummers in 1957. Alladin's painting focuses on the hands and drums of faceless tassa drummers in the Hosay parade. By the early 1990s Isaiah Boodhoo, another Trinidadian artist, would produce a painting titled *Moon Dance* in his Caroni series. He was educated in the United States and came under the influence of de Kooning, Rauschenburg, and Jasper Johns (more like Atteck than Alladin). Boodhoo's painting is gestural rather than figurative, the movement and the color summoning up the drums that accompany the dance of the crescent moon. That all painters have focused on the gesture and geometric patterns created by the color and movement rather

Fig. 13.15. Obeisance before moon wreath at Hosay festival. Photo courtesy Noor Kumar Mahabir.

than on figurative details of face and body is perhaps coincidental, but it is certainly mindful of the aesthetic of the Islamic faith that eschews figurations of the human body.

The elements of architecture, the dominant symbols of domes, minarets, the crescent moon and five-pointed star, the colors of white and green and the single splash of red—white for purity, green for fertility and gardens, red for blood—are still sustained as the dominant Islamic iconic markers in this society today.

In the next section I look at the evolution of dress. One of the original signifiers of the Islamic presence, dress and fashions adopted by Islamic followers surfaced again in the late twentieth and early twenty-first centuries as another iconic marker of Islam.

Dress as a Symbol of Islamic Piety

In Trinidad those identified as black Muslims or Muslimeen are allegedly not linked to the black Muslim movement in the United States. Ken Boodhoo writes that the Muslimeen are one of the fourteen members of the "United Islamic Organization . . . more radical Muslim organisations, some of which were formed as a consequence of missionary activity from Middle East Islamic groups" (Boodhoo 1992: 34). What this "new world Islam" has introduced in the Caribbean for the first time is a reversion to a traditional form of Islam characterized by a radical unification of religion and politics and, outwardly, an invigorated patriarchal control over women. The women of these organizations must cover their heads, bodies, and in some groups their faces from the wider population.

Indo-Trinidadian Muslim women, according to Aisha Khan, "were attired in fancier versions of Western dress, although wearing *ohrnis* [headscarves]. Even as the person to whom this ritual was devoted, Jasmine wore a rather plain, standard Western-style dress, though again with ohrni. Had this been a function in a masjid hall, or one sponsored by a middle class family, the women would have worn shalwar chemise, and many not with ohrni but with hijab" (Khan 2004: 199). At present, the hijab has become the most evocative symbol of the correctly pious woman among all Muslims, although the headgear is still eschewed by many on nonreligious occasions. The Islamic female body acquired more symbolic value of the religion's difference by the late twentieth century, as the religion also became more organized and competitive for identity and space among other religions.

Women's commitment to adopting dress styles that demonstrate piousness indicates either their collusion or lack of power in challenging the requirement of covering their bodies. Figures 13.16–13.19 give some indication of current practices. In figure 13.16, Zuleikha Mohammed wears an *ohrni* and *shalwar* chemise with simple pearl necklace, bracelet, and a watch as adornment. This outfit was donned for a religious occasion in her home and would be similar to her garb for attending normal masjid prayers such as *juma* (Friday prayers). It would not be her daily dress style, whether at home doing chores or attending other nonreligious public events. At a wedding or other Islamic function that requires more elaborate attire, she would wear an intricately decorated *shalwar* chemise, rarely a *sari*, the latter still signified as the dress style of Hindu women. As Aisha Khan (2004) has observed, a Zuleikha has virtually adopted Western dress and manners on an everyday basis but for religious occasions will ensure that her head is covered by an ohrni.

Fig. 13.16. Zuleikha Mohammed wears a *shalwar* chemise and ohrni. Photo courtesy Aneel Karim.

Fig. 13.17. Two Afro-Trinidadian Islamic women wear the full burkha. Photo courtesy Jeanne P. Baptiste, 2010.

Some of her counterparts who may be obliged by convention (for instance those who have made Hajj) may wear the hijab for every public occasion. Very rarely are older Muslim women of Indian descent viewed with the full burkha, as shown in figure 13.17. This represents an extremist form of Islamic wear among women and is generally, although not exclusively, associated with Afro-Trinidadian rather than Indo-Trinidadian Muslims.

In sharp contrast and representing iconic African Islamic dress traditions, figures 13.18 and 13.19 show young girls and one young boy taken at a mosque event among Afro-Trinidadian Muslim followers in north Trinidad.[11] The colors are vibrant, the hijabs are flattering, and in one case the young girl (figure 13.19) wears a jeweled headdress, reminiscent of the Egyptian and Turkish beadwork of headscarves. Women's dress and fashion as markers of Islamic identity are strong iconic fields for rendering Islam in the contemporary landscape. The need to control women cannot only be viewed as a signal of piety or conformity. The concept of *fitna,* originally meaning enticing or tempting

Fig. 13.18. A black Muslim family. Photo courtesy Jeanne P. Baptiste, 2010.

Fig. 13.19. Ornate headscarves and finely embroidered fabrics are used. Photo courtesy Jeanne P. Baptiste, 2010.

away from the teachings of the Prophet Muhammed, when associated with women refers to the chaos provoked by sexual disorder, which women's presence is said to cause men. How Muslim women in Trinidad have appropriated these markers, and have the freedom to do so, is an element of the iconoclasm that Trinidadian culture and society allows. A long history of Western colonization has left its mark on women's emancipation, and these gains are not easily retracted.

Masculine Power and Piety

Male dress is more straightforward in its symbolic presentation. If women have to cover their heads and faces with fabric, the beard, or male covering with facial hair is representative of the piety of masculinity. The beard signifies adherence to the faith and is a sign of wisdom, being associated with age and maturity, the stroking of the beard suggesting the act of thoughtful reflection. In figures 13.1, 13.2, and 13.20 the beard is a recurrent symbol. In figure 13.20 we see an elder of the black Muslim group, undifferentiated in many ways from the Indo-Trinidadian elders and imams shown in figure 13.2. His dress style contains patterns more reminiscent of Yoruba embroidery from Africa than those worn by Indo-Trinidadian Muslim men, whose designs follow either Persian or Indian influence in male *kurta pyjamas*. Nonetheless, there is a close circuitry in the patriarchal presence and in the iconic trappings that present Islamic patriarchy, both in the past and in contemporary society and among the different ethnic groups.

We began with the first symbolic marker of the Islamic religion as masculine, African, a recognition of dress, literacy of the Quran, and leadership of community. This has come full circle and there is a great similarity in the iconic aspects of this religion today among both Afro-Trinidadian and Indo-Trinidadian Muslims.

Conclusion: From Muted Visibility to a Defined Presence in Twenty-First Century Trinidad

In the transition from early settlement in the eighteenth and nineteenth centuries through a passage of continuous change and growth in the twentieth century, the Islamic presence in Trinidad can no longer be described as muted. Its iconic references are more visible. This has not only been a result of the increased presence of Muslims in schools, mosques, and politics and of Islamic men as community leaders but is also due to the distinctive archi-

Fig. 13.20. Elder of the black Muslim group. Photo courtesy Jeanne P. Baptiste, 2010.

tectural and apparel statements of the religion. Trinidad's history, as in the rest of the Caribbean, has been negotiated as a challenge to the dominant European colonial ideology of Christianity as civilized and superior to other religions. By the twenty-first century the multiracial and multicultural policies of a constantly extemporizing state ideology in Trinidad (in concert with contemporary processes of globalization) have allowed Trinidadians to view differentiated culture, religion, and lifestyle through the lens of tolerance, so that different sects and religions continue to coexist with great harmony compared to that which obtains in other societies.

The dominant iconic reference for Islam is an intangible one but always linked to text—the Quran—and to Arabic, the language in which the Quran is written. The interpretation of the text and the possession of knowledge of the text are recurrent features in the early and later presence of Islam in this society. The Quran is the primary apparatus around which Islam is built and continues to propagate faith and bring Muslim communities together, although this is still transmitted primarily by men. From 2005 on, the Islamic Broadcast

Fig. 13.21. Devotional stance of Islamic adherent Ayoob Mohammed. Photo courtesy Aneel Karim.

Network was introduced as a religious television channel. While catering to a wider population, it engages Muslim audiences through Quranic readings, debates, and news that virtually connect Muslims across the world. Research on Islamic iconography through an analysis of this channel's programming might provide a window onto the new symbols that will emerge in the future. With greater affluence and organized trips to Mecca to perform Hajj, Muslims return with souvenirs of the Kaaba and other pilgrimage mementos. There has also been an influx of consumer goods marked by an Islamic aesthetic, brought by merchants from India and catering to Muslim diasporas.

Nonetheless, one feature has remained consistent in my consideration of the iconography of Islam in Trinidad, an elusive one rather than one drawn from the concrete and tangible objects that can be handled. Figure 13.21 is that of Ayoob Mohammed, the writer of the Arabic script featured in figure 13.5. The photograph of him was taken at a large religious function held in his home in Chaguanas, Trinidad, in 2011. His visage, his disconnection from the audience even in the midst of onlookers, and his dress and demeanor, speak to both piety and a surrender to the compassion from Allah that is promised to believers. His open hands, held over his heart as he prays, mirror an open book, and in his closed eyes tilted slightly upward is the willingness to receive knowledge and guidance through the word of Allah, as the Prophet Muhammed received the word from a heavenly rather than earthly source. While there will continue to be debates and dissension surrounding this religion, there is no doubt that one of its most compelling iconic features is a firm belief that the transcribed words of Allah cannot be contested, and that the logic of the religion's wisdom will continuously summon believers and draw others into its fold.

Notes

1. Nor is it possible to trace purity or linearity of development in the growth and expansion of any cultural phenomenon, especially religion.

2. Trinidad is the larger island of a twin-island state. I write primarily about Trinidad as this is the site of recorded growth of this religion well into the twentieth century. There is little evidence of early Islamic practice in Tobago.

3. The use of Muslim and Moslem is not so much interchangeable as specific to time and reference; where Moslem is used, it is from quoted text. In general Muslim became the more accepted word for those of the Islamic faith as we progressed later into the twentieth century.

4. This is one of the most widely used photographs of newly arrived Indian immigrants.

5. The relevant Islamic hadith: "He who has made an image will be called upon, on the day of Resurrection, to give it a soul, but he will not be able to do so.... Woe unto him who has painted a living being!... Paint only trees and flowers and inanimate objects."

6. Regarding Arabic, Peter Hogg notes that upon his arrival in London in 1733, Sir Hans Sloane, a doctor who had served for some time in Jamaica, employed Job Jalla, his real name being Ayuba Suleiman Diallo, a well-born Senegalese Muslim who had been liberated, to translate "several manuscripts and inscriptions upon medals in Arabic in his collection" (Hogg 1979: 6).

7. This is drawn from my experience of the Anjuman Sunnat ul Jamaat mosque located on High Street in Princes Town. During my childhood the mosque was a modest one, not even visible from the road. By the 1990s it had expanded to a several-storied building with a huge copper-colored dome that was unmistakably evident for miles around.

8. On April 21, 1950, the Trinidad Muslim League was incorporated by Act of Parliament Number 26 of 1950 to represent the Ghair-Mukallid or Non-Conformist Muslims of Trinidad and Tobago.

9. Shiites around the world observe Hosay in different ways. In Kerbala, Iraq, mourners shed blood by beating themselves with swords. In Lucknow, India, the center of Shiite culture in India, it is observed with great passion with *tadjahs* (*taziyas*), drums, and mourners who reenact the Battle of Kerbala with chants of "Hussain!" This custom was

brought to Trinidad by East Indian Shiites who migrated from India in the nineteenth century. See Hosay, http://www.bestoftrinidad.com/hosay.html.

10. *The Moon Dance*, original title *Indian Festival*, oil on board, 50 × 40 in, Sybil Atteck, 1959, Collection of the National Art Gallery and Museum of Trinidad and Tobago.

11. I am grateful to Dr. Jeanne P. Baptiste, who shared with me all the photos of black Muslims from her research carried out on this population for her PhD thesis at Rutgers completed in 2013. I thank my father, Ayoob Mohammed, and my mother, Zuleikha Mohammed, for allowing me use of their photographs in this paper and for the firsthand experience of the practices of Islam in Trinidad society.

References Cited

Baptiste, Fitzroy André
N.d. "Trinidad and Tobago as the Hinge of a Primary and Secondary Diaspora between Africa, the Caribbean and South America, especially Venezuela circa 1797 to 1914" (rtf). bibliotecavirtual.clacso.org.ar/ar/libros/aladaa/andre.
Bennett, John W., Leo A. Despres, and Michio Nagai
1998 *Classic Anthropology: Critical Essays, 1944–1996*. Brunswick: Transactions Publishers.
Boodhoo, Ken I.
1992 "Islamic Fundamentalism in the Caribbean." Dialogue 135; LACC Occasional papers series 34. http://digitalcommons.fiu.edu/laccopsd/34.
Bowen, John
1989 "Salaat in Indonesia: The Social Meanings of an Islamic Ritual." *Man*, n.s., 24(4): 600–619.
Brereton, Bridget
2013 "East Port of Spain Built and Cultural Heritage: An Historical Framework" (draft). Prepared for University of the West Indies research project Leveraging Built and Cultural Heritage for Economic Development in Port of Spain, led by Asad Mohammed.
British Broadcasting Company
2009 Mughal Empire. BBC, Religions. http://www.bbc.co.uk/religion/religions/islam/history/mughalempire_1.shtml.
Burckhardt, Titus
1976 *Art of Islam: Language and Meaning*. Trans. from the French by Peter Hobson. London: Islamic Festival Trust.
Campbell, Carl
1974 "Jonas Mohammed Bath and the Free Mandingo in Trinidad: The Question of Their Repatriation to Africa, 1831–1838." *Pan African Journal* 7(2): 129–52.
Comins, D.
1893 *A Note on Emigration from India to Trinidad*. Calcutta: Bengal Secretarial Press.
Dalrymple, William
2002 *White Mughals: Love and Betrayal in Eighteenth-Century India*. London: Harper Collins.

Gottheil, Richard J. H.
1910 "The Origin and History of the Minaret." *Journal of the American Oriental Society* 30(2): 132–54. http://www.jstor.org/stable/3087601.

Goucher, Candice, Charles LeGuin, and Linda Walton Readings
1998 *In the Balance: Themes in Global History*. Boston: McGraw-Hill. Selections from chapter 13, "Traditions and their Transformations." Reading 2. http://www.learner.org/courses/worldhistory/support/reading_17_2.pdf.

Grey, Basil
1967 "Persian Art after 1200." In *Larousse Encyclopaedia of Modern Art*, 97–107. London: Paul Hamlyn.

Hamid, Abdul Wahid
2010 *The Mandingo Muslims of Trinidad: The Story of Muhammad Sisei, 1788–1838*. http://www.caribbeanmuslims.com/articles/1226/1/The-Mandingo-Muslims-Of-Trinidad/Page1.html.

Herskovits, Melville J., and Frances S. Herskovits
1947 *Trinidad Village*. New York: Alfred A. Knopf.

Hogg, Peter
1979 *Slavery: The Afro-American Experience*. London: British Library.

Jha, J. C.
2005 "The Indian Heritage in Trinidad." In *Calcutta to Caroni and the Indian Diaspora*, ed. John La Guerre. St Augustine, Trinidad: Multimedia Production Centre, School of Education, Faculty of Humanities and Education.

Kassim, Halima
1999 "Education, Community Organizations and Gender among the Indo Muslims of Trinidad, 1917–1962." M.Phil. thesis, University of the West Indies, St. Augustine, Trinidad.
2008 Muslim and Missionaries of Trinidad. http://www.caribbeanmuslims.com/articles/1029/1/Muslim-and-Missionaries-of-Trinidad/Page1.html.
N.d. "From Cohesion to Discord and Disunity." http://www.caribbeanmuslims.com/articles/1029/1/Muslim-and-Missionaries-of-Trinidad/Page1.html.

Khan, Aisha
2004 *Callaloo Nation: Metaphors of Race and Religious Identity among South Asians in Trinidad*. Durham, N.C.: Duke University Press.

Klass, Morton
1961 *East Indians in Trinidad: A Study of Cultural Persistence*. New York: Columbia University Press.

Mohammed, Patricia
2002 *Gender Negotiations among Indians in Trinidad, 1917 to 1947*. Basingstoke, UK: Palgrave Macmillan.
2010 *Imaging the Caribbean: Culture and Visual Translation*. Oxford, UK: Macmillan.

Mustapha, Nasser
2009 Education among Early Muslims in Trinidad. March 4. http://www.caribbeanmuslims.com/articles/1117/1/Education-Among-Early-Muslims-In-Trinidad/Page1.html.

Muzaffar, Sheik Hashim
2009 [1966] "History of the El Socorro Jamaat 1966." http://www.caribbeanmuslims.com/articles/1153/1/History-of-the-El-Socorro-Jamaat-1966/Page1.html.

Newsday
2008 "Muslims Arrival Tied to Indentured Experience: ASJA Commemorates Arrival Day." *Newsday* (Trinidad and Tobago), May 29.

Samaroo, Brinsley
1996 "Early African and East Indian Muslims in Trinidad and Tobago." In *Across the Dark Waters: Ethnicity and Indian Identity in the Caribbean,* ed. Brinsley Samaroo and David Dabydeen, 201–12. London: Macmillan.

Stark, James
ca. 1897 *Stark's Guide and History of Trinidad*. Boston: J. H. Stark.

Thaiss, Gustav
1999 "Muharram Rituals and the Carnivalesque in Trinidad." *ISIM Newsletter* 3: 93–94.

Warner-Lewis, Maureen
1966 *Trinidad Yoruba: From Mother Tongue to Memory*. Tuscaloosa: University of Alabama Press.

Wiet, Gaston
1967 "The Moslem World: From the Mediterranean to Iran." In *Larousse Encyclopedia of Modern Art*, 93–96. London: Paul Hamlyn.

Contributors

Jerusa Ali is a doctoral candidate in legal studies at Carleton University. Her LLM dissertation focused on cultural, religious, and legal barriers to the realization of human rights in the Caribbean. Raised in the Bahamas, she has also lived, worked, and traveled throughout the Caribbean, Latin America, Europe, and East Asia.

Jeanne P. Baptiste is a doctoral candidate in women's and gender studies at Rutgers University. Her research interests include feminist theory, epistemology and methodology, gender and development in the Caribbean, and the intersections of gender, religion, race, ethnicity, class, and nation.

Yarimar Bonilla is assistant professor of anthropology and Caribbean studies at Rutgers University, where she is also on the Advisory Board for the Critical Caribbean Studies Initiative and the Institute for Research on Women. She has published in cultural anthropology, Caribbean studies, and interventions and is currently completing a manuscript about political activism and historical memory in the French Antilles.

Sandra Cañas Cuevas is originally from Mexico City. She received her PhD in anthropology from the University of Texas at Austin and has conducted extensive research among indigenous people in southern Mexico since 1997. Her research focuses on the intersections between ethnicity, religion, and gender. Broadly, her theoretical interests include feminist scholarship, the anthropology of cities and citizenship, and indigenous struggles and movements in the Americas.

Nathaniel Deutsch is professor of history and the Neufeld-Levin Endowed Chair of Holocaust Studies at the University of California, Santa Cruz. He is the author of five books, including *Inventing America's Worst Family: The Fall and Rise of the Tribe of Ishmael* and *The Jewish Dark Continent: Life and Death in the Russian Pale of Settlement*, for which he received a Guggenheim Fellowship.

Jacob S. Dorman studies alternative African American religions and argues for conceptualizing them as instances of polyculturalism rather than syncretism. Professor of African American history and American studies at the University of Kansas, he is the author of *Chosen People: The Rise of American Black Israelite Movements*. His next book connects Orientalism in American popular culture with the rise of African American Islam in the twentieth century.

Rosemarijn Hoefte is a senior researcher at KITLV/Royal Netherlands Institute of Southeast Asian and Caribbean Studies in Leiden, the Netherlands, and managing editor of the *New West-Indian Guide/NWIG*. She has published extensively on the Caribbean, with a special focus on post-slavery Suriname, and in 2010 coordinated a three-country pilot project on the life stories of Javanese migrants in Suriname, Indonesia, and the Netherlands (www.Javanenenindiaspora.nl). Twelve of these stories are published in *Migratie en cultureel erfgoed: Verhalen van Javanen in Suriname, Indonesië en Nederland* (Migration and cultural heritage: Stories of Javanese in Suriname, Indonesia, and the Netherlands). In 2014 she published the monograph *Suriname in the Long Twentieth Century: Domination, Contestation, and Globalization*.

Gabrielle Jamela Hosein is a lecturer at the Institute for Gender and Development Studies, University of the West Indies, St. Augustine, Trinidad. She is principal investigator for the research project Politics, Power, and Gender Justice in the Anglophone Caribbean. Her research on young Indo-Trinidadian womanhood is published in the edited collections *Gender in the Twenty-first Century* and *Bindi: The Multifaceted Lives of Indo-Caribbean Women*. Her writings on political authority and public life are published in several journals and in the edited volume *Anthropology and the Individual: A Material Culture Perspective*.

Aisha Khan is associate professor of anthropology at New York University. She is the author of *Callaloo Nation: Metaphors of Race and Religious Identity among South Asians in Trinidad*, co-editor of *Empirical Futures: Anthropologists and Historians Engage the Work of Sidney W. Mintz,* and co-editor of *Women Anthropologists: Biographical Sketches.*

Patricia Mohammed is a scholar, writer, and filmmaker. She is currently professor of gender and cultural studies at the Institute of Gender and Development Studies, University of the West Indies, St. Augustine, Trinidad. A pioneer in second-wave feminist activism and scholarship for over two decades, she has published widely in gender studies. Among her major publications are *Caribbean Women at the Crossroads* (co-authored with Althea Perkins); *Gender Negotiations among Indians in Trinidad, 1917–1947*; *Gendered Realities: Essays in Caribbean Feminist Thought*; *Gender in Caribbean Development* (co-edited with Catherine Shepherd); and *Imaging the Caribbean: Culture and Visual Translation.* She has directed and produced twelve documentary films, including the award-winning *Coolie Pink and Green.*

Omar Ramadan-Santiago is a doctoral candidate in the Department of Anthropology at the City University of New York Graduate Center. He has conducted ethnographic research in Puerto Rico, the United States, and Egypt. His research interests include the construction and performance of identity and the intersection of race, ethnicity, and religion in popular culture.

Rhoda Reddock is professor of gender, social change, and development and deputy campus principal of the University of the West Indies, St. Augustine, Trinidad and Tobago. Her research interests are interdisciplinary and reflect commitment to multidisciplinary collaboration with colleagues. An activist in the Caribbean women's movement, she has as core themes in her work social justice, gender and feminism, women's social and political history, labor, ethnicity and nationalism, masculinities, sexualities, and environmental studies. Her publications include eight books (two of which won awards), three monographs, four special journal issues, and more than sixty peer-reviewed articles and book chapters.

Index

Abdel-Malek, Anouar, 63
Abd-el-Wahab, 111n8
Abduh, Muhammad, 95, 104
Abdul Aleen Siddiqui, Maulana, 277
Abdul Haqq, Daud, 209n7
Abdullah, Asim, 240
Abdullah, Fareed, 192
Abdullah, Sharifa Ali, 240, 241–42
Abolition, of slavery, 34, 86n2, 189, 208n5; France and, 146, 147, 149; Great Britain and, 188, 224, 244n11, 273
Abolition Day, 149–50, 152, 154
Abu/aboo (father), 205
Abu Bakr (Almoravid leader), 275
Abu Bakr, Fuad, 271, 279
Abu-Bakr, Yasin (Philip, Lennox), 271, 272, 310
Abu Bakr II (King of Mali), 135n3
Adas, Michael, 86n4
Adultery, 14, 79, 172
Al-Afghani, Jamal ad-Din, 95, 96, 101, 108
Afghanistan, 32, 64
African Americans, 97, 105, 107, 275; Freemasons, 49, 55–57, 60; Shriners, 54–64; stereotypes, 58. *See also* Hip Hop; Nation of Islam
African Blood Brotherhood, 108
Africans, 196; in Puerto Rico, 10, 121; slaves, 122, 151, 188, 224–25, 253, 274, 276–77, 297–98
The African Times and Orient Review, 107
African Trinidadians, 276–77, 279, 287, 290n3
Africanus, Leo, 300–301
Afroz, Sultana, 202
Al-Ahasan, Abdullah, 202

Ahmad, Mirza Gulam, 88n19
Ahmadiyya reformist movement, 33, 75, 88n19
Ahmed, Akbar, 29
Aisha. *See* Ayesha
Aitchison, Cara Carmichael, 269
Alcohol, 7, 79, 123, 174
Ali, Ameer, 227, 228
Ali, Basharat, 245n37
Ali, Duse Mohammed, 107
Ali, Hafiz Yacoob, 300
Ali, Jerusa, 14–15
Ali, Moulvi Ameer, 16, 238, 245n18, 245n22, 245n37, 308; with emancipation of Islamic women, 226–31; influence of, 217, 239; with TML, 233, 236
Ali, Noble Drew (Drew, Timothy), 62, 275, 291n10
Ali, Nurrn Nahar, 228
Ali, Yacoob, 226
Ali, Zaffar, 245n18
Ali, Zubair, 192
Alienation, 15, 192–94
Alim, Samy, 121, 131, 134
Ali-Mohammed, Haffizool, 291n12
Alladin, M. P., 315
Allah/Allaah, 61, 130, 169, 205, 218, 261; mosques and, 224, 244n7; Quran and, 118, 132, 225. *See also* Nur E Islam Masjid
Allen, Harry, 130
Almazan, Pascual, 34
Amulets, 188
Anderson, Benedict, 120–21
Anglican Church of St. John the Divine, 244n4
Animism, 7, 73

Anjuman Sunnat ul-Jamaat (ASJA), 17, 228, 230, 264n1, 266n15, 323n7; elections, 249, 251–61, 264; Nur E Islam Masjid and, 233; Quran and, 300
Ansar Laah, 272
Anthony, Susan B., 106
Antimodern, 29–30
Anti-slavery legislation, 149, 188, 208n5, 273
Apartheid, 219
Appropriation, 175; of Hip Hop, 124; of Islam, 6–7, 13, 174, 181, 182
'Aqidah/'aqeedah (creed), 193, 200, 206
Arabic, 73, 104, 167, 197, 270, 323n6; Arabization and, 89n43; with education, 192; Muslims and, 169, 180, 183n9, 183n10, 203–4, 208n3, 296, *303*, 304, 321, 322; slavery and, 188, 189
Arabic Thought in the Liberal Age (Hourani), 111n3
Arabization, 7, 15, 83, 89n43, 193
Arabs, 12, 58, 116, 201, 203–4
Architecture, 20; with Hosay festival as performance art, 311, *312*, *313*, *314*, *315*, 316; Islamic iconography with, 307–11
Arrival Day, 149–50
Arslan, Shakib, 104–5
Art, 306, 308, 315. *See also* Performance art, Hosay festival as
Artists. *See* Graffiti artists; Muslim Puerto Rican hip-hop artists
Asad, Talal, 1, 29–30, 39, 40
Ashura, 206
Asian Marriage Law, 8, 72–73, 85
Asiatics, 98–99, 102, 109, 275
ASJA. *See* Anjuman Sunnat ul-Jamaat
Askew, Kelly, 120
'Assabiyah/'assabiyaah (prejudice), 203, 206
As-Saleh, Saleh, 193
As-Siddiq, 'Aisha bint Abu Bakar, 200
Association of Indonesians. *See* Persatuan Indonesia
Atlantic Charter, 76
Atteck, Sybil, 315
Authenticity: of Arab Muslims, 201, 203–4; marriage and, 200–201; Muslim Puerto Rican hip-hop artists and, 10, 117–19, 120
Avoidance protest, 70, 86n4

Aydin, Cemil, 93, 94, 95, 104, 111n4
Ayesha (Aisha), 218, 225
Aziz, Syed Abdul, 264n2

Back to the Fatherland. *See* Yayasan Tanah Air
Bada/Id ul Fitre, 83, 89n42
Al-Badiya, Bahithat. *See* Nasif, Malak Hifni
Badran, Margot, 217, 219, 222, 227, 244n17
Bahamas, 188, 189
Bahamian and Brazilian muslimahs/muslimas: with cultural identity as "moving vehicle" of difference, 187, 193–98; ideal, 15, 187, 193, 198–202, 205; identity and, 14–15, 186–87, 193–98; Islam and, 188–93; with ummah and cultural space, 202–5
Bal, Ellen, 38
Ballack, Lorris, 279
Bambaataa, Afrika, 124, 128, 131, 132
Bamboo Settlement, 239–42
Bandung Conference, 110
Banquet invitation, Shriners, 59
Baptiste, Fitzroy, 297
Baptiste, Jeanne, 18–19
Barber, Benjamin, 29
Barlas, Asma, 282, 286, 287
Bath, Yunus (Jonas) Mohammad, 224, 276, 296, 297
Battle of Kerbala, 306, 314, 323n9
B-boy/b-girling, 116, 124, 125, 126, 128
Beards, 320
Be glorified and exalted. *See* SWT
Begum, Nawabzadu Nushat Ara, 245n21
Beinart, Peter, 38
Benefit societies, 192
Bernabé, Jean, 148
Betances, Emeterio, 118
Bid'a/bid'ah, 206
Bin Laden, Osama, 11–12, 141–42, *143*, 144
Black Muslims, 275, 298, 316, 321
Black nationalism, 104–9
Black power movements, 126, 227, 277, 278
Blacks, 94, 99, 109, 290n6. *See also* African Americans
Black Shrinerdom, 62–64
Blavatsky, Helena, 51
Blyden, Edward Wilmot, 106–7, 275

Bonilla, Yarimar, 11–12
Boodhoo, Isaiah, 315
Boodhoo, Ken, 316
Boricuas, 121, 132, 134, 135
Borikén Island, 121–22, 132, 134, 135
Boston, Anthony, 128
Boston bombings, 38
Boukman, 24, 26
Bowen, John, 304
Boys, 319. *See also* B-boy/b-girling; Children
Bozales, 122
Brand Nubian, 128
Brazil, 190, 192, 208n1; race in, 195–96; slavery in, 34, 188–89. *See also* Bahamian and Brazilian muslimahs/muslimas
Brereton, Bridget, 224, 244n12, 298
Briggs, Cyril, 107–8
British Abolition of Slavery Act, 188, 224, 244n11, 273
Bronx, Hip Hop and, 116, 124, 126, 127
Brooks, Ethel, 290n2
Brooks, Joanna, 57
Bua, Kala Akii, 279
Buddhism, 7, 73, 104
Bunt, Gary, 195
Burkhas, 287, *318*
Bush, George W., 37

Calligraphy, 306
Calypsos, 291n9
Campbell, Carl, 296, 297
Campbell, Clive. *See* Kool Herc
Campos, Pedro Albizu, 118, 123
Canaanite Temple. *See* Moorish Science Temple
Canada, 24, 25
Canadian Presbyterian Mission, 226, 237
Cañas Cuevas, Sandra, 12–14
Capitalism, 74, 120–21
Capoeira, 125
Caribbean, 128, 159n3, 199, 238, 244n12; children in, 201; colonies, 77; Hip Hop and, 120, 126, 127, 131; influence of, 106; Islam in, 295, 296, 298; Muslims in, 33–34, 39, 115, 118, 122, 134, 275, 276, 297; populations, 116, 148; slavery in, 189

Caribbean Religious History: An Introduction (Murrell), 32
Castro, Fidel, 123
Catholic Church, 12, 83, 117, 118, 163, 175
CCI. *See* Islamic Cultural Center
Chamoiseau, Patrick, 148
Charlieville Mosque, *311*
Charter of Rights and Freedoms, 25
Cheltenham, Richard, 291n12
Chen Keli, 223–24
Children, 84, 167, 178, 201; education of, 195–96, 228, 237, 239; orphans, 282
Children of the Islamic Renaissance, 278
China, 96, 104, 221–22, 223
Christianity, 5, 25, 28, 95, 106, 196; conversions, 41n5, 84, 122, 189; Islam and, 25, 107–9; missionaries, 83, 244n12; modernity influencing, 29; populations, 89n33; social mobility and, 88n24; as Western religion, 30, 32
Christianity, Islam and the Negro Race (Blyden), 106–7
Cities, antimodern, 29–30
Citizenship status, 37, 80, 149
Civilization, 94–95, 96
Claremont Main Road Mosque, 219, 231
"Clash of civilizations" model, 96
Clothing, 20, 158n1, 271, 286, 288; burkhas, 287, *318*; immigrants and, 298; kaftans, 297; Maya Muslims and, 165, 169, 172, 182n5; as symbol of Islamic piety, 316, *317*, *318*, *319*, 320. *See also* Fez; Khimaar/hijab; Ohrni; Veils
Colonies, 76, 77, 88n20, 265n4. *See also specific colonies*
Colors, 310, 311, 314, 315, 316
Columbus, Christopher, 34, 121–22, 123, 135n3, 149
Commission of Enquiry, 279, 291n8, 291n12
Communities, 41n7, 69, 77–80. *See also* Imagined communities/ummahs/nations
Confiant, Raphaël, 148
Confucianism, 222
Congolese, 148
Conservatives, 100, 106, 169, 174, 199, 245n20

Conversions, 12, 13–14, 119, 163, 277; Christian, 41n5, 84, 122, 189; Muslim, 164–66, 173, 174, 177, 180, 181, 286–90
Cook, Karoline P., 122
Coolie Pink and Green (film), 329
Coolies, 148, 299
Cotto, Correa, 116, 118, 123, 129
Council of Muslims in Suriname. *See* Madjlies Muslimin Suriname
Coup d'état of 1990. *See* Trinidad and Tobago
Craton, Michael, 189
Creed. *See* 'Aqidah/'aqeedah
Creoles, 69, 72, 76, 77, 87n12, 89n39; identity, 148–49; Indo-Trinidadian Muslims with gender, modernity and Creolization, 250–55, 258–59; language, 145, 152; with voting, 78. *See also* Indo-Trinidadian Muslims
Crescent moon, 308, 309, 310–11, 314, 315, 316
Criminality, spaces of, 272, 274
Crusader, 108
Crusades, 51
Cuevas, Cañas, 13–14
Cuffee, Paul, 275
Cultural differences, 13–14, 25–26
Cultural identity: as "moving vehicle" of difference, 187, 193–98; religion and, 118
Cultural space, 202–5, 292n18
Culture, 40, 135n1
Curtis, Edward, 110
Curtius, Anny D., 149

Dalrymple, William, 299
Dance, 125, 133, 135n6, 299, 314, 315. *See also* "Moon Dance"
Dar, Rashid, 23, 26
Dar al-Fikr Press, 111n10
Dark, 304, 306
Da'wah, 164, 206; Hip Hop as, 10, 117, 123–24, 135; women and, 190, 192, 193
De Bruijne, Ad, 85–86
Debs, Eugene V., 106
The Decline of the West (Spengler), 98
Deen/Din, 200, 201, 206
"Deeper Roots of Islam in the Caribbean," 199

De Kom, Anton, 70
Delany, Martin R., 49
Delgrés, Louis, 152
Democracy, 29, 256, 257–58, 261, 264
Derveld, F., 80
Desa (villages), 71–72, 87n6, 89n41
Deutsch, Nathaniel, 8–9
Devoir de memoire (duty of memory), 149
Diallo, Ayuba Suleiman (Jalla, Job), 323n6
Din. *See* Deen/Din
Diouf, Sylviane, 188
Dirlik, Arif, 2
Divorce, 219, 227, 228, 282, 283, 310. *See also* Marriage
DJing, 116, 124, 125, 126, 128
Dorman, Jacob, 6–7
Dougla, 271, 290n5
Downloading, music, 123
Drew, Timothy. *See* Ali, Noble Drew
Du Bois, W.E.B., 97, 108, 111n12
Dunya (worldliness), 278, 281, 283, 284, 287
Duranni, Maulana, 226
Durrani, Karim Khan, 300, 308
Dutch Antilles, 38–39
Duty of memory. *See Devoir de memoire*
Dyson, Michael Eric, 132, 133

East, the, 27–28, 41n1, 50. *See also* Orientalism; the Orient
East Indians, 78, 87n6, 141, 159n3
East worshippers (reformists), 8, 84, 86n3; Islam and, 7, 79; prayer and, 7, 70, 75, 76; West and, 76, 80, 83, 85
Edmonds, Ennis B., 32
Education, 78, 123, 261, 265n13, 300, 307; with African history, 196; of children, 195–96, 228, 237, 239; of Hindus, 83; of Muslims, 83, 168, 175, 192, 253; racism in, 72; religion and, 196, 222, 227; social mobility and, 72, 85–86, 88n24
Egalité, Guadeloupe and, 147–51
Egypt, 56, 58, 60, 87, 95, 231
Eickelman, Dale, 35
Eid al Adha, 270
Eid ul Fitr, 90, 188, 206, 245n38, 254, 265n9

Elections, ASJA, 249; democracy and, 257–58, 261, 264; gender and, 251, 252–55; with leaders and spirituality, 256–61
The Elephant in the Room, 129
Elia, Nadia, 188
Éloge de la Créolité ("In Praise of Creoleness") (Bernabé, Chamoiseau, Confiant), 148
Employment, 178–79
Enlightenment, 28, 30, 93
European Orientalism, 93–96
Evangelicals, 163, 164, 170, 173–74, 177, 178
Exodus, 58, 60
Exploration, 34, 121–22

Face veil. *See* Niqab/Niqaab
FAMBRAS. *See* Federação das Associações Muçulmanas do Brasil
Family, 81, 117, 175, 177, 219, 263
Father. *See* Abu/aboo
Fatiman, Cecile, 24
Fat Joe, 129–30
Fear: fear of brown planet and New World of Islam, 96–103; of Islam with 9/11, 9–10, 18, 37
Federação das Associações Muçulmanas do Brasil (FAMBRAS), 192
Federatie van Islamitische Gemeenten in Suriname (Federation of Islamic Congregations in Suriname), 84
Feldman, Allen, 153–54
Feminism and Nationalism in the Third World (Jayawardena), 226
Festivals. *See* Hosay festival
Fez, 51, 62, 64
Fields, Barbara, 37
Fields, Karen, 37
Fields, Milton, F., 56
Final Call, 129
Fish, Stanley, 41n7
Fitzgerald, F. Scott, 92
Five Percent Nation (Nation of Gods and Earths), 116, 129, 130, 133
Five Pillars of Islam, 7, 39, 76, 79; Jamaat al Muslimeen and, 271; Muslim Puerto Rican hip-hop artists and, 130–33
Flags, 308, 310
Fleming, Walter M., 49

Florence, William J. "Billy," 49
Flores, Juan, 116, 127
Floyd-Thomas, Juan, 130
Force-feeding, 156, 159n11
Ford, Arnold Josiah, 107
Foucault, Michel, 63
Foundation of Islamic Congregation in Suriname. *See* Stichting Islamitische Gemeenten in Suriname
Four pillars of Hip Hop, 124, 126. *See also* B-boy/b-girling; DJing; Graffiti artists; MCing
France, 11, 141, 143; secularism, 158n2, 159n5; slavery and, 142, 146, 147, 149. *See also* Guadeloupe
Fraternal organizations, 50–53. *See also* Shriners
Freemasons: African Americans, 49, 55–57, 60; irregular, 62–63. *See also* Shriners
Freethought Movement, 106
French Antilles, 144, 147–49, 159n3
The French Revolution in San Domingo (Stoddard), 96
Friendships, 176–77, 183n19
Fukkô Ajia no Shomondai (Problems of a resurgent Asia) (Ôkawa Shûmei), 104
Fula/Fulani, 122, 301
Fulani, 297
Funeral. *See* Janazah

Galileo, 95–96
Gambling, 7, 79
Gandhi, Mahatma, 12, 150, 154, 159n8
Garvey, Marcus, 106, 107, 275
Geissinger, Aisha, 200
Gender, 193, 265n6; gender-segregated worship space, 17, 167–68, 183n12, 204, 218–20, 237–39, 242; Maya Muslims with mosque teachings and, 166–70; with modernity and Creolization, 250–55, 258–59; negotiations with modernity, 261–63; segregation with indentured workers, 230–31
Ghair-Mukallid, 323n8
Ghaneabassiri, Kambiz, 3
Ghusl, 288, 291n14
Ghutrah. *See* Thobe, kufi, keffiyeh/ghutrah
Girls. *See* B-boy/b-girling; Children

Globo Network Brasil. *See O Clone*
Golden Law, 188, 208n5
Gomez, Michael, 34
Gonzalez, Michelle A., 32
Goodman, Mark J., 3
Gourbeyre, Jean-Baptiste-Marie-Augustin, 157
Graeber, David, 159n12
Graffiti artists, 116, 124–25, 126, 128, 133
Grand Masjid Equal Access for Women Project, 220–21
Grant, Madison, 92, 97, 98, 104, 108, 111n7
Great Britain, 88n20, 188, 244n11, 244n12, 273
The Great Gatsby (Fitzgerald), 92
Green, 310, 314, 316
Ground Zero mosque (Park51), 23, 29
Groupe d'Intervention de la Gendarmerie Nationale, 142, 143
Guadeloupe, 141, 142–43; as boiling pot, 144–46; with liberté and egalité, 147–51; "Madassamy Affair" and, 11, 12, 151–58; syndicalism in, 144–45; unions in, 144–47, 151, 152, 153, 155
Guardian. *See Hafiz*
Guterl, Matthew, 97, 107, 111n12
Guyana, 237, 253
Gwo ka music, 145, 157
Gymns, 286

Hadith/hadeeth, 40, 167, 182n8, 200, 206, 323n5
Hafiz (guardian), 226, 235, 244n15
Haitian Revolution, 24, 26, 149
Haji Gookool Meah Mosque, *307*
Hajj, 206, 253, 265n7, 271, 283, 322
Halal, 198, 204, 206
Hamas, 197
Handler, Richard, 41n7
Hanifa, Abu, 88n18
Haqq, Daud Abdul, 199
Hardjo, Salikin, 79, 81–82, 83, 86
Harmony. *See Rukun*
Harrison, Hubert, 9, 95, 97, 105; on Islam, 106–7; Stoddard and, 108–9, 110
Hashimi, Muhammad Ali al-, 193
Hassan, Peer, 300

Hausa, 297–98
Hawthorne, Julian, 54
Hawthorne, Nathaniel, 54
Head covering. *See* Khimaar/hijab; Ohrni
Headscarf ban, 158n1
Henan Province, 221
Hendrix, Noor, 84
Henry, Paget, 280
Hepburn, Amir Faisal, 197
Un Hereje y un Musulman (A heretic and a Muslim) (Almazan), 34
Higham, John, 92, 104
Highland, Henry, 275
Hijab. *See* Khimaar/hijab
Hindostaans-Javaanse Centrale Raad (Hindustani-Javanese Central Council), 76
Hinduism, 73, 83, 84, 148, 302, 304
Hindus, 76, 77, 88n21, *303*, *304*; with education, 83; Muslims and, 299–300, 302; populations, 38–39
Hindustani-Javanese Central Council. *See* Hindostaans-Javaanse Centrale Raad
Hindustani Muslims, 75, 88n19
Hip Hop, 120–21, 135n1; appropriation of, 124; Bronx and, 116, 124, 126, 127; history of Puerto Ricans, 116, 117–19, 126–29; Islam and, 116–17, 123, 130–33; Jamaicans and, 125, 127, 130; Muslims and, 116, 129–30; Nation of Islam and, 116, 129, 132. *See also* Muslim Puerto Rican hip-hop artists
Hirschkind, Charles, 182
Hirsi Ali, Ayaan, 29
Historicality, of religious tradition, 39–40
Histories, 10, 124–25; Borikén Island's Islamic, 121–22; Jamaat al Muslimeen, transnationalism and, 274–76; Puerto Ricans with hip-hop, 116, 117–19, 126–29
History of the Imperial Council (Shriners), 53
The History of Women's Mosques in Chinese Islam: A Mosque of Her Own (Jaschok and Shui Jingjun), 221
Hitam, Banteng, 80
Hoch, Danny, 125, 126
Hoefte, Rosemarijn, 7, 8
Hogg, Peter, 323n6
Holi Phagwa, 83, 89n42

Hoodfar, Homa, 171
Hopkins, Peter E., 269
Hosay festival, 20, 295, 306, 323n9; as passion play, 296; as performance art, 311, 312, 313, 314, 315, 316
Hosein, Gabrielle, 18
Hosein, Maulana Imran, 264n2
Hosein, Mohammed Haniff, 233
Hourani, Albert, 111n3, 111n6
Hudson, Thomas J., 56
Hunger strikes, 152, 153–57
Huntington, Samuel, 111n7

Ibadah/ibada (worship), 206
Ibrahim, Mohammed, 307
Ibrahim Ali, Amina, 276–77, 291n11
Iconography. *See* Islamic iconography, in Trinidad
Ideal Muslimah (al-Hashimi), 193
Ideal muslimahs/muslimas, 15, 187, 193, 198–202, 205
Identity, 74, 109, 150–51, 155, 280; Bahamian and Brazilian muslimahs/muslimas and, 14–15, 186–87, 193–98; Creoles, 148–49; cultural, 118, 187, 193–98; Maya Muslims, 165–66, 172, 174, 180, 181–82; Muslimeenism and, 269; Muslim Puerto Rican hip-hop artists and, 9–10, 124; Muslims, 83, 103, 111n4, 116, 166, 180, 202, 253, 272–74; Puerto Ricans, 115, 121, 123, 134
Idioms, 40, 124
Idolatry. *See* Shirk
Idrisi, al- 34
Id ul Fitre. *See* Bada/Id ul Fitre
Iftar, 35, 254, 265n9
Illiteracy, 78, 168, 181
Imagined communities/ummahs/nations, 6, 60, 62, 63, 120–21
Imam/Imaam, 206, 278, 282, 284, 285
Immigrants, 5, 37, 125, 190, 265n4, 323n4; clothing and, 298; organizations for, 74; population of local Muslims and, 35–36
Immigration, 179; Islam and, 29; with Javanese settlement and migration, 70–76
Indentured workers, 147–48, 149, 190, 244n10, 265n5; gender segregation and, 230–31; in Suriname, 7, 70, 86n2

Independence, 88n23; Islamic women with emancipation and, 226–31; for Suriname, 76–77, 83, 88n31, 89n39
"Indian Arrival," 149–50
Indianité, 147–51
"Indian News and Views," 245n23
Indians, 144, 147, 159n4, 323n4; identity, 150–51; as silent, 148, 149. *See also* East Indians
Indonesia, 74, 88n23; Javanese, 83, 87n10, 88n21; PBIS, 78–82, 85; PII, 8, 75, 87n16; Tongar, 69–70, 82, 85; unions in, 77, 79–81, 82, 85
Indonesian Islamic Organization. *See* Perkumpulan Islam Indonesia
Indo-Trinidadian Muslims, 249, 264, 290n3; Creolization among, 250–55, 258–59; gender negotiations with modernity and, 261–63; with leaders and spirituality, 256–61
"In Praise of Creoleness." *See Éloge de la Créolité*
Insurgents, 273, 291n8
Internet, 195–96, 219, 238
Iraq, 34, 64, 134, 245n21, 323n9
Isfahani, Maulana, 237
Islam, 3, 74, 167, 199, 206, 209n7; appropriation of, 6–7, 13, 174, 181, 182; Bahamian and Brazilian muslimahs/muslimas and, 188–93; Borikén Island's history of, 121–22; in Caribbean, 295, 296, 298; Christianity and, 25, 107–9; democracy compatible with, 29, 256; East worshippers and, 7, 79; fear and, 9–10, 18, 37, 96–103; Federatie van Islamitische Gemeenten in Suriname, 84; Five Pillars of Islam, 7, 39, 76, 79, 130–33, 271; Harrison on, 106–7; Hip Hop and, 116–17, 123, 130–33; immigration and, 29; New World of, 96–103, 316; after 9/11, 9–10, 18, 37; orthodox, 276; PII, 8, 75, 87n16; race and, 8, 37–38, 94–95, 109; racialization of, 277–80; revivalism, 192–93, 222, 231–32; Sahabutal, 87n16; Shriners and, 6–7, 58, 60; SIV, 75, 85, 88n19; stereotypes, 2, 25; Stichting Islamitische Gemeenten in Suriname, 84; Stoddard and, 93, 97–102,

Islam—*continued*
　104, 105, 108; symbols of, 270, 308, *309*, 310, 311, 314, 316; TIA, 226, 227–28, 233, 300; transnationalism and, 274–76; in Trinidad and Tobago, 217, 224–36, 253, 276–80, 296–306, 298, 323n2; weddings, 299–300; the West and, 26, 30, 34–35. *See also* Islamic iconography, in Trinidad; Nation of Islam; Nur E Islam Masjid; Pan-Islamic movement; *specific Muslims*
Islam and science. *See* "L'Islamisme et la science"
Islam For Peace. *See* Islam Pou Lape
Islamic Broadcast Network, 321–22
Islamic Cultural Center (CCI), 166, 182n2
Islamic iconography, in Trinidad, 19, 295, 321–23; architectural presence with, 307–11; with architecture and Hosay festival as performance art, 311, *312*, *313*, *314*, *315*, 316; with clothing as symbol of piety, 316, *317*, *318*, *319*, 320; with early iconic elements in growth of Islam, 296–302; masculine power and piety with, 320; minimalism and, 302–6
Islamic law, 73, 87n11
Islamic Trust, 245n29
Islamic Youth Movement (IYM), 233, 234
"L'Islamisme et la science" (Islam and science) (Renan), 94
Islamization, 110, 221, 222, 223; projects, 231–32; of syndicalism, 158n2
Islam Pou Lape (Islam For Peace), 3
IYM. *See* Islamic Youth Movement

Jacobs-Huey, Lanita, 41n7
Jalla, Job. *See* Diallo, Ayuba Suleiman
Jama 'Ahlus Sunnah, 192
Jamaat al Muslimeen, 18, 290n2; conversions, 286–90; with coup d'état of 1990, 246n43, 270, 273–74, 279, 310; defined, 246n43; without gender segregation in worship spaces, 242; with history and transnationalism, 274–76; identity and legacy of, 272–74; with Islam in Trinidad, 276–77; with Islam racialized, 277–80; pious sexuality and, 19, 280–83; setting of, 270–71; women and, 291n15; with women and sexuality, 284–88
Jamaat/jama'at/jama'a, 16, 75, 206, 230, 233, 290n2
Jamaat-ul-Islam, 192
Jamaicans, 125, 127, 130, 202
Jama Masjid, 17–18, 249, 254, 260, 277
James, Winston, 106
Jamia. *See* Masjid/jamia
Janazah (funeral), 282
Jap-A-Joe, Harold, 88n19
Jaschok, Maria, 221, 223
Javanese, 83, 87n10, 88n21. *See also* Suriname
Jayawardena, Kumari, 226
Jemmal-Edding (Sheikh), 96
Jewelry, 288
Jha, J. C., 225, 244n14
Jihad, 12, 29, 197
Jim Crow, 56, 58
Jinnah, Mohammad Ali, 310
Jinnah, Quaid-I-Azam Mohammed Ali, 308
Jinnah Memorial Masjid, 217, 236–39, 308
Johnson, Latif, 196
Jones, John George, 54–55, 56, 57–58, 60
Judaism, 30, 41n4, 58, 60
Juma/jummah/juma'a, 203, 206, 218, 271, 282, 317

Kaftans, 297
Karam, John Tofik, 208n1
Kariodimedjo, Johannes, 81, 82, 85, 89n35
Kassim, Halima, 225, 228–29, 255, 265n8, 300
Kaum (religious leader), 71, 85, 87n6, 296
Keffiyeh. *See* Thobe, kufi, keffiyeh/ghutrah
Keli, Abdul, 189
Kettani, M. Ali, 31, 191
Khalfani, Mustafa Khalil, 192, 196
Khan, Aisha, 159n5, 250, 297, 302, 316, 317
Khan, Mohammed Hakeem, 236, 308
Khan, Shahnaz, 281
Khanam, Daud Sharifa, 219
Khimaar/hijab (head covering), 167, 192, 206, 230, 287, *319*; connotations, 141,

194, 286, 316; motivations for wearing, 17, 20, 24, 198, 243, 278, 289, 318
Khutbah, 203, 206, 218, 219, 237, 282
Kielstra, J. C., 71–73, 76
Knowledge, 124, 261–63, 300–301
Kool Herc (Campbell, Clive), 124, 125, 130
Koran, 61–62, 76, 133, 307. *See also* Quran
Korom, Frank, 225
Kufi. *See* Thobe, kufi, keffiyeh/ghutrah
Kunya/Kunyah, 192–93, 206
Kwan, Mei-Po, 269

Ladies organizations, 217, 229, 230, 233–34, 245n31, 265n8
Ladinos, 122
Land, 104, 270, 272, 298, 310; for masjid/jamia, 233, 236–37; Maya Muslims and, 165, 170, 179
Lane, Erik-Jan, 87n11
Langkoeas, 81, 82, 89n34
Languages, 120–21, 128–29, 145, 152. *See also* Arabic; Tsotsil; Urdu
Lauzière, Henri, 105
Lawlor, Mary, 41n7
Leaders: *kaum*, 71, 85, 87n6, 296; *lurah*, 71, 72, 78; *pundits/pandits*, 299; spirituality and, 256–61
Lebanon, 122, 191
Lebrón, Lolita, 118, 123
Legislation, 25, 56, 58; anti-slavery, 149, 188, 208n5, 273; marriage, 8, 72–73, 85, 227, 228
Leonard, Karen, 37
L'Étang, G., 148
Lewis, Bernard, 111n7
Liberation Theology, 175
Liberté, Guadeloupe and, 147–51
Light, 304, 306, 307, 308. *See also* Nur E Islam Masjid
Linggadjati Agreement of 1946, 78
Literacy, 300, 307
Little traditions, 301
Lorde, Audre, 21n1
Lovejoy, Paul, 224
Lurah (village leader), 71, 72, 78

Madassamy, Michel, 12, 146; arrest of, 142–43, 151, 152, 153; Bin Laden compared to, 142, *143*, 144; with hunger strike, 152, 153–57; "Madassamy Affair" and, 11, 12, 151–58; silence and, 155, 158
Madhab/mazhab/madh'hab, 203, 206–7
Madjlies Muslimin Suriname (Council of Muslims in Suriname), 84
Mahabir-Wyatt, Diana, 291n12
Mahmood, Saba, 182, 223, 278
Maize, 165, 172, 182
Makandal, Francois, 24
Makeup, 286
Maktabs, 230, 242, 253, 265n7
Makumba, Emir Samba, 297
Male gaze, 289
Mamluk art, 308
Mandingos, 122, 224–25, 276, 297
Manger, Leif, 134
Mansa Musa (King of Mali), 135n3
Marginalization. *See* Social marginalization
Maroon Council, 34
Marr, Timothy, 25
Marriage, 191, 200–201, 271; divorce and, 219, 227, 228, 282, 283, 310; Islamic weddings, 299–300; legislation, 8, 72–73, 85, 227, 228; Maya Muslims and, 14, 174–78; polygamy and, 172–74, 180; stage marriages, 227, 238. *See also* Polygamy; Polygyny
Marx, Karl, 11
Masculine power, 251, 320
Masjid/jamia, 16, 207, 243n1, 290n2; gender-segregated worship, 17, 167–68, 183n12, 204, 218–20, 237–39, 242; Grand Masjid Equal Access for Women Project, 220–21; Jama Masjid, 17–18, 249, 254, 260, 277; Jinnah Memorial Masjid, 217, 236–39, 308; land for, 233, 236–37; Nur E Islam Masjid, 217, 232–36, *309*; women in space of, 217–21, 232, 237–39. *See also* Trinidad and Tobago
Massignon, Louis, 105
Mattingly, Cheryl, 41n7
Maududi, Maulana Abul Ala, 231

May Allah be pleased with. *See* Radiya Allahu 'anho
Maya Muslims: clothing, 165, 169, 172, 182n5; with conversions, 164–66, 173, 174, 177, 180, 181; education and, 168, 175; employment and, 178–79; with gender dynamics and teachings at mosques, 166–70; identity, 165–66, 172, 174, 180, 181–82; land and, 165, 170, 179; marriage and, 14, 174–78; men, 13, 14, 166–70, 172–79, 182n7, 183n19; migration of, 179; with Paradise, 173, 175, 183n18; polygamy and, 172–74, 180; prayer and, 167–69; social marginalization and, 13, 170; Spanish and, 13–14, 164, 165–66, 171, 177; veiling politics and, 171–72; women, 13, 14, 165–81, 182n5, 183n19
May the peace and blessing of God be upon him. *See* SAWS
McCloud, Aminah Beverly, 39, 200–201
MCing, 116, 124, 125–26, 127, 128; rhyming and, 126, 132; as tool, 133. *See also specific MCs*
McKenzie, Eastlyn, 291n12
McNeal, Keith, 250
McWorld, 29
Meacham, Jon, 29
Meah, Haji Gokool, 307
Meah, Haji Rooknudin, 300
Mecca, 50, 52, 62, 89n34, 102–3, 218
Media, 121, 158n2, 194, 197, 321–22
Medina, 217, 218, 220, 237
Meijer, Wilna, 195
Memberships, 12–13
Memory, 149
Men, 183n12, 218, 257–58; clothing for, 297, *319*, 320; with fraternal organizations, 50–53; male gaze and, 289; masculine power and, 251, 320; Maya Muslim, 13, 14, 166–70, 172–79, 182n7, 183n19; sexuality and, 280–83. *See also* Gender; Marriage; Polygamy; Polygyny; Shriners
Mence and Moore, 236
Mernissi, Fatima, 220, 289

"Merry-Go-Round," 125
The Message to the Black Man in America (Muhammad, E.), 106
Mexico, 12, 163–66, 182n2. *See also* Maya Muslims
Middle East, 29–30, 34–35, 122, 231
Migration: Javanese settlement and, 70–76; of Maya Muslims, 179. *See also* Immigration
Minaj, Nicki, 130
Minimalism, Islamic iconography and, 302–6
Minorities, among Muslims, 31, 35, 40, 186, 195–96
Mishra, Pankaj, 29
Missionaries, 83, 164, 244n12, 253
Mitchell, Tony, 124
Mitchell, Yusuf, 277
Mitterrand, François, 145, 146
Modernity: Christianity influenced by, 29; Creolization among Indo-Trinidadian Muslims and gender differential, 250–55, 258–59; gender negotiations with, 261–63; McWorld with modernity gone bad, 29; tradition versus, 28–30, 31; U.S. as generator of, 31
Modood, Tariq, 29
Moghissi, Haideh, 3
Mohamed, Bilali, 188
Mohammad (Prophet). *See* Muhammad (Prophet)
Mohammed, Ayoob, 305, 322, 323
Mohammed, Feroza "Rose," 217, 230–31, 237–39, 245n34
Mohammed, Kamaluddin, 233
Mohammed, Nafeesa, 233–34
Mohammed, Patricia, 19–20, 250
Mohammed, Zuleikha, *317*
Monogamy, 173, 174, 283
Moon. *See* Crescent moon
"Moon Dance," 315, 324n10
Moorish Science Temple (Canaanite Temple), 62, 64, 94
Moors, 275
Moriscos, 34, 41n5, 122
Morton, John, 226
Moslems, 323n3. *See also* Muslims

Mosques, 87n16, 207, 243n1, 290n2, *311*; Allah/Allaah and, 224, 244n7; gender segregation in, 167–68, 183n12; Ground Zero, 23, 29; Maya Muslims with gender dynamics and teachings in, 166–70; with Muslim organizations, 245n30; at Valencia, *303*, *304*, *305*; women and, 219–23, 231, 287. *See also* Jamaat al Muslimeen; Masjid/jamia; *specific mosques*

Mother. *See* Umm

Le Mot Phrasé, 142

Moulood functions, 234, 245n32

Mourners, 282, 323n9

Moutoussamy, Ernest, 150–51, 159n7

Movement, 233, 234, 244n10. *See also specific movements*

Movement of the Indonesian People in Suriname. *See* Pergerakan Bangsa Indonesia Suriname

"Moving vehicle" of difference, 187, 193–98

Muezzin, 167, 308

Mughals, 299, 301

Muhammad (Prophet), 63, 133, 164, 182n3, 182n8; Quran and, 131–32, 225; SAWS and, 218, 244n6; Shriners and link to, 50, 61

Muhammad, David, 116, 118, 132, 133

Muhammad, Elijah (Poole, Elijah), 92, 106, 110, 275–76, 277

Muhammad, Warith Deen, 276

Muhammad, W. D. Fard, 275, 291n10

Muhammadiyah movement, 87n16

Munasinghe, Virangini, 147

Muneera, 261–62

Murabitun Movement, 164, 182n3

Murphy, W. O., 62

Murrell, N. Samuel, 32

Music, 123, 135n6, 145, 157, 291n9. *See also* Hip Hop; Muslim Puerto Rican hip-hop artists; Rapping

Muslimahs/Muslimas, 207. *See also* Bahamian and Brazilian muslimahs/muslimas

Muslimah Women's Alliance, 220

Muslim Brotherhood, 231

Muslimeenism, 269. *See also* Jamaat al Muslimeen

Muslim Ladies body, 229, 230

Muslim Marriage and Divorce Act of 1936, 227, 228

Muslim Puerto Rican hip-hop artists: authenticity and, 10, 117–19, 120; with Five Pillars of Islam, 130–33; with Hip Hop as da'wah, 10, 117, 123–24, 135; identity and, 9–10, 124; imagined communities/ummahs/nations and, 120–21; with Islamic history of Borikén Island, 121–22; with Muslim gimmick in Hip Hop, 129–30; reggaeton and, 128–29; remixed histories and, 124–26; with reverting/going back, 119–20; with social marginalization, 9, 11, 117, 124

Muslims, 84, 88n21, 207, 228, 231, 323n3; Arabic and, 169, 180, 183n9, 183n10, 203–4, 208n3, 296, *303*, *304*, 321, 322; Arabs as authentic, 201, 203–4; black, 275, 298, 316, *321*; in Caribbean, 33–34, 39, 115, 118, 122, 134, 275, 276, 297; conversions, 164–66, 173, 174, 177, 180, 181, 286–90; education of, 83, 168, 175, 192, 253; Hindus and, 299–300, 302; Hindustani, 75, 88n19; Hip Hop and, 116, 129–30; identity, 83, 103, 111n4, 116, 166, 180, 202, 253; Identity, 272–74; minorities among, 31, 35, 40, 186, 195–96; with New World exploration before Columbus, 34, 121–22; with 9/11 fallout, 37, 64, 197; with non-Muslims, 194, 195, 198, 269, 275, 297; organizations, 191–92, 200, 217, 229, 230, 233–34, 245n30, 245n31, 245n34, 254, 260, 261, 265n8; population, 24, 35–36, 38–39, 182n2, 208n1, 253, 264n1, 277–78, 296, 298; racialization of, 37–38; slavery and, 33, 122, 135n4, 188, 274–75, 276–77, 297; stereotypes, 2, 194–95, 197–98; terrorism and, 37, 197–98, 273, 274; TML, 217, 227, 230, 233, 236–39, 300, 323n8. *See also* Bahamian and Brazilian muslimahs/muslimas; Indo-Trinidadian Muslims; Jamaat al Muslimeen; Maya Muslims; Muslim Puerto Rican hip-hop artists; Spanish Muslims; Sunni Muslims

Mustapha, Nasser, 226, 230, 237, 238, 245n36

Muzaffar, Hassim (Sheik), 300
Mythology, 49–51, 155

Nabbie, Sarah, 235–36, 245n38, 245n41; with Bamboo Settlement, 240–41, 242; on women and mosques, 231
Nageeb, Salma, 221, 223, 232
Namaaz. *See* Salat/salaah/namaaz
Names, for slaves, 189–90
Nance, Susan, 51
Napoleonic wars, 298
Nasif, Malak Hifni (Al-Badiya, Bahithat), 217, 243n3
Nationale Partij Suriname (NPS, National Party Suriname), 76, 77
National Islamic Association, 209n7
National Muslim Women's Association, 230, 245n34
National Party Suriname. *See* Nationale Partij Suriname
Nation of Gods and Earths. *See* Five Percent Nation
Nation of Islam, 37, 92, 94, 103, 106, 109; Hip Hop and, 116, 129, 132; influence, 272; origins, 275–76, 291n10
Nations. *See* Imagined communities/ummahs/nations
Naturalness, 10, 119
"The Negro a Conservative: Christianity Still Enslaves the Minds of Those Whose Bodies It Long Held Bound" (Harrison), 106
Negro World, 107, 108
Netherlands, 8, 88n23; colonies, 76, 77; Surinamese in, 70, 83, 89n40
Netherlands Antilles, 76, 77
Netherlands East Indies, 71, 75, 76, 87n6
"New Negro Movement," 97, 105
The New World of Islam (Stoddard), 93, 101, 102, 105, 108; influence of, 97, 104; with Wahabi movement, 100
New World, 19, 104; cultural differences with Old World and, 25–26; of Islam, 96–103, 316; Muslims with pre-Columbus exploration of, 34, 121–22
Ngadi, Sakri, 79–80
Nijhoff and Nijhoff, 230

9/11: fallout, 4, 37, 64, 141, 197–98; Islam after, 9–10, 18, 37; "Special Registration" program and, 37, 41n9; terror talk and, 33
1920s. *See* "the Tribal Twenties"
Niqab/Niqaab (face veil), 192, 194, 198, 206, 287. *See also* Veils
Niranjana, Tejaswini, 251–52
Nomani, Asma, 218
Nonconformists, 236, 240, 245n33
Non-Muslims, 194, 195, 198, 269, 275, 297. *See also* Jamaat al Muslimeen
NPS. *See* Nationale Partij Suriname
Nur E Islam (Light of Allah) Masjid, 217, 232–36, *309*
Nuwayhid, Ajjaj, 104, 105, 107

Obama, Barack, 35
O'Brien, W. W., 54
O Clone (Globo Network Brasil), 194
Ohrni (head covering), 230, 245n25, 298, 316, *319*
Ôkawa Shûmei, 104
"Old-school," 119–20
Old World, 25–26, 29–30
The One Thousand and One Nights, 34
Organizations, 50–53, 74; ladies, 217, 229, 230, 233–34, 245n31, 265n8; Muslim, 191–92, 200, 217, 229, 230, 233–34, 245n30, 245n31, 245n34, 254, 260, 261, 265n8; terrorism, 12, 141, 197, 207–8. *See also specific organizations*
Orientalism, 93–96; African American Shriner, 57–62; Black Prince Hall Shriners and, 54–57, 62, 63, 64; with religion in black Shrinerdom, 62–64; with Shriner mythology, 49–51; in U.S., 51–54
Orient, the, 36, 41n1
Orphans, 282
Orthodox Islam, 276
Ottoman Empire, 93–95, 99, 189, 310

Pabón, Jorge "PopMaster Fabel," 132
Pakistan, 191, 231–32, 244n4, 253, 299
Palestine, 52, 55, 57, 64, 122
Pan-Asianism, 93, 96, 104
Pandits. See Pundits/pandits

Pan-Islamic movement, 8, 9, 101, 107; European Orientalism and, 93–96; Stoddard on, 98, 99
Papastergiadis, Nikos, 202
Paradise, 173, 175, 183n18
Park51. *See* Ground Zero mosque
Pasha, Rofelt, 57
The Passing of the Great Race (Grant), 92, 98
Passion play, 296
Patmo, Soehirman, 80
Patronage, 77, 265n13
PBIS. *See* Pergerakan Bangsa Indonesia Suriname
People of the Book, 30, 281
Perez, Hamza, 116
Performance art, Hosay festival as, 311, *312, 313, 314, 315,* 316
Pergerakan Bangsa Indonesia Suriname (PBIS, Movement of the Indonesian People in Suriname), 78–82, 85
Perkumpulan Islam Indonesia (PII, Indonesian Islamic Organization), 8, 75, 87n16
Perry, Jeffrey, 107
Persatuan Indonesia (Association of Indonesians), 78, 79
Philip, Lennox. *See* Abu-Bakr, Yasin
Phillips, Eugene, 59–60
Piety, 257, 260, 278; clothing as symbol of Islamic, 316, *317, 318, 319,* 320; masculine power and, 320; pious sexuality, 19, 280–83; purity and, 253, 258, 261
PII. *See* Perkumpulan Islam Indonesia
Pillars. *See* Five Pillars of Islam; Four pillars of Hip Hop
Poetry, 125, 133, 227, 231, 245n19, 245n32
Police, 75, 123, 142–43, 152, 220
Politics, 2–3, 55–56, 60, 74; coup d'état of 1990, 246n43, 270, 273–74, 279, 310; with Javanese and community schisms, 69, 77–80; of veiling, 171–72. *See also specific political parties*
Polygamy, 281, 285; imams with, 284; Maya Muslims and, 172–74, 180; responsibilities with, 280; women and, 14, 278
Polygyny, 278, 280–82, 285
Poole, Elijah. *See* Muhammad, Elijah

Populations, 64, 86n2, 116, 148, 163; Hindus, 38–39; Muslims, 24, 35–36, 38–39, 182n2, 208n1, 253, 264n1, 277–78, 296, 298; slaves, 122, 188; Surinamese, 84, 88n31, 89n33, 89n40; in Trinidad and Tobago, 264n1, 265n4, 296, 298
Port of Spain, 297, 310, 313
Poverty, 123, 127, 176
Power, 126, 227, 251, 277, 278, 320
Prayer, 183n11, 218, 244n4, 290n2; East worshippers with, 7, 70, 75, 76; Maya Muslims and, 167–69; West worshippers with, 7, 70, 75
Prejudice. *See* 'Assabiyah/'assabiyaah
Presbyterians, 13, 237
Prince Hall Shriners, 54–57, 62, 63, 64
Print capitalism, 120–21
Problems of a resurgent Asia. *See Fukkô Ajia no Shomondai*
Profound, 116, 119–20
Protestant Church, 12–13, 83, 302
Protests, 70, 86n4, 220–21
The Protocols of the Elders of Zion, 104
Public Enemy, 128
Puerto Ricans: with hip-hop history, 116, 117–19, 126–29; identity, 115, 121, 123, 134. *See also* Muslim Puerto Rican hip-hop artists
Puerto Rico, 10, 115, 121–22
Pundits/pandits, 299
Purdah, 200, 207, 228, 229, 235, 242
Purity, 120, 153, 167, 252, 323n1; Christianity and, 25; piety and, 253, 258, 261

Al Qaeda, 12, 141, 197
Qasim, Umm, 191, 197
Quick, Abdullah Hakim, 122, 199, 208n4
Quran, 39, 73, 200, 209n8, 244n15, 296; Allah/Allaah and, 118, 132, 225; ASJA and, 300; children and, 84; green and, 310; Hip Hop and, 131, 133; Muhammad and, 131–32, 225; slavery and, 188; surahs, 167, 188, 256, 265n12, 291n8, 305; women and, 24, 198, 202, 204, 218, 221, 223, 227, 228, 231, 242, 259, 262, 282, 284–86. *See also* Koran

Qur'an and Woman: Re-reading the Sacred Text from a Woman's Perspective (Wadud), 218

Race, 103, 106–7, 195–96; Islam and, 8, 37–38, 94–95, 109; "uplift the race," 58–60
Race theory, 96–99
Racialization: of Islam, 277–80; of Muslims, 37–38
Racism, 72, 92, 93, 103, 107, 275. *See also* White supremacy
Radiya Allahu 'anho (May Allah be pleased with), 207
Rafeek, Mohammed, 236
Rafeeq, Mohammed, 308
Raffi, Haji, 260
Rahamut, Amina, 229
Rahman Tiab, 265n13
Rahnema, Saeed, 3
Ramadan/Ramadhan, 89n42, 188, 207, 265n9, 265n10, 274
Ramadan-Santiago, Omar, 9–10
Ramadhan. *See* Ramadan/Ramadhan
Ramsoedh, Hans, 77
Randolph, A. Philip, 106
Rapping, 125–26, 127, 128, 131, 133
Rashad, Munir Ahmad, 192
Rawoot, Ilham, 219, 244n7
Rawson, Albert, 49, 51
Reaganomics, 126
Red, 314, 316
Reddock, Rhoda, 16–17, 265n8
Redissi, Hamadi, 87n11
Reformists, 33, 75, 88n19, 88n21. *See also* East worshippers
Refugees, 64
Reggaeton, 128–29
Reis, Joao Jose, 34
Religions, 2–3, 41n4, 118, 163, 175; in black Shrinerdom, 62–64; Christianity as Western, 30, 32; education, 196, 222, 227; historicality of traditions in, 39–40. *See also specific religions*
Religious leader. *See* Kaum
Reminder, 193
Renan, Ernest, 94–96, 100, 108, 111n6

Repatriation: of Javanese, 69–70, 78, 81–82; of Mandingos, 224–25
Reverting/going back, 119–20
Revivalism, Islamic, 192–93, 222, 231–32
Rhyming, 123, 126, 131, 132
Rida, Rashid, 105
The Rising Tide of Color against White World-Supremacy (Stoddard), 100, 101, 102; influence of, 106, 108, 109, 110; World War I and, 97–98
Ritual meal. *See* Slametan
Rivera, Raquel, 127
Rock Steady Crew, 132, 135n7
Rockwell, Norman, 104
Rodriguez, Ricardo, 128
Rose, Tricia, 121, 126
Rosenbaum, Brenda, 173, 177
Rotterdamsche Lloyd, 89n34
Rukun (harmony), 69, 70, 73, 83
Rushdie, Salman, 29

Sacralization, 153
Sacred texts, 167–68, 170, 183n9
Sahadev, Indrajeet, 150
Saheeh. *See* Sahih/saheeh
Sahib, Haji Ruknuddeen, 307–8
Sahih/saheeh, 207
Said, Edward, 27, 63
Salaah. *See* Salat/salaah/namaaz
Saladdin, Bashan, 192
Salaf, 207
Salafi/Salafiyyah, 105, 198–99, 207
Salat/salaah/namaaz, 207, 271
Sallalahu 'alayhi wa sallam. *See* SAWS
Samaroo, Brinsley, 291n11, 296–97
Sampath, Niels, 251
Sandalwood, 304
Sanger, Margaret, 106
San Juan Muslim Ladies Organization (SJMLO), 217, 233–34, 245n31
Saudi Arabia, 191–92, 220–21, 222, 231
Saunders, Gail, 189
Savannah, 292n18
SAWS (Sallalahu 'alayhi wa sallam) (May the peace and blessing of God be upon him), 198, 207, 218, 244n6

Schalkwijk, Aart, 85–86
Scheherazade, 34
Schools, 87n11, 88n18, 219, 225, 244n16, 308. *See also* "Old-school"
Schwartz, Aisha, 220
Science, 94, 95, 96, 111n3, 111n6, 130. *See also* Moorish Science Temple
Scotland, 53
Scott, David, 41n8
Scratching, 125, 135n5
Secularism, 148, 158n2, 159n5
Segal, Daniel, 41n7
Segregation: indentured workers and gender, 230–31; worship spaces and gender, 17, 167–68, 183n12, 204, 218–20, 237–39, 242. *See also* Purdah
Self-determination, 6, 76, 88n20
Settlement, Javanese migration and, 70–76
Seventh Day Adventists, 13, 164
Sexuality, 103, 123, 130, 320; men's, 280–83; pious, 19, 280–83; women's, 19, 220, 222, 252, 280–88, 289, 290, 291n16, 300; *wudu* and, 288
Shabazz, Jamal, 279, 291n8
Shabazz, Muhammad, 279
Shafi, 87n11
Shaikh. *See* Sheikh/shaikh
Sharia, 73, 75, 87n11, 253
Sharifa, Daud, 220
Sheikh/shaikh, 207
Sheik-ul-Islam, 107
Shi'a/Shi'ah/Shiite, 33, 207, 323n9
Shirk (idolatry), 203, 207, 276
Shriners: African American Shriner Orientalism, 57–62; banquet invitation, 59; Black Prince Hall, 54–57, 62, 63, 64; Freemasons with, 49, 55–57, 60, 62–63; with Islam, 6–7, 58, 60; Muhammad and link to, 50, 61; Orientalism in U.S. and, 51–54; Orientalist mythology of, 49–51; religion in black Shrinerdom, 62–64; temples of, 52–53, 55, 57; white, 49, 51, 54, 55, 56–57, 61, 64
Shui Jingjun, 221, 223

Silence: Indians and, 148, 149; Madassamy and, 155, 158; women and, 173, 174–75, 237, 255, 282
Simmons, David, 291n12
Sinha-Kerkhoff, Kathinka, 38
SIV. *See* Surinaamse Islamitische Vereniging
SJMLO. *See* San Juan Muslim Ladies Organization
Slametan (ritual meal), 73, 79, 80, 83, 85
Slavery, 142, 152, 190; abolition of, 34, 86n2, 146, 147, 149, 188, 189, 208n5, 224, 244n11, 273; Africans, 122, 151, 188, 224–25, 253, 274, 276–77, 297–98; anti-slavery legislation, 149, 188, 208n5, 273; Muslims and, 33, 122, 135n4, 188, 274–75, 276–77, 297; populations, 122, 188. *See also* Indentured workers
Slingshot Hip Hop (film), 116
Sloane, Hans, 323n6
Smith, John, 25, 26
Social marginalization, 13, 170, 193; graffiti artists and, 124–25; Muslim Puerto Rican hip-hop artists with, 9, 11, 117, 124
Social mobility, 72, 85–86, 88n24
Soemita, Iding, 79, 80, 82, 83, 86
Soemita, Willy, 82–83
Solomon, Thomas, 121
Somohardjo, Paul, 83
South Africa, 203, 218, 219, 231
Spaces, 262, 263, 291n17; of criminality, 272, 274; cultural, 202–5, 292n18; gender segregation and worship, 17, 167–68, 183n12, 204, 218–20, 237–39, 242; women in masjid, 217–21, 232, 237–39
Spanish Muslims, 172, 173; Maya and, 13–14, 164, 165–66, 171, 177; as missionaries, 164
Speak Out: Perspectives of a Muslim Woman from the Caribbean (Mohammed, F.), 238
"Special Registration" program, 37, 41n9
Spencer, Herbert, 106
Spengler, Oswald, 98
Spirituality, leaders and, 256–61
Spiro, Jonathan, 92
Stage marriages, 227, 238
Standing Alone in Mecca (Nomani), 218
Star, 308, *309*, 310, 316

Stereotypes, 12, 58, 109, 171; Islam, 2, 25; Muslims, 2, 194–95, 197–98
Stichting Islamitische Gemeenten in Suriname (Foundation of Islamic Congregation in Suriname), 84
Stoddard, Lothrop, 8, 9, 95, 111n7, 111n8, 111n12; Islam and, 93, 97–102, 104, 105, 108; legacy, 104–5, 106, 107–9, 110; race theory and, 96–99; racism and, 92, 93, 103, 107; white supremacy and, 97–98, 100–102, 106, 108–10
Strangers in the Land (Higham), 104
Subhana wa ta'ala. *See* SWT
Sudan, 221, 223, 275
as-Sufi, Abdalqadir, 182n3
Sukarno, 74–75, 81
Sundaram Tagore Gallery, 244n4
Sunnah Society Conference, 199
Sunni Muslims, 33, 75, 133, 200, 207
Suparlan, Parsudi, 79, 80, 81, 83, 85, 86n3, 87n16
Supreme Court, U.S., 56
Surahs, 167, 188, 256, 265n12, 291n8, 305
Surinaamse Islamitische Vereniging (SIV, Surinamese Islamic Association), 75, 85, 88n19
Suriname, 88n21; indentured workers in, 7, 70, 86n2; independence for, 76–77, 83, 88n31, 89n39; Javanese community schisms in, 69, 77–80; Javanese migration and settlement in, 70–76; with Javanese repatriation, 69–70, 78, 81–82; PBIS, 78–82, 85; population, 84, 88n31, 89n33, 89n40; with Surinamese in Netherlands, 70, 83, 89n40; unions in, 76; voting in, 77, 78–79, 88n25. *See also specific Surinamese political parties*
Surinamese Islamic Association. *See* Surinaamse Islamitische Vereniging
SWT (Subhana wa ta'ala) (Be glorified and exalted), 207
Symbols, 315; clothing as symbol of Islamic piety, 316, *317, 318, 319,* 320; of Islam, 270, 308, *309,* 310, 311, 314, 316
Syndicalism, 144–45, 158n2
Syria, 122, 189, 208n1

Tabligh Movement, 234, 235
Tabligihi Jamaat, 192
Tabliqh, 232, 245n28
Tackveeyatul Islamia Association (TIA), 226, 227–28, 233, 300
Tadjahs (tombs), *313,* 314
Taínos, 121, 135n3
Taliban, 197, 207–8
Tantawi, Sayed (Sheik), 244n4
Taxis, 272–73, 290n7
Teachings, 88n19, 166–70
Teelucksingh, Yvonne, 238
Telles, Edward, 195
Temples, 302, *303, 304*; Moorish Science Temple, 62, 64, 94; of Shriners, 52–53, 55, 57
Terrorism, 38; Muslims and, 37, 197–98, 273, 274; organizations, 12, 141, 197, 207–8. *See also* 9/11
Terror talk, 33
Theosophical Society, 51
Thobe, kufi, keffiyeh/ghutrah, 201, 207
"300 Brolic," 129–30
TIA. *See* Tackveeyatul Islamia Association
Tibawi, A. L., 63
Tjokroaminoto, 74
TML. *See* Trinidad Muslim League
Toasting, 125, 135n6
Tobago. *See* Trinidad and Tobago
Tombs. *See* Tadjahs
Toner, Jerry, 41n1
Tongar, 69–70, 82, 85
Traditionalists. *See* West worshippers
Traditions, 1, 16, 251, 301; historicality of religious, 39–40; modernity versus, 28–30, 31
Transcendence, 158
Transglobal hip hop umma, 121
Transnationalism, Islam and, 274–76
"Tribal Twenties" (1920s), 92, 104–9
Trinidad and Tobago, 147, 265n5, 290n7; with Bamboo Settlement, 239–42; coup d'état of 1990 in, 246n43, 270, 273–74, 279, 310; Islamic women emancipated in, 226–31; Islam in, 217, 224–36, 253, 276–80, 296–306, 298, 323n2; with Jinnah Memorial Masjid, 217, 236–39, 308; Nur

E Islam Masjid in, 217, 232–36, *309*; populations, 264n1, 265n4, 296, 298; with revival of Islam and Islamization projects, 231–32; women and masjid space in, 217–21, 232, 237–39; with women's mosque, 221–23; with women's mosque movements, 219–21. *See also* Indo-Trinidadian Muslims; Islamic iconography, in Trinidad; Jamaat al Muslimeen
Trinidad Muslim League (TML), 227, 230, 300, *309*, 323n8; Ali, Moulvi Ameer, and, 233, 236; Jinnah Memorial Masjid and, 217, 236–39, 308
Trotman, David, 224
Trouillot, Michel-Rolph, 5
Tsarnaev brothers, 38
Tsotsil, 13, 167–68, 172, 182n4
Tufail, Maulana (Sheik), 245n37
Turner, Richard, 107, 130, 275
23rd Street Mosque, 219

Umm (mother), 200, 208
Ummahs. *See* Imagined communities/ummahs/nations
Ummah/ummat al-mu'minin, 11, 182n3, 208; cultural space and, 202–5; imagined, 120–21
Unions, 74, 158n2; in Guadeloupe, 144–47, 151, 152, 153, 155; in Indonesia, 77, 79–81, 82, 85; in Suriname, 76
United States (U.S.), 25, 31, 37, 38–39, 88n20; Orientalism in, 51–54; Puerto Rican identity in, 115; U.S. Supreme Court, 56
Universalism, 148, 150, 275
Universal Zulu Nation, 116, 128, 132
"Uplift the race," 58–60
Urdu, 75, 232, 307
Al-Urwa al-Wuthqa, 95

Valencia Mosque, *303*, 304, *305*
Van Waning, Marjoleine, 84
Varisco, Daniel, 32
Veils, 17, 188, 280, 291n17; motivations for wearing, 24–25, 171–72, 281, 287;
niqab/niqaab, 192, 194, 198, 206, 287; non-Muslims with, 194, 198
Village leader. *See Lurah*
Villages. *See Desa*
Vogt, Patrick, 156–57
Voll, John, 134
Voting, 77, 78–79, 88n25, 259–60

Wadud, Amina, 218, 219
Wahab, Abdul, 235
Wahabi movement, 98, 100, 102, 232
Wajib, 208
Walkes, Joseph A., 56, 60, 63
Warner-Lewis, Maureen, 297
Weddings, Islamic, 299–300. *See also* Marriage
Welter-Kielstra plan, 71–72
West Africa, 125–26, 189, 224, 275, 296
West India Regiment, 224, 244n12, 298
West, the: Christianity as religion of, 30, 32; East and, 27–28; Islam and, 26, 30, 34–35; Judaism as religion of, 41n4
West worshippers (traditionalists), 8, 79, 86n3; East and, 76, 80, 83, 85; Federatie van Islamitische Gemeenten in Suriname and, 84; prayer and, 7, 70, 75
When Africa Awakes (Harrison), 107
White (color), 310, 316
White Mughals (Dalrymple), 299
Whites, 38, 103; Shriners, 49, 51, 54, 55, 56–57, 61, 64; U.S. with immigrants and definition of, 37
White supremacy, 94, 104, 275; with fear of brown planet, 96–103; pan-Islamic movement and, 107; racism and, 72, 92, 93, 103, 107, 275; Stoddard and, 97–98, 100–102, 106, 108–10; under threat, 109
Widows, 282
Wiet, Gaston, 308
Wikileaks, 197
Williams, Raymond, 16
Williamson, Harry, 63
Women, 207, 245n34, 291n15, 291n17; with ASJA election, 249, 251, 252–55, 257, 258; with Bamboo Settlement, 239–42; clothing for, 20, 158n1, 165, 169, 172,

Women—*continued*
182n5, 271, 286, 287, 288, 298, 316, *317, 318, 319,* 320; da'wah and, 190, 192, 193; ladies organizations, 217, 229, 230, 233–34, 245n31, 265n8; in masjid space, 217–21, 232, 237–39; Maya Muslims, 13, 14, 165–81, 182n5, 183n19; mosques and, 219–23, 231, 287; polygamy and, 14, 278; Quran and, 24, 198, 202, 204, 218, 221, 223, 227, 228, 231, 242, 259, 262, 282, 284–86; sexuality and, 19, 220, 222, 252, 280–88, 289, 290, 291n16, 300; silence of, 173, 174–75, 237, 255, 282; in Trinidad and Tobago, 217–23, 226–32, 237–39; voting and, 259–60; widows, 282; YWMA, 230, 254, 260, 261, 265n8. *See also* Bahamian and Brazilian muslimahs/muslimas; Gender; Marriage; Polygamy; Polygyny; Veils

World Assembly of Muslim Youth, 191, 200

Worldliness. *See* Dunya

World War I, 97–98, 107, 109

Worship. *See* East worshippers; Ibadah/ibada; Masjid/jamia; Prayer; West worshippers

Wright, Jacob F., 58

Wu, Frank, 111n7

Wudu, 167, 271, 288, 291n14

X, Malcolm, 8, 95, 110, 123, 276; Mecca and, 102–3; Stoddard and, 9, 92, 93, 97

Yayasan Tanah Air (Back to the Fatherland), 81, 89n37

Yoruba, 297

Young, Robert, 103

Young Muslim Women's Organization, 230

Young Women's Muslim Association (YWMA), 254, 260, 261, 265n8

Zapatista uprising, 12, 164, 165

Zeinab, Umm, 200

NEW WORLD DIASPORAS

Edited by Kevin A. Yelvington

This series seeks to stimulate critical perspectives on diaspora processes in the New World. Representations of race and ethnicity, the origins and consequences of nationalism, migratory streams and the advent of transnationalism, the dialectics of homelands and diasporas, trade networks, gender relations in immigrant communities, the politics of displacement and exile, and the utilization of the past to serve the present are among the phenomena addressed by original, provocative research in disciplines such as anthropology, history, political science, and sociology.

International Editorial Board
Herman L. Bennett, Rutgers University
Gayle K. Brunelle, California State University at Fullerton
Jorge Duany, Universidad de Puerto Rico
Sherri Grasmuck, Temple University
Daniel Mato, Universidad Central de Venezuela
Kyeyoung Park, University of California at Los Angeles
Richard Price, College of William and Mary
Sally Price, College of William and Mary
Vicki L. Ruiz, Arizona State University
John F. Stack Jr., Florida International University
Mia Tuan, University of Oregon
Peter Wade, University of Manchester

More Than Black: Afro-Cubans in Tampa, by Susan D. Greenbaum (2002)
Carnival and the Formation of a Caribbean Transnation, by Philip W. Scher (2003)
Dominican Migration: Transnational Perspectives, edited by Ernesto Sagás and Sintia E. Molina (2004)
Salvadoran Migration to Southern California: Redefining El Hermano Lejano, by Beth Baker-Cristales (2004)
The Chrysanthemum and the Song: Music, Memory, and Identity in the South American Japanese Diaspora, by Dale A. Olsen (2004)
Andean Diaspora: The Tiwanaku Colonies and the Origins of South American Empire, by Paul S. Goldstein (2005)
Migration and Vodou, by Karen E. Richman (2005)
True-Born Maroons, by Kenneth M. Bilby (2005)
The Tears of Hispaniola: Haitian and Dominican Diaspora Memory, by Lucía M. Suárez (2006)
Dominican-Americans and the Politics of Empowerment, by Ana Aparicio (2006)
Nuer-American Passages: Globalizing Sudanese Migration, by Dianna J. Shandy (2006)
Religion and the Politics of Ethnic Identity in Bahia, Brazil, by Stephen Selka (2007)
Reconstructing Racial Identity and the African Past in the Dominican Republic, by Kimberly Eison Simmons (2009)
Haiti and the Haitian Diaspora in the Wider Caribbean, edited by Philippe Zacaïr (2010)

From Douglass to Duvalier: U.S. African Americans, Haiti, and Pan Americanism, 1870–1964, by Millery Polyné (2010)

New Immigrants, New Land: A Study of Brazilians in Massachusetts, by Ana Cristina Braga Martes (2010)

Yo Soy Negro: Blackness in Peru, by Tanya Maria Golash-Boza (2011; first paperback edition, 2012)

Trance and Modernity in the Southern Caribbean: African and Hindu Popular Religions in Trinidad and Tobago, by Keith E. McNeal (2011; first paperback edition, 2015)

Kosher Feijoada and Other Paradoxes of Jewish Life in São Paulo, by Misha Klein (2012; first paperback edition, 2016)

African-Brazilian Culture and Regional Identity in Bahia, Brazil, by Scott Ickes (2013; first paperback edition, 2015)

Islam and the Americas, edited by Aisha Khan (2015; first paperback edition, 2017)

Building a Nation: Caribbean Federation in the Black Diaspora, by Eric D. Duke (2015)

www.ingramcontent.com/pod-product-compliance
Lightning Source LLC
Chambersburg PA
CBHW031753220426
43662CB00007B/388